MARKETS

Also by Martin Mayer

Business and Finance

THE MONEY BAZAARS
THE FATE OF THE DOLLAR
THE BUILDERS
CONFLICTS OF INTEREST: THE BROKER-DEALER NEXUS
THE BANKERS
NEW BREED ON WALL STREET *(with Cornell Capa)*
MADISON AVENUE, USA
WALL STREET: MEN AND MONEY

Other Nonfiction

MAKING NEWS
GRANDISSIMO PAVAROTTI *(with Gerald Fitzgerald)*
THE DIPLOMATS
THE MET: 100 YEARS OF GRAND OPERA IN NEW YORK
ABOUT TELEVISION
BRICKS, MORTAR AND THE PERFORMING ARTS
ALL YOU KNOW IS FACTS
THE TEACHERS STRIKE
EMORY BUCKNER
DIPLOMA
THE LAWYERS
WHERE, WHEN & WHY: SOCIAL STUDIES IN AMERICAN SCHOOLS
THE SCHOOLS

Fiction

TRIGGER POINTS
A VOICE THAT FILLS THE HOUSE
THE EXPERTS

W·W·NORTON & COMPANY
New York · London

MARKETS

Who plays...

Who risks...

Who gains...

Who loses...

MARTIN MAYER

Passages of varying length in this book, from paragraphs to pages, have appeared in *American Banker, American Heritage, Barron's, Business Month, Financier, Forbes, Fortune, Los Angeles Times, New York Times* Business World, *U.S. News & World Report,* and the *Wall Street Journal.*

The text of this book is composed in Times Roman, with display type set in Fenice Bold Italic. Composition and manufacturing by The Haddon Craftsmen, Inc.
Book design by Jacques Chazaud.

First Edition

Library of Congress Cataloging-in-Publication Data

Mayer, Martin, 1928–

  Markets: who plays, who risks, who gains, who loses

  Includes bibliographical references and index.
  1. Stock–exchange. 2. Securities. I. Title.
HG4551.M39   1988   332.63'2   88–5207

ISBN 0-393-02602-7

W. W. Norton & Company, Inc., 500 Fifth Avenue, New York, N. Y. 10110
W. W. Norton & Company Ltd., 37 Great Russell Street, London WC1B 3NU

1 2 3 4 5 6 7 8 9 0

for Henry Axel Lissakers Mayer
his first book
with love

Contents

ix

Preface

Black Monday was about as ill a wind as could blow in peacetime, but there were those to whom it blew good. There were people who had bought puts in Chicago as well as people who had "written" them, people who were short, people who thought the Treasuries market had bottomed and were riding the rocket in long-bond futures. If these terms are strange to you, read on, for they are herewith explained. We are fresh out of rose gardens to promise you, and there is no way the instruments and procedures of markets can be understood without work, but if you want to work, it's here.

I don't buy puts, or stock, or T-bond futures, or anything else in these markets, because I write about the subjects and I don't think writers should place themselves in a position where they could benefit as investors or speculators by what they have written. But I, too, was a beneficiary of the hurricane on Black Monday, for I was midway into my work on this book—I had spent my weeks in London for Big Bang, and in Japan during the greatest burst of activity the Tokyo Stock Exchange had ever seen, and in Chicago acquiring expertise on these strange markets that only professionals knew. Suddenly when I spoke at table, it was as though I were the old E.F. Hutton: People listened.

PREFACE

Though the crash did not come entirely as a surprise—I had stopped paying much attention to the stock market in summer 1987 because I knew the prices were crazy—the violence of the vomiting was of course unexpected and frightening. It still is. So this book was redirected, as you might turn the battleship *Iowa* in the water, to face somewhat different targets. It was a noisy, frantic, preoccupied time; we loaded a lot of cannon. I look around me today and marvel at how much the children have grown.

The organization here is unusual. A Prologue introduces the terms of art from the point of view of a public that buys these instruments retail and hopes to profit by them personally. Those who have read books about investing probably have nothing to learn from it. Chapters 1 and 2 then survey similar ground from the outside to report on attitudes, institutions, purposes, some of the people who labor in the vineyards and why they are paid for it. Chapters 3 and 4 detail the why and how of the greatest market collapse in American history, with perhaps a little less tender loving care for the participants than has been shown by the official reports. The reports were quite helpful as supplements, but the chapters had been completed in first draft before they appeared and required little change in direction or focus. If you were hanging around the markets in October, you heard the stories.

The following six chapters are geographically based, because Chicago, Tokyo, London, and New York have undertaken rather different functions. And then there are, indeed, conclusions.

At the end, for perusal at any time a need is felt, there is a personal and discursive Glossary of the most important terms of art in the book.

I first came to the financial district to work in 1947, and my first book on these subjects was written in 1953. I have been in and out quite a lot since. Though all of this book is fresh baked, and rests on several hundred interviews in 1986 and 1987, there is also of course a sense in which it relies on what the old educational psychologists would have called my apperceptive mass. In my original planning, I had anticipated an even wider range of coverage, with chapters on Singapore, Montreal, and Paris, all fascinating if not quite essential markets rather different from the dominating marketplaces that would then have formed the core rather than the entirety of this book. Perhaps another time. And I had expected to adopt an authoritative tone proper to my age and station. Given what I found around me after October 1987, a somewhat more argumentative, even polemical approach seemed justified. "Do you not know," asked Oxenstierna of his son in some surprise as he neared the end of his services to the kings of Sweden in 1648, "with how little wisdom the world is governed?"

Over forty years of wandering around the markets have left me with too many people to thank. For special help on this book and matters associated with it, I should like to mention in no particular order Yoshitoki Chino, Duke Chapman, George S. Moore, Leo Melamed, John Heimann, Roger Rutz, Richard Sandor, Mel Adams, Bill Clark, Sandy Lewis, Tone Grant, Brandon Becker, Bill Brodsky, Kate Hathaway, Bill Zimmerman, Scott Pardee, Shiro Inoue, Jean-François Bernheim, Charles Ramond, Alan Newman, Christine Bogdanowicz-Bindert and Detlef Bindert, Hiroko Tanaka, Maurice Mann, Dennis Donahue, Sir Martin Jacombe, Jack Hennessey, Sir Kenneth Berrill. Many of them will hate it.

And, of course, Tom and Jerri and Louis, Jim and Faith and Elena; and Karin and Fredrica and Henry. Hi, guys; Daddy's home.

Martin Mayer
New York
February 1988

Prologue: A Guide for the Bewildered

"More mental masturbation goes on in this business than in any other. You've got all these mind trades that go on—Did *he* buy it? Did *he* sell it? The really smart guys don't pay attention. They think about what *they* want to do."

> —Bernard Madoff, securities dealer
> and arbitrageur, 1986

1

*I*n 1967, in the course of writing an article about Bernard Cornfeld's Investors Overseas Services, I went from Geneva to Bonn on a Learjet with James Roosevelt. Franklin Roosevelt's son had been hired to use his entree and then his charm to persuade Chancellor Ludwig Erhard that the Germans had some kind of obligation to give access to American securities salesmen. Myself, I went to talk with the German head of the IOS office in Bonn, and I asked him to consider me a customer and give me the sales spiel. He did.

Most of it was out of the IOS sales manual, a recitation of the wonders of the American economy and markets, and the advantages of buying a "fund of funds," a mutual fund that invested in other mutual funds. But the peroration was unique to this sales manager in this city.

"Can I giff you a guarantee?" this earnest young man asked

rhetorically, leaning over his desk, brown hair slicked back, brown eyes big behind the horn-rimmed glasses. He had worked himself up to the point where he regarded me, I think, not as a reporter but as one more natural prey. "No! There is no guarantee. But when you take de bridge over de Rhine, do you haff a guarantee that your car will come to de odder side? No! Yet every day, thousands of people drive on de bridge over de Rhine, and they come to de odder side."

It was indisputable, and so I think are most other sales pitches for investments. This is not a book about investments. It is a book about markets, which means it is about prices and where they come from, about trading and traders and the institutions that make trading more or less efficient. And on a deeper level, it is about institutions and people that thrive financially and psychologically on volatility, levels of unpredictability that disturb and frighten the average sensual man.

The prices that emerge from these fluctuations are at least as important for those who sell their labor or rent their land—or just go shopping—as they are for investors. It is by no means clear that investors should pay that much attention to the fluctuating approximations by which markets find the prices that bring the parts of the economy together for productive purposes. Certainly no one should try to buy at the bottom or sell at the top; as Wall Street has it, bulls can make money and bears can make money, but hogs always lose. The investor's problem is that at the moment of entry and the moment of departure the price at which he buys and the price he receives when he sells are determined by this world of institutions that do nothing but price, price, price, all day long.

2

All the house rules for valuing investments are right, and all of them are wrong.

Obviously, one wishes to ride a trend. Equally obviously, when everyone else believes the market is going up, you are in danger of becoming the last to come on board before the ship sinks.

There is no doubt that investors should buy value, and seek out companies with stock that sells at a discount to book value or at a very low multiple of earnings or both. "Look," writes Burton Malkiel of Yale's business school, "for growth situations with low price-earnings multiples." Better look fast, too, because that's going to be a moving target. Even then, it is also true, as Martin Shubik of Yale once observed, that "a bargain which is perceived as about to become a bigger bargain is no bargain." The market may have reasons you don't know for putting a lower value on this stock than you do or Malkiel does. It has to be a mistake to "quarrel with the market," but if you do what everybody else does, you can't get better than average results.

Some companies are household names with products people need and big research-and-development departments that yield steady growth. The portfolio managers in the 1970s called those "one-decision stocks"—you bought them and you put them away. But when you took them out again, some fraction of them might be useful only as wallpaper. Even the people who spoke of one-decision stocks on Monday might by Wednesday—oh, maybe Thursday—be telling you about the need to monitor your investments continuously.

The only safety is in diversification, and no one should put all his eggs in one or even a very few baskets. But you also should concentrate your investments in what you really understand, as Warren Buffett does, which means that you are on dangerous ground when you get beyond three or perhaps four.

The market is "efficient," and prices at any given time express all the information available to investors; therefore it's a mistake to try to "beat the market" and the best thing to do is buy into an index fund, which owns the whole range of securities. But looking backward with a few years or even months of hindsight, there were always "undervalued" stocks that would have improved the return on your investments and "overvalued" stocks that should have been avoided. And when the index can drop more than 20 percent in one day, it doesn't yield much security.

One of the first rules everyone is taught is to ride the winners and discard the losers. This requires discipline, because selling at a loss confesses a mistake, and people find confession hard. Some must force themselves to get out by leaving "stop orders" that sell automatically at a specified trigger price, or otherwise imposing an external compulsion.

"Averaging down," buying more shares as the price drops to cut the average price per share, is considered the quintessential sucker's game. But most stocks are cyclical, and even currencies fall to rise again. Virtually every study shows that maintaining an even flow of money into the market—which means buying more of it at lower prices and less at higher prices—is likely to be a successful strategy over time. Except that almost nobody can do it, because the factors that drive down prices also usually diminish the supply of investment funds in the hands of the purchasers.

Obviously, if you're in on a good thing you multiply your profits by purchasing "on margin," with borrowed money. If you're in on a bad thing, however, buying with borrowed money multiplies your losses.

Many people put their faith in "technical analysis," charts that predict the next movement of prices. The oldest and most established of these technical approaches is the Dow theory, which measures the performance of two indices, a group of industrial stocks and a group of transportation stocks. In its simplest form, the theory holds that the stocks of the more highly capitalized companies will tend to trade over a moderately short period of time within a fairly narrow range of prices. If the trend is up, then prices will tend to break out of this range on the up side, and will make "new highs." When they decline again (and prices, of course, never move in a straight line), the lows on the new move will not be as far down as they were the last time the stock paused. This makes it possible to draw a "trend line," an upwardly sloping channel with all the highs within the top of the channel and all the lows still within it down at the bottom.

Should this pattern reverse—should upward movements fail to penetrate the level of the last new high, while downward movements begin to move prices below "the neckline," the level of prices that marks the last low—the Dow theory calls for at least a temporary redirection of the channel. Thus one hears of "support levels" and "resistance levels," "testing the highs [or lows]," "double bottoms," "head-and-shoulder formations," and the like.

Meanwhile, a group of transportation stocks is separately followed along the same lines. If the same reversal appears in the transportation index, then a new trend is considered "confirmed," and the keepers of the flame will declare a shift from a bull market to a bear market (or vice versa). Though the railroads are not today the economic force they were when John D. Rockefeller, Sr., had major interests in all the lines that shipped tank cars of petroleum, public expectations of the future prosperity or problems of the companies that move goods and people are certainly a reasonable measure of where the economy is likely to go. Some bull markets or bear markets are "primary" and will last a long time; others may be "secondary," deceptive movements that give false guidance to long-term investors.

Dow theory uses market movements as an indication of where the economy is going, and the expected impact on prices feeds back through the real world. Other technical systems ignore what is happening in the economy, and regard the stock market as an independent, narcissistic, autoerotic arena, a special circus with its own internal lions and lion tamers, trapeze artists, tightrope walkers, and clowns.

The most publicized such system in 1987 was the Elliott wave theory, which simply proclaims on the basis of curve fitting that market movements fit the mathematical patterns of a Fibonacci series, the work of an early thirteenth-century pioneer in arithmetic. The advantages of true belief in such a theory were demonstrated after the humongous crash. Robert Prechter, for example, whose proclamation that the Dow-Jones Index of the prices of thirty large-capitalization industrial stocks would inevitably go to 3600 lured many customers to his published service and thence to the brokers, suddenly discovered after October 19 that he had begun his measurements from 1982 rather than (as he should) from 1974, and that he had therefore been led away from the true answer (2700) to a false one. Every technical analyst says after the market has shown him to have made a mistake that his real problem was in failing to follow the true guidance of his own system.

The same technical "rules" are applied to all markets, and in all of them there are repetitive examples of how wrong the technicians are. In the energy pits on the New York Mercantile Exchange on December 15, when near-term crude oil futures fell below $17 on a volume of almost 150 million barrels (!), broker Joel Faber noted that "two weeks ago the price was up to nineteen dollars and four cents, and the technicians were all saying, 'There's your classic reverse head and shoulders, it's gone beyond the neckline, the price is going certainly to twenty, probably higher.' Today they're all saying that the indicators all point to thirteen."

A college roomate of mine made his living for many years as a tape reader for a Wall Street house, relying on an extraordinary memory for patterns of movement—the probability that in each of several hundred active stocks two "up ticks" (sales at higher prices) would be followed by a third move ahead or a move back. Thousands, perhaps tens of thousands, of Americans sit before screens with chart books open on tables before them, writing X's and O's in columns, and laying rulers on the graph to draw lines that connect tops and bottoms of each day's trading in a given stock or index with the tops and bottoms of the trading in that stock or index at the day's opening and at its close—or maybe week by week, or month by month, or on a ten-day or hundred-day or one-year "moving average."

Yale's Malkiel points out the fundamental flaw in such analysis, which is that the chartist gets his news only after the trader has acted on his instincts and the fundamentalist has acted on his information. Still, *recent* late information may be worth more than stale late information. No doubt, technical forecasting of the stock market is numerology—but so is the analysis by which the Federal Reserve System attempts to calculate the impact on the economy of a change in the money supply. All government planning—indeed, all corporate planning not devoted to innovation—rests on the belief that markets will respond to stimuli tomorrow much the same way that they responded to similar stimuli yesterday and the day before. Malkiel goes a little far when he writes that "past movements in stock prices cannot be used to foretell future movements." Confronted with the prospect of a strike that would suspend the publication of his newspaper, the *New York Times* columnist James Reston asked plaintively, "How can I know what I think until I read what I write?" The market, one suspects, is a little like that, too.

3

In the United States, the stock exchanges are, more or less, "cash markets." Buying stock on an exchange is more like buying a couch or a car than it is like buying a pork loin or a toy for Junior to give Sally at her birthday party. Though in fact the technology exists to transfer the ownership to you today and collect from you today, the stock exchanges insist they have to do something with the upholstery and the dealer prep before you get it. You buy it or sell it now, and you commit to pay for it or deliver it now, but in fact you won't have the shares registered to or out of your account for at least four business days (which can be a matter of considerable importance because dividends are paid to "shareholders of record" as of a certain date), and your broker doesn't have to receive your money until the third or fourth or (if you're a big customer who wires funds) even fifth business day after the transaction. Until 1980, he didn't pay you the proceeds of your sales for some days after that—in the 1970s, the largest single source of revenue at the big brokerage houses was "interest on customer free balances"—but since the perfection of the money-market mutual fund most brokers have arrangements to "sweep" customer accounts into interest-earning assets at least by the start of the next week.

As a purchaser, you may borrow much of the cost, up to a maximum (it has been 50 percent for a long time) set by formal action of the Federal Reserve Board. And as a seller you can borrow the stock you deliver, "selling short," through arrangements by which you pay a kind of rent for the use of the stock and leave the receipts with the broker to give him comfort that when the time comes you will replace what you borrowed. It is very important to do this: The oldest doggerel on Wall Street, from old Dan'l Drew in the nineteenth century, proclaims that "he who sells what isn't his'n/ must buy it in or go to pris'n."

Stock exchanges are markets for "direct investment"—you own what you buy, and your return is a function of the success of the company in which you have purchased shares. But the exchanges guarantee—it is their reason for being—that this investment will be reasonably liquid, that if you wish to sell there will be buyers. For this purpose, they provide "market makers" of one kind of another who stand ready to make a bid for what you own (or make an offer of what you want to buy) whether or not there are customers from the great public out there ready to take the other side of your trade at the time you wish to get out or in. American exchanges operate as continuous auctions, with prices that move all the time, presumably reflecting the relative weights of public desire to buy or to sell the securities being traded.

None of these conditions is required for investing, or for markets. Money-market mutual funds, for example, always sell at the same price of $1 a share; what changes after you buy is the number of shares you own, and that number expresses the interest earnings on the short-term paper the fund buys plus or minus any change in the market price of that paper. Often enough, the interest paid on such paper is expressed as a "discount"—instead of paying you $400 additional when returning your original $10,000, a six-month Treasury bill at 8 percent annual interest will sell for $9,600 and grow in value to $10,000 through the six months. Note that this is in fact more than an 8 percent return, because $400 is a higher proportion of $9,600 than it is of $10,000.

When market interest rates rise, the price of fixed-rate paper declines; when they fall, the price rises. The shorter the term of the paper—money-market mutual funds are restricted by the Securities and Exchange Commission to paper that pays out in nine months or less—the less the price changes, and the more rapidly the shares in the fund earn the new rather than the old rate of interest. The very ingenious idea of measuring the value of the shareowner's holdings by number of shares at $1 each rather than by price per share appears to have sprung from the fertile marketing imagination of Howard Stein, a quiet, tough-minded salesman who succeeded Jack Dreyfus at the head of Dreyfus Fund. Valuing the fund by number of shares was a marketing tool of extraordinary power, making it possible to offer customers the right to withdraw their funds by writing a check, and to pay bills on the chassis of an investment rather than from a transaction account at a bank.

Money-market mutual funds got their start because the government held down the interest rates banks could pay on savings accounts (and prohibited the payment of interest on transaction accounts) at a time when the government's own inflationary policies were forcing up all the other interest rates in the money markets, including the interest the Treasury itself had to pay. But Treasury bills, not to mention commercial paper and negotiable bank certificates of deposit and bankers' acceptances, came only in large denominations and were a pain in the neck to buy and sell. The funds were a way that ordinary people could pool their resources and for a very small fee to the management of the fund earn market rates rather than government-imposed rates on their savings. Since 1980 with some limits, and since 1987 absolutely, banks and thrift institutions have been free to pay what they wish, but the funds thrive, because a mutual fund is a lot cheaper to run than a bank. One of the reasons a fund is cheaper, of course (not the only reason), is that it doesn't bear the costs of deposit insurance.

But the message apparently given by deposit insurance is wrong. The money-market fund is not only less of a gamble than a share of stock; it is also, over time, not quite so obviously, less of a gamble than a bank account with a fixed interest payment. On any given day, the bank account can be redeemed for the face amount on the passbook or according to the schedule associated with a certificate. But the value of the money is not guaranteed. The amount of money an investor will receive when he cashes in a money-market fund is a function of the interest the fund has earned, and because interest rates go up in a time of inflation the odds are reasonably good that a money-market mutual fund held for a period of time will be stable in terms of the purchasing power of the dollars that can be taken out of it. Thus a money-market fund is a market-related form of investing, and a bank savings account is not.

By the same logic, the purchase of cash gold in the form of coins or bullion is also a form of investment, though I must say I regard the presence of gold in an investment portfolio as a sign of misanthropy. Gold is a bet against your fellowman, giving you a stake in disorder and inflation. Gold investments become profitable only if the government fails in what is economically its prime function, to maintain the value of the money it enforces as "legal tender." Unlike any other investment except perhaps undeveloped land (also antisocial, especially if it is held off the market for speculative purposes), gold yields its holder no stream of income. The damage done to society by a flight to gold is now no longer so heavy as it was when all money and credit rested on a base of gold and the disappearance of the metal from the vaults of banks and governments shrank the money supply at precisely the moment when the economy needed liquidity. But it's hard to avoid the feeling that the purchaser of gold intends harm, though he can no longer wreak it.

In all cash markets, investors participate essentially as purchasers to hold (in the agricultural markets, purchasers to eat; in the metals markets, purchasers to fabricate into manufactured goods) and as sellers of what they own. Short sellers are in overwhelming proportion professionals who make their livings in the markets and speculators using markets to place bets. The ratio of "long" to "short" positions at the stock exchanges runs about twenty to one. Moreover, the stock market is an institution where in theory all purchasers can win. The social purpose served by its existence is that it helps finance economic growth, which requires increases in capital. The investor who sells a stock that later rises is by no means necessarily a loser: He may have taken his profits and invested them in a stock that went up even more.

If the system functioned ideally, investors in new ventures would gain by the prosperity of those ventures through a rise in the price of their ownership shares. They would collect that gain by selling to less adventurous investors when the securities were "seasoned." Then they would return their cash to work with the next crop of entrepreneurs. This happens only in textbooks and in promotional literature, but it's a sound theory. And it's also a reasonable excuse for the optimism of brokers, whose buy recommendations exceed their sell recommendations by about the same twenty to one that longs exceed shorts. The real reason for the optimism of brokers, however, is that buy recommendations can be promoted to the whole universe of possible customers (and commission payers), while recommendations on the sell side essentially interest only those who already own the stock.

4

Futures markets, in contrast to cash markets, do not offer their patrons the commodity that underlies their activity. Instead, they trade contracts to purchase or sell that commodity on a future date. The contract is inescapable. Those who purchase must stand ready to receive the commodity at a specified delivery point at this price on a specified date (or to buy an offsetting obligation from someone who has a contract to deliver to that point on that date, thus permitting the "clearing corporation" that serves the exchange to extinguish both contracts). Those who sell futures contracts must stand ready to deliver the commodity to the delivery point for this price on the specified date (or buy in someone else's contract to accept delivery). As a result, futures markets are not situations where everyone can win. If the price goes down, the purchaser pays more on delivery than the cash market price that day, while the seller collects more; if the price rises, the seller is paid less than that day's market for his wheat or hogs or bonds, and the buyer gets a bargain. Futures markets are zero-sum games. Thus they draw a somewhat different personality type from what you might find in the stock market.

One does not borrow to buy futures contracts, and too many people in and out of the markets—analysts as well as journalists and politicians—have allowed themselves to be confused by the fact that the same word "margin" is used to specify both the fraction of a stock purchase price the buyer must post in cash and the binder on a futures contract. The binder is what a building contractor or an exporter would call a "performance bond," a good-faith deposit that will be forfeited if the contracting party does not live up to his contract.

The problem for the commodities exchanges—and there are a bunch of them: the Chicago Board of Trade and Mercantile Exchange, the Kansas City Board of Trade, the Minneapolis Grain Exchange, the New York Commodities Exchange and Mercantile Exchange and Coffee, Sugar, and Cocoa Exchange and Cotton Exchange, etc.—is that the purchasers of the contracts have to be better than their bonds. They cannot be permitted to walk away from their binders (which people do, after all—quite a number of Wall Street players forfeited their deposits on co-op apartments and summer houses after October 19) if the prices of the contracts they bought move so far that their losses exceed their stake. This happened in 1986 in London at the Metals Exchange, where the governments of the world, joined by treaty in a Tin Council formed to control prices, walked away from their tin contracts when they no longer had enough money in their kitty to keep the price up, dropping losses like rain on brokers and investors who thought they had profited by sales to a government-sponsored agency.

Well-run commodities exchanges (a category that obviously did not include the old London Metals Exchange) therefore require investors to "mark to market" every night, revaluing the contract at today's price. All changes in price come out of or add to the performance bond, and if that falls below a certain percentage of the current market value of the contract its owner will be called on to put up additional "margin," to increase his stake. Or, if the price rises, he will be allowed to take some money out. We shall have occasion in the Chicago chapters to look at the exceedingly clever institutional arrangements by which this system has been made safe and sound.

The stock exchange has twenty times as many longs as shorts, but on the commodities exchanges the ratio of longs to shorts is necessarily fifty/fifty, and the advice given by Futures Commission Merchants, the term of art for "broker" on the commodity exchanges, splits about evenly between buy recommendations and sell recommendations. Futures markets play a significant economic role, and in agricultural commodities something like half the futures transactions by people other than the traders themselves reflect the legitimate needs of producers and consumers of the commodity being traded. But for the outsider buying contracts through a broker, the futures markets are a bet, whether what are traded are metals or grains or livestock or financial instruments.

Thus the odds against the "investor" are much worse in the commodities markets than they are in the stock market. There is no way everybody can win in the commodities market, and the outsider is always playing against professionals. Futures markets are most interesting as gambling instruments when the price fluctuations are widest. In the early 1970s, when the Russians decided to maintain their animal herds despite a catastrophic drop in grain production, the Chicago and Kansas City grain pits drew speculative interest worldwide, and in the late 1970s universal distrust of the world's governments provoked a flight to gold that sent prices soaring in daily moves of a percentage point or more.

Oil trading—in a futures market that did not exist before the late 1970s—went berserk in the mid-1980s as producers, refiners, and users tried to mitigate the effects of a decline in spot prices that took away more than half the value of a barrel of oil in less than six months. (Significantly, the futures price dropped even more—abstract markets overshoot, because there is no one who *must* buy right now what someone else *must* sell right now, which is one of the things that make them attractive to gamblers.) At the same time, the government price-support program that kept the farmers in business (at great cost to the Treasury) cut the attractiveness of the grain pits, where prices bounced only gently above the support level.

Prices of futures contracts are of course a function of prices in the cash markets for the underlying commodity. In a well-ordered universe, and most of the time in most places ours is not so pathetically ill-ordered as publicity might lead you to believe, this relationship is determined by the "cost of carry." Wheat to be delivered in sixty days should cost roughly what wheat costs today in the cash market, plus the costs of storing it for sixty days, plus the interest that can be earned on the money that doesn't have to be put up for sixty days. If the contract runs ninety days, the price should be higher than the sixty-day price by the costs of carry for an additional thirty days. In principle, arbitrageurs will keep the relationships among current prices and future prices at different contract maturities roughly in line with the costs of carry, buying in the market where the price is low and selling in the market where the price is high until equal values sell at the same price.

The arbitrage looks easy between two different months of a

contract in the same commodity, and there are people in the pits who make a living by "spreading," buying one contract and selling the other (no risk) when the prices get out of line with each other. Arbitraging directly between the cash market and the futures market is more complicated because it involves the physical movement of quantities of a commodity, encompassing questions of what is available for delivery right now and what is expected to be available in sixty or ninety days or six months or whenever. Gaps greater or less than the cost of carry will often develop because of differences of opinion about what is going to happen in the world—whether, for example, oil prices will go up or down after an OPEC meeting forty days after the oil now being sold in the cash market has been refined and burned.

With the arrival of financial futures in the 1980s, contracts for future deliveries of bonds or stocks or loans or currencies, the costs of physical storage were withdrawn from the equations. Intricate questions of what could be delivered against the contract were intricately answered, all the stakes were raised, and to some extent the nature of the game changed. Below the exoticisms of "carry," after all, the essence of the relationship between futures on commodities and the cash market in those commodities was that what was bought for cash was consumed and disappeared. In financial futures, which now account for almost three-quarters of all the trading on the "commodity" markets, the items traded in the cash market are mostly long term, or roll over virtually without cost, like Treasury bills or Eurodollar bank deposits. Thus a change in price stimulates not consumption or hoarding but trading activity. In Chapters 5, 6, and 11, we shall have occasion to look at what is implied by the change from physical commodity to financial instrument in the operations of these markets.

For present purposes, it is enough to note that the creation of financial futures made it possible for outsiders to use markets to hedge against losses of value in large real investments. By their nature, then—a fact still imperfectly understood in many brokerage houses as well as in Congress—the futures markets are insider markets, most likely to be used by institutions and corporations, servants of business strategies rather than for individual investment needs or individual speculation. And by 1987, less than 10 percent of the action in the futures market pits was the execution of orders from individuals.

PROLOGUE

5

Where the private investor came into his own again in the 1980s, perhaps unfortunately, was at the options exchange, which has the greatest Unique Selling Proposition in the history of financial marketing: limited risk, unlimited potential gain. An option is just that—the right, but not the obligation, to buy (or sell) a security or a commodity, or a futures contract for a security or a commodity, at a price fixed at the moment of purchasing the option. In the "European" style (options have been around a while), the option becomes effective only on the day it expires. In the "American" style, it may be used, at the holder's discretion, any time prior to expiration. For the buyer, as noted, the risk of loss is limited to the price of the option, called the "premium," because you don't exercise the option unless doing so makes you a winner. For the option "writer," however, who agrees to sell or buy at a fixed price in the future, the risks are definitely not limited unless steps are taken to limit them.

Like futures, options can be used to hedge risks, at greater immediate cost but with greater maintenance of profit possibility. If the futures market goes against the hedger using it, he loses the gains he would otherwise make on the instrument he has hedged—if the householder worried about inflation sells T-bond futures to protect him against higher interest rates on his variable-rate mortgage, and the rates in fact go down, he has to pay out on his losing contract all he saves from the lower rates. If he hedges by means of an option, however, he merely tears up his option contract and pockets his savings on interest.

In the stock market context, someone who owns a stock and would be willing to sell it for a small profit can write a "call," giving its purchaser the right to buy that stock at the present (or some other) price up to the date of expiration of the option. If the price doesn't go up, the call writer has in effect reduced the cost of the stock he holds by the amount of the premium; if it does go up, he has made his little profit. The purchaser of the call has been able to make a play on a possible large rise in the price of the stock (or protect himself against heavy losses if he's short the stock) at a cost limited by the premium. Conversely, someone who is short the stock can lock in a small profit by writing and selling a "put" that gives its purchaser the right to sell the stock to him at a set price (and if the price goes up he has reduced his loss on his short position by the amount of the premium).

The writer of a "naked" option (the call writer who does not already own the stock and will have to buy it to deliver to the purchaser of the call if the price goes up, and the put writer who is not short the stock and will have to pay cash for what has become overpriced merchandise if the price goes down) can lose not only his shirt but much else besides. A couple of months after last year's Black Monday, David Ruder, the new chairman of the Securities and Exchange Commission, which regulates the options markets as well as the stock exchanges, opined that naked options were too risky a strategy for the amateur to attempt. It's not fair to ask where he was when we needed him, for in fact he was until summer 1987 a professor at Northwestern University; but it's reasonable to inquire why his predecessor and his predecessor's colleagues allowed brokerage houses to encourage beginners to ski on these slopes.

We shall look later at some intellectual accomplishments of the options markets, which have moved from sideshows unnoticed in the news to central elements in computer-based market strategies. (Fifteen years ago, no newspaper carried options prices as news, and the handful of options dealers bought little ads in the paper to list what they had for sale.) Suffice it here to note the different categories into which these hybrid instruments must be slotted:

1. Obviously, by *purpose*. A "call" gives the right to buy the underlying stock or commodity, and a "put" gives the right to sell.

2. By *duration*. One factor in the price of an option (its "premium") is the length of time over which it may be exercised, and, clearly, the longer the period, the more valuable the contract. Options may be written for periods as long as a year from the first day they are offered, but the premiums on longer term options are necessarily high and the action tends to concentrate in the nearby months.

3. By *price* of the item on which the option is purchased. Options for each month are offered nowadays at a variety of prices, ascending and descending from the current market quotation. Thus, if shares of stock in General Electric are selling for roughly 50, there might be active option contracts at 40, 45, 50, 55, and 60 (for each of a number of months). A call at 40 is "in the money" by $10, and its price will of course reflect that. A call at 60 has no immediate

value and is "out of the money." Conversely, a put at 40 is worthless if the option is expiring today, while a put at 60 is worth $10.

Duration and price will not, by themselves, dictate the premium paid for an option, for the market value of an option is very much a function of participants' beliefs about the likely volatility of the market for this stock or index or commodity over the life of the contract. Indeed, options professionals tend to be more interested in volatility than in the direction of the market: Back in the days when options were sold over the counter rather than traded on an exchange, it was not uncommon for some in the then-small club of players to buy "straddles," which permitted their owner both to buy and to sell, at different times. And option players still create straddles, buying and selling both calls and puts. In 1987, obviously, the premium required to buy almost any option rose—quite dramatically after October 19—because greater volatility made it more likely that safely out-of-the-money options might indeed become in-the-money options at some point during the life of the contract even if the stock ended up on expiration day just about where it was on the day the option was written.

Once the premium has been paid, the options like the futures markets are zero-sum games marked to market every night, and like the clearing instrumentalities of the futures exchanges the Options Clearing Corporation (which processes the trades on all the exchanges that deal in "listed options") requires "margin" deposits from those who have written contracts and are at risk. Losers among option writers must add to their "margin" overnight and winners among purchasers of options on stock indexes can cash in their gains from the previous day's trading.

As noted earlier, people who write puts and calls and collect the premiums divide into two groups—those who are "covered," who can satisfy the contract from their existing holdings (or have hedged their options risks elsewhere), and those who are "naked." Both pay their brokers very large commissions (as a fraction of the premium) to do such work for them. It has been a very good business—in 1987, about 310 million options contracts, one and a quarter for every man, woman, and child in the United States, were traded on the various exchanges. Prior to October 19, a number of customers' men (salesmen; formally, "registered representatives") at carelessly run brokerage houses made a bundle by advising their clients to write out-of-the-money naked puts, which through the five years of the big bull market generated a small earnings stream much appreciated by the elderly and by individuals trying to live on a limited estate. When the market collapsed these people found themselves with obligations to the Options Clearing Corporation that they could not possibly meet. Unquestionably the worst victims of the crash were these innocents, and the cumulative loss was undoubtedly in the hundreds of millions of dollars.

6

"Derivative" instruments, like futures and options, are not a fad, and will not disappear. They are among the many still-strange results of the new computer-based information and communications technology. Derivative instruments have opened up new opportunities for individuals, but have also set new traps for the unwary—and sometimes even for the wary. As "risk-transfer" devices, they will eventually offer strategies of money management to people as well as to institutions. The homeowner with an adjustable-rate mortgage, for example, can already and inexpensively go short a Treasury-bond futures contract dated the same month as the recalculation of his mortgage interest payments; if interest rates rise, the price of the futures contract will decline, and the profit on the short position will pay the increase in the mortgage costs. Not many amateurs do things like this yet, but someday they will.

Perhaps the strongest criticism to be made of the derivative instruments is that they confuse people, even professionals, about what they are doing. Joel A. Bleeke, a principal in the management consultant firm of McKinsey & Co., suggested in the *Wall Street Journal* shortly after the 1987 crash that "an *investor* could hold 85% of his portfolio in short-term money-market investments and use the remainder to purchase call options or options on index futures. The call options increase in value in a rising market; the short-term investments safeguard capital and pay interest." Quite apart from the fact that this will be a losing strategy in all but quite volatile markets, the person who follows it is in no sense an "investor." Call options buy neither plant nor machinery; they express the ownership of pieces of paper, not of anything real. As the chairman of Imperial Chemicals said a few years ago at a London occasion where the hosts were the brokerage firm Greenwell's, "In the end, you know, somebody has to make the widgets."

In addition, there has been a problem of perception at the institutions that now trade more than half and hold more than a quarter of the nation's listed stocks. With the creation of portfolio insurance techniques that involve hedging the value of a stock portfolio through the sale of index futures and options, pension-fund and mutual-fund managers came to consider their equity holdings much safer than they can be. For generations, the first investment advice from bankers and good brokers has been not to put into the stock market money you can't afford to lose. It is of the nature of equity that the investment is at risk, especially in an economy so highly leveraged as ours, where immense debt-service charges must be met before the allocation of income to owners.

Excessive efforts to transfer risk, paradoxically, have made the markets much more dangerous, though not hopeless, for the individual investor. Even for professionals: "My personal finances," says Gus Mitsopoulos, who manages what the firm does in the interest-rate futures pits for Refco, the largest commodities broker, "are a function of what I think of the bond market. How I finance my seven-year-old's education. But if there's too much volatility, you can't do business."

7

There are few businesses anyone can be in where there is no value to a reasonably good grasp of the markets that set the prices everyone pays. There is also comfort, intellectual entertainment, and probably profit in understanding how markets happen, as machinery and as workplaces for specified, real, live human beings. And, of course, the importance of the subject far transcends the question of whether this individual or that—even you or I—makes money.

Markets are central institutions of a modern society. If you understand markets, you have a chance of understanding what is happening in your time. If you don't, you don't. You may think you do, but you don't.

MARKETS

1

The Names
of the Games

"I went in one morning to see Randolph Burgess, who had come to our
bank from the Federal Reserve and ran our trading desk even though he
was vice-chairman of the bank, because he knew more about it than anybody else. He said, 'George, I can't see you now. We've got a pile of
Treasuries and the market is going down and I've got to sell them.' So I
came back in the afternoon, and he said, 'George, let's do it tomorrow.
We're short Treasuries and the market's shooting up, and I've got to buy
them.' I said, 'This morning, you were saying the price was going down and
you had to sell them.' He looked up at me pityingly. 'George,' he said,
'you'll never be a trader.' "

—George Moore, first chairman of Citicorp,
reminiscing in 1986

1

One morning shortly after stock prices collapsed on October
19, 1987, I watched the dawn rise over the markets from a
vantage point at the offices of Troster, Singer & Co., the
largest dealer in stocks not listed on an exchange. About three thousand of these usually but not always lesser companies are actively
traded "over the counter," an anachronistic misnomer for a system
that now flows the bids and offers of some five hundred "market
makers" through a mainframe in Trumbull, Connecticut, and then
out again to computer screens all across the country. Only members
of the National Association of Securities Dealers can have these

3

MARKETS

"NASDAQ" (NASD Automated Quotations) screens. The public participates as customers of one of the 6,500 member firms, who may act as dealers (selling at a markup or buying at a markdown from the wholesale price) or as brokers (charging a commission). In either case, wholesale firms like Troster, Singer are the proximate source of the stock the public customer buys or sells.

Prior to October 19, Troster, Singer routinely bought and sold about fifteen million shares of stock every day (in early 1988, volume was little more than half that; in both cases the total was about 10 percent of the trading done in NASDAQ shares). Much of this buying and selling was done through the firm's own "INside" computer, which permits about twenty of its best customers (mutual funds and discount brokers buying and selling for *their* customers) to execute orders at Troster, Singer on the best bid or best offer any of the competing market makers is showing on the NASD's screen— that is, the "inside" price. Meanwhile, of course, the firm's own traders must be active in the market to replenish the positions buyers are depleting (or to distribute the stock that accumulates as the customers sell). This is not a new business, but one can fairly say it's changed. In 1952, when I visited Troster, Singer in its rather dingy Wall Street offices and spent some time with Colonel Oliver Troster, the house was proud of a daily volume that sometimes hit as much as sixty thousand shares, which was then 10 percent of all the trading done over the counter. A dozen or so traders, in jackets and ties as I recall it, all men of course, sat facing each other over banks of telephones along a table with Colonel Troster's desk at one end and at the other end a blackboard on which a man chalked the prices on the more active stocks. Colonel Troster had a megaphone beside his telephone, through which he could call instructions to his troops.

The Troster, Singer offices were moved just across the Hudson River to Jersey City in the 1960s to escape a New York State tax on stock transfers, and remained in New Jersey after the transfer tax had been repealed. It doesn't much matter in this day of wires and satellites and screens where a securities dealer is located. The heart of the enterprise is an amphitheater of a trading room on the top floor of a twelve-story office building, with semicircular rows of tables armed with about seventy screens and keyboards and telephone keypads rising step by carpeted step. At the front of the room a square panel of moving lights carries the Reuters news summary for cursory inspection by those who don't wish to clutter their working

4

screens with words. Forty-eight traders, men and women, the men in shirt-sleeves, sit at the screens, watching the prices and transactions in "their" stocks, trading for the firm's account and processing calls from broker/dealers not on the "INside" system. Despite the carpeted steps and the soundproofed ceiling, it's pretty noisy.

Some of the companies involved are quite substantial and are traded heavily within a wide range of prices—for example, Apple Computer, Intel, Itel, Reuters, MCI Communications, and the American Depository Receipts of Jaguar (for which prices are quoted not in the conventional eighths of a point but in thirty-seconds of a point, like a government bond). Others, including a number of regional banks and public utilities, are usually stodgy (nothing was stodgy in October 1987, though the public utilities suffered less than most), and some of the largest are lightly traded. But this is also the market that makes possible the capitalization of the new ventures, technological and otherwise, because it gives the investors and speculators who buy stock in such companies a place where if desired (or necessary) they can get their money back. The real damage done by the October avalanche was here, in the opportunities to "go public" that disappeared from the prospects of hundreds of promising new companies because the firms that made those markets disappeared. Over the two weeks after October 14, prices in the NASDAQ market dropped almost half again as much as the price indices of stock traded on the New York Stock Exchange, and the carnage was greatest in the stocks with the lowest capitalization and shortest history. Early 1988 saw somewhat better prices on light volume, but the IPO (Initial Public Offering) business did not recover.

The president and chief executive officer of Troster, Singer is Arthur Kontos, a quick, compact man in his fifties with dark hair and a thick mustache, who wears shirt-sleeves and a bright red tie. In addition to his office that in 1987 still looked over the river to the New York skyline (a view that will soon be blocked by the continuing construction of "Harborside," New Jersey's federally assisted answer to Wall Street), Kontos keeps a desk and screen in a corner on the top rung of the traders' amphitheater. Everyone in the trading room can see him and consult as needed. (As a possible auxiliary for the computerized information system, Kontos still has Colonel Troster's megaphone atop the computer screen at the desk behind him.) Troster, Singer traders have great leeway to take positions with the firm's

5

capital, and Kontos had his information system designed so that they do not in fact know during the day whether or not their work this day has made money. "Traders have enough to worry about," Kontos says, "without thinking about P and L. I'll worry about P and L." By contrast, the Merrill Lynch computer system for its over-the-counter traders tells them minute-by-minute whether the stocks in which they make a market showed a profit to the firm from the day's trading, the month's trading, the year's trading.

Personally, Kontos is following the fortunes of Apple Computer and of Genentech, a genetic engineering firm about to receive Food and Drug Administration approval for an anticoagulant product helpful to heart attack victims. He pushes the button that shows him the trades so far today on the INside system, and notes that the customers of the discount brokers are buying. "Let's keep our position in Genentech," he calls to a young assistant at the next table, who nods and picks up the phone to go shopping.

One of the traders calls from two rungs below in the amphitheater: "Bear Stearns has sixty thousand SMSI to sell; do we want it?"

Kontos says, "I'll take a look," and punches up on the screen the recent trading patterns of this rather lightly traded stock (only 3,500 shares of it had changed hands the previous day).

At Kontos's elbow, I say, "I don't recognize that symbol. What is SMSI?"

Kontos looks at me with a degree of impatience. "It's something," he explains, "that Bear Stearns has sixty thousand of."

But it is this attitude, this search for the trader's edge rather than for fundamental values, that keeps markets alive through good times and bad. "I have a time horizon of about fifteen minutes," Kontos says. "If I put my head above that, it gets shot off." The profit in making a market will be, over time, the exploitation of the "spread" on each "turn"—that is, if the market is 40 bid, 40-¼ asked, and customers come in with "market" orders, the proprietor buys at 40, sells at 40-¼, and pockets twenty-five cents per share. If the stock is trending higher, which means no one will sell at the 40 bid, the market maker in an active stock will normally be able to by at 40-⅛ and sell at 40-¼; if it is going down, and no one will buy at 40-¼, he will still usually be able to sell at 40-⅛ and buy back at 40. If the stock is very active and the spread is only one "tick" (prices on the stock exchanges move by eights of a point), the market maker will do a number of trades without profit on the turn, simply holding the franchise. "The jobber's turn," to use the British phrase, pays the rent and the clerical expenses and the fees associated with being in the market. Profit then comes out of being a fraction of a step ahead of the daily fluctuations, *feeling* what the market will do next, or out of handling big transactions for big customers.

Many traders like to go to bed at night without any positions in what they trade. Some will take a little loss on their last sales to clear out the inventory, or on their last purchases to buy in a short position, saving themselves risk to capital, interest charges if they borrow, peace of mind in general. Since 1982, the Chicago Mercantile Exchange has been trading a futures contract in the prices of the 500 stocks of large American corporations weighted to form the Standard & Poors index. The Merc stays open for fifteen minutes beyond the close of the New York Stock Exchange, to help traders hedge the general market risk of the next opening by selling futures if they have inventory, and buying futures if they're short. In early years, this end-of-day activity constituted a large part of the trading in that "pit." Though every so often one finds people who really want to fly their little plane under the bridges—the cowboys in the oil pit who play what that market calls "the Texas hedge," buying the cash and buying the future at the same time—this is not, for all its reputation, a gambling business. "When somebody tells me he has the guts to take risks," says Bernard Madoff, who runs a business like Troster, Singer's (but he also deals in a hundred big stocks listed on the New York Stock Exchange), "I don't want him here. Any trader can take risks. All he has to be is stupid."

Even people who seem to be doing risky things are often playing it very safe, if you know the whole story. Ed Thorp, an ardent, nervous math professor who first came to public attention as the man who was barred from the world's gambling casinos because he had learned to beat the blackjack tables by remembering which cards had already come out of the shoe, runs a private arbitrage fund called Princeton/Newport Partners, "in business to find mispriced securities by analysis, computing, and logical thinking. In 1973, the French issued a gold-backed bond, the Giscard. It was to pay in January 1988 in either cash or gold. We found it trading at a discount to its price in gold in 1985, and figured that properly leveraged we could make sixty percent by buying bonds and selling gold futures. But the French could default by taxing foreign holders. So we borrowed from French banks, collateralized ninety percent with the bonds. . . . The gap closed, we made our profit, and we left." Thorp tries to take care of the usual hazards, too. "We called Goldman, Sachs, and asked what happened to our records if a nuclear bomb hit New York. They said they made copies of everything, and stored them in Iron Mountain. We said, 'That's okay, then.' "

I sat one Friday afternoon with T. Brett Haire, the startlingly handsome wavy-haired, square-shouldered, blue-eyed director of trading for First Boston, in his glass-walled office in that firm's New York trading room. Haire had an open line to a phone clerk at the Chicago Merc, and he was selling the near month S&P futures, fifty contracts (then valued at about $7 million) a pop. When the report of this sale hit his screen at a price that showed he hadn't moved the market (the ticker symbol is SPZ, pronounced "spooz"), Haire spoke into the phone, "Another fifty." If the price had begun to move, he would have stopped, but it held firm till the bell shut him off at 4:15, New York time. Whatever is wrong with them, and there are some problems, the Chicago markets are deep and wide.

One of First Boston's customers, on First Boston's recommendation, was well on in the process of accumulating a $150 million position in the stock of a very big business. Haire was confident about his firm's judgment of the value of this company vis-à-vis other possible investments, but didn't wish to spend the weekend worrying about whether some movement in the market as a whole might make his purchases much less of a bargain. The shares of this company almost always moved with the market, and in spring of 1987, with the Japanese so active and the Tokyo Stock Exchange trading twice before New York reopened, prices sometimes changed dramatically over the weekend. If the market went up at the opening on Monday, anything lost on the sale of the futures would be gained by an increase in the value of the $150 million purchase; if the market went down, the effective purchase price of the stock would have gone down with it. By selling the futures, Haire guaranteed the validity of the price he had just paid for the stock. "Margin" on the sale in Chicago would be about $3 million, so the cost of the insurance was about $650 (one day's interest on $3 million at 7 percent), plus a little commission money—for coverage on a possible decline in value on about $65 million worth of stock.

In the futures pits where commodities from random-width plywood to soybeans to interest-rate futures are traded by men and women yelling at one another, "pit scalpers" form a significant category of the "locals," the traders who spend the whole day in the pit and provide liquidity by buying and selling exclusively for their own account. These hyperactive players of the game jump in and out of their positions in intervals measured by minutes or even seconds rather than by hours or even quarter-hours. "I'm going to write a book called *The One-Minute Speculator,*" says Jack Sandner, the blond, bearded ex-prizefighter (and lawyer) who is chairman of the Chicago Mercantile Exchange. Other traders may hold an inventory of positions, long (what the trader has committed himself to buy) or short (what the trader has committed himself to sell).

The trader with a long position hopes (he will say "expects") to see prices rise, enabling him to sell at a markup to his contract price; the trader with a short position hopes to see prices fall, allowing him to buy below the price at which he has agreed to sell. But even traders who expect to profit on the increasing price of their inventories will be active in the market all day, "buying on weakness" and "selling on strength" to reduce the effective cost of their positions, looking for ways to hedge an exposure and guarantee a profit whichever way the market moves. Mostly, the trader makes his money by judging the very short-term turn, whether the next "tick" will be up or down, whether his bid should be raised or lowered at this instant to profit by the passing trend.

On a day when there has been a 2 percent rise or fall in the price of an active stock (or the price of a contract for future delivery of $100,000 in Treasury bonds or 40,000 pounds of bacon or 42,000 gallons of crude oil), a pit trader may be in and out a hundred times, averaging a profit per round-trip that runs one-tenth of 1 percent (or less) of the value of what he is trading. Good markets from a trader's point of view are those where volatility draws volume, the opportunity to ride the wave ("the trend is your friend"), to do a lot of trades in and out with a small profit on each. The tradition of riding the wave began in the agricultural pits in Chicago because agricultural products show well-defined seasonal trends that traders can safely— well, more or less safely—ride in short bursts. Leo Melamed of the Chicago Mercantile Exchange, who invented currencies futures on commodities exchanges in the early 1970s, still remembers fondly his time as a pork-bellies trader: "That was a great contract. I used to say it had nine bull markets and six bear markets, all in one year."

Because trading in and out in volatile markets is what he and his people do for a living, Troster, Singer's Kontos kept his shop in business throughout October 19, 1987, and continued buying through his INside system from brokers whose customers wanted out any way they could get out. It was, of course, an enormous strain, on people and on systems, though Kontos can think of a parallel: "October 19th," he remembers, "was the day after Christmas, and everyone wanted to return his stock certificates." Because the market had felt weak the entire preceding month, Troster, Singer had in fact gone into Black Monday with large short positions in several of the stocks in which it was one of the market makers. Even so, Troster ended the day owning quite a lot of shares that had gone down from the price at which the firm had bought them. "That morning at the opening," Kontos remembered with a shiver, "we did forty-five hundred transactions in five minutes. . . . We made the decision that if we were going to go out of the business we would do it in style."

Later that day, when everybody else did seem to be out of business and there was no place a man could lay off the purchases he made on his mechanical system, Kontos apparently decided that style might not be enough justification for the risks. INside functioned through the crash, unlike most of the over-the-counter market, but according to the SEC staff report on these events, Kontos at noon cut the maximum order he would automatically execute from 3,000 shares to 1,500 on the most active stocks, 1,000 to 500 on the rest—and then cut again, down to 600 and 200, after two in the afternoon. And the spreads widened in this market as elsewhere, of course. It's still an admirable record, if not exactly what Troster, Singer advertised. And in an admirable display of resiliency, all systems were back to normal by Thursday, October 22.

2

Day in, day out, while the winds of change gust and the spotlight of reportage dances about like lightning, the most important news in the world, certainly the most useful news in the world, is prices. Other news tells you what the world did yesterday. Prices tell you firmly if not quite precisely what the world will do today and tomorrow. Prices are determined—"discovered" is the preferred word among the theoreticians—by people in markets. Markets are thus the central institutions of capitalist societies, and what happens in markets is more significant most of the time than what happens in agencies of government. Dishonest or badly informed markets warp the allocation of a community's resources, and governments that try to "plan" such allocations without guidance from markets wind up with "command economies" in which much of the citizenry's most purposive efforts go toward evading the government's commands.

But since the first dukes and counts began protecting the trade routes, it has been obvious that markets exist only at the sufferance of governments. They are creatures of what Milton Katz at the Harvard Law School likes to call "the legal order." And because they require a medium of exchange, they can function effectively only in regimes that value the integrity of their money.

Of all the mysteries, that of the market is perhaps the most resented. The market makers and speculators and brokers are quite different people from those whose efforts are evaluated and influenced by the movements of market prices—the farmer, the entrepreneur, the builder, the candy maker, the pensioner, the miller, the homebuyer. The camaraderie of the market makers seems to hide a conspiracy—and sometimes does. The visible winners in the markets tend to be those who play in them, who neither sow nor reap, but merely cash in. The perceived losers are often a much larger community of identifiable producers and consumers. The explanations of what happens in markets are often arcane and rarely correct.

Because the aim in the market is always to buy cheap and sell dear, the motives of the marketplace fall under the anathema of greed. "Merchants of human misery," President Harry Truman called the grain traders who had built big profitable positions in the wheat pit while the U.S. government was trying to feed hungry Europe in 1948. The players in the markets are, by definition, people who know the price of everything and the value of nothing. For them, all the world's a souk; and all the people in it, hagglers.

"Friend of mine is vice-president of the Independent Kansas Oil and Gas Producers," said Kalo Hineman, acting chairman of the Commodity Futures Trading Commission during the crisis days of October 1987. "He called back in 1986, said, 'These guys have talked the market down to ten dollars a barrel and now they're trying to talk it down to eight.' When he'd finished, I said, 'You sound just like a wheat farmer.' And that's right. The independent oil producer, like the wheat farmer, has always been a price taker."

There is a great deal of gamesmanship in the business. In his reminiscences of the London Stock Exchange, Donald Cobbett tells

11

the story of Julian Berger, the largest jobber (dealer, or specialist in New York Stock Exchange terms) in the shares of Rio Tinto, an Australian mining company: "He bid the price up successively. . . . 'Three-eights buy Rio, at a half buy Rio, buy five thou at five-eights . . .' In the midst of this racket, a broker cautiously approached Julian's henchman, Gerald Brown, remarking unhopefully that he was a buyer of ten thousand at a half.

" 'What did that chap want?' asked Julian when the broker had left his pitch.

" 'No interest to you, sir,' replied Gerald. 'Said he was a buyer of a tenner at a half.'

" 'Well, sell 'em to him, sell 'em,' snapped Berger.

" 'But you're bidding five-eights,' expostulated Gerald.

" 'I know that,' retorted Julian, testily. 'How'd you think I can sell 'em otherwise?' "

Mark Twain called it feeding buckshot to the other fellow's frog before a jumping contest. Ivan Boesky before his fall was a master of the art of appearing to buy while his "beards," as they used to call such agents at the racetracks, were out selling. It happens on all markets, everywhere.

Moreover, the traders are mostly tough cookies. The economist and money-market consultant Marcia Stigum quotes an unnamed dealer: "A trader is the archetype I-will-kill-you player of tennis, backgammon, and other games. He knows this is a killer business, and to him winning is everything—it's his mission in life, and when he wins, he won't even be nice about it." The work requires the most unremitting concentration, and it drains those who do it—even after good days, the crowd coming down the escalator at the Merc looks gray and beat, and few people smile. But it commands extravagant attachment: When the Chicago Board of Trade began night trading to catch the big fish from Tokyo at the hours when they bite, the same people—volunteers, most of them—returned to the floor at six o'clock to start all over again. "Once you've worked on the floor you never get it out of your system," says Ken Lazzara, a dark, efficient young man who now does long-range planning for Refco, the largest of the commodities brokers. "I still toy with becoming a local, every day." Kate Hathaway of the Commodity Futures Trading Commission says it's murder to hang on to the Commission's examiners: "They all want to go off and be traders themselves."

Traders' egos are involved in their work: Mostly, they lie to each other and to themselves about how well they've done. The only measurement is money. With few exceptions, successful traders flaunt their wealth and its appurtenances. Socially, they are almost all braggarts, most often about the sure things, the spreads and hedges that couldn't lose much money at worst and actually made a bundle. "Traders can tell you all about a whole trading session a month ago in which they made money like a golfer who can tell you how high the grass was when he made a great chip shot," says James Chakos, a large, confident man in shirt-sleeves who spent twenty-five years in the "pulpit," the black cage cantilevered over the T-bond pit at the Chicago Board of Trade, reporting trades instantaneously for the ticker tape. When people were glad to see the "yuppies" get theirs in fall 1987, the objects of their contempt were the traders in the markets.

This is not new, either. In 1841, looking back on the South Sea Bubble of more than a century before, Charles Mackay wrote of "The overbearing insolence of ignorant men, who had risen to sudden wealth by successful gambling, made men of true gentility of mind and manners blush that gold should have power to raise the unworthy in the scale of society. The haughtiness of some of these 'cyphering cits,' as they were termed by Sir Richard Steele, was remembered against them in the days of their adversity."

And when a trader works for others, as most do, he knows that if something goes wrong he takes the spear. "A trader is always remembered for his losses, not his profits," says John Arnold of the foreign exchange division of Morgan Guaranty. "It's always a joint decision with the man looking over your shoulder when you're right, and when you're wrong, it's 'Why did you do that?' So I never make predictions."

Yet the truth is that the real producers and real consumers run the greatest risks when there are no traders and no "artificial" futures markets, when they must buy and sell at the moment when the crops ripen, without the intermediation that abstracts their output and needs into mere pieces of paper. "Speculation," said that great phrase maker Oliver Wendell Holmes, Jr., "is the self-adjustment of society to the probable." Markets shift the risks of changing prices from the producers and consumers of commodities to people who are merely buying and selling titles to the merchandise. They allow people who operate on different time horizons to do business with each other through intermediaries, "traders." Thinking themselves clever and

1 3

independent, the traders are in fact the servants of both sides, accepting violent fluctuations in their own income so the ultimate parties to the transaction can smooth their own costs and receipts. Owning shares of stock in a publicly traded company is almost always safer than having a partnership in a venture. The merchants who crowded the docks of the seaports waiting to see what their goods had brought them when sold overseas had to charge much greater margins than any manufacturer could imagine today, to compensate for their risks. Information is most useful when there is time to act on it.

In the markets that look ahead, the veteran buys (or sells) on the rumor, knowing that he will draw imitators, and closes out his position on the news, which will have been "discounted"—incorporated in the prices—before its arrival. In the cash markets where producers deliver and consumers take, prices at each moment reflect immediate supply and demand and instantaneous expectation (rumors and news are the same)—and the market power of the people who are always there. "Exchanges," says Leslie Rosenthal, wearing his purple cotton jacket (bright colors help a man get recognized in a pit), a gray-haired, florid, barrel-chested Rumanian refugee grain trader who was for some years chairman of the Chicago Board of Trade, "are a price-discovery mechanism where you do the discovering publicly. When you start a futures contract for a commodity that never had one before, you always get opposition from the club of dealers that already exists in that business. The more people know what is and isn't a fair price, the harder it is for the dealer."

In the wholesale meat market, the price is a function of how many carcasses are hanging on the hook. If prices go high, vendors rush to deliver to the market, and prices fall—further and further as the meat ages, until finally the scavengers, the buyers for the school lunch services and the nursing homes, the hospitals and the prisons, the fast-food chains and the Soviet Union, come by and take what's left before it rots. A story about an outbreak of hoof-and-mouth disease in Iowa (God forbid) will move prices both in what survives of the stockyards and at the Chicago Mercantile Exchange, where live cattle ready for slaughter and feeder cattle ready for fattening are traded for future delivery. But the buyers of futures will be able to hedge their bets in ways that the buyers of carcasses cannot—buying corn, for example, while they buy cattle, because corn prices will be depressed by the same rumor that boosts cattle prices (fewer cattle to feed), and will rise if the rumor proves false. The little guy putting the animals he has raised into the market is at the mercy of the day, while the big guy can always wait. Futures markets to a degree equalize the competition. "I'm a wheat farmer and a cattle farmer," said Kalo Hineman of the Commodity Futures Trading Commission. "My son's running it for me now. And the way to get rich in cattle farming is the way Bernard Baruch said you got rich in the stock market—you sell too soon." Futures markets make that possible.

Repeatedly in the nineteenth century, the state legislatures closed the futures markets in agricultural products, because the price of wheat or corn went down. The result of these prohibitions was greater oscillation in the cash price paid by the millers and the cattle feeders—and, dangerously from a societal point of view, a reduction in the stocks carried over from one year to the next as insurance for the users. In the absence of a market that deals with some representational construct rather than the real product, producers and consumers always become, in the words of economist Paul Samuelson, "unwilling gamblers."

Where information flows smoothly, market prices tend to move continuously; where information is subject to interruption, they jump. Time and place, of course, happen to us all: Those who sell ice in the wintertime are not paid well for it, and those who want sun-ripened strawberries in December will be charged the air freight from the southern hemisphere. Prices of manufactured goods are elevated by the fact that competition is monopolistic, by the sunk cost of the capital investment required before competitors can effectively enter the market (and perhaps the marketing costs imposed by an economy where establishing a brand is the precondition for sales). Prices of natural monopolies—electric power, local telephone service, franchised transportation—are of course controlled by the state.

Some markets are naturally "lumpy," like commercial real estate, where the individual transaction is very large and the time scale of the investment makes interest rates the determining factor in both the real and imputed costs (that is, the interest you have to pay to borrow year after year and the interest you give up year after year on the cash you have in the deal). Some markets are "elastic," in that price movements rapidly produce increases (or decreases) in supply or demand. When the Hunts put silver through the roof, tons of it appeared as people melted down tableware; when fares are raised on public transportation, fewer people ride the bus; when you move to negotiated commission rates volume doubles—in London, volume tripled—on the stock exchange. Others are "inelastic," in that price movements take a long time to work their way through to real production or consumption, and any major change in supply or demand will push prices hard and far. In the 1970s, it was argued that the market for oil was very inelastic, that extreme price rises did not reduce demand because energy requirements were relatively fixed in a society and did not expand supply because the provision of alternative energy sources was either impossible or hopelessly expensive or so time consuming as not to affect pricing even on a futures horizon. Thus OPEC, first as majority supplier to the world and then as controller of the marginal product that would determine the price, could forever hold the developed world by the shorthairs.

Into this atmosphere came the rapidly deteriorating New York Mercantile Exchange, eking out a precarious existence on the second floor of a hideous steel-and-glass box built on the site of its once glorious and gewgawed Victorian red-brick home, its leading contract (in potatoes) having been manipulated more or less criminally. Looking for something to trade, the NYMEX, as it has come to be called, offered contracts in petroleum futures. The first time around this was not well done, involving contracts for heating oil delivered at the port of Rotterdam, because it was the biggest oil port. The international oil companies were not ready even to recognize the idea of market prices for oil, and, of course, the OPEC cartel, like the previous oil company "concessions," was an attempt to deny the logic of market pricing. In November 1978, the NYMEX tried again, with a contract for Texas intermediate sweet crude of a specified gravity and sulfur content delivered in Cushing, Oklahoma. "The timing," says broker Leon Faber, "was magnificent. We face east every day to the Ayatollah. He really made our market." Even though Texas intermediate accounts for only 2 percent of the world's oil production, the existence of the NYMEX contract made it the "benchmark," the reference point, for all pricing of crude oil. Later NYMEX expanded its "energy complex" to futures and options contracts for heating oil, gasoline, etc., all arranged to offer the buyer and seller a complete choice of forthcoming months, up to sixteen months hence, in which the contract would expire.

In late 1987, when an OPEC meeting broke up in disarray, daily trading in crude oil futures at NYMEX reached the astonishing total of 150 million barrels, roughly ten days' OPEC production. Earlier in the year, the "open interest" in these contracts—the amount of oil, gasoline, and propane in participants' inventories of contracts to buy and sell—totaled 398 million barrels, roughly the entire above-ground supply of oil and product in the non-Communist world.

The number is not really that large, because futures or options contracts on heating oil or gasoline may exist entirely for the purpose of hedging other contracts in crude oil. That is, a trader with contracts that require or permit him to *sell* heating oil or gasoline at a fixed price some months hence may simultaneously, to reduce his risk or lock in an arbitrage profit, acquire contracts permitting or requiring him to *buy* crude oil at another price in another month. As the crude oil and refined products prices are very likely to move in the same direction, the trader holding positions on different sides in the two commodities is guaranteed not to lose much money on the deal—being a professional, indeed, he will probably catch the prices in the different contracts in such a way that the "spread" guarantees him a modest but useful return. Most of the "locals" on the floors of the commodities markets make their livings by spotting illogical differences between the prices of slightly different contracts, and playing such spreads. NYMEX has a special place on its dirty red-carpeted floor, a kind of platform between the crude pit and the product pits, for those who play or help their customers play "the crack spread." And each spread transaction, of course, creates what looks like a pair of contracts that may have to be fulfilled with actual delivery.

In the terms of art of the business, the "open interest" numbers from the NYMEX reflect both "paper barrels," contracts that will be settled through extinction before their expiration, and "wet barrels," contracts that represent actual oil or product to be delivered to a purchaser through an "exchange for physicals," or actual delivery via the NYMEX facility. Historically, commitments to buy more than the supply available on the day the futures contract expires produce what the markets call a "squeeze," which can run prices to the sky. The Hunts thought they could do that in silver, which was very dumb of them and eventually transferred the billions of dollars their father had left them from their hands to more intelligent ownership.

In normal times, the players and the clearing corporations try to maintain a stable ratio between open interest subject to possible calls for delivery and real inventory at the warehouses. Terry Martell, the rotund former Alabama professor who became research director of the New York Commodity Exchange (COMEX), where gold and silver trade (locus of the Hunts' trouble), reports that "we have 2.8 million ounces of silver in our warehouses, enough silver to plate a battleship, and lots of gold [though probably not enough to cover the $75 billion worth of open interest listed by the COMEX clearinghouse], all in lower Manhattan. This would be a hell of a city to sack."

Over time, what will matter most in the oil business is the fact that the key prices for oil have become those that emerge from the open outcry of continuous auction at NYMEX, not those paid today by the refiners or the consumers. The newspapers still carry daily reports on the spot prices for Brent oil from the North Sea, west Texas intermediate crude, and Arabian light. But oil companies, power-and-light companies, airlines, auto manufacturers, and natural gas pipeline companies make their plans looking into the next months on the prices revealed on the floor of the NYMEX, now ensconced (and crowded) on a quarter of the commodity futures trading floor of the World Trade Center to the west of Wall Street.

Interestingly, the oil trade has not got used to its freedom. For years, the price of oil was derived from the "posted price," which was what the big oil companies charged themselves for the oil they drew from under the sands of the Arabian desert (on a basis that allowed them to charge part of what they paid as a "tax" they could deduct from their U.S. taxes). To keep prices up, the Texas Railroad Commission limited the amount of oil the big companies could take from Texas in any month (when the Israeli-French-British invasion of Egypt choked off the transport of oil from the Persian Gulf in 1956, the United States had so much surplus capacity socked away to preserve Texas prices that it could supply its European allies for more than a year without creating shortages at home). Even now, the old-timers feel that if they knew exactly how much oil was coming out of the ground, they would really have their hands on what was going on. M. S. Robinson, recently retired president of Shell International Trading in London, complained to the *Wall Street Journal* in fall 1987 that because of the secrecy of OPEC, "we don't know whether too much oil is being produced until the market breaks."

But that's what a properly functioning market does: It tells everybody that too much or too little is being produced, in a way that cannot be ignored simply because somebody doesn't like the news. Governments kill markets because they cannot live with the information they provide: Rather than force wheat farmers out of business because there's a glut of wheat and the price yields a living only to the lowest-cost producers, the government (in the United States or Europe or Japan or, God save us, Saudi Arabia) sets up a price support and buys for its own account at that price—and then immense quantities overhang the market. And until what the government has bought has admittedly rotted, few farmers can make a good living.

3

Among the major changes technology has wrought is the increased chance to make markets without a marketplace. About a month after the British government opened British securities markets to a raft of new players in the "Big Bang" of fall 1986, which we shall visit later, the London Stock Exchange abandoned its trading floor. The Troster, Singer operation works entirely through telecommunications. And it is almost two generations since there was a significant trading floor in the United States for the cash money markets. Today, it's "upstairs," the trading rooms of individual firms linked together by telecommunications, that provides the locus of trading in Treasury bills and bonds, foreign exchange, bank reserves ("Fed Funds"), and very short-term interbank loans both at home ("repurchase agreements," or "repos") and abroad ("Eurodollars"). The volumes of trading in these instruments outrun the human imagination. On a routine day in 1987, the New York Stock Exchange traded $5 billion to $6 billion worth of stock, the S&P pit at the Chicago Mercantile Exchange did perhaps $8 billion of index futures at market value, and the Treasury-bond pit at the Chicago Board of Trade moved about $25 billion in T-bond futures contracts. But the Fed Funds market in which banks trade in and out of their own accounts at the Federal Reserve Banks ran $80 billion a day, the "repo" market in Treasuries was at least twice that, and foreign exchange trading involved $200 billion.

Most of the U.S. Treasury paper cash trading is done with the assistance of a Telerate screen, a news service that reports the inside prices quoted by banks and dealers for money-market instruments—the prices at which dealers will buy from and sell to each other.

Telerate was begun in 1969 by the bond house of Cantor, Fitzgerald, essentially as a marketing tool, a way to distribute their own quotes. Other firms paid to have their quotes "published" on the Telerate screens, and in theory they still do, though in fact the major players are present by invitation. The computer-generated composite pages, which present the best quotes presently in the system, half a dozen or so separately on buy and sell sides, are in practice the marketplace for U.S. Treasuries. Even the traders for the Federal Reserve, who used to be on the telephone all the time collecting quotes from dealers, now sit and watch the screens.

Thanks to the Cantor, Fitzgerald connection (and the discounts New York State had to offer to rent space at the World Trade Center when the buildings were new), Telerate occupies exotic quarters, one floor below Cantor's own 105th-floor offices in one of the two tallest buildings in New York. About a dozen "reporters" sit in a goldfish bowl, a room with glass walls to the public hall, watching screens with green letters and numbers, headsets strapped on, keyboards at the ready to update the quotes. Between what some hundreds of market makers supply directly to the Telerate computer and what the reporters take down over the telephone, the service changes well over half a million quotes on its screens every day.

Companies that sell market-related statistical services can use the Telerate system as a kind of publication for subscribers, buying a "page" accessible only to those among the twenty thousand Telerate screens that also pay for this information. Telerate itself offers an upgrade of its basic information service that calculates spreads, signals arbitrage opportunities, and manipulates the streams of price information to demonstrate their meaning in connection with prearranged trading strategies. But customers cannot do their actual trading through Telerate facilities; for that, one still needs a separate telephone line. By the mid-1980s, Telerate had become bigger than its founders, who sold control in early 1987 to Dow, Jones & Co., the publishers of the *Wall Street Journal.*

Internationally, the long-established British press agency Reuters is a far more important service. Since 1973, its screens have been the locus for cash bids and offers of foreign exchange from all over the world, and immense volumes of foreign-exchange transactions now occur through the Reuters wires. Reuters subscribers cannot, like the "INside" customers of Troster, Singer, simply hit a button to execute a currency purchase or sale at the price on the screen, because banks have credit limits on their dealings with each other and management wants to exercise constant supervision over what their foreign-exchange traders are doing. Citicorp chairman George Moore, who was also president of New York's Metropolitan Opera, once explained that there are four kinds of people with whom you cannot use reason: great chefs, beautiful women, opera singers, and foreign-exchange traders.

Dealing, therefore, occurs through keyboards. A bank or broker looking to buy or sell foreign exchange can bring up the current quotes on his screen, and then directly query any one of the scores of traders in this currency by punching out the four-letter code that identifies this participant in the market. (The message types out: "Hi Frds [Friends], Bank of Montreal here . . .") Having established the size trade for which the quote is good, the searcher can hit the bid or take the offer on the screen, and confirmation of the trade then prints out of the computer printer in both shops simultaneously. Reuters' own computers, however, do not keep a record of the trades, only of the volume of "contacts" among the roughly fifteen hundred subscribers to the foreign exchange—a volume that in 1987 ran well over sixty thousand a day.

The cash prices for foreign currency reported in the newspapers and on broadcast news services, whatever the country in which the trading is alleged to have occurred, are in fact the prices on Reuters screens. The difference between "the Tokyo market" and "the New York market" is that more traders are awake in Tokyo during the hours the news reports quote the Tokyo prices and more are awake in New York during the hours the news reports quote the New York prices. But there is only one foreign-exchange market now, and it resides mysteriously in the wires and transistors and communications ganglia of the Reuters Monitor. It works round-the-clock and round-the-globe: "If I'm hot and I'm trading currencies," says Steve Rosenberg, who went from trading metals for Shearson to trading for himself at the New York Commodity Exchange (COMEX) and then trading at home from a screen, "I'll stay up twenty hours. There are fifty places that want that business, and they don't even charge commissions, they make it on the bid-and-asked."

Foreign exchange will doubtless continue to be Reuters' central business: "Foreign-exchange markets," says its Australian-born CEO Glen Renfrew, a newsman with experience on four continents, "are so much bigger than these piddling securities markets." But

21

with the passage of time, Reuters has expanded its price reporting to virtually all the securities and commodities markets anywhere in the world. According to the prospectus published in 1986 in connection with the first public sale of the company's stock, Reuters in December 1985 was reporting on-line the prices of 38,900 securities and 11,600 exchange-traded options from 210 locations in 65 countries around the world to everyone in the world who had a Reuters' screen. The general news-gathering capability, while it now amounts to less than 6 percent of Reuters' revenues, is essential (and is why Telerate, hoping to remain a viable competitor to Reuters in the supply of price information, yielded control to Dow-Jones, which has its own large news staff and an Associated Press link). "People around the world today," says Renfrew, "won't trade unless they have instant information—total information."

Reuters Monitor and Reuters Alert have become the indispensable tools of traders everywhere. Leo Melamed of the Chicago Merc says that he has a Reuter's Monitor screen in his bedroom, and looks at it when he gets up at five in the morning—"after I take a leak, of course; sometimes before I take a leak, depending on my position." Tony Bruck, a young trader who came to the commodities markets from a Ph.D. in linguistics at the University of Chicago, reports that some of his friends have their Reuters Monitor rigged up with bells that will wake them when there's a major move during the night in something in which they have a position.

In 1987, Reuters acquired a company called Instinet, which had a system that allowed customers to pull up bid and asked quotes on their screens and then buy or sell shares at those prices at the touch of a button, through a properly programmed and modemed personal computer. Some time in 1988, the Chicago Merc and Reuters will launch a service that permits people anywhere in the world to buy or sell futures contracts and options traded on the Merc, through screens and telecommunications facilities, at any hour that the exchange itself is not open. These will be the same contracts, with the same commitments to the Merc's clearing corporation, that are traded in the pits. For legal purposes and with reference to any limits the exchange may set on the daily movement of prices, trades after the market has closed in Chicago will count as part of the next day's trading.

In a sense, the deal with Reuters was a follow-up to the Merc's two-year-old arrangement with the Singapore Mercantile Exchange (or SIMEX), by which the Merc's most popular cash-settlement contracts, especially the Eurodollar and S&P 500 futures contracts, are bought and sold in Singapore for clearance in Chicago—and the SIMEX's most popular contract, futures of the Japanese Nikkei-Dow index of prices on the Tokyo Stock Exchange, will be traded in Chicago. Meanwhile, Reuters retains some freedom to deal with other exchanges: As 1988 began, Renfrew and Andre Villeneuve, an English newsman with Oxbridge credentials who is director of Reuters' American operations, began negotiations with president Rosemary MacFadden of the New York Mercantile Exchange for a Reuters extension of the NYMEX trading hours on oil futures.

These are immensely important developments, and we must leave to the final chapter consideration of what they portend and whether we are likely to be happy about what happens. If substantial trading volumes from other countries are stimulated by the availability of these contracts at the hours when people other than residents of the Western Hemisphere do business, the CME-Reuters link will levitate the Chicago markets out of the American Midwest and make them in truth the global markets everyone has been talking about. And except in foreign exchange, that will indeed be something new.

Right now, though there are experiments going on almost out of sight (Montreal, which does 12 million shares a day, has links with Antwerp, Vancouver, and Sydney that make it possible to trade listed Canadian shares twenty hours a day), global markets tend to be internal to the participating brokers and dealers. Merrill Lynch, for example, will maintain a unified trading "book" in the shares of, say, Credit Suisse, Ducretet-Thompson, Fiat, Matsushita, Volkswagen, British Petroleum, and Apple Computer. New York pretty much shuts down its trading at the close of the market at 4 P.M., which is 10 P.M. most of the year in London and 6 A.M. in Tokyo. The international department in Tokyo and the Hong Kong office will kick in at about 7 P.M. New York time and do their own business in the same stock, passing the torch and a possibly much amended Merrill Lynch trading position to London at 3 A.M. New York time. And what returns to New York when the U.S. markets shake themselves awake at 9:30 (for stocks: Chicago starts trading the bond futures at 9 A.M. New York time and one stock index product at 9:15 A.M.) may be a quite different position from what New York left to Merrill Lynch worldwide seventeen and a half hours earlier. In any major Merrill office anywhere, a touch of a button on a keyboard will summon forth the report of the day's activity in each market—and how much the firm made or lost on it.

The *idea* of international markets, of course, is not as new as today's participants like to think. In London before World War II, there was a "Yankee market" on the floor of the stock exchange, which opened at three o'clock. Donald Cobbett remembered a scene dominated by the jobber George Rothschild, a stocky man "half hidden by his outsize gray carnation. . . . Wall Street was coming in better. Clerks would be quickly decoding the first cables. This side the market has been bearish and prices were below parity. The cables fluttered in the jobbers' hands. Suddenly it was as if a match were set to dynamite; the whole market erupted in a clangorous roar . . . George's staccato bidding topping the lot . . . 'Half buy Radio!' . . . 'At a half buy Radio!' " Stephen Raven of S. G. Warburg remembers that when he started on the London Stock Exchange twenty years ago, he worked for Ackroyd & Smithers, a jobber with a specialty in U.S. shares: "We made a market in London, laid it off in New York, settled in London." Because the settlement period in London was at least a weekend and usually a week or more longer than it was in New York, there were edges a jobber in London enjoyed in such trading.

Despite editorial pressure to the contrary, there are not now and will not be for some time to come "global" markets in corporate securities. Various parts of the legal order that govern securities and markets, including such simple things as the settlement system by which the securities are delivered and paid for, are too different from one country to another. Merrill Lynch, for example, has a unified worldwide book in Fiat, but its book shows trades executed on the Milan Stock Exchange as long as a year ago, for which the securities have not yet been delivered and the money has not been paid, because the clearing facilities in Milan are primitive.

Even the futures market in U.S. Treasury bonds is not quite the same between the Chicago Board of Trade and the London International Financial Futures Exchange (LIFFE, pronounced "life"), which trades the same contract and will if necessary enforce delivery in Chicago by its members on expiration date. The several hours additional time that the London seller has to put together a deliverable package on the day the futures contract comes due gives the London seller a little more chance to make money, and the spread between the London and Chicago contracts may run as high as

6/32nds of a point. And there is, of course, at all times an information barrier that mere electronics will not necessarily transcend. "Each market has peculiarities," says Scott Pardee, a big, soft-spoken, straightforward veteran of the Federal Reserve Bank of New York (where he managed the nation's official foreign-exchange trading), who is now vice-chairman of Yamaichi Securities, America. "It costs you money to learn them. The Reuters screens tell you this and that, but you have to live where the market is and read the local papers. If you're trading dollars and marks in Hong Kong and suddenly a guy calls from New York with a big order, you wonder, What does he know that I don't know?"

Still, where there are cash settlement contracts with clearing-houses rather than with the individuals on the other side of the trade—a situation we shall be looking at later—there is no inherent barrier to full internationalization, especially now that the major currencies are convertible to one another instantaneously at a cost that works out to something like twenty dollars for every million dollars traded (2/100ths of 1 percent). Sir David Scholey, who by force of intelligence has made the rather small British house of S. G. Warburg a major player worldwide, points out the key fact: "that you can now unbundle IBM from dollars or Fiat from lire."

The Reuters Monitor has made this possible, together with the institutional system that made the dollar the reserve currency of the world. Currency trading is done almost entirely in dollars (that is, someone selling yen for marks normally uses his yen to buy dollars which in turn buy the marks), and settlement is in effect at CHIPS, the Clearing House Interbank Payments System computer in New York that processes about $400 billion of mostly international payments every day. To the extent that the other markets are internationalized, it is because commodities are denominated in dollars. For example, the price of gold in South African rand is simply the price of gold in dollars times the number of rand to the dollar; thus the gold-mining companies do great when the exchange value of the rand declines. Similarly, the price of oil in yen is the price of oil in dollars times the number of yen to the dollar, which means that when the dollar declines with reference to the yen the Japanese get their energy cheaper. And the prices of all a nation's securities, corporate or governmental, debt or equity, are strongly influenced by the interest rates in that currency—which in an age of easy convertibility among currencies are a function of whether this one is strengthening or

25

weakening as the trading proceeds on the Reuters screens.

More than a quarter of a century ago, according to Arthur Schlesinger, Jr., President John F. Kennedy "half humorously derided the notion that nuclear weapons were essential to international strength. 'What really matters,' he said, 'is the strength of the currency.' " As the United States learned most uncomfortably in the last months of 1987, the "globalization" of the world's markets has taken what humor there might have been in Kennedy's comment and turned it sour.

Meanwhile, individually, each with its own purpose, every weekday, the markets go on.

2

Upstairs, Downstairs

"Markets have been going through two things—globalization and institutionalization. They interact. One of the results is that thought processes are becoming en masse—it isn't an individual thinking any more."

—Leo Melamed, special counsel,
Chicago Mercantile Exchange, 1987

"Those fellows you see in that pit with gray hair? Don't be confused. They're twenty-eight years old, too."

—Mike Heeger, floor manager, Refco,
at the Chicago Mercantile Exchange, 1986

1

*T*he things that unite auction markets in which prices are found—as distinguished from wholesale and retail markets in which prices are given and taken—are far greater than the things that divide them. The auction markets are almost infinitely varied in terms of the products they price, the participants in the auction, the procedures they follow, and the institutions they become. But they are, very significantly, sisters under the skin.

2

Six days a week just before eight in the morning, twenty or so men in jeans and sports shirts appropriate to the season gather at the New Bedford Seafood Exchange in a small steel-walled green shed attached to the larger steel-walled green shed of Yellowbird Trucks in the industrial park beside the harbor of this old Massachusetts city. They have come for an auction in which the catch of ten to twenty of the city's fleet of 130-odd trawlers, returned from the sea the previous night, will be sold to one of the 23 firms that have paid an $8,500 initiation fee to become a member of the exchange. Between 150,000 and 300,000 pounds of fish will be sold here at a typical auction. The prices at which transactions are concluded here will be broadcast to the world through the facilities of the U.S. Department of Commerce, and will strongly influence the price of fish in wholesale markets up and down the Atlantic Coast.

The exchange is a small square room, inexpensively wood paneled, with a nubby brown Berber carpet. Behind is an even smaller narrow room for observers, including men from the ships that have put their catch up for sale, who communicate back to their captains in Portuguese on walkie-talkies as the auction proceeds. On one wall of the main room is a row of telephones with long cords, each tied to the home office of one of the member firms. At the front of the room is a long green chalkboard divided by vertical lines into about three dozen compartments. When the members arrive, the names of the boats up for auction today are already on the board, with a listing below each of them of the species the captain says he caught on this trip, and the total weight of each kind of fish. A railing separates the men in the main room from the area where the chalkmen stand to mark the board.

When the bell rings at eight o'clock, the bidders leaning against the railing begin yelling at the three men by the chalkboard, who choose one of them as the flag bearer, in effect, for each of the boats. The chalkman writes down the price that bidder offers for each of the species on the boat, and then writes the bidder's initial on the bottom. Any member who now wishes to bid for this boat need merely increase the price offered for one of the species. That commits him to meet the existing price on all the other species. The original bidder keeps his initial on the boat by calling "ten," which adds a tenth of a cent to the price just bid by his opponent.

People who think that calculating the value of options on interest-rate futures is complicated should consider what is asked of the bidders in New Bedford. If they win, they take the whole "trip," usually 12,000–20,000 pounds of fish, both the species they need for their customers and the species they will have to scramble to lay off.

Meanwhile, they have to watch what their rivals are paying for species on another boat, for everyone will be on the phone to New York and Boston and elsewhere with the same wholesale merchants. "You've got to go jump on the other guy's trip," says Joe Rugnetta, a soft-spoken older man in large glasses whose father and grandfather were New York fishmongers, "so he can't beat you in the market. That boat may be bid at too much for sand dabs, and you may not want it, but you can be damned sure his flounder are no bargain." Various opportunities exist: "You can sometimes get a boat you want by bidding three dollars for a species where there's only two hundred fifty pounds of it on the boat." Some people bid high because they need fish, some because they have inventory and they're protecting the price.

The bidders are men of experience (women are definitely not permitted: It is generally agreed by the fish merchants, many of whom would blush to hear what gets shouted in the coed foreign-exchange trading rooms, that women couldn't take the language the men talk on the floor). They know how long each boat has been out and how much ice it carried on departure; they know that some of these captains take better care of their fish than others, so that the value of 3,500 pounds of cod on one boat may be quite different from the value of a similar quantity on another boat. And, of course, everybody watches the weather forecasts, knows the number of boats that went out yesterday and seem likely to go out today, and listens to the reports available by radio from the boats now at sea.

After the initial flurry of bids, the men on the floor, most of whom are of Italian background, schmooze a little and smoke, talk a little about the Red Sox or the Celtics or the Patriots, then drift over to the telephones and discuss the opening with home offices. Someone with a receiver in his ear, dragging the long cord across the room, may make a preemptive strike on a single vessel. Another flurry of bids may precede the two-minute break at 8:15, when the captains whose boats are on the board get an opportunity to withdraw them, either because they don't like the prices or because they don't like the house that seems the probable winner of the auction. For auction purposes, the fish on board are guaranteed Grade-A, and prices can be renegotiated after the boat pulls up to the winner's dock if the quality is found lacking. Some processors have a reputation with the captains as chiselers. The grim-looking young men with the walkie-talkies in the back room are discussing these matters with the captain, who can weigh anchor and sail to the next morning's auction in Boston, or go on to Gloucester, where large wholesale dealers have the resources to buy an entire trip.

At 8:17, the auction resumes, for five more very active minutes. The last minute is full of screaming ("You see men turn into animals here," says Bruno Fustaci, Joe Rugnetta's son-in-law, who is being broken into the business). The auctioneers don't have to turn away from their board to know who is screaming. They keep erasing numbers, adding tenths to prices, sometimes adding much more to prices, until the bell rings and the room rather suddenly quiets. The bidders look at who won the trips, and may sound each other out a little on the availability of some species they are committed to for their out-of-town customers, though serious bargaining of that kind is more likely to be done over the telephone from the privacy of one's office than out on the auction floor. After one such call this morning, Rugnetta's auction bidder Victor Varano, an overweight, energetic man with graying tight curly hair, furthered young Fustaci's education with the comment, "I never trusted a fucking Norwegian in my life. Only Italians, I tell you." But then Varano made a deal with his Norwegian friend. "Fishmongers are always at each other's throats," Rugnetta said, "but usually, everybody in this town helps each other, to a certain extent."

In the New Bedford Seafood Exchange, meanwhile, the chalk-men are making a record of the results of the auction so that participants can verify what they sold and what they bought at what price. They then call a telephone number at the Department of Commerce, which communicates the prices to WPMS, the local radio station, for broadcast to the Cape Cod area at 8:40 A.M., and records the price list on a cassette tape so that fish wholesalers elsewhere in the country can call an 800 number and hear the official report through the earpieces of their telephones. Commerce also prints up the prices on its "green sheets" for distribution by mail all over the country. But by the next day, when the green sheets arrive, the prices will have changed.

The captains' boats tie up at the landings beside the processing plants the merchants own, and the crews begin hoisting baskets of gleaming fish from the hold to the sluices that lead to the rooms where fillets are sliced away and steaks cut, and heads, bones, and (where not already jettisoned to the gulls) guts are sent off to the cat-food makers. When the boat is unloaded, the captain will be paid, with a check that will be good funds today—you can get cash for it immediately—at one of the local banks. Thirty-five dollars of each check has been paid out in advance to the Seafood Exchange for its services. The merchants will have to wait, usually thirty days, long after the fish are eaten, before their customers pay them.

Joe Rugnetta's dark-haired rose-lipped daughter came to work for him recently, leaving a job at the New York headquarters of First Boston's Real Estate Development and Mortgage Finance division (which wanted to send her to London to work on the giant Canary Wharf project that is to move half the City's money men a mile east and well into the Thames). "In a lot of ways," she says, "New Bedford and First Boston are the same. The pressure's the same".

3

The market superficially most like that of the New Bedford Seafood Exchange is the gold-fixing market in London. Since 1919, with a hiatus between World War II and 1954, a small number of gold bullion dealers have met daily, then twice daily, at a round table in a large room on the top floor of the offices of N. M. Rothschild & Sons in New Court in London. Oriental rugs lie on the marble floor, and the walls are hung with portraits of the former royal families of Europe, once the Rothschild clients. Until 1987, there were only five "members" of this market, but in 1987, following the noisome failure of the banking affiliate of one of the five (Johnson, Matthey), it was considered wise to provide a broader base. The five (including a replacement for Johnson, Matthey) will still meet at Rothschild's, but they will be in direct consultation with some fifty-odd dealers recognized by the Bank of England as a London Bullion Market Association.

Like the fish brokers, the gold dealers are tied to their home offices by an umbilical cord of telephone wire. The chairman, a representative of Rothschild's, proposes a price, and dealers say whether at that price, speaking of course for their customers around the world, they would be buyers or sellers. If there are more buyers than sellers, the chairman suggests a higher price; if there are more sellers, a lower price is suggested. Before each dealer there is a stand with a small Union Jack. When the price declared is one at which the firm would stand prepared either to buy or to sell, he dips his flag. As long as anyone's flag is still erect, the bidding continues. When all the flags are dipped, the chairman announces a "fixing." The five dealers are then committed to buy or sell, in a prearranged proportion, whatever is offered to the group or bid from the group at that price.

Like the New Bedford market, the London fixing does not really determine the price that even intermediaries will pay later in the day: It is a guideline. As William M. Clarke and George Pulay wrote in 1970, *after* the price is fixed "the forces of supply and demand come into real play and the price will fluctuate accordingly." Other fish markets are different. In Tokyo, for example, there is a "display" market, patronized by retail fishmongers and restaurateurs rather than processors, and the fish are exposed to potential buyers, who wander around and look at them (checking for fattiness by cutting into the tails of the frozen tuna lying gray-white on the asphalt beside the dock) and bid by individual lot at one of a series of several dozen auctions proceeding simultaneously on the paving along the waterfront, the auctioneers standing on packing crates and puffingly pumping themselves up to be heard by the rear rank of bidders in the next bay. Other metals markets are different, too, with trading floors and brokers making bids and offers and prices varying continuously as buyers and sellers strike individual deals. But the London gold "fixing," like the New Bedford auction, sets a price for a bundle of transactions to guide wholesalers in their activity, then goes away until the time comes to price the next bundle.

As a matter of common sense, the decision on how to bid for a single homogeneous commodity like gold should be much simpler than the decision on valuing a dozen species of fish. But a much larger mix of factors influences the gold price. Gold is gold because of its durability: Not only individuals and corporations but central banks and governments buy gold to hold it, bringing into play a great complex of techniques for calculating present value. While feedback from the "real" market of ultimate consumers does influence bidding by buyers at the fish auction, it is yesterday's information, and once and for all. And the supply of fish, which is in the short run relatively independent of price, varies far more drastically than demand.

At Rothschild's the men behind the little flags are listening through their telephones to word from the cash and futures and options markets that run round-the-clock, in New York and Chicago, Hong Kong and Sydney, Bahrain and Zurich. New Bedford deals only with dollars, but the gold market must consider movements and expected movements in the exchange value of currencies. From the point of view of a German investor, a 10 percent rise in the price of gold as denominated in dollars is meaningless if there is an accompanying decline of 10 percent in the price of dollars as denominated in marks. Interest rates don't matter much in New Bedford, but they are highly significant to gold traders, because they purchase gold mostly "on margin," with borrowed money.

And, of course, giant inventories hang over the gold market, where players worry about the activities of "the Red man [Russia], the Black man [South Africa], and the Yellow man [Singapore]," all of which have government agencies that are strong participants in the private market. Gold is a store of value: "Only in so far as paper money represents gold," Karl Marx wrote quite sternly, "is it a symbol of value." It is also an industrial commodity, used for jewelry, as a lining for containers that hold certain highly corrosive chemicals, and as a plating for the bottom of space rockets to protect them from the gases in the propellant. And it is a manufactured product, for changes in the technology of leaching gold-bearing soils have greatly increased the output of what were once marginal mines, all over the world: Higher prices will bring increased supplies.

As a free market in terms of dollar pricing, gold goes back only to 1973, when the United States—which had inundated itself with gold in 1934 by raising the price to $35 an ounce (from the previous $20.75)—got tired of selling its hoard to the rest of the world for $42.22, a figure that virtually ignored forty years' inflation in other commodity prices. "The United States," economic adviser Milton Gilbert of the Bank for International Settlements wrote the American banker George S. Moore in 1969, "has only been prepared to pay the 1934 price for gold and in consequence it has not gotten any. If it similarly insisted on paying only the 1934 price for coffee, diamonds, steel, Chevrolets, champagne, bus drivers, civil servants or trips to outer space, it would not get any of those either." Finally, the gold market, unlike the fish market, is full of amateur players who bid up the prices of bullion and coins and buy and sell futures contracts and options contracts giving the right to buy gold itself or gold futures.

Still, as a matter of form, the gold fixing is a market with the same characteristics as the New Bedford fish auction. One notes in passing that both of these markets fulfill their functions without making trouble for anybody. They are both anchors, in a world where most markets have become a sea of shifting tides.

4

The classic continuous market is the New York Stock Exchange. Here during trading hours, the buyer can always find the merchandise listed as traded on this floor, and the owner can always sell any listed security for cash at a price determined in a never-ending auction. The terms of choice are "depth, breadth, and resiliency"—people can sell very large quantities of a very large variety of securities, and the price will tend to return to its previous level relatively quickly if the only factor moving it off its previous level was the size of the block that changed ownership. This is a grand trading floor, built (for what then seemed the immense cost of $2 million) at the turn of the century, a well-proportioned room seven stories high with cathedral windows, an ornamented ceiling, and a famous loggia much beloved of the television news shows, where an officer of the exchange sounds a bell for the opening and another bell for the closing.

About twenty-five hundred people work on the floor and in its annexes in adjoining buildings, trading on an average day in 1987 perhaps $6 billion worth of shares in the largest corporate enterprises of America and, increasingly, the rest of the industrialized world. Requirements for "listing" a corporation's shares at the NYSE include a minimum market value for the company's shares of $18 million, minimum pre-tax profits of $2 million, at least 1,100,000 shares in the hands of the public, and 2,200 members of the public who hold the shares. A company can fall below some of these numbers and keep its listing, but not too far for too long. The Exchange will also wish to approve the transfer agent who registers the change in ownership when a share is sold, and in the case of foreign corporations the arrangements that have been made to create a piece of paper that conforms to American law.

Rules changes in the mid-1980s for the first time permitted big customers to call their brokers on the floor directly, but most call their customer's man upstairs and let him relay the message. At one time or another, the price of one of the 1,366 "seats" on the exchange (obviously, nobody sits; what is meant is the right to buy or sell listed securities from or to other members within these precincts) has gone over a million dollars. Only individuals can be members: The "member firms" are considered extensions of the individual, not his employers. On the other hand, members cannot do business with the public unless they form firms. There have been women members since the mid-1960s, when Muriel ("Mickey") Seibert, a large, tough blond who had seen the coming eruption of the air-freight business and made herself the outstanding expert on the stocks of those companies, broke the barrier.

The creation of the legal infrastructure that supports this market was one of the great intellectual achievements of the nineteenth century, not perfected until well into this one. The word "stock" is an Americanism. In proper English, "stock" is a debt instrument, and British government bonds are still called "stock"; what are traded on the exchanges where they speak British English are "shares," and "common" for stock becomes "ordinary" for shares. But the limited liability corporation in which people own "stock" was initially a British creation, adopted and adapted by the sovereign American states, which charter corporations. American businessmen cannot imagine a world without the notion of a corporate entity that survives the death of its mortal owners and managers, and maintains its own legal persona, so that its owners are not individually responsible for its debts. Within the memory of living men (though they're getting very long in the tooth), bank stocks could not be traded on an exchange because bank charters, unlike other corporate charters, required shareholders to come up with more money if the bank failed and depositors had to be paid off. People now talk about options limiting a purchaser's risk, and options sell consistently for more than their intrinsic worth because this safety feature is valued. But a limit on risk is inherent in the corporate structure: The shareholder can't lose more than he's put on the table.

The key figure in Anglo-American stock exchanges is the officially sanctioned "market maker," who stands ready at all times to bid for a stock a member offers for sale, or sell a stock a member bids to buy. In London, this role until "Big Bang" in fall 1986 was fulfilled by a jobber, who did no business with the public but traded as a dealer, adding to or subtracting from his own inventory, with the brokers who handled public orders. The brokers were strictly intermediaries: They could not sell from their inventory or keep what their customers sold through them. Stocks with larger capitalization usually commanded the services of several jobbers, who might stand at different "pitches" on the floor. Each of the nine pitches as the market neared Götterdämmerung in 1986 was a gray eight-sided structure serving as a desk for clerks inside, topped by an octagonal marquee on which mechanically driven price boards gave information to seekers for it. London being a floor that retained its boys'-club atmosphere to the end, the posts where the shares most in demand were traded might bear an ornament identifying them—a large Styrofoam bowler hat, for example, when the Trusteed Savings Banks first became a publicly held corporation and all those who had been allocated shares at the underwriting were rushing to "stag" their holdings (sell on the immediate rise in price that for some years in the British bull market always followed issuance of new shares by a major corporation or by the government privatizing some state-owned enterprise).

The London Stock Exchange had a dirty secret, which was that it processed a tiny value of trades, about as much as the Philadelphia Stock Exchange or Pacific Stock Exchange in the United States. (The LSE also had a thriving business in auction trading of British government bonds, however). In October 1986, for reasons and in ways we shall examine later, changes in British securities laws and the rules of the exchange destroyed this institution, moving the trading of shares upstairs into office towers where "market makers" (no longer called jobbers) sat at screens and answered or did not answer the telephone, many of them now dealing directly with customers. And at this writing the floor of the London Stock Exchange serves as a giant filing cabinet where clerks hunt among the papers the British system was unable to process in the aftermath of the threefold increase in trading in 1987. By the time this book is published, however, the mess will probably have been cleared up, for reasons not entirely satisfactory to the exchange: Volume dropped by more than a third after the crash.

At the New York Stock Exchange, market making is in the hands of a "specialist," who like the London jobber normally did no business with the public (though this was a custom rather than a rule, and recently some of the big brokerage firms have taken over specialist posts, continuing to operate them independently). Each stock is assigned to one such firm and trades only at its post, in this case a mahogany enclosure surrounded by CRT screens that poke over the heads of the brokers and clerks walking past on the floor. Fifty-five specialist firms ranging in size from two to twenty-four members handle the fifteen hundred or so common stocks. The biggest specialist firm, Spear, Leeds & Kellogg, makes markets in more than 130 stocks (and also, incidentally, controls the over-the-counter house of Troster, Singer, visited in Chapter 1). Specialists stand in front of their posts, waiting hospitably for brokers to visit.

In principle, trading at the New York Stock Exchange is initiated by a broker who asks the price of a stock (quoted in eighths of a dollar, bid and asked—40-⅛, 40-⅜) and the number of shares for which those bid and asked are good. Sometimes the bids are from other brokers in the "crowd" at the post; sometimes they are from the specialist himself, who is charged with maintaining a "fair and orderly" market. In a situation where the separation between the bid and asked is two ticks, he will probably try for a sale in the middle, in this case at 40-¼. Failing that, if his customer has given him a "market" order, he will probably hit the bid or take the offer for any size up to the maximum for which the other brokers or the specialist are quoting these prices. If he has more than the maximum to buy or sell quickly, he may make his intentions known to the specialist or to other brokers standing near this post, or he may bide his time. Large customers pay brokers for their judgment on the direction of the market and its depth. If his customer wants to pay only 39-½, or sell for 42, and has given him a "limit" order rather than a "market" order, the broker may leave the order with the specialist to execute when and if the price of the trading by the brokers before the post hits that limit. When there is no public bid or offer, the specialist as market maker is obliged to make a bid or an offer on his own account, normally within a tick or two of the last sale price.

In principle, again, the specialist has the help of his "book"— the orders left with him at prices off the current market—to help him judge the prices at which new buy orders or sell orders will be available. During placid times, he has an easy living, buying at 40-⅛, then selling at 40-⅜, making $25 a turn on each pair of hundred-share transactions. During volatile times, he is massively at risk. But because he stands at the eye of the storm, presumably he knows more about how the market is moving than anyone else (he says so, for sure), can get in and out more adroitly and more profitably, and can indeed exact something not far short of tribute from brokers who have big orders to move.

For practice increasingly diverges from principle in the modern stock exchange, where most of the buying and selling—nearly two-thirds of all shares traded by the public (as distinct from the specialists and the brokerage houses trading for their own accounts)—are on the order of grand institutions that usually trade in big blocks of stock. In the 1960s, when pension funds ballooned and charitable trusts turned from bonds to stocks and insurance companies were permitted to buy equities, there was some question whether the continuous auction at a stock exchange post could accommodate the new ownership patterns. The need to bring bids and offers to the post and "expose" them meant that the institutions had to tip their hand, giving wise guys on the floor (and their best friends off it) a chance for a free ride. Moreover, commissions until the 1970s were fixed by the hundred-share "round lot," which meant that the pension fund buying 10,000 shares paid a hundred times as much commission as the dentist buying 100, even though the amount of work for the brokers who collected the commission was nowhere near two orders of magnitude greater. As late as 1965, there were fewer than ten 10,000-share block trades on the average day. In the 1968 bull market, one day in September saw an astonishing 120 such trades. In 1987, there were more than 3,500 per day.

Brokers in the 1960s could be ordered to "give up" to other brokers some part of these commissions, and of course they could use the money within their own shops to offer customers whatever services customers might want. These could be very serious research services, or things a lot more exotic. "Soft dollars" were inevitably a source of corruption on Wall Street and off. Asked whether he didn't resent having to give up some of his commission revenues on trades for big customers, one broker told an SEC hearing, "I don't want the full commission—I couldn't even *count* it all." At the end of 1968, under pressure from the Securities and Exchange Commission, the New York Stock Exchange prohibited customer-directed "give-ups," which was, as Shakespeare once put it, a perilous shot out of a popgun.

What really persuaded the exchange that the world had to change was the visible fact that high commission rates on block trades gave competitors a chance to take away the most profitable and arguably the most important business the exchange had. Broker/dealers who were not members of the exchange could profitably negotiate trades back and forth between big holders and big buyers for much less than New York Stock Exchange commissions. For a while major business flowed to so-called "third-market" dealers who were not members of the exchange. The one advantage members had was capital enough to take "positions," to hold some of the deal themselves and feed it out slowly on the floor. But some nonmembers were big enough to take positions, too—firms as large as First Boston, Blyth, and Morgan Stanley did not hold seats on exchanges.

Moreover, the specialist system was an irrelevancy in the age of block trades. William M. Donaldson, who had recently founded Donaldson, Lufkin, Jenrette, said in 1968 that "gigantic traders can't do business through mom-and-pop stores like specialists." As early as the mid-1960s, firms were granted the right to make block trades upstairs in their offices, and take them to the floor only after the deal was finished. By 1969 the big customers were getting discounts on their commissions. Through the 1970s the institutions, the competition, and the government beat on the exchange to drop its commission schedule entirely, and on May Day 1975, with much sackcloth and ashes and wailing, the exchange did so.

Between them, however, the specialists and the floor brokers who relied on commission revenues had the political strength—one member, one vote—to require that the old forms be followed, and that the specialist retain the appearance of a function. Rule 390 requires block traders to bring their deal to the post and present it to the specialist; and if the specialist has any public orders on his book for this stock that are at a better price than the block deal, the block traders must give some piece of the deal to the book. At the same price, the public does not have priority: The rule is that "size take precedence." As a practical matter, however, the specialist can use this opportunity to demand some of the shares for himself if he thinks the deal is a bargain or sell off some shares if he thinks it's overpriced. The block positioners consider themselves market makers and resent this strongly, but usually if the demand isn't too gross they will cut the specialist in. It's his post.

Specialists are not always popular (though some are), and all those I knew thirty-five years ago have retired rich or died rich. Still, the fact is that when the markets collapsed in October 1987 almost the only place that a man with shares of stock could sell them for cash was the floor of the New York Stock Exchange, because in the end the specialists took their responsibilities seriously. One specialist—an old-timer, in business for half a century—said that on October 26 he signed a check for $26 million, to pay the losses his firm

39

had incurred trading on October 19. (New York Stock Exchange trades settle five working days, or one week, after their execution on the floor, a hangover from a time when people had to get stock certificates across the country to make delivery.) In Chicago many traders fled the pits and went off to drown their sorrows while the market was open; upstairs where the unlisted securities are traded on the telephone and through the screens, many over-the-counter dealers took the telephone off the hook. But the specialists at the New York Stock Exchange remained at their posts and continued to make bids. The bids were sometimes very low, and they dropped very quickly on very low volume—in the last hour of trading on October 19, "Adam Smith" pointed out in his television show, the Dow-Jones average dropped one point every nineteen seconds—and as we shall see some people behaved much better than others. But the men who made the bids were without exception at that point loaded with inventory for which they had paid very much more than they were now bidding. They made their markets.

Tokyo's auction does without market makers: The "saitori" who keep the records of the bid-and-asked for the stocks traded at their post work for one of four member firms (companies, not individuals, are members of the Tokyo Stock Exchange). But they do not in fact buy and sell, and they have no obligations to maintain a market—indeed, quite the contrary: If the best bid they have is 10 percent below the closing price of the day before, they are required not to open the stock at all. This is one of the reasons the Tokyo market went down less than New York or London the week of October 19: There were days when half the stocks didn't trade at all, which meant that the price of the Nikkei-Dow index, the most common measure of the exchange, was kept high by the apparent stability (no motion at all) in the shares of some of its most important components.

The Tokyo Stock Exchange floor is a trapezoidal high-ceilinged giant only a few years old, in a strange low, stone-walled building more like an Egyptian temple than anything one thinks of as Oriental. Along the two long walls are tier on tier of desks with clerks at telephones, sending hand signals to and receiving hand signals from the brokers on the floor. The hand signals convey large orders to the floor and confirmations from the posts. Small orders are handled by printouts from terminals along the edges of the floor and are run to the posts by runners, mostly young women, who like the clerks on the New York Stock Exchange are absolutely forbidden to run. Hand signals also convey to the clerks at the desks information that the home office wants to know about the condition of the saitori's "book," and this may be, as we shall see later, their most important function. Everyone in the room wears either a brown (for clerk) or blue (for broker) jacket. There are only five posts, huge five-sided desks with clerks along all the surfaces, plus a desk against the wall in the rear for trading the listed stocks of foreign companies. Everything is very busy except the desk for foreign securities, which is virtually deserted, largely because commissions are still fixed in Tokyo and Japanese institutional investors can do their business in foreign securities more cheaply where those securities are domiciled.

Working on the floor of the Tokyo Stock Exchange is not a high-status occupation, and the career path in the securities houses runs out the door at an early age. The average age of those who work on the floor is little if any over thirty. Discretion in the execution of orders is unusual; indeed, most orders are "matched" upstairs in the brokerage houses before they come to the floor at all, an activity that except in the case of large blocks would be strictly illegal in the United States. In times of stress, like fall 1987, the fact that a broker can delay entering a customer's order at the exchange until he rustles up another customer to take the other side gives the Ministry of Finance a way to brake the action when the market is going downhill. In April 1987, prices were booming on the Tokyo Stock Exchange at a daily volume of one and a half billion shares. In November 1987, prices were lower to steady, and through various mechanisms volume was being held to 250 or 300 million shares a day. By March 1988, prices but not volume had almost entirely recovered.

Only the seven hundred or so most highly capitalized Japanese corporations are traded on the TSE floor; the other two thousand or so stocks trade quietly at a "second section" through row on row of computer screens in a low-ceilinged, carpeted room below the main floor. Nobody works here except employees of the four saitori firms, seated neatly on identical chairs before identical tables bearing identical screens, all dressed in brown jackets and wearing slippers in the older Japanese fashion. (A giant rack of pigeonholes for shoes stands by the entrance.) David Silver, president of the Investment Company Institute and author some years ago of the exchanges section of the SEC Special Study of the securities market, visited Tokyo not long

41

ago and asked what these fellows did. They waited, he was told, until they saw identical bids and offers on the screen, and then hit the button that said "Execute." Silver wondered idly why a person was necessary to make that sort of match, which the computer could so easily do unattended. His companion nodded and whispered, "Employment." Given that orders are matched prior to their entry at the exchange, and that the saitori on the floor have no market-making function, there is no obvious reason why the entire business of the Tokyo Stock Exchange cannot be conducted on machines. For some of the more thoughtful participants in what has been a pretty wild and woolly market, the computerized services of the second section are a comforting backup against the day when some scandal on the floor reaches earthquake proportions. We shall look at some of that later.

5

Down the hall from the second section of the Tokyo Stock Exchange, in a room lined with acoustical tiles, visible from the corridor beside it through acoustically insulated glass, the market that trades the world's greatest value of paper plays itself out as a pantomime for the occasional observer. This is the yen-bond futures market, created in September 1985 and by mid-1987 a monster that traded more than $30 billion worth of contracts every day. About three dozen men, all employees of the exchange, identically dressed in dark brown jackets and lighter brown trousers, white shirt and tie, sit wearing headsets at telephone consoles that stand on long semicircular tables. They face a blackboard and a changing group of three to five men who make chalk marks on it, moving the prices for different durations of contract in response to calls from the desks. They wave their hands a lot, they are obviously yelling, and every once in a while somebody stands up.

What is traded is a futures contract on a "benchmark" bond, one of scores of ten-year government bonds issued by the Ministry of Finance to fund what has been a very large Japanese government deficit almost every year since the oil shock of 1973. Only this bond is deliverable against the futures contract, and its price fluctuates wildly with the movement of the futures prices—regardless of what other Japanese government bonds are doing in the cash market. This does not seem to matter. The buyers and sellers of the yen-bond futures contract are hedging or speculating (mostly, by some margin, hedging) the direction and speed of interest-rate movements in Japan, and for that hedge to be valid the use of contract prices rather than real prices will do fine, so long as everyone accepts the conventions. The secret of the conventions' success, probably, is the fact that cash trading in Japanese government bonds is thin: The holders, corporations, and insurance companies as well as individuals tend to lock them up in the closet and keep them there, because the Ministry of Finance likes it that way.

All futures trading has a degree of artifice to it, because there is no physically established limit to the number of contracts the traders may hold (the "open interest" remaining at the close of the day, after the longs sell and the shorts buy and both cancel their previous contracts by presenting these reverse contracts to the clearinghouse). In cash markets, today's supply is limited and usually knowable; in futures markets, supply is directly created by demand. There can be paper calling for the delivery of less of the commodity than is in the warehouse (no problem—more of the commodity goes on the cash market) or paper calling for the delivery of more of the commodity than is in the warehouse (big problem as delivery date nears—the buyers can squeeze the sellers, running up the price of both the contracts and the commodity). Commodities futures exchanges limit the positions individual traders can hold to make sure nobody exploits this artificiality, and may even put a stop to the growth of open interest by demanding that all purchases in a pit be for the purpose of extinguishing existing short positions until a better balance is achieved.

Until recently, all American futures markets were built on a substratum of deliverable commodities. The favorite gag of the "pits" was always the newcomer who failed to sell his contract in time and wound up with 40,000 pounds of pork bellies or 25,000 bushels of soybeans dropped off on his lawn. This is not the way the game works: Commodities acquired through satisfaction of a futures contract (and big grain users like Pillsbury and General Mills may in fact acquire wheat this way) are delivered to one of a number of specified warehouses, where the purchaser will find and remove them. Proper specification of delivery points may be essential for the use of the contract by the players most intimately connected with the use of the commodity. Leo Melamed, who brought foreign currency futures, Eurodollar futures, and finally the S&P 500 contract to the

Chicago Mercantile Exchange, first established himself with his fellows by expanding the permissible delivery points for the feeder cattle contract the exchange had begun to trade in the early 1960s, but had not previously been able to build to profitable activity.

The U.S. Treasury-bond futures contract, still the world's most important such instrument though the Japanese contract shows a greater volume of transactions, is traded at the Chicago Board of Trade, in a pit that would have flabbergasted Dante, a ring of seven steps, the top one forming an octagon with a diameter of perhaps three dozen feet. The total space within the circle is 1,150 square feet, and in these confines more than five hundred men (women don't try it) may stand from 7:30 in the morning (the market opens at eight but members may get there early to guard their place on the ring) until half past two in the afternoon. During this time, with a handful of exceptions, they will not eat or drink or go to the bathroom. People sometimes fall backward off the top step (there is no way anyone could fall forward) and get hurt. Every so often, in an awesome sight that the participants may not be entirely conscious of, the entire group on the upper steps, packed tight against each other, sways in uncertain rhythm, now right, now left.

The pit is in a corner of the great room, a creation of the 1920s at their most grandiloquent, and along the two walls are rows of phone booths sticking out like stacks of bookcases in a library, clerks jammed back-to-back in narrow aisles. Big customers can access this floor directly, without going through the brokers' upstairs offices. The men on the top rung of the pit are brokers, communicating with the clerks by hand signals, occasionally flipping, Frisbee style, laminated cards on which they have scribbled notations of trades. The cards fly back into the rows of booths with noteworthy but not unerring accuracy. On the lower levels and in the pit the "locals" bid for their own account, scalping, riding trends, trying to outguess the brokers.

High above the pit, a black cage ("the pulpit") is cantilevered forward for the clerks at their keyboards and screens, who try to pick out from the din and the melee the trades that have been consummated, size and price and which of fourteen possible delivery months is involved, and put them into the electronic reporting system. Both sides of every trade are responsible for signaling it to the clerk in the pulpit. "If we're lucky," says James Chakos, who worked there twenty-five years and now supervises the others, "we get fifty percent. It's a job that takes total concentration, back and forth: You're hollering at the trader and the trader is hollering at you. We put out four, five thousand quotations a day with only a handful of corrections. I look for a guy who's got a high energy level, and a sense of numbers—fractions."

This is a continuing open-outcry auction, where the participants wear large identifying labels clipped to their cotton jackets so they can know and write down the other side of the trades they have just yelled and gestured (palm out to sell, palm in to buy) at each other. Among the factors that sustain the noise level is that a trader's bid is good only while he is yelling it: Unlike a system where a specialist registers bids and offers and keeps them in effect until satisfied or canceled, the open-outcry system recognizes only what is being called right this minute. Sales are recorded only within half-hour time intervals on the brokers' and traders' cards; for audit trail purposes, the Board of Trade and the Chicago Merc have joined with a somewhat skeptical Commodity Futures Trading Commission in the design of a "computerized trade reconstruction" system.

What this frenzied group of leather-lunged and mostly large men trade is a construct created by a still almost-young academic economist named Richard Sandor, who started with the Board of Trade as a professor on leave from the University of California at Berkeley and is now an executive director of Drexel Burnham Lambert in its Chicago office. The construct is a thirty-year bond with an 8 percent coupon—that is, a bond that pays interest at a rate of 4 percent of its face value every six months. The contract is for $100,000 of face value, and the price moves in intervals of $\frac{1}{32}$nd of a point, or $31.25 per "tick." The maximum permitted movement in the price of the contract is three points ($3,000) per day; if the market "locks" three points off its previous close, trading halts until people are willing to bid or offer within the limits. The deposit necessary to purchase or sell this contract varies according to how much prices have been moving; it usually runs about $7,500, which protects the exchange through a second day. After two such days, the trader will have to come up with some more money or have his contract sold out from under him at whatever loss is required to dispose of it.

T-bond futures contracts are written on four time horizons— September, December, March, and June. A package of bonds approved by the Board of Trade Clearing Corporation may be delivered, at the seller's option, at any time during the last thirty days of the contract, and the holder of the contract must then pony up the remainder of the money and take delivery. Usually, because it's easier for both parties—and because the hedging value of buying an interest-rate futures contract is realized perfectly by a cash payment—both the buyer of the contract and the seller will sell before expiration to third parties seeking to extinguish *their* contracts. Not infrequently, contracts are rolled over into the next time period. Because deliverable packages can be put together, a continuous loose arbitrage links the cash market in Treasury bonds and the futures market, but the mathematics of what each series of bonds should be "worth" in terms of the future is complicated.

The T-bond pit was the first of the Chicago financial futures markets to become institutionally dominated, because the world is full of large pools of money with proprietors who would rather earn the normally higher interest rates paid by long bonds but fear locking themselves into long-term instruments that can lose value rapidly when the damned fool government runs its affairs in such a way that interest rates rise. Before the arrival of the futures market, moreover, government bonds could be expensive to sell. Back in the 1960s, when he had recently risen to leadership in the family firm, William (always "Billy") Salomon of Salomon Brothers noted that people thought bond trading was at bottom a safer activity than stock market trading, because the government always paid the face value of the paper. "But the fact is that if nobody needs the maturity or the coupon you want to sell," Salomon said, "there may be no bids at all, and if you absolutely must sell it you may have to take a serious loss."

The T-bond futures contract is an insurance policy that works. Because the gap between bid and asked is 1/32nd of a point and commissions are trivial and the Clearing Corporation will accept a letter of credit in lieu of cash deposit, a life insurance company or a savings and loan or a bank with a bond yielding 9 percent can guarantee that whatever happens to interest rates in the next three months its investment portfolio will be able to maintain a yield of, say, 8.91 percent. Once the futures are well established, the CBOT begins to trade options on those futures in an adjacent pit. Because options require the payment of a premium, the portfolio manager can't lock in a rate as close to his coupon, but in normal times he could probably insure himself something like 8.65 percent, with the possibility of a large profit if bond prices rose.

We shall have occasion to look at the mechanics of these markets, their origins, and their influence, later.

6

The best time to see the Chicago Board Options Exchange is a time when almost no one, in fact, does see it: a half hour or so after the close. It's easy to walk around, through the immense litter of newspapers and reports and scribbled scraps, from the semicircular IBM pit facing two dozen screens to the sizable amphitheater where brokers and locals meet to trade options in the Standard & Poors 100 index. Rising from the black floor are tier on tier of semi-enclosed cubicles with screens of their own and desks from which the clerks can signal their brokers. The total collection of screens is the largest in the world outside NASA headquarters in Houston. Time-stamp machines stand on pedestals beside the trading-floor clerks who report the sales and prices, and they do not stop clicking just because nobody is there to put paper in them. The screens, most of them hung from girders on spiderwebs of steel, glare at the paper on the floor as the clocks click in a miscellany of arbitrary rhythms. One awaits the appearance of a space-suited commander. From Mars.

Large-scale options trading, too, comes out of Chicago, though there are important options markets now in New York and San Francisco (common stocks), in Montreal and Philadelphia (stocks and currencies), in Paris (bonds), and in London (everything). The concept of the option is, of course, a commonplace, and the word is part of ordinary English usage as "futures" is not. In the futures context, both purchaser and seller of the contract are entirely at risk. If the price of the commodity falls, the purchaser of the contract has committed to pay more than the commodity now costs, and must either compensate the seller for the reduced price he will receive in the cash market or take possession with the knowledge that he can resell only at a loss. If the price of the commodity rises, the seller of the contract must either compensate the supplier for the difference between today's price and the price in the contract, or buy the commodity at the higher price and deliver it at a loss. By contrast, the options contract is asymmetrical. The purchaser of the option (the call option giving the right to buy or the put option giving the right to sell) is at risk only for the price of the option itself; if the market goes against him, he simply declines to exercise the option.

But the seller of the option (call or put) is in the same position as the purchaser of a futures contract: If the party on the other side does exercise the option, he is on the hook for the losses.

The European option was historically very specific, permitting the purchase (a "call") or sale (a "put") of something (a stock, a bond, a physical asset) at a price set today for some specified future date. American options are significantly different, in that their holders can exercise the option, call the stock from the counterparty or put it to him, at any time up to expiration date. Though the locus was wrong, the bumper sticker on an English car in the financial district had it about right: "Options traders do it until they expire."

Until the 1970s, the options business was a little over-the-counter specialty headquartered in New York and dominated by four or five small firms. Though there was a traditional standard price—$137.50 per hundred shares for a ninety-day option—in fact the contracts were nonstandard, some for longer and some for shorter durations, some at the market, some above it, some below, the offerings dictated essentially by what the broker's experience had been in response to advertising. It was a way for a poor man to lose his money, pretending to play the stock market.

To some extent, options are still a way for a poor man to lose his money, pretending to play whatever market allows options on its traded entities. But the instruments created in Chicago in the 1970s are an ingenious system for broadening their appeal and their use. Under the arrangements first put in place by the Chicago Board Options Exchange (CBOE), options on a given stock are traded in a series of prices, usually at $5 intervals. With IBM selling at 120, for example, options might be offered at 100, 105, 110, 115, 120, 125, 130, 135, and 140. (CBOE options trading on IBM runs more than 50,000 contracts or 5 million shares a day, reflecting the common view that the movement of IBM's price tells you what the institutions are doing; actually, Cray Research is a better proxy—institutions own almost 97 percent of Cray's stock—but the commonality doesn't know that, and the IBM contract is, of course, much more liquid.) At each price for the stock, there are separate options running into various months, which is why the exchange needs all those screens.

The price of an option begins with the relationship between the "strike price" of the stock and the real price at which it is now trading—a call option, a right to buy IBM at 140, is "out of the money" and not worth a hell of a lot if the stock is now selling at

120, but a call at 110 is "in the money" and worth $10 cash "intrinsically." Add to this a premium, a time value that relates to the historic volatility of this stock, the price of the stock itself (an option on CBS shares in March 1988 controlled $16,500 "worth" of stock while one on Citicorp controlled only $2,000), and the anticipated volatility of the market as a whole. Then subtract the commission savings for the professional (but not the outside customer) who acquires stock through the exercise of an option rather than by purchase, and all the factors that should move the price of an option are present. Of course, rational pricing models do not always predict prices.

One notes again the total difference between the buyer and the seller of an option. The buyer has an entirely limited risk: If the market moves away from him, the worst that can happen is that he loses his premium and the commission he paid. This will probably happen, just as the lottery ticket will probably be thrown away, but there's always a chance it won't. The seller, on the other hand, receives a steady stream of money from the premiums and probably wins—but he can take a horrendous shellacking if he has sold a put and the market falls, or sold a call and it rises.

If the option is "covered"—that is, if the seller already owns the shares on which he "writes" a call, and can satisfy the call by delivering them, or has already gone short the stock and can pay the holder of the put option out of the profits on his short sale—the loss is strictly the sacrifice of an opportunity for gain. (And this "strategy" is defensible: Cash received from the sale of an out-of-the-money call reduces the effective cost of this stock in the portfolio, and cash received from the sale of an out-of-the-money put can solace the short seller for some unexpected robustness in the price of the stock he has shorted.) But if the option is "naked"—and in the aftermath of October 19 it appeared that eminent brokerage houses permitted their employees to help unsophisticated customers sell naked puts— there can be a lot of work for the bankruptcy courts before the sun sets. It was the options market that came closest to destruction when the stock market collapsed in October 1987.

3

Meltdown: 1. The Fuel

"Mr. Ford had his own private religion. He believed strongly in reincarnation. He used to expound his views on this to me at great length. One of the 'proofs' he used was this: 'When the automobile was new,' he'd say, 'and one of them came down the road, a chicken would run straight for home—and usually get killed. But today when a car comes along, a chicken will run for the nearest side of the road. That chicken has been hit in the ass in a previous life.' "

—Harry Bennett
(Henry Ford's bodyguard), 1951

1

*A*sked one day in the early years of this century why the stock market had gone down, the elder J. P. Morgan gave the one known foolproof answer. He said, "There were more sellers than buyers." On a similar level of analysis, John Kenneth Galbraith told *Barron's* magazine in early December 1987 that the previous summer, when stocks had been at their historic highs, "people and institutions were in the market for no reason except that it was going up."

But there is, of course, as Galbraith hastened to add, more to it than that. One can pick up the story of the crash of 1987 at many points. The seeds were sown, no doubt, in the refusal of the Johnson administration to pay the costs of the Vietnam War in the mid-1960s, by the insistence that Americans could have both guns and butter—an insistence picked up again by the Reagan administration. In between, we had a loss of discipline from Richard Nixon's 1971 abandonment of the long-standing American pledge to sell gold for dollars to foreign official agencies. Next, perhaps inevitably, came the worldwide abdication of monetary restraint in 1972 that led to the leap in commodity prices and then the success of the oil cartel in 1973, and the Carter administration's successful effort to talk down the dollar in 1977–1978, followed as the night the day by the disastrous inflation of 1979–1982. One must not forget the spectacular tax bill of August 1981, when Democrats and Republicans in the Congress vied to see who could cut the revenues farthest, and finally compromised on a measure that over three years would reduce the government's tax take by almost exactly twice as much as the bill Ronald Reagan's Treasury Department had sent over to start the process.

But the obvious place to begin is the nationalist disinflation-in-one-country crusade of Paul Volcker, appointed chairman of the Federal Reserve Board by President Carter in 1979 and reappointed by President Reagan. In every way larger than life, Volcker had risen from the ranks of research economists at the Federal Reserve Bank of New York, worked briefly at the Chase Manhattan Bank as an economic forecaster, and served in the Treasury Department as undersecretary for monetary affairs when John Connolly was Richard Nixon's Treasury secretary. Volcker understood that the central task of the Federal Reserve Board is to maintain the value of the currency. Under the Constitution, Congress and Congress alone has the power "to coin money [and] regulate the value thereof," but this power has essentially been "farmed," as Congressman Wright Patman liked to put it, to the Fed. By the time Ronald Reagan took office in 1981, the American people were heartily sick of inflation, and while the president's budget makers factored in a heavy dose of it when making their spending and tax plans, Volcker in effect had a free hand in putting an end to it.

Given the domination of "supply-side" economists in the early years of the Reagan administration, Volcker had no way to control inflation other than a sharp restriction of the measured money supply and an escalation of interest rates to levels the United States had never known before. The rising interest rates, coupled with the federal government's need to borrow after the Reagan tax cut, brought the country the worst recession it had experienced since World War II—and also, drawn by the rates, a flood of foreign money. To keep the money supply from rising and the interest rates from falling,

Volcker's Fed "sterilized" the inflow of funds, selling enough of its own holdings of Treasury paper to sop up the funds the foreigners were sending. The United States was a creditor nation in the early 1980s, and high dollar interest rates helped improve the American balance of payments. But in addition to the harm done at home, the interest rates were hugely damaging to the debtors in the less developed countries, and they disrupted money relations in the Common Market, where the French franc, Italian lira, and British pound tended to lose value in dollar terms more rapidly than the German mark, the Dutch guilder, or the Danish krone. It was suggested to Volcker in fall 1981 that he would not be able to maintain the pressure because he would bankrupt the third world and distort the trading patterns among the European economies. "They have their problems," the chairman of the Fed said. "We have our problems. I am hired to take care of our problems."

A very strong currency in effect subsidizes imports and taxes exports, and over a wide range of the manufacturing spectrum foreign goods competed successfully against American products. The income elasticity of demand for imports in the United States was very high—that is, for every extra thousand dollars an American household earned, it had a tendency to spend a high fraction, perhaps 15 percent, on imports, while a German or Japanese family of comparable dimensions and income might spend on imports only 5 percent or so of an income increase. Since 1972, when the United States became a net importer of oil, domestic prosperity had always taken the nation's balance of trade into deficit, reducing the value of the dollar and eventually heightening domestic inflation—but recession had restored the country to the status of a net exporter as domestic demand fell. Now, in 1981–1982, because Volcker's success at driving up the exchange value of the currency kept dollar prices higher than prices in other currencies, even a serious recession could not bring American international trade back into balance. For those who were tourists abroad during those years, it was great fun while it lasted.

Then in August 1982 Mexican finance minister Jesus de Silva Herzog came to Washington and, in the words of a Treasury Department official, "turned his pockets inside out." Volcker immediately saw he could go no further in holding dollar interest rates high and began flooding the system with money. The stock market, which was deep in the doldrums, the Dow-Jones industrial average hanging at or even below 800, started a climb that would take it almost exactly five years later to 2722. But the dollar stubbornly remained high for another three years, sustained by inflows of foreign money drawn by American interest rates that were still, on an inflation-adjusted basis, the highest in the world. Finally, in fall 1985, at a meeting in New York's Plaza Hotel, the finance ministers of the leading powers agreed to take concerted steps that would bring down the value of the dollar, and they did. Once U.S. interest rates came down, there was nothing to hold the dollar up.

Thereafter, movements in the foreign-exchange market began to create a kind of tariff on imports to America and give a growing subsidy to American exports. If anyone suggested that Congress pass a ten percent subsidy for all exports and charge a 10 percent tariff on all imports, the editorial writers would be up in arms about "protectionism"; when it's done through the foreign-exchange market, somehow, the innocents in the newspapers and in the White House think it's all right. One notes in passing that the tactics Treasury Secretary James Baker followed in 1987 were known in the 1930s as "beggar-thy-neighbor" policies, and that the International Monetary Fund was created to prevent them. But currency manipulation didn't work, largely because political leadership underestimated the extent of the transformation in American producing and consuming that would be required to make the foreign trade numbers better when a ten percent increase in exports and a 10 percent decrease in imports merely maintained the size of the trade deficit as measured in dollars.

The federal budget deficit and the foreign trade deficit fed on each other, not for the first time: Charles Schultze, chairman of Jimmy Carter's Council of Economic Advisers, told Congress in early 1978 that a large budget deficit would be necessary to give foreigners a place to put the extra money that would be burning a hole in their pockets as a result of the foreign trade deficit, which was then estimated at a horrifying $18 billion for the year. By 1987, we had a trade deficit that was only a few hundred million dollars less than that in the month of October alone.

For more than a year, the world waited patiently for the devaluation of the dollar to remedy the trade deficit. To finance continuing American imports, foreign money poured in to acquire American government and then corporate bonds, buy real estate, and build automobile and other factories. Thanks to the immense federal deficit, which during the eight years of Reagan doubled the American national debt from one to two trillion dollars, American real interest rates remained above those in Japan and Germany, though not as far above as they had been in Volcker's heyday. As the trade deficit continued to grow, interest rates had to keep rising to draw foreign funds. Early in 1987, market forces began to drive the dollar down again. And again, the finance ministers met, and patched up an ad hoc system of intervention and rhetoric, this time at the Louvre in Paris, but now nothing worked.

Everyone knew that the dollar would get weaker. Between rising interest rates (which mean falling bond prices) and the declining dollar, the Japanese insurance companies that had been the main purchasers of American government paper at the quarterly auctions of long-term U.S. Treasury bonds had suffered an enormous loss—not far off $20 billion—between September 1986 and April 1987. Private inflow into fixed-income investments slowed dramatically (the Japanese Ministry of Finance coerced the Japanese securities houses into taking down more than half of the big U.S. Treasury auction in May 1987, but they sold off the bonds immediately). Japanese investors fled the American fixed-income market. In March 1987, for the first time, Japanese investors spent more money to buy shares of American stocks than they spent on bonds.

Meanwhile, despite the United States' deficit status, Americans began acquiring assets abroad at a great clip, expecting that their earnings on such investments would be further enhanced, in dollar terms, by the appreciation of the foreign currency in which the investment was denominated. In its annual review of which investments did the best in the preceding year, Salomon Brothers highlighted British "gilts" (government bonds). Between the relatively higher interest rate on British government paper and the increased value of the pound, an American investing dollars and measuring his gain in dollars showed a total return on gilts of 45.2 percent for calendar 1987. This obviously drew customers. When foreigners do what Americans did in 1987, we call it "capital flight." When Americans do it, we speak of "international diversification."

The oversupply of dollars abroad may have been made even worse by the growing tendency of interest rates on Eurodollar deposits (dollars held outside the United States where the Federal Reserve might not be available as a lender of last resort) to rise more rapidly than interest rates in the United States. Among those tempted to leave dollars abroad were the foreign government central banks that were taking a pasting on the reduced value of their dollar holdings. (German accountants make the Bundesbank reveal these losses; for calendar 1987, the total was about $3 billion.) This sort of thing had also happened in the early 1970s, before Arthur Burns, then chairman of the Fed, convinced his opposite numbers that by creating a possible dollar multiplier in the offshore banking system they were adding to the downward pressures on the U.S. currency. In the confusions of 1987, with a Treasury Department entirely unequipped for such heavy lifting taking the lead role in international negotiations, Burns's lesson was forgotten.

What carried the stock market from 1900 at the end of December 1986 to 2700 in mid-summer 1987 was in part a better than expected year in the American economy (fueled by an increase in the export industries, for the volume of American exports did respond nicely to the devaluation of the dollar), but in larger part what the pundits came to call "the weight of money." The Japanese especially, with a savings rate well over 15 percent of their income and a bilateral surplus with the United States running to roughly $60 billion a year, moved to the American stock market the dollars they were piling up from their exports. Their net purchases of stocks may well have run $20 billion in the first eight months of the year.

Still, the fact was that capital outflows from the United States balanced the inflows of foreign investment. The end result in the first half of 1987 was that foreign central banks had to acquire enough dollars to fund the $80 billion-plus of the American deficit in that period. Unlike Volcker, the heads of the European and Japanese central banks did not seek to sterilize the inflow of dollars. Instead, they printed marks and yen and other such currencies to the extent necessary to buy the dollars. Both the German and the Japanese money supply rose by more than 10 percent year on year. Though price levels in their currencies were well protected by the considerable drop in the number of marks or yen they had to spend to acquire the commodities in international trade, which are priced in dollars, they became concerned about the long-range implications of so large a growth in their monetary aggregates. In the summer, both Germany and Japan began absorbing some of the inflow of dollars, using tactics analogous to what Volcker had done in the United States half a dozen years earlier. The Japanese market responded with a dramatic drop in the price of yen bonds, and interest rates began to crawl up the scale in Germany.

In the United States, doubtless as part of the Louvre arrangements, the Federal Reserve held the dollar aggregates steady. As German and Japanese rates rose, U.S. rates rose further. In July, Volcker announced that he would not seek renomination as chairman of the Fed (Alan Abelson, managing editor of *Barron's*, later nominated him as "market timer of the year"), and in August he was succeeded by Alan Greenspan, who pledged to maintain anti-inflationary policies. In earnest of those intentions, the Fed in September raised its symbolic discount rate, the rate at which it lends money to banks with good collateral when they have temporary difficulty meeting the reserve requirements the law imposes on all depository institutions. This turned out to be insufficient. The Japanese, on whose willingness to purchase U.S. securities the financing of American government and investment depended, became net sellers in the U.S. market in September. And in that third quarter, the United States' balance of trade in services turned negative for the first time since World War I: The interest and dividends and repatriated earnings foreigners took from America exceeded the interest and dividends and repatriated earnings from American overseas investment. (In the fourth quarter, the service amount "improved": Because the dollar went down, the dollar value of earnings on American overseas investment rose. Ah, statistics!)

Within American markets there had long been relatively stable ratios between corporate earnings and share prices, and also between interest rates in the long-term bond market and dividend yields on stocks. By summer 1987, these ratios were being grossly violated. Thirty-year Treasury bonds were selling to yield more than four times as much as the dividend payouts on the S&P 500 stocks, and such a ratio had never been seen, let alone sustained, before. And the S&P index was selling for 23 times the annual earnings of the underlying corporations.

Such overvaluation necessarily has a number of causes. Takeover frenzy and the growth of junk bonds as a means of financing the purchase of stock were contributors. Anthony Delis of the Boston money-management firm Delis & Kontes suggested six months before the crash that the growth of futures and options meant that "equities and options have been acting more and more like commodities," and that in commodities markets "ascending curve patterns climb vertically, exhaust themselves, and then drop just as vertically." And there may also have been a certain amount of rigging of the stock market by the big U.S. brokerage houses and their institutional clients. The brokerage houses nowadays make more money as a group trading for their own accounts than they do from the commissions paid by their customers.

If there was rigging, it went under the name of "guaranteeing the close," a term of art relating to the fact that investment funds are priced according to the prices of the component stocks at the close of the market. Index funds especially, with their guarantee that they would deliver the results indicated by the index somewhat "enhanced" by their arbitrage activity, cared deeply that the results they printed lived up to the advertising. This was not so easily done when such a fund was involved in buying or selling, because even at the very small commissions they paid, the costs of trading could be great enough to move their performance just under that of the index itself. (Some funds, moreover, were being sliced up by their brokers, as we shall see in Chapter 11.) The remedy for the fund, recommended by the brokers, was to purchase selected stocks, well weighted in their index, during the last few minutes of trading. Early in the day, the fund would notify the broker that he had perhaps $50 million to spend at the end of the day, "to guarantee the close."

The broker could then "front-run" the client in ways difficult to trace, typically through the purchase of one of the stock index futures contracts late in the trading day—usually the contract for the Major Market index (MMI), traded at the Chicago Board of Trade, which measured the prices of only twenty stocks, all but three of them part of the Dow-Jones industrial average. These are all heavily traded; nobody would notice a little added burst of activity at the close. Indeed, as 1987 wore on, sophisticates came to *expect* a lot of extra trading and some price movement in those stocks toward the close of the day. Though the "Missiles," as MMI futures were called, were not very active by comparison with the S&P 500, they were popular with certain heavy hitters who tended to come in with orders if they discerned a trend. When the price of the stock went up at the end, the value of the MMI rose with it. Trading in MMI futures began fifteen minutes before the opening of the New York Stock Exchange each morning, and was likely to reflect the overnight value of the "cash" index, which had been raised when the broker guaranteed the close the night before. So the broker could sell out at a profit.

Once the community of insiders knew about this custom, the MMI futures contract became a likely candidate to rise to a premium over the actual measured index toward the end of the day, opening an opportunity for arbitrage profits for brokers on days when they did not have orders from the index funds. The arithmetic is complex but not difficult. In spring 1987, each MMI contract represented roughly $100,000 worth of stock, and could be bought with a down payment of about $5,000. If the futures contract with one month to run sold for, say, 1 percent more than the total price of the twenty underlying stocks, an arbitrageur could sell the future for $101,000, buy the stock for $100,000, and guarantee himself $1,000 per contract traded. As a "market maker" on *some* exchange (the SEC was permissive in these definitions, and the Federal Reserve permitted SEC rules to govern), a brokerage house could borrow as much of the cost of the stock as a bank would lend. The Board of Trade permitted 25 percent of an MMI purchase deposit to be made in the form of a letter of credit. With three-quarters of the purchase price of the stock borrowed at 8 percent, the interest cost for a month would be $500; the letter of credit would be $12.50. If the components had to be held to the expiration of the contract, at which time the price of the future and the cash would necessarily "converge," the "carry" on the deal would be $512.50, the profit $487.50 on a capital commitment of $28,750. Multiply the profit by 12 times a year, and you get $5,850, which is a slightly better than 20 percent return on capital. By committing $10 million to this activity, a big broker/dealer got a guaranteed $2 million-plus profit, and he could take nearly all of that right down to the bottom line.

In fact, he probably did better than our example. You don't *have* to "unwind" the two sides of this sort of arbitrage, cashing in or paying off on the contract and selling the stock, until the last day— but you *can* do so anytime it's profitable. Which may well be tomorrow morning. As the Japanese were mostly purchasers at the opening, the odds were good in 1987 that the blue-chip stocks in the MMI could be sold at an up-tick or two tomorrow morning. Because the MMI began trading before the stock market opened and the Japanese were not players in Chicago, the odds were pretty good that one could unwind the transaction the next morning, buying in the Missiles at the opening and selling the shares, at a nice profit. One hundred times a year. Now the return is about 150 percent on capital. And that doesn't count the profits on the options, which can be pushed from "intrinsically" worthless to a substantial premium in the last two minutes of the trading day. You can afford to pay people to do nothing else. All the big brokerage houses developed "index arbitrage" teams and allocated capital to them. These teams were active all day long, most frequently playing the S&P 500 index against some basket of S&P stocks, but it may well be—some very sophisticated people think so—that they made their real money at the close.

This sort of activity was much facilitated by the electronic order-delivery system on the New York Stock Exchange, which had been installed originally to take care of small orders from small customers but had been expanded to serve the index trading needs of the big brokers. What makes the manipulation story plausible is a certain amount of internal evidence from trading patterns, and the very unusual course traced by the mature bull market in 1987. Normally prices toward the end of a long upward movement rise much more strongly among the smaller capitalization stocks, which presumably come to people's attention after their better known brethren have reached something that looks to market players like a fully priced condition. But in the 1986–1987 bull market the most striking performers were the stocks in the indices (and the more indices they were in, the better they tended to do), while the smaller companies, though heavily traded, rose much less. We shall have occasion later to look at index arbitrage in other contexts. It is at least possible that practice at manipulating the Missiles came in very handy during the market meltdown.

After the crash, the Salomon Brothers research department produced a graph covering fifty years, showing a pair of jagged black lines tracing numbers 20 percent above and 20 percent below a center that measured fourteen times the earnings of the companies that made up the S&P index. A blue line in that channel showed the actual market prices as the years passed. The blue line had remained within the channel except for a minor spike below in the 1960s and a giant spike that rose way above in 1986–1987. Leo Melamed of the Chicago Mercantile Exchange, who lost money through the first half of the year fighting the tape in the futures pit ("I'm a new kind of alchemist," he told Brett Haire of First Boston; "I make gold in the currency pits and turn it into shit in the S&Ps"), liked to say that if somebody offered to pay him twenty-three times the earnings of his little business, he would sell out in a minute, so he couldn't understand why people were buying stocks. Then, he added, he went to Japan, where the Merc was opening an office, and expressed his concern to one of his Japanese hosts, who said, "You don't understand; we've moved to an entirely new way of valuing stocks." Melamed relaxed: "I knew then we had to be near the end," he said.

Yet on October 2, twelve days before the start of the landslide, Salomon Brothers published a quarterly "asset allocation" recommendation to its institutional clients, urging them to put more money into equities, worldwide. Merrill Lynch's very intelligent research department saw the market rising rapidly, buoyed by increased earnings further heightened by accounting changes relating to pension reserves. Morgan Stanley urged all its clients to stay or become 100 percent invested in common stocks. Six weeks after the crash, George J. W. Goodman (aka "Adam Smith"), who was on Morgan Stanley's mailing list, received an enthusiastic, even urgent buy recommendation for a stock the house was beginning to cover in its research program. He said he wanted to pretend he was a customer, and send back a note reading "With what? You had me one hundred percent invested in October and I lost half my money. How am I supposed to buy something now?"

2

On October 5, the Dow-Jones average was still only about 3 percent below its August high. As in 1929, there had been a dip in September, and then a brief renewed rise. The week of October 5 saw a drop of 6 percent, with a 92-point loss on Tuesday. The market steadied on diminished volume on Monday, October 12, then rose smartly on Tuesday, October 13. Then the roof fell in—down 95 points Wednesday on 207 million shares, 58 points Thursday on 263 million shares, 108 points Friday on an unprecedented 338 million shares. It was still not quite certain, Alan Abelson wrote in *Barron's,* whether the numbers meant a correction or a bear market. "In a correction," he explained, "other people's stocks go down; in a bear market, your stocks go down." Monday's *Wall Street Journal* thought the bull market was "seriously if not mortally wounded," though "no one is forecasting a crash like that in 1929–30." Then the market dropped 508 points on a volume of 604 million shares.

There are of course disagreements about the proximate cause of the slide. The economic recovery Volcker had pushed onto the rails in 1982 had turned five years old, and whatever the pigeon entrails may say when the economists look at them—and there is no doubt the economy was extremely strong in third quarter 1987—the up-slopes of the business cycle rarely last longer than five years. The editorial writers of the *Wall Street Journal* (a very different group from the news staff) thought the disaster had something to do with the Senate's rejection of President Reagan's nomination of Judge Robert Bork to the Supreme Court, though that had been anticipated for some time. Failing that explanation, the *Journal* and some in the financial community (including the members of the Brady Commission that later analyzed the crash for President Reagan) blamed a tax bill in the House of Representatives, which would have penalized the issuance of bonds to finance the takeover of companies previously owned by shareholders. The market, it was said, had risen in significant part through the hope that companies would subsequently be bought by others at a price that reflected not the anticipated cash flow from the business itself but the asset values that could be realized by dismemberment and sale.

Without defending the specific proposal, it can be noted that these supposed "free-market" deals were in fact schemes for exploiting the tax break the government unwisely gives to companies financed by bonds (which pay interest from income before tax) rather than stock (which pays dividends from post-tax income). And also that the pricing of stocks to reflect the breakup value of the enterprise rather than its potential profits is something that looks rational only when the central bank is diminishing the value of income streams by maintaining high real interest rates. If in fact the shattering of speculators' beliefs that stock prices could ride this particular rocket to the moon was the trigger for the market collapse, one can only regret that Representative Dan Rostenkowski had not pushed his proposals through the Ways and Means Committee much sooner, when there was less of a bubble to pop.

For me, the triggering event was the feud that blew up the week of October 12 between Karl Otto Pöhl of the German Bundesbank and U.S. Treasury Secretary James Baker. Early in the week, Pöhl made a speech permeated with an essentially unconcealed contempt for Baker and the conduct of American economic policy. As the Latin countries have learned in their relations with the United States, that sort of contempt is among the privileges of creditors and the burdens of debtors. But Americans, including the American government, did not understand that their status in the world had changed. Over the weekend, Baker on television talk shows threatened the Germans with the devaluation of the dollar unless they shaped up and stimulated their economy by fiscal as well as monetary means—a step that might or might not be rational policy for the Germans, but certainly would not make a significant contribution to the reduction of the American trade deficit. "What caused the crash," says Leo Melamed of the Chicago Merc, putting a similar thought somewhat differently, "was all that fucking around with the currencies of the world."

Sunday night in New York was Monday morning in Japan. Most brokers report that there was an eerie silence on the wires from Tokyo. "We think they saw it coming," says one executive in a large firm, "and the Ministry of Finance said, 'Hold off—with all our other problems, we don't want to get blamed for this one.' " But there may have been some Japanese participation in the torrent of sell orders that roared in from Europe before four in the morning on October 19. Several American mutual funds had been fully invested, and were already stretched to meet redemption demand from the previous week. From Boston, Fidelity Magellan Fund, which had been 98.6 percent invested and had already exhausted its reserve, notified brokers that it would have to sell $1 billion worth of securities to raise cash. Even before the New York Stock Exchange opened, Fidelity dumped $90 million worth of U.S. shares openly traded in London on the stock exchange there, and may well have sold more on London's unreported over-the-counter market. Morgan Stanley sold hundreds of millions of dollars worth of stocks in London before the New York market opened, with no public record of the sales.

The brokerage houses alerted their institutional clients, many of which had adopted programs of "dynamic hedging" that instructed them to sell index futures contracts on the Chicago Mercantile Exchange as the market value of their stocks diminished. That way, the mathematicians claimed, the gains from short positions in the falling index would compensate the institution for its losses in its portfolio of actual stocks. Knowing what the published formulas would lead the mathematicians to do—and how much was left to do after the previous week's 235-point drop—traders waited in the wings, withholding their orders to buy, certain that there would be a cascading of offers in the futures pits at progressively lower prices. No purpose in buying now.

Both the New York Stock Exchange and the S&P pit at the Merc opened at 9:30 A.M. New York time. None of the Dow-Jones stocks *could* open for trading at the bell, because the specialists responsible for maintaining the markets, already stuffed with stock they had bought the three previous trading days, were in no position to absorb the fantastic surge of sell orders—and those who had been buyers last week were mostly sellers now. Only seven of the thirty were trading before 9:45—American Express, AT&T, Bethlehem Steel, International Paper, U.S. Steel, Union Carbide, and Woolworth. Eleven had still not opened an hour into the trading day—Alcoa, DuPont, Eastman Kodak, General Electric, Goodyear, IBM, Merck, Philip Morris, Sears, Texaco, and Westinghouse. Even so, volume in the first hour was almost 100 million shares, and the tape ran twenty minutes late. By the end of a 604-million-share day—more than three times the normal volume in what had been a very busy year—the tape was more than two hours late. For people in brokerage houses and their customers, the most frustrating aspect of the day was the total lack of relationship between the appallingly low bid-and-asked quotes, which were kept current by the clerks at the post, and the reports of trades, which were literally hours late. Many people waited forty-eight hours to get confirmation of the price at which they had sold, and then very often it was less good a price than they had thought they were getting.

Part of the problem in New York was that there were four different markets for each listed stock. One was the negotiated block trade upstairs, which often, even in quiet times, transferred the ownership of securities at prices a percentage point or two or three off the current market. New York Stock Exchange Rule 390 required the block brokers to bring these transactions to the floor to be printed on the tape, and one of the things the brokers held against the specialists was that they sometimes insisted on taking a piece of the block for themselves, on one side or the other, relying on the fact that prices normally sprang back to where they had been after a block trade at an off-price was printed. This off-the-floor market traded October 19, especially in the afternoon, on a principle of no-even-remotely-plausible bid will be refused. When such crossed sales came to the floor, they absorbed what few bids existed between their price and the price of the previous sale. Mostly, upstairs just dumped it on the specialist.

The second market was the usual trading by the "crowd," the brokers with orders from their home office to buy or sell at the current asked or bid or at some other price. To the extent that these orders were "not held" (that is, left the broker with discretion to get the best price), they tended to pile up, because the people on the floor couldn't believe the prices. People at the posts with sell orders would then panic, the market having fallen so far below the prices in effect when their clients put their orders in. The insulation of the floor from the customers—the fact that floor brokers communicate through the customers' men upstairs in the offices—made it impossible for brokers to ascertain customers' intentions in a reasonable time frame. But it was this market, which was very busy with brokers desperately trying to sell and other brokers wondering whether the time to buy had come, that the specialist had to monitor and smooth. It took all his time and attention.

Yet a third market was on screens at the post, the Intermarket Trading System showing the bids and askeds of market makers on the other stock exchanges and of over-the-counter dealers who deal in listed stocks (and maintain a membership on the entirely computerized Cincinnati Stock Exchange as their access to these screens). Presumably, orders arriving at the post are to be executed by the specialist or dealer with the best quote on the screen at that time. But the specialists in the lesser exchanges and the dealers, even when they are not deliberately pricing off the market (offering at a slightly higher price and bidding at a slightly lower one), normally guarantee their quote for only 100—exceptionally, as much as 1,000—shares. If the order is bigger than that, and most are, the ITS screen may be irrelevant. Its function usually is to permit the specialists on the lesser exchanges, and the over-the-counter dealers in listed stocks, to lay off their trades automatically on the specialist in New York. On October 19, this system essentially shut down, by accident or by design, preventing the out-of-town specialists and the over-the-counter dealers who handle listed securities from unloading on the New York Stock Exchange.

At the Pacific Stock Exchange, when the traders on the options floor tried to lay off their risks by selling shares to the specialists on the stock in San Francisco, they were asked not to do that, because the specialists had been cut off from their usual lines to New York

and were already eating great quantities of stock brokers had directed their way because the PSE's SCOREX electronic order system
automatically executed trades the specialists would later have to
honor. Not surprisingly, this system also broke down during the day.
The president of the Philadelphia Stock Exchange wrote a pious
piece in the Sunday *New York Times* in which he lamented that the
failure of ITS had meant "specialists on other exchanges could not
provide . . . help [to] their New York Stock Exchange counterparts,"
which was one of the few laughs anyone got that week.

Finally, the specialist had at the back of his post a printer that
spat out slips from the electronic Designated Order Turnaround
(DOT) system the exchange had installed as long ago as 1976 to
enable brokers to process small orders from small customers at low
cost after the end of fixed commissions. At the request of the big
brokerage houses that were now large traders for their own account,
DOT's capacity had been expanded to 2,099 shares for orders "at the
market." Meanwhile, a LIST system had been created to enable
brokers to enter orders for many different stocks at once, most
significantly in the S&P 500 stocks that could be arbitraged against
the S&P futures contract. This played a considerable role in deepen-
ing the disaster of October 19, and which we shall consider presently.

In theory, the specialist fed orders from DOT into the "crowd"
of brokers before his post. In fact, on October 19, when orders for
396 million shares were sent through the system, there was no way
for the specialist to keep up with the slips coming off the machine.
For some stocks, DOT orders arrived on a screen before the post
rather than on a slip; the specialist couldn't keep up with the screen,
either. All orders were time-stamped. If the specialist did not find a
way to fill a market order in three minutes, he was compelled by the
rules of the exchange to buy at the existing bid or sell at the offer for
his own account. During the course of October 19, DOT malfunc-
tioned, largely because the computer printers were not fast enough
to keep up. But the specialists were still compelled at settlement time
a week later to buy such stock, at the prices prevailing when the
brokers' time-stamped orders were entered at their end of the system.
Fortunately, they didn't know it on October 19.

The harm done by the DOT system, however, went far beyond
the aggregation of selling orders dumped onto the floor. In the life
of the post, it was generally understood that at a time of order
imbalance there was no purpose served by hammering prices down

(or up). Assume eight brokers in the crowd working this post, all with orders to sell from 1,000 to 5,000 shares, 20,000 in all, and no buyers. The specialist shrugs his shoulders and says, "No way. Not at this price, or anything like it. Wait." Then an order to buy at market or at a limit near the existing price arrives, for, say, 2,500 shares. The brokers at the post can bid against each other for the order, progressively lowering their price if they have authorization to do so, or they can divide the buy order among themselves ("participate it out") at a price near the previous sale. Normally, they will operate in concert to maintain the orderly market, each disposing of 200 to 500 shares from his larger order to sell, then wait for another buyer to emerge at perhaps a lower but not extravagantly lower price. When the DOT system clicks out the orders at the back of the post, however, the human adjustment to market movements is frustrated, and everybody has to bid against the electronically delivered slip for the whole of each buy order. The result can be—and was—to create panic from imbalance, terror from panic.

When all is said and done, of course, a specialist has assumed a legal obligation to maintain a fair and orderly market "so far as practicable," which means in times of stress an obligation to buy when others are selling and sell when others are buying. In return, he has a monopoly on the little turns discussed earlier, plus a little license to poach from the upstairs market makers who put together the block trades. In the aftermath of Black Monday, *Fortune* magazine was given a peek at the books of "one of the five leading specialist firms" for the years 1981–1986. They showed a return on capital that never fell below 33.6 percent and went as high as 95.2 percent, a return on revenues consistently over 40 percent. The Brady Commission found that while specialists as a group acquired $489 million worth of stock on the floor of the New York Stock Exchange on October 19 (most of it in the first two hours, though they also bought fairly heavily toward the end when there were no other bids), no less than 30 percent of the specialist community were in fact net *sellers* into the market break. David Silver, who ran the specialist portion of the SEC's *Special Study* of the securities markets in 1963, remembers that this was about the proportion that had sought to capitalize on the strange panic that seized the market in May 1962.

Despite the enormous overload of 155 million shares in the first ninety minutes and a drop of 200 points in the Dow-Jones index, the system bounced back from 11:00 until almost noon, and the Dow regained 80 points. At 1:15 it was still 30 or so points above its low, and then the roof fell in. During the next hour, the Dow dropped more than 5 percent—but the S&P 500 futures contract in Chicago dropped more than 10 percent. Trading during that period slacked off just a little; for the day as a whole, the NYSE averaged more than 93 million shares an hour, while the hour from 1 to 2 P.M. totaled about 80 million. During that time, index-related sales accounted for almost two-fifths of all sales. According to the SEC report on the crash, computer programs generated more than half the selling of stocks in the S&P 500 between 1:10 and 1:50 on Black Monday.

For October 19 as a whole, index-related sales entered through DOT totaled 89 million shares, or about 15 percent of all the selling on the New York Stock Exchange. It is a measure of the academic prestige of the mathematicians and economists who designed the portfolio insurance and index arbitrage systems that the press almost without exception agreed from early on that "program trading" was *not* a major problem October 19, and one of the great accomplishments of the Brady Commission that against the weight of academia and publicity it said, Your father's mustache, guys. Here's the evidence.

4

Meltdown: 2. The Wreckage

"I was on the options floor a lot that day, to see what problems people were having, and of course it's an isolated place in the middle of a building, you don't have any contact with the outside world. My most vivid memory is when one of the young fellows who I guess had read his history books came up to me in the afternoon, solemnly, and asked, 'How long are the lines?'

" 'What lines?' I said.

" 'You know,' he said. 'At the banks.' "

—David Rich, vice-president for regulation,
Pacific Stock Exchange

Subscribers here by thousands float,
  And jostle one another down,
Each paddling in his leaky boat,
  And here they fish for gold and drown . . .

Meantime, secure on Garraway cliffs,
  A savage race, by shipwrecks fed,
Lie waiting for the foundred skiffs,
  And strip the bodies of the dead.

—Jonathan Swift, on the end
of the South Sea Bubble

1

At the Chicago Merc, the day opened sourly. Traders and dealers had met on Saturday in an extraordinary session to attempt to reconcile an unprecedented volume of "out-trades"—trades where the participants disagreed as to price or even nature, with both parties claiming to have sold (somehow there weren't any cases where both parties claimed to have bought). Something like ten thousand trades, with a market value of almost one and a half billion dollars, were still in dispute among the parties when the bell rang for the start of trading at 8:30 Monday morning.

Pit brokers for a Salomon Brothers subsidiary, acting on behalf of a large institution fulfilling its portfolio insurance program, led the action by selling December futures for the S&P index in hundred-contract lots. Each of these contracts presumably had a face value of $140,000 or so ($500 per point times the 280 points of the index as of the close of October 16). The price of the futures contract in the pit sank like a stone, opening $10,000 below the cash index. But these numbers were misleading, for many of the most important stocks in the index had not yet opened in New York, and the cash value of the stocks in the index was still being calculated as of the prices at which these stocks had closed on Friday. In any event, like the New York Stock Exchange, the Merc more or less recovered by eleven o'clock, and the S&P December contract was briefly a touch higher than the underlying, "real" index. (Interestingly, the Brady Commission reports that purchases by one unidentified big foreign investor brought it up.) Then the Spooz began the first of what would be several precipitous drops, much faster than the drops in the underlying stocks.

Locals speculating for their own accounts are the market makers in the futures pits, and even now, in highly institutionalized Chicago, they are involved as buyers or sellers (or both) in two-fifths of all the trades. On October 19 the larger locals who gave information to the Brady Commission appear to have been net buyers to the extent of about $200 million worth of S&P contracts. The big buyers were "trading-oriented investors" and "arbitrageurs" (categories that undoubtedly included a number of large broker/dealer firms trading for their own account) who bought between them about 29,000 contracts. The big sellers were the "dynamic hedgers," the portfolio insurers, who sold almost 34,000 contracts, amounting to roughly $4 billion face value.

For those who worked in the pit and were net long and not hedged, the afternoon was an incomprehensible horror, and the disappearance of bids from locals in the late going was the reason the futures closed an unbelievable 24 points below cash value. The cash

S&P index lost 20.39 percent on October 19; the December futures lost 28.61 percent. About 40 of the 400 members who normally work in the S&P pit left during the course of the day—probably 20 percent of the locals—and among those who stayed, said one observer, "You never saw so many people with their hands in their armpits." The community of locals in the S&P pit ultimately got well, but only because later in the week George Soros, the Hungarian refugee guru of Quantum Fund, star of magazine article and television interview, panicked and dumped immense quantities of contracts at Thursday's opening through the intermediation of a kid broker from Shearson Lehman who didn't know enough to stop selling when the market went hopelessly out of line. The situation became apparent in the pit, and locals gobbled up contracts as much as 60 points—$30,000— below cash value. For many of them, the profits of the next half hour covered the losses of the preceding two weeks.

Volume on October 19 in the S&P contract was 162,000 contracts, a record but only marginally higher than the 156,000 traded on October 9 (or the 157,000 traded on September 11, 1986). The open interest at the close of the day, however, was up 26,000 contracts, about twice as much as any previous increase. It measures the damage done that the 172,000 contracts of open interest as the pit shut down Monday had a market value of more than $6 billion *less* than the 146,000 contracts of open interest at the close the previous Friday. It measures the resourcefulness of the Merc and the authority of its clearing corporation that the total margin on deposit against S&P contracts at the close on October 19 was up $1.65 billion, from just under $3 billion Friday to more than $4.5 billion on Monday, even though the value of the contracts was down. As the price of the contract dropped, the longs had to put in new money to replace what had been deducted from their accounts to pay their losses to the shorts, and the shorts wouldn't get a chance to take their profits out until the next day.

With a little help from their banks, the clearing firms, the Futures Commission Merchants (that is, brokers), and their customers buttressed the clearing corporations of the three Chicago markets by more than $3 billion, most of it on an intra-day basis, while the markets were still open; funds were wired in or credit was extended within half an hour or an hour of the call for a "variation margin." It was very hairy. Harris Bank reports that its branch in the Board of Trade building cashed a number of checks in the hundreds of thousands of dollars ("from very distraught people," says public-relations director Mary Uhlmann), and rented out a number of new safe deposit boxes.

In the bond pit at the Chicago Board of Trade, the surge started in Monday evening's trading session, as the Japanese began the flight to quality, lifting a Treasury-bond futures contract that had fallen as low as 77, and would rise in the succeeding weeks by about 15 percent. On two occasions, on the way down the week of the 12th and up the week of the 19th, trading in the T-bond pit would reach over 650,000 contracts, or $65 billion worth of bonds; counting the options, the open interest reached *$100 billion* worth of bonds. But this is overwhelmingly a market in which the participants are hedged: The banks and insurance companies and investment houses that are short futures are simultaneously long the cash bonds, and vice versa. Even the locals in the pit are usually one way or another playing the "basis," the difference between the interest rate implied by the futures price and the interest rate specified by the price for equivalent bonds in the cash market. Moreover, the T-bond pit followed the commodity market tradition of "limit moves," so that once the price had risen by three points—$3,000 per contract—trading was shut off until someone was prepared to sell for less or the next day came. "As an economist," says Robert Rutz, the blond, lightly mustachioed president of the Board of Trade Clearing Corporation, "I've had varying views on price limits. As the head of a clearinghouse, I'm for them; they give me time to collect the funds."

The worst carnage, inevitably, came at the Chicago Board Options Exchange. This is probably the most heavily populated of the exchanges, with 931 regular members, 700 "exercisers" who acquired rights to trade on the exchange by virtue of their prior membership in the Board of Trade, and 400 "specials," beneficiaries of a deal by which the Midwest Stock Exchange, where they had been trading, agreed to get out of the options business. About three-fifths of the business was in the option on the S&P 100, an index of the hundred most heavily capitalized stocks on the New York Stock Exchange, which in its various months at various striking prices could trade more than 300,000 contracts a day, by far the greatest fraction of them to small players rather than institutional hedgers.

As the price of the contract is the index times the number of stocks, the option on the S&P 100 by definition controls a face value only one-fifth that of the future on the S&P 500. Going into the crisis weeks, someone buying an option that was out of the money by about 3 percent could hope to have a monthlong play on the movement of $30,000–$35,000 face value of stock indices for a risk of perhaps $1,500, counting commissions. "This is," says Alger ("Duke") Chapman, its president, "a retail market predominantly." With a position limit of 10,000 contracts, the maximum an institution could have hedged here on October 19 was $280 million, which is pocket money for the big boys: Commodity Futures Trading Commission figures showed seventeen institutional investors with short positions about that big or bigger in the S&P 500 contract at the Merc.

Of course, small players can be hedgers, too—indeed, the greatest single function of the Chicago Board Options Exchange has probably been the opportunity it has given people who own stock to protect themselves by buying inexpensive out-of-the-money puts, giving them the right to sell their stock at something only a little less than today's price even if the market moves against them. Most hedging by the local players who stand in the amphitheater of the index options pit at the CBOE, looking at the unbelievable ganglia of screens that show premiums at different "strike prices" for different months, is necessarily done in the options market itself: A man who is short the November contract 260 can hedge quite effectively by buying the 255 December contract.

Strategies involving the simultaneous purchase of one option and sale of another are solemnly peddled by brokers who make commissions on both as "bull spreads" or "bear spreads," which let the customer make a little money at little risk if prices rise or fall. Old-timers in a business that goes back only to the early 1970s call most of them "alligator spreads," because the commission eats the customer alive. For the traders in the pits, who do not pay commissions (it makes all the difference), the desired hedging strategies may involve simultaneous trading in the futures pits or at the stock exchange, and for them the chaos of October 19 was ruinous.

The day begins at the Chicago Board Options Exchange, which handles something more than three-fifths of the nation's options trading, with a kind of roll-call: a "rotation" through the list of options, to let the exchange's clerks who hold the overnight orders from the public feed them out to the market makers. No trading can occur in any option until it has been called in the rotation. The rules of the options exchange provide that if a stock has not yet opened in its primary trading location, the option cannot be traded, either.

Index trading is permitted regardless of the condition of the underlying market, but on October 19 and 20 it was necessary to add a large number of new "strike prices," at which options could be bought for each month of expiration—and given the condition of the markets, the CBOE decided to run separate rotations for puts and calls. On a normal day, the rotation was complete in less than fifteen minutes; on October 19, the index options rotation took an hour and a half, and on October 20, two hours and forty-two minutes. And even then, free trading was not permitted, because the market had moved so far on the 19th (and trading had been suspended on the 20th) that "reopening rotations" were called.

Meanwhile, the public was essentially frozen out. CBOE has perhaps the best of the automatic public order systems, the RAES (for "Retail Automatic Execution System"), which permits public customers to purchase up to ten contracts at the price on the screens when the order arrives. Market makers who have signed up to supply this service are assigned these orders in rotation, and pick them up every so often from a kind of open postbox on the floor, to see how their position has changed while they were bidding in the amphitheater. The arrangement with the market makers was that they signed up to supply this service by the week—that is, if they agreed to accept these orders on Monday, they would have to continue executing them through Friday. Prior to October 19, about four hundred market makers at the CBOE participated in the RAES system. (The reader should note that the small customer, who supplies the life blood of this market, is usually wrong. Filling his orders tends to be profitable.) After the bloodbath of the preceding week, almost nobody was prepared to sign up for all of the next week, and CBOE got volunteers only by offering them the chance to back out at any time. By Friday the 23rd, only forty-six were still participating.

On the 19th and 20th the low participation did not matter so much, because the RAES works only during free trading, and the rotations took up nearly the whole day. Later it didn't matter so much because the premiums market makers charged to write options had gone beyond reason. At 11:53 A.M. on Tuesday, October 20, with the S&P 100 cash index valued at 218, a November put contract at 195 was sold at a premium of 85—that is, to buy the right to sell in four weeks for $19,500 something that was at that moment worth $21,800, the purchaser paid $8,500.

What such premiums reflected, of course, was the immense carnage that had been visited upon the writers of puts the day before—and, indeed, in the late morning of October 20. The purchasers of the puts were safe and would be able to cash them in, though as we shall see it took a long time for the New York banks to believe this, because the Options Clearing Corporation, like the clearing corporations at the commodities exchanges, stands between the buyer and seller of every option and guarantees that the terms of the contract will be met. The clearing firms that do the paperwork for the traders, and for the "introducing brokers" whose customers trade with them, in turn stand responsible to the clearing corporation. Presumably, the brokers can collect from their customers, but some thousands of people who wrote options simply did not have the resources to pay off in the aftermath of the crash, and some of those who did were strongly resisting their brokers' demands, on the grounds that nobody had ever told them they had these enormous potential liabilities. Probably half the $122 million that E. F. Hutton lost in fourth-quarter 1987 on its way to the glue factory was the result of their high-priced customers' men leading those who listened into temptation.

On December 2, the *Wall Street Journal* gave the headline "The Black Hole" to a front-page article about ordinary people who found themselves bankrupt after writing naked puts and calls at the urging of their brokers (who collected commissions on each of these contracts, of course—commissions a good deal larger, in proportion to the price of the instrument, than those charged elsewhere in the securities business). Wayne Lutheringhausen, president of the Options Clearing Corporation, said, "One New York wire house told me, 'If we do an options business for the rest of history, we'll never make up what we lost that week.' But the existence of our market is the reason he had all those two hundred million share days in New York, and he made a lot of money on that." The bottom line is that the options markets lost their salesmen; volume probably will never recover.

Some big fellows were hurt by their exposure as clearing firms for traders with the wrong risk-preference schedule. Teh Huei Wang of Hong Kong put Charles Schwab in a position where the clearing corporations needed $84 million in margin calls, and all Schwab could get out of the man finally was $67 million. In all, Schwab's customers ran out on $22 million worth of margin calls. First Options Corp., which had been acquired by Continental-Illinois Bank for $135 million only months before, wound up with a loss of more than $50 million on the trading of Hwalin Lee, a Taiwanese-American who was a denizen of the pit. Mr. Lee, it turned out later, had been sanctioned twelve times by the CBOE for various rules violations, most commonly exceeding limit positions, and was being sued by Merrill Lynch for $1.4 million in connection with some troubles in his clearing account in 1983.

There was some tendency to regard this as bad luck—Continental-Illinois had, after all, inherited this fellow from the previous owners of First Options—but there is some other evidence that people had suspicions of how that clearing firm was being managed. An options trader at the Pacific Stock Exchange noted in passing that the morning of October 19 on his way to work he had stopped off at First Options, which was his clearing firm, and instantly removed his $800,000 of excess margin, just to make sure it didn't go down with the ship. And the *Wall Street Journal,* in its gutsy piece on December 2, noted that First Options, unlike other brokers and clearers, was still permitting its customers to write naked puts and calls on, in effect, the credit of Continental-Illinois.

2

"The gravest crisis of Thursday, October 24," wrote Vincent P. Carosso of the panic of 1907, "occurred on the New York Stock Exchange, where the call money rate had soared to 125 percent bid, with none offered. The sudden lack of money was caused chiefly by frightened trust company officials, intent upon strengthening their own cash reserves, demanding payment of their outstanding loans and refusing to make new ones. Unable to borrow any money, brokers and security dealers could not conduct business, nor could the stock exchange."

At the New York Stock Exchange in 1987, that day was Tuesday, October 20. Alan Greenspan, chairman of the Federal Reserve Board, announced early in the morning that the Fed would supply enough liquidity to the market to enable business to be done, and the New York Fed was out early making three-day repurchase agreements to pump cash into the banks. But the New York banks were feeling the terror of a non-swimmer who has just stepped in over his head.

In 1984, the Federal Reserve System had published a staff *Review and Evaluation of Federal Margin Regulations,* which in the world-weary way of this decade's academic market studies produced a finding that "casts some doubt on the importance of margin ratios for stock prices," and argued that "on balance, the activity of margin traders may help stock prices in anticipating future price levels. . ." Cooler heads on the Board prevailed, however, and the Fed continued to enforce, not very vigorously, a 50 percent margin requirement for exchange-traded and some over-the-counter stocks—that is, banks and brokers were forbidden to lend buyers more than half the purchase price. Except that some buyers were exempt. Specialists, brokers who facilitated the purchase or sale of big blocks by "positioning" stock in their own account until they could dispose of it, and "market makers" were permitted to buy or sell securities with a "good-faith" margin—which meant whatever the banks were willing to lend. In 1977, after a long and fairly heated argument, the Fed had agreed to let the SEC grant exemptions also to options traders in the pits (most traders in an options pit are theoretically market makers) who were buying stocks to hedge their option holdings.

In theory, none of this matters much. The options exemption is good only "share for share" and Rule 390 of the New York Stock Exchange prohibits anyone but the designated specialist from holding himself out as a "market maker" in NYSE-listed securities. But in practice there is not just a loophole but an inviting open door. As part of its drive to prevent NYSE monopoly on the trading of the most important shares, the SEC has defended the right of regional exchanges, the Philadelphia, Pacific Coast, Chicago, and even the nonexistent computer-simulated Cincinnati exchange, to trade NYSE stocks. And broker/dealers, even "risk arbitrageurs," can claim to be market makers on those exchanges if they buy from and sell to lots of other market participants. In the end, said the Brady Commission in a comment that privately "shocked" the Fed and "surprised" the NYSE, "professionals are not subject to the 50 percent margin requirement applicable to individuals. Professionals. . . can invest in stocks on 20 percent to 25 percent margin." The SEC Report also notes "effective 20–25% levels at which. . .self-clearing broker-dealers generally are able to finance their stock positions."

Meanwhile, under Rule 431 E-5 of the New York Stock Exchange, member firms were permitted to treat as market makers other broker/dealers who were their customers, and to lend them 75 percent of the price of their purchases. Margin lending was very profitable for brokers, who charged their customers a 1-½ to 2 percent surcharge over bank rates, and by custom got also the right to lend the customer's stock to short-sellers. Total margin lending in October 1987 was $47 billion, or about 1.9 percent of market value— roughly one-third the percentage in October 1929. The "risk arbitrageurs" and *soi-disant* investment bankers, who "put companies in play" for takeovers and leveraged buyouts, were of course the most heavily margined of all. A 20 percent drop in the market wiped out the collateral securing the loans of such professionals. No wonder the banks panicked.

And panic they did. Calls for repayments or more margin began going out to the arbs Monday mid-afternoon, compelling them to sell whatever they could sell; this was probably the most powerful depressant in the 200-point drop that ended the day. Tuesday morning, Greenspan or no Greenspan, bankers deluged the market with demands for more money, more collateral. Specialists who inquired about borrowing some money to carry much larger positions than they had ever been forced to hold before were told to get lost, even if they had prior arrangements for lines of credit. After all, chairman John Reed of Citicorp told the *Wall Street Journal,* his stockholders would not have thanked him if he had lost $100 million supporting the stock market. Branches of foreign banks, which had become significant lenders to brokers and to specialists (it was an easy way to build an asset portfolio in New York), turned tail and simply disappeared.

The bank that ran farthest and fastest, interestingly, was Bankers Trust, which was both one of the largest lenders to the market and in its investment management service one of the largest offerers of portfolio insurance programs that called for heavy and repeated selling into a decline. In theory, there is a "Chinese wall" between the trust department that runs such programs and the division of the bank that lends to the markets, but in the conditions of October 20 it seems at least possible that top corporate management, responsible for both parts of the bank, took an interest in what the trust people planned to do that day. Earthquakes demolish Chinese walls, and, as the English like to say, grapevines grow over them. Eventually, E. Gerald Corrigan, president of the Federal Reserve Bank of New York, caught all the banks and wrenched their elbows above their shoulder blades, and they resumed lending to the market.

In Chicago, by contrast, the banks came through. The futures and options exchanges were institutions that "marked to market" every night—indeed, marked to market during the day, when necessary, as it was October 19. The rules required that the binders or performance bonds posted by the purchasers of contracts would be cut down immediately as the result of any losses suffered, or increased immediately to reflect any gains. Thus "margin calls" went out every night routinely from the clearing corporations of the exchanges, and the banks were accustomed to financing what the exchanges and the clearing firms had to do to transfer money from losers to winners. Price movements in Chicago, after all, were a zero-sum game: For every long who had to put up money marking to market in the meltdown, there was a short who had cash coming to him at the same time. The winners had a great stake in keeping the game going by helping the banks finance the losers. And prior to Black Monday it wasn't much money: At the Chicago Mercantile Exchange, for example, the average margin call in 1987 prior to the month of October was only $93 million, and the record for the year had been $299 million on May 26. On October 19, the total call reached $2.5 billion.

The three big Chicago markets are much larger customers in proportion to the size of their banks than the New York markets are for their giant money-center institutions. "Long before we have problems," says Bruce Osborne, a plump, reasonably relaxed shirt-sleeved banker in his forties who supervises lending to these markets by Harris Bank, the special heroes of the meltdown, "we take a lot of time and effort in understanding our customers and our customers' customers." Moreover, the people who invented the instruments they trade in Chicago are still around and active—most of them market-hardened academics, street-smart Ph.D.s. They really understand their markets in ways relatively few people in New York understand theirs. Even before the Federal Reserve System had officially turned on the spigot, the Federal Reserve Bank of Chicago was being accommodating about daylight overdrafts to meet the margin calls from the Merc. "It was very clear early in the day," Osborne adds, "that everyone needed to work together—the customers, the clearing corporations, and the Fed. If liquidity had dried up, it would have been a problem. But all the participants were performing. There was gridlock, but we oiled the system." As Richard Thomas, president of the First National Bank of Chicago, put it, "A lot of credit decisions had to be made. The banks supported their customers."

The very fact that October 19 was an institutional panic, with only minor public participation, helped get credit to Chicago, where the facts were understood. If the winners had not been able to collect Tuesday morning in Chicago, when the clearing corporations settled accounts, there would have been no hope of restoring orderly markets anywhere for days, perhaps weeks or months, to come. Indeed, there were troubles on Tuesday, partly because the New York banks that served some of the Chicago member firms were clutching their liquidity and partly because the Merc at first sent incomplete information to the banks. The clearinghouse forgot the interim credits the winners had earned but had not received at the intra-day reckonings on Monday and ordered the banks to pay out only what was owed from the Tuesday morning settlement, then had to countermand the instructions and issue new payment orders—and by then FedWire, the system by which the Federal Reserve transfers money from one bank to another, had broken down. This systems failure was a particularly nasty problem because the Chicago banks used the FedWire system rather than a local clearinghouse for large dollar payments amongst themselves. This was, one suspects, the "gridlock" Osborne meant.

And after FedWire was cleared, there was still a delay because at least one of the Chicago banks was afraid of exceeding the cap the Federal Reserve Board has placed on daylight overdrafts if it proceeded with payments before receiving cover. As a result, two New York firms (one of them Kidder, Peabody) did not in fact receive their money from Chicago until well on in the afternoon. But in fact neither the Merc nor the Board of Trade had to draw on their own lines of credit at all, and anyone who called (as the two uncompensated New York houses did, a little after noon) was told quite correctly and calmly that everything was okay.

On Tuesday morning both the stock and the index markets opened with a rocket-propelled whoosh, as individual investors (not institutions) swarmed to buy blue chips at prices that had been marked down fantastically—in many cases, more than a third—over the previous ten days. Then the rally faltered and died: There was no money in New York, and in the end only New York counted. John Phelan, chairman of the New York Stock Exchange, got on the phone with E. Gerald Corrigan, president of the Federal Reserve

Bank of New York: Why wasn't the Fed supporting the market, as Greenspan had said it would? But the Fed was supporting the market; it was just that the New York banks were too scared to lend. The money for margin calls at the New York Stock Exchange was due at noon; lacking that money, the brokers began to sell out their margined customers. Meanwhile, the mutual funds were terrified of not having the funds to redeem customers' shares—$2.9 billion worth had been tendered on October 19—and were pumping stock into the market to raise cash. (Goldman, Sachs, trying to play J. P. Morgan, had offered the funds a billion dollars in low-interest loans to keep their shares off the market, but a billion dollars wasn't enough money to make a difference.) By noon a vacuum had formed under stock prices: The market had lost all its gains of the morning and was dipping toward new lows.

Stuffed with stock, lacking the resources to keep buying even if they wished to run the risks (which many clearly did not), the specialists stopped trading in many of the most important companies. Shortly before noon, someone at the Securities and Exchange Commission, which does not have the power to close exchanges (only the officers of the exchange and the president of the United States can do that), took it upon himself to notify the Chicago markets that the New York market was about to shut its doors. Leo Melamed called to check with chairman John Phelan of the New York Stock Exchange, and was told the board of directors was about to meet to consider such a proposal. The Options Exchange had already suspended. With many of the most heavily weighted stocks in the index not trading, the question of how to value the S&P futures contract was not easy to answer. At 12:13 (EDT), Melamed ordered a stop to trading in the S&P pit, pending the resumption of trading in the large capitalization stocks in New York.

What happened next is a matter of some dispute. It is known that desperate investment banks, their capitalization disappearing, called their clients and urged them to announce stock buy-back programs to give stockholders and specialists a feeling that there was support somewhere, and more than a hundred companies did. ("Expressing confidence upstairs," chief economist Roger Kubarych of the New York Stock Exchange says sardonically, "in the stocks their pension fund managers were kicking the shit out of down on the floor.") It is generally believed that the White House made a few calls, too.

And the *Wall Street Journal* has argued that the big brokers (presumably with their institutional clients) manipulated the market up with purchases in the one contract that was still open for trading—the Major Market Index (the "Missiles") at the Chicago Board of Trade, which had long been suspected as a source of manipulative procedures. The Board of Trade reported to the *Journal* that there were 808 trades between 12:30 and 1:00. The price of the MMI rose 60 points, the equivalent of a 350-point rise in the Dow-Jones industrial index, in half an hour. The sellers of those futures as they reached premium over the cash index could lock in a profit by buying the underlying stocks in New York. The *Journal* is talking about a total maximum demand from this source of less than $50 million, in a day when the value of stocks traded was more than $20 billion, and there is nothing in the figures produced two weeks later by the Commodity Futures Trading Commission to support the newspaper's thesis. On January 4, 1988, the CFTC published an analysis of the trading in Missiles on October 20, which found the purchases in question "dispersed among small transactions of one or two lots, a large proportion of which was executed by locals. This pattern is typical of MMI trading, and . . . is inconsistent with a finding of market manipulation." The Brady Commission presented totally different numbers, but also concluded that "the data reveal no suggestion of any concerted action by any major firms or anyone else to manufacture a rally."

But there are people at the Board of Trade who believe the *Journal* story, and it may be so. A staffer to Congressman John Dingell informed the press that someone from inside the Board of Trade had told him the data given to the CFTC had been cooked. A former official of the CFTC told the *Journal* he didn't like the look of the CFTC's report. Myself, I don't know and can't guess—except to note that if the Missiles were used to save the market on October 20, the manipulators did the securities business two favors: They got the markets trading again (in fact, the Dow climbed that afternoon in what was then the biggest one-day rise ever), and they generated an audit trail that may yet put a stop to shenanigans that in the past we could only suspect were massaging the market. But it will be months if not years before the dust settles and we can see what stands behind it.

At the Options Exchange, to complete the litany, the day of terror came on Thursday. After Tuesday's rise the market had really soared on Wednesday, back over 2000 on the Dow, and President Reagan had said with obvious satisfaction that this strange episode was over. Then it wasn't over at all. "On Thursday," says Wayne Lutheringhausen at the Options Clearing Corporation, "I could not get control over my stomach. People had just become conscious of the extent of the damage, and they still hadn't pulled in their risk profile. At the New York Stock Exchange, they don't even collateralize until the fifth business day after. Here, it's 'meet the calls,' 'meet the calls.' There was no money. I called the Fed. They said, 'We're pumping it in. Why isn't it getting to your guys?' It was the New York banks, they wouldn't take puts as collateral. One bank was calling on our guys to get out the puts, which were gaining value, put in stocks, which were losing value. [That is, the bank stupidly wanted real if depreciating stock certificates rather than these derivative if appreciating put contracts as the collateral behind its loan.] Fortunately, Harris Bank stood up to the line."

3

About a year before Black Monday, chairman John Phelan of the New York Stock Exchange had given a speech in which he warned that the combination of dynamic hedging tactics by the big institutions and index arbitrage—the two sides of what had come to be called "program trading"—might create a market "meltdown." We had a meltdown, and almost everybody decided that program trading had nothing to do with it. But almost everybody was wrong.

"Portfolio insurance," as the hedging tactics were called by those who sold them, purported to guarantee fund managers against significant losses in their stock portfolios. Following a formula, the managers would sell index futures whenever the stock market declined (usually the trigger was 3 percent), increasing the proportion of the portfolio hedged in this way as the decline proceeded. Any losses in value suffered in the cash market would thus be made up by gains in the derivative market. "As futures evolved," W. Gordon Binns, Jr., vice-president and chief investment funds officer for General Motors told a congressional committee in July 1987, "larger pension funds increased their participation in this [futures] market. . . . Consequently, large pension funds . . . have an ability to effectively hedge market risks. As a result of this progress, pension funds are in a better position to hold larger equity exposures."

The danger that this repetitive selling into a declining futures market might drive the prices of these contracts further down than would otherwise happen was mitigated, in portfolio theory, by index arbitrage, which would automatically create buyers for the futures the funds wanted to sell. In portfolio theory, there are few differences between owning (or owing) actual stocks and owning (or owing) a futures contract, and they can all be expressed by certain easily calculated comparative costs: The buyer of the futures needs to put up only a small fraction of the cost, while the buyer of the stocks must put up the full price, in cash and borrowings, paying or forgoing interest. The futures purchaser puts the money he doesn't have to spend for the contract into Treasury bills, which probably yield more than the dividends the stockholder receives. Then there are commission charges, etc., all easily worked out by a program that can run on quite a small computer. Each day, there is a number that states the break-even price differential between the cash market and the futures market, assuming that all positions are held to the expiration of the futures contract and "unwound" when the prices of the two must converge, at the last minute. When the difference in the prices is greater than that number, the arbitrageur through his computer program buys the future and sells the underlying stocks, or vice versa, locking in a certain if small profit.

Apart from the possible manipulation of the market through the MMI, which would be done by broker/dealers rather than by institutions, the futures contract of choice for both portfolio insurance and index arbitrage was the S&P 500, generally regarded as the best proxy for the stock market as a whole. One interesting aspect of the choice was the fact that when the Chicago Mercantile Exchange first applied for permission to trade the S&P index future, in 1981, part of the argument for approving the application was that this futures contract could never influence the daily prices in the stock market. Arbitrage would not be possible because of the difficulty of buying or selling 500 stocks at once. Indeed, over the years spokesmen for the Merc went around the world talking nasty about the Missiles because the mere twenty stocks in the rival index made the interplay of the cash and futures markets a playing field for manipulators. Early on, however, the earnest, nervous mathematician Ed Thorp, author of the book *Beat the Dealer* and master of, among other things, blackjack, developed a proxy for the S&P involving as few as thirty-six stocks, which moved with such close correlation to the index that he could profitably arbitrage the contract and the proxy whenever the contract got five or six points out of line.

Still, Thorp's programs needed a big spread, and the thing was awkward to do. A lot of individual orders had to be sent separately to the floor for execution at prices that were, after all, determined by a continuing auction. And the game as Thorp designed it really played in only one direction, because since 1938, when William O. Douglas as chairman of the SEC imposed Rule 10-a on what was then a reluctant New York Stock Exchange, brokers have been forbidden to execute short sales unless the last different price at which this stock sold was *lower* than the price at which the seller offers his borrowed stock. Because of this "up-tick rule," it might not be possible to sell any stocks in the index that you didn't already own when the math called for the purchase of an underpriced futures contract and the sale of the stock. Thorp also had the problem that brokers can't legally give a mere entrepreneur the use of the proceeds of a short sale, which means he needed a much bigger gap between the price of the future and the prices of the underlying stocks when an arbitrage program told him to sell stocks.

Presently, however—and quite inadvertently—innovations at the stock exchange and widespread acceptance of the "efficient market" hypothesis tore down the barriers that had prevented free and easy arbitrage of the cash and futures markets. The stock exchange DOT system permitted instantaneous communication of buy and sell orders in sizes sufficient to arbitrage scores of futures contracts. Not all the orders, of course, would be executed right at the prices that triggered them—the new bids might be below or the new offers might be above the previous sale. But the computers could make allowance for "breakage" and still promise profits on the executed trades at gaps between the contract and the cash that might be less than three points.

Meanwhile, the growth of "index funds" meant that huge pools of money, up to $160 billion by mid-1987, had been invested in *all* the stocks that made up the futures contract. Index funds could play Thorp's game in both directions—without even going to the trouble of developing a proxy for the index—because they never had to sell short. They could sell out of their portfolio into a falling New York market with absolute assurance that through their purchase of the futures contract in Chicago they had *already* bought the stock back at a lower price. Douglas's rule against short-selling to drive down the market—which the great majority of laborers in the vineyards at the stock exchange now consider an excellent idea, though university economists and traders of derivative instruments disagree—had in effect been subverted.

This was fine with General Motors's W. Gordon Binns and with the other operators of index funds, because their theory told them that if arbitrageurs were free to play the cash and futures markets against each other both markets would become more liquid and more "efficient." The result of permitting short sales of stock in "unwinding" index purchases, they thought, would be to raise the price of the futures. John Phelan, who had been a New York Stock Exchange specialist and the son of a specialist before he became chairman, knew better. The scenario he saw was a chain reaction.

Selling heavily in the futures pits (which happened), the computer-guided portfolio insurance firms would open the gap between futures and cash. This would (and indeed did) trigger index arbitrage in the form of purchases in the pits and sales on the floor. But the result would be predominantly to push the prices of the stocks even further down rather than to raise the price of the futures. People, not machines, buy and sell these instruments. And market behavior as witnessed for centuries—this was the reason for the Douglas rule— makes price movements asymmetric. When prices go up, there are always people willing to sell and lock in their profit, but when prices go down with any severity purchasers are scared away. Buying the futures would indeed bring new sellers into the futures pit, but selling the stock would bring few new buyers to the exchange. As the prices of the stocks went down, the mathematicians would trigger another round of "dynamic hedging," new sales of futures to protect the portfolio, which would in turn trigger a new round of index arbitrage selling of the stocks and another reduction of stock prices sufficient to give the command for still more hedging. The process could repeat itself until neither the futures contract nor the stocks had any market value at all.

Still, the process seemed limited by the fact that only index funds could play. As the Commodity Futures Trading Commission pointed out in its interim report on Black Monday, "the 'uptick' rule on the NYSE inhibits arbitrage-induced short selling of stocks in a general market decline." The evidence from the previous firestorm, on September 11 and 12, 1986, was that a meltdown might start ("index-related futures trading was instrumental in the rapid transmission of . . . changed investor perceptions to individual stock prices, and may have condensed the time period in which the decline occurred"), but the chain reaction would run out of fuel. While most index funds sold futures for insurance purposes, fewer played the arbitrage game. And only the index funds could play.

Then another large player was allowed to throw fuel on the fire. On December 17, 1986, the SEC gave Merrill Lynch a "no-action" letter—and published it for the guidance of the other big brokerage firms—permitting broker/dealers *and only broker/dealers* to sell short into a declining market, provided that any one of the many separate accounts the firm managed for its own use and benefit was long and the sales were pursuant to "unwinding" an index arbitrage. Prior to that letter, a broker/dealer, like anyone else, could sell only if its net position as a firm was long; subsequent to that letter, though its authors said they had not intended this result, it was anything goes. On October 19, institutional investors sold 21,000 new S&P contracts (about $3 billion worth) on the Merc, and bought 8,800 new contracts (undoubtedly for index arbitrage). And broker/dealers bought another 5,700 contracts, and used DOT to execute program trades.

The SEC Report on the crash is by the Division of Market Regulation, which issued the no-action letter. Though elsewhere the Report presents a chronology of sales indicating that broker/dealers sold more than 11 million shares admittedly short October 19, the great bulk of it at hours when the market was falling, the Division says that "firms have been unable to quantify the extent to which they relied, or have advised as that they did not rely, on the no-action position during October." It is doubtless only a coincidence that the total program selling by broker/dealers for their own account, both admittedly short and not admittedly short, adds up almost exactly to what would have been required to perform arbitrage on 5,700 S&P contracts bought in Chicago. The Division argues in its Report for the abolition of the up-tick rule, on the grounds that it's inconvenient in the relationship between the futures markets and the stock market, and that people who wish to evade it can do their business in London, anyway. That's rather like the IRS arguing that it's silly to try to collect taxes from high rollers because they can always stash the money in Swiss banks. The open refusal of the SEC to enforce its own rules speaks for itself.

For reasons that are by no means clear, the Brady Commission bought the academic argument that continued close articulation between the trading in the S&P 500 contract and the New York stocks would have limited the damage October 19—that the failure of the DOT system to deliver rapid executions on the floor forced sellers to use the futures market to get out, which drove the Spooz to a heavy discount from the cash. This, Brady argues, created a "billboard effect" discouraging potential buyers of stocks who saw the S&P contract predicting a decline to 1400.

The deep discount of the futures from the cash no doubt did have effects. We know that Wells Fargo investment advisers acting on behalf of General Motors's Binns, still committed to getting out pursuant to their programs, dumped stocks directly onto the New York Stock Exchange system—thirteen orders of $100 million each—because the prices were worse in Chicago than they seemed to be in New York. But if they had been able to sell at a better S&P price in Chicago because buyers of the futures were able to perform index arbitrage by selling the stocks, they would merely have shifted the doing of the dirty work from their shoulders to others'. By far the stronger case is that only the delinkage of the two markets by the breakdown of the technology that had given them a spurious identity prevented a complete collapse on October 19. If the DOT system had been working perfectly and the specialists had absorbed all the stock the funds and the broker/dealers threw at them, the futures contract prediction of 1400 on the Dow would have come to pass, probably only as a way station on the road to something still lower.

4

No one seriously argues that program trading "caused" the crash. President Reagan said the Brady Commission report made that case, but as usual he hadn't read it. Given the dimensions of the imbalances in the American economy, the stronger case by far is to say that the prices in the market on October 19 were closer to fair value than the prices had been before. But without program trading we would not have had an institutional panic, for the institutions would not have been beguiled by mathematicians into the belief that investments in equity were not money at risk. The destruction wrought by elephants running in the squirrel cage will be with us a long time. The trauma of the people who work in these markets will scar these institutions for years to come. The process of capital formation for American business has been changed in ways we have not yet begun to understand. You have to be awfully sophisticated to believe that there's no harm done to society when more than a fifth of the value of its enterprise can be melted away without any easily explicable reason in a single day of wrath.

It probably can't happen again just that way. The fund managers are sure they were right and the markets let them down (and that the press was unfair). Hayne Leland of the University of California at Berkeley, one of the founders of portfolio insurance and a partner in the money-management firm of Leland, O'Brien & Rubinstein, told the *New York Times* in reaction to the Brady Commission report that "portfolio insurance selling on October 19th was equal to just $2/10$ of 1 percent of the total value of stocks. It is hard for me to believe that such a small amount of selling drove down the market by 20 percent." That's like saying that there was no reason for the price of oil to quadruple when OPEC cut supply by about 2 percent. In times past, professors of finance understood the powerful effects of change at the margin.

But the danger of meltdown is somewhat reduced, because the masters of the funds have reined in their advisers. The institutions will put less of their money into equities in the future, and they will probably trade less. Oddly, the worst damage to the position of the mathematical fund managers was done in the days immediately after the crash, when stock prices rose. The funds had taken their profits out of their "insurance" when the contracts were marked to market, and being efficient had put the money into Treasuries, which were rising smartly. Then stock prices went up, and they had to meet margin calls on the contracts they were still short. They had to take money out of Treasuries and give it back, and for this sort of shifting of funds the managers needed the approval of corporate officers. While the stocks the funds had hedged were regaining value and the variation margin the funds were called on to supply did not represent a real loss, the corporate officers hated the idea of being told they had to put up what looked to them like fresh money, and they told their managers to be more careful next time. Out of such trivia comes significant institutional change.

5

Chicago: 1.
Present at the Creation

"Futures markets are designed to permit trading among strangers, as against other markets which permit only trading among friends."

—Terrence Martell,
research director, COMEX

"By 1975, currency futures seemed right, but what business had it in Chicago? If it was important, how could you trust it to a bunch of pork-belly traders? But they had to come to our doorstep, because we were the only ones with the tools."

—Leo Melamed,
Chicago Mercantile Exchange

1

I remember, back in the early seventies," said Anthony Frank, "I went to sell the Chicago Board of Trade the idea of trading Ginnie Mae futures. I went with Rich Sandor." Ginnie Mae = GNMA = Government National Mortgage Association; the futures would be contracts to buy or sell GNMA certificates at a price fixed today, on or before a specified distant date. Frank, who is now Postmaster General, was then head of the acorn-size Citizens Savings of San Francisco, which later, after much fertilizing, grew into the First Nationwide Savings he sold to the Ford Motor Company.

Sandor, who is now a managing director of Drexel Burnham and chief of their futures and options division, was then an economics professor from U. Cal. Berkeley on sabbatical. "Rich wanted me to explain the Ginne Mae paper to them, and I did. I told them about pass-through paper and how it worked, and how you assembled a package of mortgages big enough to give you an average likelihood of when people would repay them, so you could figure the certificate had a duration of twelve years. And how important Ginnie Mae was as a source of financing for homes for moderate-income Americans, and the history of the Federal Housing Administration, and Fannie Mae [Federal National Mortgage Association, the original government-chartered mortgage banker], and why the subsidized operation had to be spun off because of the tax interpretations, and how a futures market in Ginnie Maes would cut the cost of mortgages for American families by making them more liquid and encouraging new investors to buy them.

"They were a hard-bitten bunch of traders. 'Players,' Sandor called them; they didn't like that. They listened, but they didn't understand what we were talking about. Finally one of them leaned forward and said, 'Mr. Frank, I need the answer to one question.'

" 'Yes, sir,' I said.

" 'Do these things, these Ginnie Maes, go up and down in price?'

" 'Yes, they do,' I said.

" 'Good,' he said. 'Then we can trade them, Mr. Frank.' "

2

There are no fewer than four Chicago markets trading physical or financial commodities or derivative instruments on securities—the Board of Trade, the Mercantile Exchange, the Board Options Exchange, and the MidAmerica Exchange (which trades the Board of Trade contracts in small lots but opens forty minutes earlier and thus often points the way). The Options Exchange is supervised by the Securities and Exchange Commission and trades only options on securities registered with the SEC and index measurements of price movements in those securities. The other three still trade agricultural commodities and some metals, as they have since 1848 on the Board of Trade, 1880 on the MidAmerica, and 1919 on the Merc. They are still supervised by a Commodity Futures Trading Commission spun out of the Packers and Stockyards Division of the Department of Agriculture by Congress in 1974. But three-quarters of the trading on these floors is now in financial futures, contracts for the purchase and sale of artificial commodities that move with reference to interest rates and stock prices. The rise of these markets—and as the 1980s end they bestride the world of paper like colossi—is the most important development in finance in the second half of the twentieth century. But, of course, it's still Chicago, and there is a strong tendency for New York and London not to take it seriously. Hog butcher to the world, Carl Sandburg said.

Where the liquidity of the stock market rests on a single specialist trading quietly with a handful of brokers at his post, the liquidity of the Chicago contracts grows from the willingness of a large community of "locals," short-term speculators who own or lease memberships and stand in the pit, to acquire contracts and dispose of them for the very small price differences between trades. The New York Stock Exchange is proud of the fact that the "spread" between the bid and the asked at the posts is most often less than one-half of 1 percent of the price of the stock; but in the commodity pits the spread is usually one-twentieth to one-fiftieth of 1 percent of the face value of the contract. This is accomplished by concentrating on a handful of contracts the business that on exchanges necessarily pours out over thousands of stocks, so that many bidders clamor for a piece of the action in what is called, quite correctly, "open outcry."

Though these markets have problems we shall look at presently, it is probably worth noting at the top that this public yelling helps to disinfect markets from secrecy as sunshine, in Justice Louis D. Brandeis's great metaphor, helps to disinfect contracts from fraud. "An open outcry market," says the arbitrageur Sandy Lewis, "is probably honest; an upstairs market is probably dishonest." This is less true today than it was, thanks to computer screens that produce a sort of silent outcry, but for all its dubious characters and inexplicable bounces, Chicago is a lot more "transparent" than either Tokyo or London, where a lot happens that is not exposed to public view or hearing. Hanky-panky in the commodities pits can occur only with the knowledge and consent of a lot of people listening in. Indeed, the clearing corporations and the CFTC know who the customers were for big trades in Chicago, while in New York it's impossible to find out about the customers and only the Stock Exchange knows (and won't tell) who the brokers were.

Like Saturday night poker games, the Chicago markets thrive on a constant infusion of new suckers who will lose their money and pass on. The path to the pits leads through a test and a character check by the National Futures Association (which has been delegated this task by the Commodity Futures Trading Commission). About sixty people work for NFA doing nothing but registering applicants for the title of "Associated Person." More than 60,000 people have passed the test, most of them employees of stock brokerage firms who may have occasion to advise clients on commodities matters. (Stockbrokers are *much* bigger than Futures Commission Merchants: Refco, the largest FCM with very nearly 20 percent of the options and commodities business worldwide, takes in about $200 million a year in commissions, while Merrill Lynch, which does about 12 percent of the listed securities business, gets more than a billion dollars in commission revenues for such efforts. Merrill, because its customers are individuals who pay considerably higher commissions per trade, actually takes in from its options and commodities business about twice as much commission revenue as Refco, which moves twice as high a volume of contracts but does all of it wholesale.)

Once past the National Futures Association hurdles and a rather cursory examination by the exchanges themselves, almost anyone can rent a seat to trade anywhere on this floor or in specified groups of pits. The color of the badge clipped to the jacket indicates the playing fields to which this individual has entry. The Board of Trade has separate memberships for agricultural and for financial products; the Merc has three, for agriculturals, for currencies and interest-rate futures, and for stock index products. The rental for a membership on either exchange is at this writing $3,000 to $5,000 a month—accompanied by a deposit of at least $50,000 (which can be in the form of Treasury bills) to be left with the firm that will stand responsible for the tenant's trades and will "clear" them through a rather elaborate paperwork process. At the Merc, the newcomer wears on his jacket a special badge identifying him as, in effect, a student driver, which will lead some of his companions in the pit to be nice to him and others to bleed him. Of the people at the bottom of the pit, which is where the locals stand (because they don't have to make contact with the clerks at the telephone booths), roughly half were not here a year ago and roughly half will not be here a year from now. ("Well," says John Meilke, chief of market surveillance for the CFTC, "the failure rate of all new businesses is high, and a floor brokerage is a new business.") A few burn out; most go broke. Many come back after an interregnum as someone's employee, and go broke again.

Of course they're gamblers. In his book *The New Gatsbys,* Bob Tamarkin, who covered the Chicago exchanges for the *Chicago Tribune,* wrote of a female trader starting out at the Merc who was asked if she wanted to bet a nickel on the Super Bowl. She won, and on Monday went over to collect, and "the trader with whom she had bet handed her a check for $5,000. In the pit culture where deals were made in financial shorthand, a nickel wasn't what it seemed to be." But there is also another community. "The reason I came here," says Barry Lind of the Chicago Merc, speaking of a time in the later 1950s, "was that I thought it would be an easy place to make fifty thousand dollars a year filling customers' orders. The average age on the floor then was about fifty, and there was no competition. The markets were in decline. But if you looked at the history books, they always came back, and I figured when they did, there wouldn't be much competition."

The pits clearly are not just a place to do business; they are, to quote Ken Lazarra, a wiry young man in his early thirties who has worked all around the T-bond and the S&P pits for Refco, "a unique and very close social system. The guys in these pits know each other, they have a lot of rules and regulations among themselves that have little to do with the CFTC. A local arrives, the first thing he does is throw down his trading card where he's going to stand, and then he goes off for a cup of coffee. People know him, he's a big trader, they respect the card. If the new kid on the block tries that, he'd better start shooting some numbers immediately. Once you've worked in the ring you never get it out of your system, it's like racing cars. I still toy with becoming a local, every day."

Some pits are quiet, and their denizens horse around a lot, until somebody gets bored and begins offering contracts at prices better than the quoted market. People trade with each other back and forth, hoping that the sales flashed around the world onto the screens will provoke interest from potential customers far away. If these things are prearranged, of course, the exchange as self-regulator and the commission as preserver of the marketplace will wax very wroth and may sock the miscreants with fines and suspensions. Nothing is easier than for two or three members in the pit who have similar

93

inventory profiles to agree that they will buy from and sell to each other at steadily rising or falling prices, until the public barrels in to ride the trend and lets them sell their positions at a profit. Traders are both fined and expelled for this offense every year—and you pay the fine even though you're expelled, because it gets deducted from the sale price of your seat. It is also true that not every such arrangement is caught, and that by permitting traders to create "synthetic options" by buying and selling the same contracts, the CFTC has encouraged the creation of fraudulent "open interest."

In the pits where the big business is done, however, there's not much time for horsing around, and the volume is so heavy that little guys can't stage enough trades to move the market. Most traders work in abominably crowded, sweaty, smelly, noisy circles of hell. In terms of the physical suffering imposed and the remoteness of the likelihood of success, buying into a pit in a commodities market is like becoming a ballet dancer. But they do it by the thousands every year.

In part, the attraction is the possibility, remote but real, of becoming one of the "legendary traders," the fellow who drove a cab by night and stood in the pits by day until he had a hot streak and moved into the world of Mercedeses and yachts and country estates. But it's also an addiction, day by day. Tony Bruck, a thirty-seven-year-old trader with a doctorate in linguistics from the University of Chicago and experience in computer graphics, came to the pits through a newspaper ad by Richard Dennis, a giant of the pit (physically and financially) who had decided to train apprentices. In a bachelor apartment about two blocks from the Board of Trade, featuring screen and easel for charts and spectacular stereo equipment, Bruck was thinking about the development of night trading, and decided he rather liked it. "But I don't think I'd be for Saturday and Sunday trading, too," he said thoughtfully, then added, "of course, there are a lot of guys who would."

The question of how much and what you have to know to trade successfully draws many and varied answers, and the fact is that there have been legendary traders who never finished high school. "For most of these guys," says a clerk, looking into the pit from the vantage point of a telephone booth, "they don't give a shit if it's currencies or cattle." Among the requisites is the capacity to pump oneself up to near-frenzy, to make enough noise and motion (in cramped quarters) to get the attention of the others in the pit. As often noted, the addiction to trading can also spawn other addictions, and the administrations of the exchanges are forever in negotiations with the police about how to handle the cocaine problem.

When possible (which is not often) locals like to feel in touch with the outside world, if only because they worry about being at a disadvantage against the fellows on the top step of the pit who have steady contact with the telephone clerks and who also trade for themselves (the rules don't, though they should, forbid it). Rumors—the deaths of presidents, new giant petroleum fields, Russian troop movements—sweep the pits, not infrequently started by people with positions to clean up. There's also a serious desire for real information. "When I was president of the Board of Trade," said Robert Wilmouth, now president of the National Futures Association and before that a banker with First Chicago, "I used to get to work at six in the morning, and I was virtually trampled by traders rushing to get to their office and find out what happened in the British and German markets before they went out on the floor."

At the medical examiner's office in New York, the visitor is greeted with a message carved in marble: "Here death delights in helping the living." The Chicago commodity exchanges have long recommended themselves as places where the gambling instinct serves the world of production and consumption. But with the introduction of financial futures in the years since 1972, these markets have become something much more than that. In the most active financial pits—Treasury bonds, S&P index, Eurodollars, Treasury bills, currencies—the famous dentist in Peoria taking a flyer on soybeans is not a factor. In the pit where participation by the general public is heaviest—the S&P index—individual buyers and sellers account for roughly 7 percent of the trading; in all the others, they account for less than 5 percent. These are now markets in which institutions trade with each other through the mediation of the locals.

When the Merc began trading futures contracts in foreign currencies in 1972, the *Wall Street Journal* carried a comment by a banker who professed himself "amazed that a bunch of crapshooters in pork bellies would have the temerity to think that they can beat some of the world's most sophisticated traders at their own game." But in 1987, when the Brady Commission was soliciting comments on Black Monday to guide the president in proposing cures for a disease some thought had spread from a point of infection in the

Chicago pits, the most ardent defenders of the Merc were the big banks, the pension funds, and the insurance companies. And the *Wall Street Journal.* The crapshooters in pork bellies had become the chosen agents of the financial establishment. This did not happen by accident.

What is missing from most discussions of the Chicago markets and their influence is any understanding of the intellectual accomplishment that lies behind them. The foundation of their success is the substitution of an exchange's own clearing corporation for the counterparty—the purchaser of what you sold, the seller of what you bought—in every trade in every pit. The guarantee of the integrity of the markets is the process of continuously pricing everybody's "open interest" (the contracts the players are holding at the end of the day's trading), valuing all positions at the price at which they closed that day, and settling up immediately the next morning. Those whose contracts have diminished in value are required to put up more cash to keep their deposit at the prescribed percentage of value; those whose contracts have increased in value are permitted to take out yesterday's winnings. "We have only one rule around here," says Board of Trade Clearing Corporation president Robert Rutz, who used to teach banking at the University of Wisconsin, and now occupies a large office with an easel for presentations and a window looking out onto the huge trading floor from high above. "You pay up before seven o'clock and you don't get in any trouble." The salability of the product traded on these exchanges results from the ingenious construction of uniform contracts that can be traded as surrogates for a heterodox world. And all of this was planned.

In 1986 the tin contract at the London Metals Exchange collapsed when the International Tin Council, an agency of a group of governments of both producing and consuming countries, set up in the heyday of the U.N.'s New World Economic Order to maintain stable and rising prices for this commodity, confessed itself unable to pay for the contracts it had purchased. The losses to the sellers, which included significant American brokerage houses like Drexel, Burnham and Shearson, Lehman, ran into the hundreds of millions of dollars. This was a time when American banks were threatening death and damnation to any Latin country that reneged on its indebtedness, but when the brokers sued the British government, which was one of the guarantors of the Tin Council, the House of Lords told them they could go whistle for their money—didn't they know governments had sovereign immunity?

The brokers were out of pocket because they had in effect extended credit to the Tin Council when selling it contracts for future delivery of tin. This had been convenient, because it meant that neither purchasers nor sellers of contracts ever had to soil their hands with money until the actual delivery of the commodity, which was a much more common end to futures trading at the London Metals Exchange than it is at other exchanges. ("Tight margin manufacturing concerns such as UK copper fabricators have not been used to putting money up front in their LME operations," as a sympathetic commentator put it.) And so long as the only participants were private parties, sitting around a circle on red leather benches and shouting at each other in five-minute bidding frenzies, a commodities exchange where "principals" trusted one another was safe enough. But by the time you have reason to doubt the creditworthiness of a government or a government agency, it's too late for self-protection.

Credit is not entirely unknown in Chicago, either. Clearing firms may extend credit to those for whom they clear, if they wish, and banks may extend credit to the clearing firms—but the markets are structured so that the buyers of the contracts will be absolutely safe. Their trades are registered not as obligations of the broker or his customer on the other side of the deal, but as obligations of the exchange's clearing corporation, which interposes itself as the counterparty on every transaction. The purchaser of a contract to accept delivery of Treasury bonds at today's price commits to buy from the Board of Trade Clearing Corporation, and the buyer of a contract to deliver Treasury bonds at today's price commits to deliver to the Clearing Corporation. When the time comes to purchase or make delivery, the Board of Trade Clearing Corporation will find someone on the other side of the market to close the transaction. (The original seller may have extinguished his contract, which is of course easy to do when the counterparty is the clearing corporation rather than the individual from whom you bought originally. You don't care what the trader on the other side does after the contract clears: If he purchases a countervailing contract, delivers it to the clearing corporation, and disappears, your position continues unchanged.) If either side reneges on the deal, the other side still gets what he bought because all the members of the clearing corporation are jointly and severally liable for its obligations. As Tone Grant of Refco says, "We guarantee our customers to the clearing corporation, and we guarantee the clearing corporation to our customers." Merc vice-president John Davidson points out that "membership does not give you the right to enter the trading floor"; traders can do business only if their accounts are guaranteed by one of the eighty well-capitalized "clearing members."

Prudential Insurance can buy from or sell to Joe Sixpack on the floor of the Merc or the Board of Trade as easily as it can deal with General Motors Acceptance Corporation, because the resulting contract has nothing to do with Joe or, for that matter, with GMAC. In the words of the Merc's basic promotion piece *Trading in Tomorrows: Your Guide to Futures,* "Traders need never worry about who was originally on the other side of the transaction." Says Leslie Rosenthal, former chairman of the Board of Trade, "We can say, 'You—billion-dollar corporation—are not making a transaction with this one hundred forty thousand dollar net worth individual, you're making a deal with *everybody.*'" The system goes back to 1925, and was much resented when new by traders who were used to trading on their charm and their connections.

After a broker/dealer called Volume Investors went noisily bust in the gold pit at New York's COMEX, concern about the possible extent of these obligations led Merrill Lynch to spin off its commodities brokerage operation as a separately capitalized entity. But in fact the danger to the clearing corporation and its members is all but invisible. The Tin Council could buy contract after contract on its good name alone, but in the Chicago markets both buyers and sellers must maintain their earnest money at a fraction of the contract value that normally exceeds the maximum plausible daily price movement. Four times a day at the Merc, all contracts are "marked to market" in a simulated clearing, which means that the computers deduct losses from and add winnings to each customer's deposit money according to the movement of prices since the last clearing. When the deposit money falls to the "maintenance margin," the fraction of the original down payment that must be kept in the contract (usually half), the clearing corporation will call for additional money (a "variation margin") not only at the close of trading but during the day. That additional money must be delivered within an hour, or the clearing firm will be ordered to sell the position. Both the Board of Trade and the Merc track the trading and the margin of all the larger customers (whose identities and trades must be "registered" with the exchange), and can give a clearing firm warning that one of its clients is nearing the edge. Meanwhile, the major clearing firms have their own computer runs, and may make customers put up more deposit money than the exchange itself requires.

At the Merc, though it is generally regarded as the junior and racier of the two big commodities exchanges, this margin is absolute—every customer has to have the money there for all his contracts, even if some have been purchased to hedge others. At the Board of Trade and the Options Clearing Corporation, holders are permitted to net their long and short positions and the clearing firm must deposit only such additional margin as the net figures demand. In those contracts where daily price changes are limited by the rules of the exchange, which is true in all but a handful of the pits (the price of the T-bond contract, for example, can change only three points, or $3,000, per day), the deposit money is always greater than the limit. It has been known to happen, especially when a contract moves "lock limit" day after day, blocking the poor customer from selling out, that losses exceed margins, in which case the clearing firm takes the hit. At New York's COMEX, Volume Investors urged a number of customers to sell gold futures just before the market jumped $39 an ounce. Presently, the clearing firm, which had taken its own advice, declared bankruptcy with $10 million in assets and $28 million in liabilities to its customers, the clearing corporation, and other brokers. The COMEX membership found the funds to pay off the counterparties in the trades, but the customers of Volume itself were stuck with losses. Indeed, *all* customers of Volume Investors, whether involved in these trades or not, found themselves with their accounts frozen by court order, which is why Merrill Lynch spun off its commodities brokerages into separate operations.

The uniformity of the contracts, crucial to the operation of these exchanges and central to the international expansion of their markets, comes easily for some commodities and not so easily for others. Gold, obviously, is traded in units of so-many ounces of a metal of a specified purity. Currencies are currencies. Pork bellies are a processed product. Live cattle and live hogs are sold by weight for a given breed of animal. But where does the seller make delivery if called upon to do so, and where does the buyer take delivery? "If you have one delivery point, it's too far," says Kalo Hineman of the Commodity Futures Trading Commission, himself a cattle raiser from Kansas. "I don't want to ship cattle a thousand miles. With one delivery point, though, you can find out the inventory. When you have ten delivery points, you never know what you're going to get."

Wheat has always been special, because farmers grow a lot of different kinds of wheat, and millers use different varieties for different purposes. The Board of Trade contract since time immemorial has been for hard winter wheat, but the bakers who make the abominable white bread Americans eat have always used soft wheats. (And the Minneapolis Grain Exchange has a separate, not very active contract for "white wheat.") For the wheat contract to be useful as a hedge for the millers and bakers, there has to be an established "conversion" factor (in the language of the trade, to quote CFTC commissioner Robert Davis, once a commodities specialist at Harris Bank, "an understandable basis relationship between the soft wheat market and hard red winter wheat"), by which all the wheat crops can be hedged in a single transaction. Some range of mix of wheats is permitted in the delivered package of five thousand bushels per contract, and the art of putting such packages together is practiced by grain storage warehouse owners. The Board of Trade has always had contracts where the commodity is not only deliverable but redeliverable by the initial purchaser to another buyer.

"Warehouse receipts always trade at the lowest common denominator," says former chairman Les Rosenthal, "because that's what you're going to get. New York says you can't do that, can't have someone who isn't a member of an exchange come in and make a package. But we're not too greedy. If someone's silo can put together something with a penny premium, we say that helps the market, it builds liquidity."

Curly-haired and confident, a free-market capitalist in what was then, briefly, a red sea, Richard Sandor in 1969 was a young economist at the University of California at Berkeley, with a grant from the Center for Real Estate and Urban Economics to work on housing problems. Among these in the early days of Nixon was the gap between the interest rate householders had to pay on mortgages and the rates in the bond market, even though the mortgages were federally insured. The hope was that by "securitizing" mortgages this gap could be reduced.

Both the problem and the proposed solution had a considerable history, dating back to the original federal housing legislation of the 1930s, which had authorized the creation of federally chartered mortgage associations that would issue bonds and use the proceeds to purchase federally insured mortgages from the banks and savings and loans that had originally written them. In effect, each Federal National Mortgage Association would tap the bond market for a new supply of funds the banks and thrifts could use to help people acquire housing. No private parties had stepped forward to start such associations, so the government had eventually chartered one of its own. Special programs within FNMA, funded by the government, helped subsidize interest rates on Federal Housing Administration mortgages for moderate-income households. Then a court ruling put the FNMA deficit into the federal budget, the association was privatized and listed on the New York Stock Exchange, and the subsidized program had to be moved out. It landed at the Government National Mortgage Association, which was to issue "pass-through certificates," shares in pools of federally insured mortgages put together by a mortgage banker, who pledged to "pass through" after taking only a tiny service charge all payments made by the homeowner on his mortgage, both principal and interest. This was a doubly guaranteed piece of paper, specifically backed by the credit of the United States as well as insured by the FHA. To everybody's surprise, you couldn't sell it at all.

The answer, clearly, was the creation of a secondary market in which institutions that purchased packages of these mortgages could price them and sell them. Without such a market, purchasers were stuck holding mortgages they might not want whether or not someone had "securitized" them. But Ginnie Maes by their nature were not standardized instruments. As pass-throughs, they paid off according to how long the borrower kept the house—when he sold, the income stream from interest payments ceased and the owner of the paper got that part of his money back for reinvestment, which he might or might not wish. If interest rates fell, the homeowner might refinance his mortgage, which also took it out of the Ginnie Mae package the investor had bought. Even before the Ginnie Maes were issued, Sandor had worked with Tony Frank at Citizens Savings to develop criteria by which the duration of mortgages could be estimated: "We took his portfolio and we ran fifty thousand regressions, found that quality measures, the ratio of the loan to the value of the house, were as important as quantity measures like the neighborhood." There wasn't and couldn't be any standard Ginnie Mae.

Sandor, on sabbatical, went to the New York Stock Exchange,

which wasn't interested in trading Ginnie Maes, and then he thought of Chicago. He had taken occasional flyers in the grain contracts himself, and he knew the history of the Board of Trade. "I suddenly realized that if you took the preamble of the charter of the Board of Trade, from the 1840s, you could substitute the letters GNMA for wheat. It was a 'heterogeneous market' with a 'growing supply' where the product sold at 'discounts and premiums.' People talk about 'originating grain'—that's what they say the grain elevators do. The operator of a grain elevator is a mortgage banker; a mortgage banker 'originates loans.' " One could *create* a uniform Ginnie Mae contract with an assumed interest rate and duration, a proxy for the mortgages customers wanted to buy or sell as the wheat contract was a proxy for their grain needs. Delivery against such a contract could be in the form of a warehouse receipt for certificates "graded" like grains or soybean meal. "The conversion factors," says John Hobson of the Division of Economic Analysis at the CFTC, "are analogous to quality substitution in the agricultural commodities markets." And what was delivered could then be resold, like the grains. "At the Board of Trade," Sandor comments, "they had no trouble with the concept that there's a primary dealer somewhere who does the mixing and matching."

"This teacher at U. Cal. Berkeley," says Les Rosenthal, who may have been the man who asked Tony Frank if the prices fluctuated, "he had the one original idea. All the other contracts are derivatives." Savings and loans and insurance companies and banks badly needed some way to hedge their exposure to fixed-rate mortgages that yielded a steady stream of interest payments at a time when the cost of the funds they lent was jumping wildly up and down. Sandor's Ginnie Mae futures contract gave them that. It was especially useful because buying real certificates was such a clumsy process, requiring the offering of a specific instrument that had to be narrowly described. "Futures markets," Sandor observes from experience, "succeed where the cash market is transactionally inefficient."

Other financial futures had been attempted by other exchanges, on their own motion, without seeking government approval of any kind: The Agriculture Department, which supervised the commodity markets, was interested only in agricultural products. But this was about to change as Sandor, who had first taken a second year's sabbatical and then changed venue to the Board of Trade as its economist, worked out the details of this exceedingly complicated instrument. With help from the Merc, the Board of Trade lobbied the Congress to include in the legislation that established the new Commodity Futures Trading Commission a phrase about contracts for "tangible and intangible" products—and to have several congressmen specifically mention "mortgages" in the debates.

The Ginnie Mae futures contract was among the first the CFTC approved after its formation in 1975. The Securities and Exchange Commission woke up twenty-four hours before trading was to begin in what most people would have considered—probably wrongly, as noted—a "security" rather than a "commodity." The SEC sued to block the start of trading, but was unable to do so. Sandor's Drexel, Burnham office is a rather modest (but corner) room in one of Chicago's space-age new office buildings where the halls have metallic plastic walls and the air seems imported. On the wall, where his gaze often rests on it, is the ad he wrote for the opening of trading. It shows a Sweet Charity type in a miniskirt, her handbag flung over her shoulder, Ginnie Mae to the life, with the proclamation by the Board of Trade that "There's nothing plain grain about us any more."

The Ginnie Mae contract started well because there was a need for it, but in fact the calculations were too complicated—a 16 percent mortgage could not be calibrated with an 8 percent mortgage, because the homeowner was too likely to pay it off in advance. And while futures markets thrive on the transactional inefficiency of cash markets, there are limits, and the settlement system for Ginnie Mae trades, which was still in a state of flux in 1987 after a computerized clearinghouse aborted, left holders of the contracts unable to lay off their risks in the cash market. So Sandor moved on, this time to a contract on U.S. Treasury-bond futures. The construct was a $100,-000 face-value bond of fifteen years' duration, with an 8 percent coupon. If interest rates went higher, the price of the bond would fall; if they dropped, the price of the bond would rise. The deliverable package was again something that had to be graded and adjusted.

"We had to normalize all bonds," Sandor recalls. "Everybody said they wanted yield equivalence. [That is, the package of bonds delivered in satisfaction of the expiring futures contract had to yield the purchaser the 8 percent to maturity specified in the contract.] We had a crazy factor system that made higher coupons and longer bonds the cheapest to deliver. [That is, the cash market consistently sold a bond at a smaller premium than its higher-than-8-percent coupon justified, and also valued longer bonds at less than what the actuaries said they should be worth.] It was one of the better chess games you'll ever see. Every time we gave the short something [that is, applied a grading factor that made the deliverable bonds cheaper], we had to give the long something [apply a grading factor that made the deliverable bonds more expensive]. But we couldn't make the contract so perfect it became a cash instrument—you had to leave room for arbitrage." T-bond futures began trading in 1977, and within five years they were the most heavily traded "commodity" in the world. And it's the T-bond futures (and the options on them) that were the product the Board of Trade offered Japan in 1987 when it moved to a night session to catch the morning market hours in Tokyo. By then, the Ginnie Maes had withered on the vine, not surprisingly, because most investors need an interest-rate hedge rather than a specific mortgage hedge, and with Treasury bonds you didn't have to worry about when they would be paid back.

"When I started," Sandor said, "nobody thought Ginnie Maes would lead to bonds or Kansas City's Value Line index or the Merc's S&P. What we thought was, 'Look how complicated it is to borrow a bond and short it.'"

3

Interest-rate futures were Sandor's baby, but financial futures as a category were mostly the creation of Leo Melamed of the Chicago Merc. A small, black-haired man of immense determination, Melamed rose through the ranks of traders and elected officials at the Merc: He made policy himself. Indeed, though his titles at this writing are the carefully non-executive chairman of the executive committee and special counsel—and what he really wants to do is trade and write a follow-up to a science fiction novel called *The Tenth Planet* which Bonus Books of Chicago published in 1987— Melamed still makes policy. When the futures industry came under attack after the market meltdown, it was Melamed who fluttered from television show to newspaper office to congressional conference room to give his industry's side of the story. Very effectively, too.

Leo Melamed was born in Bialystock, Poland, the son of Yiddish teachers who in 1939 looked around Warsaw, where they were living, and said, basically, "This is not going to be a good place for

Yiddish teachers." They made it to the Soviet Union, also not a good place for Yiddish teachers, and thence via Vladivostock to Japan, an even worse place for Yiddish teachers, before arriving in Chicago (not a bad place for Yiddish teachers) shortly before Pearl Harbor. "As a small boy," Melamed says, "I lived for two years holding my mother's hand." As Melamdovich, in the Slavic patronymic, young Leo went to Chicago public schools, then to the Chicago campus of the University of Illinois on the old Navy Pier, then to John Marshall Law School in an afternoon program.

As a law student, Melamed thought he should have a morning job with a law firm, and at the age of twenty he answered an ad from Merrill Lynch, Pierce, Fenner & Beane (as it then was), which sounded like a law firm to him. ("I got there for the interview, I thought, My God, it doesn't *look* like a law firm.") They hired him, and sent him to work for their man on the floor of the Merc, Joseph F. Sieger, who was chairman of the exchange. These were not good days on the Merc, which traded futures contracts for butter and eggs and onions (all perishables, it will be noted, though there are those at the Merc who will argue that chilled eggs were storables in the winter). The onions pit in particular was a scandal: "They'd allowed corners and squeezes and whatever else," Melamed says. "I had to watch; it was a lesson." (Later, in an action Melamed professed to find a horror, Congress legislated an end to futures trading in onions.) But he was hooked from the first day.

A year later, he borrowed $3,100 from his father ("all the money he had, I think") and bought a seat, and traded eggs. And went to law school, and drove a cab at night: "I'd got married, and we'd got a child right away." In the early months of his trading, Melamed made money. "I remember saying, 'I'm doing better than the professor who's teaching me at law school.' Then I went broke. What happens when you go broke? It depends how old you are. I went broke three times, but when you're in your twenties you can handle it." He worked his way out of it in part by taking jobs for others at the exchange, and in part by practicing law in the evenings—"personal injury, real estate, divorce, bankruptcy, whatever the street offered me." In 1965, when Melamed was thirty-two (probably—he's shy about his age), he quit the practice of law, telling his partner, "I will never be a trader and successful at it until I depend on it for my living. If I know my whole livelihood depends on my ability to be a trader, then I'll be a good trader."

By 1965, Everette B. Harris, who was president of the Merc for twenty-five years, had developed the livestock contracts—pork bellies, live cattle, feeder cattle—that saved the exchange. Melamed made his first real money as a trader in the pork-bellies pit. (At about that time, the advertising genius Bill Bernbach was selling a wretched rye bread called Levy's with pictures of black and Chinese kids eating it and a slogan "You don't have to be Jewish to love Levy's." Melamed's success in the pork-bellies pit presumably proves that you don't have to be goyish, either.) But the Merc was still a stodgy and unimportant place, run by a board of directors mostly descended from the butter-and-egg traders who had founded it in 1919. Melamed organized what they called a "Brokers Club" of younger members, who staged a palace coup in 1967, putting in a new chairman sympathetic to their concerns, who in turn appointed committees to find new contracts to trade and to improve the existing ones. Melamed came up with improvements to the moribund live cattle contract (mostly a widening of the delivery points) that brought that pit a surge of new activity. In 1969, he was elected chairman of the Merc. Its budget was about $180,000. Eighteen years later, the budget was more than $75 million.

In 1969, the New York Produce Exchange (later the New York Mercantile Exchange), which was in even worse trouble than the Merc, offered the first contracts on currency futures. The Bretton Woods accord, signed at the end of World War I, had tied all the world's currencies to the dollar in ratios that were presumably binding on governments and could be changed in legal markets (there were black markets of various kinds in various places) only by government action. The U.S. dollar, in turn, was tied to gold, and the United States had pledged to sell its gold at a fixed price (then $32 an ounce) to governments and central banks that wished to hold gold rather than dollars. Banks bought and sold currencies with one another at slight price differences for the use of their customers in commercial transactions, and sometimes acquired significant long or short positions in their belief that a devaluation or upward revaluation was in the cards, but the published prices were the official exchange rates rather than the results of bidding and offering in a market. This system had got in grievous trouble in 1968, and had been rescued only by a strange agreement by the leading industrial nations to segregate "monetary gold" from "non-monetary gold," but relative currency values were still controlled within a percentage point or two by the willingness of the governments to act in concert to "defend the rates." There wasn't enough business to feed an exchange, and the contract lapsed.

Melamed says that as a trader he had seen in 1967 that the British pound had to be devalued, and had been outraged to find that as a private citizen of a free country there was no way he could back his judgment with cash. His friend Henry Jarecki, a former psychiatrist who now runs Mocatta Metals in New York, says that he actually went to the First New Haven Bank and asked to sell a hundred thousand pounds. "The bank said, 'What is your purpose?' When I told them I thought the pound would be devalued, they said, 'That's speculation, and we can't support that.' Ridiculous: They thought it wasn't good for *me.*" Meanwhile, Milton Friedman of the University of Chicago had been proclaiming that fixed exchange rates were leading to undue and harmful government intervention in national economies for the purpose of maintaining these artificial ratios, and that currencies should be floated to find their own levels vis-à-vis each other in a free market. Floating exchange rates, he told a congressional committee in 1963, "are an automatic mechanism for protecting the domestic economy from the possibility that [trade] liberalization will produce a serious imbalance in international payments. . . . It is not the least of the virtues of floating exchange rates that we would again become masters in our own house."

In 1971, President Nixon slammed closed the gold window and announced that the United States would no longer redeem dollars in gold. Though his Secretary of the Treasury, John Connolly (aided by *his* Undersecretary for Monetary Affairs, Paul Volcker), organized a revival of the principles of Bretton Woods at a meeting in the Smithsonian Institution late that year, it was clear to the more far-sighted that Humpty Dumpty for better or worse was off the wall. That fall, Melamed and Everette Harris went to Friedman and asked him to do a paper on the feasibility and advantages of futures markets in currencies. As anticipated, Friedman thought it was one of the best ideas since flush toilets. "I knew Milton Friedman was God," Melamed says, "so how the hell could I be wrong?"

Others believed in other gods. Bankers almost without exception thought a currency futures market was foolish—their own forward markets for currencies met the needs of business fully (and were hugely profitable for the banks). "I went along with the idea because I would follow Leo anywhere," says trader Barry Lind, who served on the organizing committee for the new market. "But I didn't think it would work until our board took a trip to Europe together to try to sell the idea there, and I saw what the banks were charging people to change their money." The Europeans were no more enthusiastic than American bankers—Lind remembers that at most of their meetings the Merc board outnumbered the audience. The great moment on the trip came at the Bank of England. The bank's board received Melamed only for the purpose of telling him they weren't interested, then at the end of the meeting courteously asked if there was anything else they could do for him. He said jokingly, "Yes, you could float the pound," and was icily ushered to the door. The next day it was all over the papers that the Bank of England had floated the pound: The board had taken Melamed's joke as evidence that some scoundrel had leaked the information.

Currency futures' time had come—and in 1972 the Merc did not need approval from any government agency to open its doors to currency trading. But these things do not just happen. The rest of the Merc, while willing to let Melamed lead and give his project houseroom, was not willing to take the risks to its reputation, its banking relations, and its pocketbook that might follow from the introduction of currency futures amidst the agricultural pits. Melamed as a lawyer saw the escape hatch: He incorporated a separate "International Money Market" that would offer memberships to the five hundred members of the Merc for $100. "I had a sense of how you can make a market successful," he says. "I loved the pit, I loved the members of the pit, I knew a great majority of them admired me, and would do what I wanted them to do for patriotic reasons. I pleaded, cajoled, and convinced them that some day it would pay off in terms of money."

But members of the Merc were making good money trading pork bellies and live cattle; they would put up $100 to join, but they really didn't want to hang around a currency pit. By 1972, memberships at the Merc were selling for $100,000. So Melamed recruited a separate membership for the IMM, people who would be in the finance ring all day ("as long as they have hope"), because that was the only place they were permitted to trade. These separate IMM seats were offered to the public for $10,000 ("let them beg and borrow it for their dreams") for the first year after trading began on May 16, 1972, and then the roster was closed. About 150 IMM memberships were sold, and they were a good buy. Less than a year after the Merc started trading currencies, the arrangements Connolly had crammed down the throats of American trading partners at the Smithsonian (and Richard Nixon had called "the most significant monetary agreement in the history of the world") were in a state of collapse; in effect, if not juridically, currencies were floating, and though business did not grow rapidly there was a lot to trade. In 1987, IMM memberships (either the IMM piece of a Merc membership or one of these special seats) sold for as much as a quarter of a million dollars.

Perhaps the most remarkable of Melamed's inventions for the IMM was the "Class B membership" by which what could be called "official arbitrageurs" were inserted between the IMM and the banks. "At the beginning," Melamed says, "no bank would become a member. Bob Abboud [then president of the First National Bank of Chicago] was on our board, but his foreign-exchange trader wasn't interested. Without participation by the banks, we ran a risk that our transactions might not have any connection with reality. Was our price for Swiss francs the real price, or just a Merc price? So I said to the banks, 'We'll insert someone who is a customer of yours. He will buy D-marks from you in the cash market and sell D-mark futures in our place, or vice versa. I will let you look at his position every day, so you can assure yourself you are never at risk, and he will have the backing of the commodity firms at the Merc who are your customers.' "

At this period in history, it was worth a lot to be a friend of Leo Melamed. "There was a bridge player, Bert Norton, a top bridge player here in Chicago," Melamed recalls, "and I played tournaments with his wife, Carol Norton, who later became the first woman on our floor. Bert wanted to come to the Merc, and said, 'Should I just go into the pits and trade?' I said, 'No—you'll go broke. But I have an idea for you.' He listened to what I told him about the Class B membership and arbitrage, and he said, 'That's too complicated.' I said, 'Cut it out. You're one of the top bridge players.' My firm made a deal for him with Continental Bank."

Henry Jarecki of Mocatta Metals believes that if the banks had participated in the futures market from the beginning they could have killed off the traders (of whom he was one—he was an original IMM board member). "You can prove mathematically," he says, "that a guy just standing in a pit and trading when the futures market is not the primary market can be picked off by the guys in the primary market." Instead, the Class B arbitrageurs picked off the banks, in effect making a market inside the bank's forward market in all the currencies traded on the IMM. That is, the traders in the pit would sell you a futures contract with more marks for your dollar in ninety days than the bank would promise to give you at that time, and buy a futures contract from you with more dollars for your mark in ninety days than the bank would promise. Traders may be greedy, but they are not as greedy as banks. Class B status took virtually no capital, because Melamed had guaranteed the banks that these arbitrageurs would lay off their positions every night. As many as forty men, including Melamed's friend Norton, worked at keeping the real and futures prices together for their own profit as Class B arbitrageurs. They all made fortunes. Then the banks woke up to what was happening, joined the IMM themselves, and put the outside arbitrageurs out of business. The banks eventually came to dominate these pits, because the Reuters screen made the cash market too big and too narrow in its spreads to leave much profit for traders.

By then, Melamed had moved the IMM on to interest-rate futures, starting in 1976 with a contract in three-month Treasury bills, which had to be and was approved by the new CFTC (under its charter to supervise the trading of "intangibles"). Milton Friedman himself rang the bell to start trading on opening day. The planning for this contract was not simple, because T-bills were quoted in the cash market by interest rates, but the futures contract would have to be based on the price of the bill itself. When interest rates go up, the price of the bill goes down, and vice versa. This meant that traders would have to think inversely, which is not an easy thing for traders to do. Melamed solved the problem by inventing an "IMM index," which is 100.00 minus the annualized yield on the T-bill. (This is, of course, the way the Treasury Department looks at T-bills, which sell on a discount basis: That is, instead of getting a $10,000 piece of paper that pays $162.50 interest in three months, the purchaser pays $9,837.50 for a piece of paper that turns into $10,000.) If traders expect the annualized interest rate to go from 5.83 percent to 6.56 percent, they reduce their bid from 94.17 to 93.44.

Currency futures Melamed had tried to sell to the Bank of England; T-bill futures, he tried to sell to Salomon Brothers. "I went to Billy Salomon. I had no credentials. He listened to me and said, 'This is not for Salomon to start. But if you prove it will work, I'll join, and I promise you Salomon will be your number-one trader.' And when we showed it would work, it gave the bond dealers a huge security blanket, he was as good as his word: Salomon did come in and did become number one."

Other interest-rate futures contracts followed, most notably the contract in ninety-day Eurodollar futures, which in effect gives its purchaser an obligation to take and its seller the obligation to make a million-dollar ninety-day loan in London at the interest rate specified in the contract on the date the contract expires. These things feed on each other: Traders (and banks) begin playing a "TED spread," the difference between the interest rate on T-bills and the interest rate on Eurodollar deposits, a ratio expressing the degree of confidence the market has in the banking system. Between them, the T-bill and Eurodollar pits trade something like 70,000 million-dollar contracts every day, with an open interest in the tens of billions of dollars every night. But the importance of the Eurodollar contract transcends its own trading revenues, for approval of Eurodollar trading by the CFTC at the end of 1981 opened the door for trading in the S&P index.

"The Eurodollar contract," says Melamed, "is one of those things one did that changed history. It was the first instrument where the buyer didn't have to take delivery in kind. We argued with the federal government, we said, 'The hedger wants protection, but he wants to go through his own brokers and institutions for the physical instrument. What he wants is insurance. Why not offer him money instead of the commodity itself?' We needed the CFTC to say, 'Yes— your idea of cash settlement is worth trying.'

"When I was a kid, a runner for Merrill Lynch at twenty-five dollars a week, I'd heard the old-timers say, 'The greatest thing to trade would be stock futures—but you can't do that, it's gambling.' But once I didn't have to make delivery of the product . . .''

It had been possible for years to make a bet on the course of the Dow-Jones index, in London, where the bookie house of Ladbroke's had stood ready to take your bet. This made it impossible for any London market to develop, by the way, because gambling winnings are not taxable in England but profits on stock contracts are. James Cayne, president of the Wall Street house of Bear Stearns and a buddy of Melamed's from the days when he was in the scrap-iron business in Chicago and cleaning up the city's bridge tournaments, called Melamed after a trip to London in 1977 to tell him about the

Ladbroke's book and suggest that the Merc try something of the sort. "He laughed," Cayne remembers, "and said, 'We're ahead of you.'"

Melamed had understood more than Cayne: Having put through the other financial futures and seen what made them go, he had learned that a stock-index future would not be just a gambler's toy, however his colleagues on the trading floor might view it—it would be a hedging tool of great power for pension funds, insurance companies, trusts, all those who needed a way to lock in the values of a portfolio for a period of time without actually selling their stock or to delay a planned purchase without risk of losing the market. Options on individual securities, which were already being traded in Chicago, could protect portions of the fund, but only at a considerable cost; futures on an index would be cheap.

In fact, the Kansas City Board of Trade got to the CFTC first, winning approval in February 1982 for a futures contract based on the Value Line index, a geometric average of percentage movements in the prices of some 1,650 stocks traded on the New York, American, and Toronto stock exchanges and over the counter, with every stock having an equal weight in the average. A price change in IBM has a significance of .06 of 1 percent in the Value Line index, but 4.4 percent in the S&P 500 index, which is weighted by the capitalization of the underlying companies. (The difference between the S&P 500 and the Value Line index would spawn an arbitrage of its own: People who think the small companies will do better than the big ones in the market can buy the Value Line and sell the Spooz.) And the Board of Trade had gone to the CFTC for approval of a contract based on the Dow, though it had not received approval from Dow-Jones for this use of its index.

Melamed again saw a step further. "As a practical matter," says Jerrold Salzman, a rather laid-back lawyer in his forties who has worked with Melamed since 1967, when he was a kid associate in Lee Freeman's dominant Chicago law office, "you had to have some way to prevent conflicts of interest. These services add or subtract companies from their index, sometimes a dozen times a year, after mergers and such. It's important to be sure that the people who do this are not buying and selling our contracts. Anyway, Leo thought it best not to have fights when you don't have to have fights; we're not crazy around here." For agreeing to permit the use of its index, S&P, a division of McGraw-Hill, gets a royalty per contract traded, which is probably the largest single contributor to its gross revenues. The royalty arrangement turned out to be more than worth the cost to the Merc, for in the end, rather to Salzman's surprise, the Supreme Court of Illinois ruled that the Board of Trade could not trade an index without the consent of its proprietor—and the S&P 500 became, if not the only, by far the biggest wheel in town.

But not all at once. Jim Cayne of Bear Stearns called the *Wall Street Journal* and asked to have an ad on the page opposite the ad the Merc would take to advertise the first day of trading in the Spooz, on April 20, 1982. The *Journal* said that obviously there would be many applicants for that spot, and they couldn't promise it to Cayne. Then there were no applicants for the spot, and at ten o'clock in the morning Melamed called Cayne. "You won't believe this," Melamed said, "but we have no orders." Bear Stearns bought some contracts. For the next weeks, Melamed greeted members of the Merc arriving at the door in the morning and grabbed them by their jacket fronts to lead them to the S&P pit to trade: "Give us fifteen minutes a day, make the liquidity that will give this market a chance."

Then came Ed Thorp and arbitrage, and the index funds, and electronic order delivery to the posts on the New York Stock Exchange. And, of course, the bull market. "It was like giving liquor to an Indian," Brett Haire said conversationally in the First Boston trading room, six months before the crash. "The bond boys had been used to dealing with the tail that wagged the dog, but the stock guys were not used to futures contracts. In 1982, it was not unusual to see price relationships that in retrospect were crazy. You had to deal with five hundred stocks controlled by these clerks called specialists. . . . When the CFTC approved the contract they thought you couldn't use it to manipulate the market. They didn't know about the DOT system . . ."

113

6

Chicago: 2. Setting All the World's Prices

"The 1970s and the 1980s were an era of the big trader and the star investment banker. Now we are in the era of the machine."

—Tone Grant, president,
Refco Group, Ltd.

"We ought to have a futures contract in Brazilian debts. Then we could tell the banks how to mark them."

—Robert Rutz, president,
Chicago Board of Trade
Clearing Corporation

1

*N*obody ever made more money trading in the Chicago pits than Thomas H. Dittmer, who started in the world without very much (he was part of the military honor guard in Lyndon Johnson's White House) but started in Chicago as a man of parts because his mother had remarried into the business. Young Dittmer's stepfather, Ray E. Friedman, was a grain and cattle trader based in Sioux City and his Refco, Inc. (an acronym from his name) cut a ponderable figure in the markets. Some of what became Dittmer's trademarks were derived from Friedman, with whom he worked in partnership for a number of years. Both men traded essentially by dominating markets, taking big positions that influenced others to trade on their side. And both were great partygivers, with Dittmer setting what is still probably the record when after a big hit he chartered a 747 and took everyone who worked for him and some friends for a weekend in Las Vegas. But Friedman's sixty-fifth birthday is well remembered, too. Bob Tamarkin in his book on the Chicago traders described the party in Sioux City for four hundred people, two hundred of them from out of town: "The dinner dance was held in a 120-foot by 60-foot tent to the right of the guest house near the two tennis courts. . . . The tent was complete with a stage and dance floor. To commemorate the commodity that afforded Friedman such luxury was a King Kong-size plastic cow."

The consensus estimate of the fortune Dittmer took out of his trading activities is about $300 million. Like most legendary traders, however, he had legendary troubles with the regulators and the officials of the exchanges. For good and sufficient reasons, because commodity markets have a history of squeezes and there are always more futures contracts which buyers can hold for ultimate delivery than there is stock in the warehouse to be delivered, all the exchanges have limits on the positions traders can acquire. Dittmer traded for himself, for Refco, and for a gaggle of partnership arrangements he had made over the years, and it is by no means clear that he always knew or cared how large his total position was. (Traders, said one of them, have the sense of organization and the patience with paperwork of a six-year-old.) And like every big player, he made some of his most important purchases and sales through what the racetrack calls "beards," participants who had no visible connection with him. Which accounts he put such trades in, how he added up what all the accounts owned or owed—answers to these questions were apparently as elusive for him as for others. In the early 1980s, as the clearing corporations and the exchanges got better computers, others were constantly calling such questions to Dittmer's attention, usually through the device of formal proceedings.

So in 1981 Dittmer hired two very well-organized, handsome, smooth-as-silk young men still in their thirties—first Phillip Bennett, an Englishman, graduate of Cambridge University where he had been a rugby player, who was then running the commodities lending end of Chase Manhattan Bank in New York; and then Tone (pronounced "Tony") Grant, another athlete, former Yale quarterback and marine, who had practiced law in Silicon Valley and then worked as general counsel for Commerce Union Bank in Nashville, Tennessee, a bank with various interests in commodities markets. Bennett, as chief financial officer, a new title, got to keep track of the money, and Grant, as general counsel, resolved the lawsuits and administrative proceedings, one by one, winning the private cases and accepting by consent a half-million-dollar fine and a six-month suspension of trading privileges in the limit violation case. Dittmer asked his two young assistants to plan the future of Refco, and presently Grant returned with an analysis and a program:

"The financial instruments will dominate the market, and the market will be global. Our product is futures and options on tangible and intangible commodities. Our business is providing access to that product, on the phone, twenty-four hours a day. We need big clients, because we have to make money on every trade, and it costs no more to do a fifty- or hundred-lot order than it does to do a five- or ten-lot order. We can't get a retail-type commission, so we can't afford to take credit risks—nobody pays us to take credit risks. A client who's a trader, eventually he makes enough money or he loses enough money and he quits. That's not a business. If you have an institution that's hedging for the long haul, that's a business. Our clients have to be institutions, not individuals, except for some big introducing brokers—and even there, it has to be the broker, not the individual, who is responsible for maintaining the margins. And we have to be in all the markets, because this is a business that lives off volatility, and you don't know which market will become volatile next." When the nuclear reactor blew at Chernobyl (all markets make money off bad news because bad news makes volatility), the grain pits in Chicago exploded into activity that briefly dwarfed the financials, and Grant had Refco ready for that, too.

Even in 1982, Refco did a substantial order-filling and clearing business for clients—but Dittmer himself was its biggest client. That would have to stop: If Refco was going to sell its services to the great institutions, it could not be identified with the activities of a legendary trader: Dittmer would have to quit cold turkey. Which he did. "All I know," he says, casual, long-headed, Western, a little jowly, seated beside one of the few pools of soft incandescent light in an office that is like a dark cave off Refco's brilliantly fluorescent Chicago trading room, "is that I went to the bathroom one day, and when I came back Tone and Phil had turned the whole business around."

But Dittmer says he had been ready to hang it up even before Grant suggested that his firm should get out of trading for its own accounts. "When you traded corn," he says, "you could be a pretty big trader and have an impact on the market. But when it's bonds or S&Ps, you can't—the world is too big. In the future there will be big institutions on both sides of all the trades; the day of the local who takes five hundred or a thousand contracts is gone. In the old days it didn't matter about information, because the information was no good. If I'd had every government crop or livestock report ahead of everybody else, I'd have gone broke. In the ag reports, they'd lose seventy-five million beans and then find them again, and they were always off five percent on the hogs, which is twenty dollars plus or minus on the contract. But in the financials, it's real information, and it's valuable for fifteen seconds."

The last straw was the change in the tax law in 1982 that made it impossible for traders to move one year's income into the next by creating "straddles," combinations of puts and calls that let you sell the loser this year for a deduction and cash in the winner next year. "The day of the speculator is gone," Dittmer says. "When Uncle Sam takes thirty-two percent of your winnings and gives you back none of your losses, you've got to go broke some day. You can be right six years in a row and wrong one year, and you're broke. The pension funds have to be the only players left in the world. Because they don't pay taxes, they have to wind up with all the money."

Putting his money to work in his business but outside the pits, Dittmer bought Refco a diversified institutional clientele. The firm became the largest Futures Commission Merchant in the country in 1984 with the acquisition of the commodities division of the Wall Street house of Donaldson, Lufkin, Jenrette (by then a division of Equitable Insurance), which had been the fifth-largest broker on the futures and options exchanges—and placed itself out of sight in the leadership stakes the following year by purchasing Conti Commodities, the third largest. To put it mildly, these acquisitions created economies of scale: Refco kept most of the clients and most of their volume, while reducing the personnel roster by roughly 85 percent in the acquired companies. One of the first magazine articles about the new Refco appeared in the trade publication *Intermarket.* Its cover illustration was a drawing of Sylvester Stallone wearing a torn Refco jacket of the kind traders wear on the exchange floors, holding a rocket launcher, while behind him the wrecked buildings of Refco acquisitions smoldered; the title was "Refco: First Blood." "One very able person," Grant says rather coldly, "can do the work of several others."

Open twenty-four hours a day in Chicago and New York and staffed with brokers who speak Japanese and the major European languages in the hours when those customers are at work, Refco in 1988 had branches in London, Paris, Zurich, Hamburg, Milan, Singapore, and Sydney as well as in the United States. The firm was by far the largest broker in the options and futures business, executing one side or the other of more than a fifth of such business through worldwide exchange memberships. And all that trading was done essentially on instructions from a roster of only five thousand customers. The only occasions when Refco buys or sells for its own account are those when positions have been acquired overnight and must be hedged or laid off in the morning, or when an accommodation has been given (this may take Dittmer's consent) to a big client who wants in or out right now but whose order might move the market if inserted all in a piece. "We do assume a basis risk," says Bennett, meaning that Refco sometimes guarantees a customer a hedge before acquiring it, predicting where the cash market will stand when it opens. Such risks are taken most often in the bond market, where prices are generally more stable in the first half hour than they are on the stock market. Because different packages of bonds can be bought to satisfy the rules for delivery against the futures contract, the "basis risk" Bennett mentions produces a profit for the firm more often than a loss. But it's business Refco would be perfectly happy to do flat, neither making money nor losing it.

Refco maintains memberships on the major stock exchanges to cut costs on hedging activities in the cash market that underlies the index futures and options, and it was until 1987 a primary dealer in U.S. government securities, recognized by the Federal Reserve Bank of New York as a direct counterparty when the Fed was conducting open-market operations, buying Treasury bills from dealers to put fresh money into the economy or selling them to sop up what the Fed regards as excess bank reserves. Primary dealer status also gives a firm access to the "inside" screens of prices bid and asked by the half-dozen "inter-dealer" brokers who help these firms square their positions with each other anonymously. This information is considered sufficiently precious by outsiders that Lazard Freres, an investment house that is not a primary dealer, has sued in federal court to compel the brokers to give it access.

But as the Japanese securities houses moved into "primary-dealer" status and the margins for the trading houses, always small, shrank still further, the Refco triumvirate decided that the word on the Telerate screens about what the Fed was doing was good enough for their purposes, that some clients would just as soon not let the Fed know what *they* were doing (one of the requirements on those who wear the epaulet of primary dealer is that their activities must be transparent to the Fed), and that the capital that had to be separately committed to this activity under Fed rules could be better employed elsewhere in the firm. It is a measure of the difference in perceptions between Washington and the markets that as Representative Charles Schumer pushed a bill to jimmy American firms into the Tokyo market by threatening to deny Japanese firms access to the status of primary dealer, Refco decided to discard the uniform and function as a civilian.

The firm is privately held—Dittmer has 51 percent of it, Grant and Bennett split the other 49 percent—and publishes no financial statements. Revenues from brokerage activities apparently ran in 1987 something like $200 million, and another $100 million was apparently taken in from management fees, arranging financing for customers, clearing fees, and specialized activities. Refco has a considerable operation in foreign exchange, a sizable presence in the metals pits in both New York and London, and a petroleum futures operation including a subsidiary that does well in "EFPs"—exchanges for physicals—by which paper barrels are converted to real oil at the expiration of the contract period. There are 350 employees worldwide. Capital in the business is about $170 million, but most of it has to be retained in the firm's own operations—"Our customers," Grant says, "like to see us with one hundred million dollars committed to clearing their trades; they don't mind it when Salomon has only five million or Goldman has twenty million, because the parent guarantees." Profits in 1987 were in the neighborhood of $40 million, which probably understates reality because expansion costs and machinery investment are expensed quickly. The crash cost nothing—Refco had no positions, and its clients delivered during the day itself and overnight, no sweat, $365 million of "variation margin" called for by the gigantic volatility of October 19. "The experi-

119

ence of the last couple of weeks," Bennett said dryly in November, "shows the benefit of our strategy."

Behind the polished exterior and the rational analysis of a long-term plan, Grant is every bit as aggressive as Dittmer ever was. "You can never rest," he says; "as long as you don't have one hundred percent of the business, there's more to do. We're in a tough world, because everybody knows who all the clients are." Refco's sales pitch for itself stresses its closely supervised teams of traders in the pits, the quality of its research on short-term market trends, and the claim that customers do better here simply because the firm takes no positions of its own. "The brokerage houses that are our main competitors for clients in the S&Ps," Bennett says, "their business in the pits is driven primarily by their own proprietary trading. Our business is customer-driven."

2

As a supplier to giant pension funds, insurance companies, and banks (and to a few big traders who want, as Dittmer did in the old days, to conceal their purchases and sales from the prying eyes of the pit), Refco has to compete on price and efficiency. The firm does not spend money on fundamental research or economic analysis, because its customers do their own, "more profoundly," says Grant, than Refco can, but it has acquired over the years a cadre of technicians, most of whom work on the floor itself because Dittmer has strong feelings about the value of hands-on experience. For the same reason, Refco's floor people are allowed to do a little trading for their own account though executives aren't. "There are no rules," says one of them, "except that if it's perceived that what you do for yourself gets in the way of what you do for the clients, you're out." Hundreds of pages of computer printout on yesterday's market movements are generated every night by Refco's computers, together with a brief news summary of items that might explain those movements, apart from the internal condition of the markets, for the use of both customers and employees. Arriving for work in the morning, the clerks and traders pick up fan-folded books of computer paper from a wheeled cart, "our traveling newsstand." Grant and Dittmer meet every day at 6:30, and call New York, where it's 7:30, to talk with Bennett at Refco's offices overlooking the harbor in the World Financial Center.

Depending on the product and the customer, Refco's commissions run between $10 and $15 per contract. (That's ¹⁄₁₀₀th of 1 percent for an S&P 500, and only about twice what a big institution pays per 100 shares on the New York Stock Exchange, which is not the least of the reasons the institutions prefer to do business in Chicago when they can.) Grant's rule is that every trade should be profitable to the firm on the commission collected, which means very heavy automation and very low variable cost. "I had said we could triple our volume without increasing our costs," Bennett reported in late fall 1987. "The week of October 19th we tripled our volume without increasing our costs." The keypunch operators in Chicago, New York, and London input directly to the mainframe in Memphis, Tennessee (an artifact of Grant's time in that state), and the mainframe sends the results back to the screens and to the printers that make hard copy around the world.

"We produce the computer run on all orders done for clients in the United States by 5:45 P.M. EST," Bennett says. "They can see it—their terminals tap into their accounts with us. If there's a mistake they can cure it by the time of our final input at 7 P.M. The total dollar value of errors here as a percent of gross commission is about zero point two percent. The industry average runs three to five percent. When we took over the other firms, we found errors they had carried for *days.* Our rule is that an error must be cleared up before the market opens, or we don't trade the account."

About 65 percent of the salesmen are accounted for, Bennett says, as independent profit centers. They are credited with their clients' commissions and debited by their shares of the overhead and all the direct costs they incur, and they get a prearranged percentage of the profits. "That controls variable expense," Bennett notes: "They look after their costs themselves, which allows us to concentrate on fixed costs, running the machines." This entrepreneurial focus kept with Refco the account executives with the biggest institutional accounts—the only ones Refco wanted—when the firm absorbed Conti and DLJ. Dittmer was quoted as saying that the people who asked how much Refco would pay them were dismissed, while those who wanted to know how much money they could make for themselves remained.

Other salesmen are considered to have educational functions and are compensated by some mix of salary and bonus. "Business risk management," which is the description of Refco's work that

Grant likes best, is quite a new concept for many of the company's potential clients, and Grant has placed what may be the largest bet in the financial services industry on the efficacy of educating people to understand the subject. His director of education is an overweight, slow-speaking, thirtyish man with a round face and brown bangs, John W. Labuszewski, whom Refco lured away from a job as senior marketing manager for the Board of Trade.

Labuszewski, who worked his way through college and an MBA writing computer programs on the side, has created (and then, as programmers will, noodled over and improved) a number of proprietary trading programs, especially in the T-bond options area, where the mix of many dates at many prices—many bonds at varying "basis" differences between their yield and the implied yield on the futures—presents mathematical problems worthy indeed of the rocket scientist. Usually his course in options and futures trading runs three or five weeks, and rests on the construction of a simulated account which the trainee plays in prearranged exercises "until his comfort level is up." Every afternoon at three the analysts returned from the floor give a lecture on how the market behaved that day, plus reasonable speculative strategies for tomorrow. For potential clients with whom, as Labuszewski puts it, "you hope to hit a home run," the training course may run as long as six months. The trainee then takes Labuszewski's programs back with him to his employer's computer. The programs, however, are time-dated, requiring periodic reinvigoration; unless Refco gets business from the company, they stop accepting information.

Major efforts have been put into training Japanese traders from the four big securities companies and the major banks—and, for a two-week rush course in January 1987, from the Ministry of Finance. They come in groups as large as twelve or fourteen, for stays of several months, and Labuszewski has two Japanese-speaking Americans who work with them as instructors and then—days are long at Refco—liase with them after they go home. (All the five or six young men who work with the trainees also handle client accounts. "A strategic decision," Grant says. "You can spend money on advertising or research. We spent ours on setting up a situation where when a man in Tokyo or London picks up the phone he knows the man he's talking to.") Among the few restrictions put on a visiting reporter at Refco are the names of these Japanese-speaking Americans. Labuszewski himself is studying Japanese.

The conclusion of the training program for the Japanese is a work of art. The trainee's employer rents a seat on one of the exchanges for each trainee at the end of his course, and puts up the $50,000 deposit at the clearing corporation the exchanges require before they will let anyone trade in the pit. Then the trainees try it, hands-on. When they lose the $50,000 (they do, with very rare exceptions) they go home, having learned what locals do and why they must follow the strategic plans of their employer rather than trade their instincts. Presumably they will seek tactical advice and enter their orders by calling their old friends in Chicago. Refco does not and will not have an office in Tokyo—"We're open here twenty-four hours," Grant says. "We tell them they're better off getting their information at the source than they can be talking to anybody in Japan." After the Ministry of Finance approved the use of futures and options by Japanese institutions in spring 1987, a dozen Japanese securities houses and banks acquired memberships on the Board of Trade and the Merc and the Options Exchange, but they haven't in fact put people in the pits and Refco does not expect them to do so in a significant way; even in New York, where they have been members for years, the Japanese houses "give up" their executions to American firms.

"My primary mission is to educate the clients," says Labuszewski; "that rings the cash register. But there are economies of scale. If you have a training program, you might as well use it in-house." Twice a week for an hour and a half, Labuszewski also trains the Refco newcomers, who are a very mixed bag—each department in the firm does its own hires, because the bosses don't want to waste money on a personnel department. The course runs thirty-five weeks and involves the mastery of a mass of loose-leaf materials as well as computer instructions. Trainees don't have to have much prior education—"People have made fortunes in commodities with no more than a high school education," Labuszewski points out—but at the end of the process they do have to pass a test, and, he says, "Some of the test is pretty tough. But I figured, what the hell, I learned it." The larger test, of course, is performance: "If you're not contributing to the bottom line after a six- to eight-month period at Refco," Labuszewski concludes, "that's it."

One of the reasons such elaborate training programs are required is that salesmen for risk-management services must be able to present strategies, tactics, and programs—they can't just be order takers. The task is further complicated by client preferences about where the person who works with them should hang his hat during working hours. Some like to have a direct line to the trading floor, where Refco has actually bought memberships (at a cost that may run several hundred thousand dollars each) for people who will be manning telephones and flashing signals to the pit. In the Refco scheme, the man at the phone has discretion, and the man in the pit does not: "I figure," says Gus Mitsopoulos, a muscular but nervous young trader with a small mustache and rimless glasses who handles institutional clients from just outside the T-bond pit, "that discretion is what they pay me for." Mitsopoulos is one of those who have been coming in every night at 6:30 to trade for the Japanese: "I don't know how much longer anybody can work these hours. It's a little tougher than putting a hot dog on a bun."

Others want to talk with people in the trading room, where desks tend to be more widely separated than they are at other firms, because the need to keep client information confidential exceeds the value of close communication among traders—Refco, after all, does not trade for its own account. Still others remember their trainers and call in to Labuszewski's five-man corner, where a group that combines the functions of teacher, salesman, and researcher sits at consoles along the wall in an area shared by students in cubicles.

Grant says that there is no ladder. "We don't believe in competition internally—competition is all around us. If you have internal competition you waste energy that should be used to compete against the people you should compete against. We cultivate a professional attitude. We never use the word 'clerk' around here. No one is without a function and a purpose, and everybody is supposed to be self-improving. People should do their own job better and get paid more for it, not be looking for another job. People who know they can develop in their area are professionally fulfilled, and if they are well compensated for it they will work for the good of the whole."

Of course, people do advance, from runner to clerk to salesman to trader, but the progression takes place through the training program, for which all are eligible. Dittmer was always known for paying his people well, in addition to perks like gold Rolex watches and the Las Vegas weekend party. The family art collection, which includes Jasper Johnses and Rauchenbergs, Robert Motherwells and Richard Serras, is on display at the office, mostly in the halls, for the edification and delight of the staff. The working day runs ten and even twelve hours, and very few people in this business break for lunch. They are working, mostly in responsible positions, for the biggest pools of money in the world. They should be well paid.

3

What went wrong with portfolio insurance on Black Monday, said Gary Ginter, was the failure of those who practiced such strategies to realize that in very volatile markets they were missing a key step. Selling big lots of contracts into the S&P 500 pit was inevitably going to drive the price of the futures well below the price of the cash. This would mean that the institution seeking to insure its portfolio had to make the sales the strategy dictated at a price for futures contracts that in fact guaranteed losses the theory said should not occur. Such a problem! How to handle?

Well, in a rational market there was at least a chance that the futures contract would bounce back to where the cash market was trading. This would leave the supposedly expert fund manager with egg on his face. To prevent that embarrassing and costly result, the manager could buy an out-of-the-money call option on the index futures at a strike price a little over the current market. To give the thing numbers, with the index in the cash market measuring 250, or $125,000 for a contract, a sale of the future at 230 will yield only $115,000. And if the futures market recovers to 250, the fund will have lost $20,000 per contract. A call option on an index future at 235, however, five points out of the money, will be relatively cheap, selling at a premium of, say, $3,000. Buying two of those, the fund manager risks a loss of $6,000 if in fact the cash market is about to confirm the Spooz—but gains back his $20,000 if the Spooz rises to 248. Funds that had followed that strategy on October 19 would have had countervailing gains in an easily cashable instrument with which to pay the margin calls on October 20 and 21 on the futures contracts their portfolio insurance program had sold.

Very clever. You can read it twice, or three times, or you can take my word for it.

Ginter, who invents such clevernesses with some help from his friends, is a burly, bearded, soft-spoken man of about forty, who was one of the original partners and is now executive vice-president of Chicago Research and Trading Group, or CRT, which has institutionalized the locals' function on futures and options markets around the world. Formed in 1977 with a capitalization of about $200,000—most of it won in less organized arbitrage activity in the spread between the price of soybeans and the prices of soybean meal and soybean oil—CRT came into 1988 with capital of more than $200 million, all of it from profits, and about $2.5 billion in total assets, nearly all precisely hedged with almost but not quite identical liabilities. There are about 550 employees. Ginter and his brother-in-law Joe Ritchie, the group's president and supervisor of trading, are still key players. Corporate headquarters is on three floors of one of the newest Chicago skyscrapers just south of the Loop, acquired cheap (that is, at a rental of only $1.35 million a year) when Chase, which had contracted for the space, decided to pull back. The furniture in the reception areas and conference rooms is elegantly modern, but the executive surroundings are a little unconventional: Ginter doesn't like desks, and works at a high easel or a kind of screenboard that makes Xerox copies for distribution; Ritchie doesn't like offices, and works at a table with a screen in the trading room.

Neither man ever went to business school or studied economics or, for that matter, mathematics; their subjects were theology (Bible school theology, not Ivy League-type divinity school theology), philosophy, and literature. Ginter and his wife and their two children live in a black slum in west-side Chicago "because my church is trying to establish a presence there." Where Refco wouldn't waste its money on a personnel department, CRT has a senior vice-president for human resources, who pulled himself out of the gutter of alcoholism and got a Ph.D. in psychology, to advise them on the character and temperament of candidates for employment. Ritchie was a deputy sheriff in a town near Chicago when Ginter called him to come work at a little metals trading company that arbitraged bags of coins against the bullion contracts in New York and Chicago. Obviously, both men had talents they never suspected in the use of computers to explore the nooks and crannies of interrelationships, but it's still a crazy story.

"The policy of the CRT group," says its official statement, "is to trade large volumes within each trading day, to limit the size of open positions and to minimize the risk of each trade. Emphasis is placed on high-volume, low-margin activities, enabling the CRT group to profit from the large volume, not from large risk. On the whole, the CRT group trades and/or clears between 100,000 and 200,000 contracts per day, resulting in total contract value cleared in excess of *$1 trillion* each year [emphasis added]. The group owns over 100 memberships on 15 exchanges and trades approximately 70 different futures and options contracts on products ranging from interest rates, equity indices and foreign exchange to metals and agricultural products. The CRT group specializes in trading contracts having complex execution and delivery requirements. In these markets, its sophisticated option valuation models, real-time information systems and efficient floor trading and clearing operations can be used to the group's best advantage."

Refco acts as broker for one side or another in more than one-fifth of the world's futures and options trades. CRT is probably the purchaser or seller on something like half those trades. Every transaction is immediately hedged, either by spreading into a similar market (selling the June option while acquiring the May option), by matching an options position against a future or a cash position, or by acquiring countervailing positions in markets that CRT knows from experience and analysis move opposite to the market in which the position was purchased. As new markets have opened up, CRT has jumped into them. *Intermarket* once noted a comment at a financial executives' conference: "My definition of a mature options market is when CRT's volume drops below 50%." When the American Stock Exchange wanted to begin trading on a new Institutional Investors index, it invited CRT to be the specialist, and the contract got off to a roaring start. The Montreal currency options market, which trades the largest contracts in that business to keep down transaction costs for the largest customers, has had CRT as the market maker from the beginning, and the firm offers a bid-and-asked spread good for a $5 million transaction either way in deutsche marks and Canadian dollars, $3 million either way in British pounds. Of course, exposures in Montreal can be and are laid off instantly in Philadelphia, where CRT is by far the largest market maker, or in the currency pits at the Merc.

What CRT has done is to broaden and computerize the locals' function in open-outcry markets. Like the local—like any market maker—CRT makes money essentially by riding the trend, but in this case with enormous sums of money and with the most elaborate hedging strategies to assure that losses if the trend expectation is wrong are more limited than gains if the expectation is right. "Before I ever got into these markets," Joe Ritchie said, "I noticed that people believed in randomness and I scratched my head, thinking it was one of the biggest jokes I've ever seen. With no mathematical background, I could look at practically any price chart for one second and know that price was not generated anywhere close to randomly. . . . Any child could look and see that this walk is not random. If you saw a man roaming about in the fashion of a market move, you might say, 'I can't figure out where that guy is going,' but anyone with any statistical sense will know that he's not walking randomly."

The entire operation is computer controlled. Orders come to the traders through radio headsets, and in some markets CRT's floor people have Texas Instruments hand-held computers programmed in-house to give them exact instructions on when to buy and what to sell for each of the contracts in the spreads. Trends are tracked incessantly, and the width of the spreads CRT needs to become active is determined by the computer-measured volatilities of the trading that is going on right now. The brilliance of what has been done can be measured by results—"It's like somebody showing you a slot machine," Ritchie said, "where all you have to do is put a dollar in and two come out. Then you put two in and four come out. And you can test it and find out that it works." And the interviewer from *Intermarket* said, "So the markets aren't efficient," and Ritchie said from the depths of delightful experience, "No. Not close." Asked to explain, he said, "It's just like the rest of life—it's horse sense. There's no magic. We used to do a lot more research when we started." And Ginter added, "Yes, we did. It never paid off, though."

Another measurement of the brilliance, obviously, is the fact that all those who have tried to imitate CRT have one way or another come a-cropper. Everything to do with arbitrage and options creates a bias toward a feeling of control, a sense that the slot machine puts out two for one and four for two, a little bit at a time, until suddenly all the little winnings are overwhelmed by the one big loss. To its proprietary computer programs that predict what is going to happen, then, CRT has added a large number of side loops that ask "What if?" CRT's first bonanza was at the New York COMEX when the Hunts were cornering silver: The Chicago house rode it up and then rode it down, making money in both directions. Theoretically, volatility is the source of profits for options traders, but as a practical matter spreaders and hedgers get blindsided when the markets move out well beyond their usual trading ranges. "When everything goes up for grabs and the abnormal becomes normal," Ritchie said, two years before Black Monday, "you not only have to understand how the market has always worked, but you have to understand why it's worked that way, so you can spot the exception coming." To which Ginter adds: "That's why academics can be taken to the cleaners in trading—they don't known when their theories can no longer serve as the only guide in trading. When the markets are quiet, Black-Scholes [the standard algorithm for determining the value of an option] is just fine. But beyond a certain level of volatility, the model though still accurate becomes increasingly irrelevant. The inability to actually execute may be more important than knowing the implied volatility."

4

Leo Melamed lives in fear that some day it will all just go away, that someone from the government will come and shut down the Merc or make it impossible for the traders and brokers to do their business. From his first days as an officer of the Merc, he has stressed the importance of keeping on good terms with Washington. Year after year, the Merc has one of the three or four biggest political action committees in the country, and the walls in Melamed's office are covered with pictures of himself with presidents, speakers, and majority and minority leaders of both parties. "Success begets vulnerability," he says. "If we don't maintain a strong voice in the Congress there are enemies out there who will stomp on us."

Henry Jarecki of New York's Mocatta Metals reports that James Stone while chairman of the CFTC "said Leo and I were the two most interesting people in the business. We were both refugees from the Germans who had been overwhelmed in our childhood by the power of the authorities to shift our lives. I reacted by attempting to undermine all authority so no one could ever have power over me. Leo reacted by becoming part of his environment and learning to control it." Melamed calls it "the Bialystock syndrome," referring to the Polish town where he was born, where people—especially Jews—have learned to expect the worst. But even the Board of Trade, socially much better established than the Merc, suffers fits of paranoia. "Despite our unparalleled trading performance, or perhaps as a result of the dramatically increased usage of our marketplace in recent years," said its 1987 annual report, "we found ourselves having to turn our efforts to Washington, D.C., to head off regulatory issues that threatened the economic function served by our exchange, the effectiveness of our markets and our very livelihoods."

The Chicago markets are still something less than a well-oiled machine, and are far from free of what bankers politely call "moral hazard." Though the only demonstrated example of deliberate abuse in the relations between the options market and the underlying stocks was an oddity on April 19, 1984, when the small New York house of Miller Tabak Hirsch bought $100 million worth of stock on the New York Stock Exchange to push into the money a bunch of previously worthless (and thus virtually free) call options on the S&P 100 at the Chicago Board Options Exchange, the lack of hard evidence of manipulation between markets may well mean only that the SEC put little effort into looking at possible excesses by the big brokerage houses after 1981, when John Shad of E. F. Hutton became chairman. The failure of the SEC to move against Miller Tabak Hirsch conveyed the message that fair would be foul and foul would be fair: A little manipulation was okay.

Petty cheating, in any event, is reputedly fairly common, at the New York Stock Exchange where contract brokers who work on the floor for more than one upstairs firm exchange information about heavy orders from institutional clients, and in the gold and silver pits of the COMEX and the S&P futures pit at the Chicago Merc. In these markets, traders say, brokers who trade for their own account often find ways to "trade ahead" of customer orders—in effect, buy for themselves with the knowledge that they can lay it off on the customer at the next sale, at the price they paid if the market is going against the customer and at a price that gives them a little profit if it is going with him. In spring 1987, the Merc took serious technical action to stop this practice, and though traders continued to complain, that may simply be the nature of traders. "Poor fills," which is the lingo for the complaint (a "fill" is the execution of the order), have so far been a source of irritation but not an impediment to growth, partly because the spread between the bid and asked in these markets is so small that the cost of doing business even after a little fiddling by the locals is less than the cost of buying and selling through good brokers in the securities markets. And customers can defend themselves up to a point, by insisting that their brokers tape-record their orders on a machine that gives continuous time reference.

This is still something less than a full defense, because trades are not time-stamped in the pits, and brokers making out their stiff cardboard trading cards to show what they've done keep their records only in half-hour time "brackets." When the exchange declares a "fast market," which is normal operating procedure at openings and closings and not uncommon during the trading day, brokers are no longer obliged to get their customers the best price reported on the screen at the time the order arrives. The "out-trade" problem is appalling: In the S&P pit, in the average day, 10 to 12 percent of the volume is protested by one side or the other (after October 19, the session to resolve out-trades began at midnight at the Merc). In 1986, the Commodity Futures Trading Commission ordered the Chicago exchanges to make brokers write the time to the minute for every trade, which is done at the New York Mercantile Exchange. ("Sure," says a trader on the Chicago Merc, "the broker writes the trade on a card and flips the card to the reporter in the center of the pit; it hits the reporter on the head and falls on the ground, and he picks it up and puts it in the computer when he gets time.") Instead, the Board of Trade and the Merc worked out a system they call CTR for Computerized Trade Reconstruction, which presumably permits the exchanges and the CFTC to know as much as they would if all the trades were time-stamped.

Down in the basement, the Chicago Board of Trade has an eighty-employee "Office of Investigation and Audits," which by law does a biennial "compliance review" of the 120 member firms registered to do customer business, looks into customer complaints, and meanwhile monitors the screens all day long. Barbara Lorenzar, who keeps track of how the clearing firms and their big customers stand in terms of their daily trading and capital adequacy, has informal working arrangements with opposite numbers at all the other exchanges around the country, so that everybody knows when anybody is worried about a given player. The Board of Trade Clearing Corporation delivers every morning a five-inch-thick book of computer printout detailing the previous day's trades, and it gets looked through during the course of the day. Meanwhile, Mary Shepherd in investigations is looking for "people trading in nonstandard ways," locals and brokers who seem to be trading too much with each other, trades that appear in different "brackets" (half-hour time periods) on the cards of the participants, etc. And the computer combines the numbers on the ticker that come from the pulpit above the pit, the time stamps that are on the orders taken by the clerks at the telephones on the trading floor, and the trading cards everyone must submit twice a day—and since May 10, 1987, the machine presumably reconstructs the sequence of the day's trades.

The volume of business in the Chicago pits in 1987 was already, clearly, a terrible strain on the system. "How many people can you put into a pit?" Leo Melamed wonders. "Five hundred? Yes. One thousand? Probably not. And you're talking about big buck capitalization. Nobody can afford to put a trader in the pit who's undercapitalized. Also you need a psychoanalyst—can he live in this atmosphere?" Increasingly, the better capitalized traders are not in the pit but upstairs looking at their screens, like Melamed himself. Well before he stopped trading, Tom Dittmer stopped spending his days in the pits: "On the screens," he says, "you see so many more markets." As noted, traders make more money between markets than they can within markets. And everybody outside the pit is a customer, potentially a consumer rather than a provider of liquidity.

Richard Sandor, inventor of the T-bond contract, says, "I take a real free-market view. It's not the number of contracts that makes problems, it's the number of orders. The S&P is one-third the size of the bonds in contract volume, but the problems are worse because the volume is done in a number of small orders. As the market becomes jumbled, transaction costs rise, there are more busted trades, I have to staff more extensively to handle errors, which means I have to widen my spreads, and customers go elsewhere." Sandor foresees automation of the process by which orders get to the floor, and perhaps a substitution of radio-frequency signals to headsets for today's hand-signal communications between clerk and trader, but no change in open outcry in the pit.

William Brodsky, president of the Merc, who like his father before him worked at the New York Stock Exchange, thinks more drastic measures are probably on the way. "When I first came here in 1982," he says, "Morgan Guaranty was just in the process of becoming a Futures Commission Merchant, to trade in the currencies and Eurodollars. Everything's happened in five years. Just as the institutional investor changed the face of the New York Stock Exchange, he's changing us now." The obvious first step is to take the small orders out of the auction, as they are at the Chicago Board Options Exchange, where the RAES (Retail Automatic Execution System) simply assigns executed trades to those market-making members who have agreed to participate. Melamed would like to go the other way, taming the institutional order with a "sunshine" rule that would compel a broker to tell the pit the size of his order, so the locals can divide it up among themselves without any need to call down liquidity from upstairs. Not bloody likely, as Eliza Doolittle put it.

Tone Grant insists that Refco has no model of the markets, and is thus entirely flexible in facing the future. It is by no means without significance that neither he nor Phillip Bennett has ever been a trader, in a business where virtually every other significant firm is run by someone who has either worked on these floors or played for his own account. Their bet is on the proposition that one can achieve true risk management via the Chicago markets and their rivals elsewhere in the world. Refco belongs just about everywhere: at the MATIF in Paris, the *marché* for futures contracts on French government bonds; at the Singapore Monetary Exchange, which has been booming even though the futures contract on the Nikkei-Dow index of Japanese stocks dropped from 26,000 to just over 5000 in three wild days in October, while the Tokyo market itself never fell below 21,000; at London's LIFFE, which will probably take over the floor of the London Stock Exchange now that the stock market there has moved upstairs to screens and telephones. But the lesson of fall 1987 may be that beyond a certain critical mass the futures and options markets become part of the risk problem rather than part of its management.

"Hedging," says Gus Mitsopoulos, "has become a buzzword, a phrase without meaning. We had a day when the thirty-year bonds popped three points in the cash markets, and the futures never moved. At the end, I had a client say to me, 'Now I understand the difference between being hedged and being flat.' " Ken Lazarra, who handles institutional accounts for Refco involving both bonds and equities, says that "volatility is great for business for a while. But the average investor can't stand to see his equity swing twenty thousand dollars a day—and the institution is in the same boat on a bigger scale. After a while people will pick up their cards and move on. Volatility is not good for long-term business."

Academics can design all sorts of hedges. One can, presumably, buy thirty-year Treasury bonds (which will decline in price if inflation returns) and also buy the futures contract on the Commodities Research Bureau index (which is a bet on higher inflation), and presumably you're safe, you've locked in the interest rate with a little edge on the side because the index will go up before the bonds go down. But the relationships among such markets are not only not established, they tend to be unstable under pressure, when liquidity squeezes out here and floods there in ways that are by no means wholly predictable. The lesson of both spring and fall 1987 was that bonds and stocks don't necessarily move together, though they should (because rising bond prices mean lower interest rates which mean higher multiples of earnings for stock prices), and historically they usually have. Caveat emptor. "Certainty," said Justice Oliver Wendell Holmes, who also defended the commodity markets, "is generally an illusion, and repose is not the destiny of man."

Refco's Grant has argued that the multiplicity of instruments in the end preserves the hedging markets from disequilibrating moves: Huge investment pools may be led by their computers along similar paths, but they will employ different tactics, buying the futures while selling the options, or buying the options while selling the underlying instruments. Black Monday leaves that argument at best in suspense. And it can be argued that institutional domination denies the intellectual accomplishment of the Chicago markets, the interposition of the clearinghouse as the other side of all the contracts, so that a GMAC could safely do business with a Dittmer, not worrying about the credit ratings of the counterparties. If the likes of GMAC are going to deal only with the likes of Nippon Life in Chicago's brave new world, the markets will lose a crucial elasticity. Grant, of course, knows this full well; commenting on the slow start at London's LIFFE, he said that "they put out these great brochures, just look at our wonderful members, but the members were the people who should have been the customers."

Chicago's futures markets have become the leaders in finding prices for financial instruments as well as agricultural products (they have never made it in the metals markets, which are still dominated by London and New York) because they have offered great efficiency, defined as low costs of execution and good prediction of the movements of the underlying cash markets of which they are "derivatives." Epigrammatically—this is, of course, what the word "futures" really means—they discover the prices the cash markets will subsequently set. All this depends on greater gravity in the cash market so that the satellites stay in plausible orbits. It is by no means clear that these markets will be efficient over the longer time horizons on which economic activity actually occurs if they become not merely leaders in measurement but leaders in influence. The SEC says with blithe acceptance that "the character of the [stock] market has changed to the point where the 'price discovery' feature of the derivative market is leading, rather than following, price trends in the underlying equity markets. Moreover, through index arbitrage, the prices 'discovered' in the futures pit are quickly transmitted to the floor of the NYSE where prices adjust to the general market sentiment in the futures arena." But for profound reasons we shall look at in Chapter 11, neither the New York nor the Chicago markets will be allowed to operate on that basis over time.

For there is make-believe as well as systemic strength in the growth of the Chicago markets. No amount of hedging can give institutions safe equity investments in an economy driven by innovation, or stable real interest rates in an era of erratic government behavior. The Chicago instruments are clearly superior as a vehicle for international trading, but one has to depart far from the common experience of mankind to argue as the professors do that globalization decreases risk. An economy fixated on protection against shock may be, oddly, a more fragile economy than one that simply pays attention to business. To whom does one transfer risk, when everyone is risk averse?

7

Tokyo: 1. The Money Dragon at Home

"[In] the early postwar period Japan . . . faced a foreign exchange crisis at least as serious as those faced by developing countries today. People were poor, prospects were grim, and low productivity prevented export competitiveness in all but the cheapest products. The outlook was so gloomy that John Foster Dulles said that suicide would not be an illogical step for those concerned with Japan's economic future."

—Robert Allan Feldman,
International Monetary Fund

"If you have free and unfettered global financial markets, then eventually the country with the highest savings rate will own the world."

—Brandon Becker,
Division of Market Regulation,
Securities and Exchange Commission

1

Y ou know, it's not so long ago that we Japanese were so poor we sold our wives and daughters to be prostitutes in Southeast Asia." This was Yasuhiko Nara speaking, vice-chairman of Merrill Lynch in Japan, formerly an ambassador to the United States, a long-headed older man of great charm and wisdom, amused by the world, experienced in managing the attitudes of Americans. He looked up to see how this went over, a very rich man at his ease testing, testing, and when it didn't seem to do very well he shrugged almost imperceptibly and moved on to more sophisticated comments about his country and its government and its policies. But there was also something in what he had said as hors d'oeuvres.

In the world of finance of the late 1980s, Japan has been the four-hundred-pound gorilla who sits wherever it wants to sit. Its banks and insurance companies and securities houses and manufacturers and real estate operators are welcome everywhere in the world, for they bring money with them—and what money they don't bring they can borrow cheaper than the natives, because they have yen assets they can pledge to their dollar or sterling debts. In 1986–1987, Japanese investors bought every quarter at least three-fifths of the term bonds the U.S. Treasury sold at auction to fund the immense American budget deficit. From all over the world of developed economies, people with overpriced deals come to the overpriced hotels of Tokyo to lay their offerings before their hosts. But it is all quite recent. Even as late as 1980, as sophisticated an observer as Eric Hayden of Bank of America (later with Bank of Boston) could comment that with the cost of oil imports up from $3 billion in 1970 to $60 billion in 1980, the Japanese had to worry "that their trade bills may overflow the New York market" and that U.S. credit-restraint programs might damage "their dollar-raising capability." And within the memory of men still active (if only just), Japan had been a really poor country full of really poor people. It had been a long road from there to here, to the elegance of the Otemachi district near the Palace and the new office building in which we were speaking, and Ambassador Nara had certain knowledge that the road had been traversed one step at a time.

A friend of mine at a cocktail party given him on the occasion of his departure from Japan after some years of working there was accosted by his young Japanese assistant, with whom he had become, he thought, rather close: He had met the young man's mother. The assistant was drunk, and took him by the lapels. "Gaijinsan," he said, "after your years here you think you know something about Japan, don't you? Be truthful—you think you know something about Japan. Well, I tell you, Gaijinsan, you don't know shit about Japan." I have made three trips of one to four weeks, on business, the first in 1976, the most recent in 1987. I have spent time with Japanese in banking, securities, music, diplomacy, broadcasting, literature, real estate, and local politics, I have enjoyed their company and admired their accomplishments. I have done a fair amount of reading, especially in the wonderful library of International House in Tokyo. Five of my books have been published in Japanese translation, which always makes an author feel at home. But if a Japanese seeing you with this book comes up and tells you "That Mayer, he don't know shit about Japan," don't let the fact that I know more than you do dissuade you from agreeing with him.

That preliminary confession and avoidance out of the way, I note the great stroke of good fortune that a young research executive in Daiwa Securities in 1960 who translated into Japanese my early book *Wall Street: Men and Money* later grew up to be Yoshitoki Chino, chairman and CEO of the second-largest brokerage house in the world. (His rival Nomura Securities remains the largest.) As a result, several dozen Daiwa executives in Tokyo, New York, and London gave not only their time and attention but considerable work in arranging special translations of documents and easy-to-follow graphs in the hopes of conveying to me what their firm did, and why, and how, and the ways that their work fit into the larger picture of Japanese financial markets. The story as pieced together from Daiwa and numerous other sources draws heavily on the insights the Daiwa executives pressed upon me—but what I have made of it, of course, is my own. As the reader will see, there are substantial sections with which they will profoundly disagree.

2

Japan was horribly beat up in the war, and in the years immediately after that the country was reorganized as profoundly as Eastern Europe by its occupying power. Land reform, labor unions with economic goals, anti-trust laws to break up the old trading companies and the Zaibatsu (the family-based conglomerates with tentacles everywhere), the separation of banking from the securities industry—these were economic legacies of Douglas MacArthur's mission to plant democracy in the land where a God-Emperor had to renounce his divinity in the act of surrender. What emerged from the turmoil, with a little help from American need for a stable back area in the Korean War, was a machine for the generation of economic growth, led by bureaucrats but fueled with the energy of a more entrepreneurial society than its history would have predicted. On the other hand, if history had not got itself so obsessed with chrysan-themums and swords, we could perhaps have seen capitalism nascent in Japanese feudalism as it was in European feudalism.

In general, equity bore the brunt of the war's losses, and indus-try was rebuilt with bank loans. Different kinds of banks did different kinds of work: There were long-term credit banks and trust banks that held investable funds and financed industrial development, while country banks supported local business, agricultural coop banks financed the very large community of farmers, and city banks concentrated on trade finance, working capital, and the support of the industrial groups with which they had been associated before MacArthur broke up the Zaibatsu. Savings were coerced from a predominantly young population by a government that offered virtu-ally nothing in the line of free social services and were facilitated by a pay system that delivered as much as a third of the year's salary in the form of large bonuses in June and December. From the war to 1979, Japanese households saved more than 20 percent of their post-tax income every year, and during no year in the 1980s did savings drop below 15 percent. This was in most years triple the savings rate of American households. These savings were channeled into banks and postal savings accounts, available in 23,000 post offices around the country. By 1987, postal accounts totaled more than $800 billion dollars. Interest on all accounts was controlled and low, but postal savings were tax exempt on accounts up to 3 million yen (at 120 to the dollar, $25,000) per person. Before the tax exemp-tion was killed in 1988, 113 million Japanese (including babes in arms and seniles in beds) had managed to accumulate no fewer than 210 million "per-person" tax-exempt accounts.

Demand for loans from business always exceeded the resources of the banks (the term of art was "overloan"), and the added money they needed was supplied to them by the central bank, the Bank of Japan, directly through its discount window or indirectly through loans from the "tanshi." These are money brokerages which help banks balance their accounts at the close of day; they are headed without exception by former Bank of Japan executives "parachuted from heaven" to their new jobs, and the Bank knows absolutely everything they do. For many banks, money borrowed from the Bank of Japan and the tanshi funded 15 to 20 percent of their loans. Even then there was a shortage of capital, and the government invited foreign banks to establish branches which would make "impact" loans to finance the importing of industrial equipment specifically approved for acquisition abroad. Such loans were funded with the currency of the lending bank, but appeared as yen-denominated assets and liabilities on the books of the branch, giving the foreign bank a base for subsequent domestic lending. Otherwise, prior to 1980, foreign banks were not permitted to take yen deposits, and Japanese banks were not allowed to convert foreign exchange to yen for lending purposes. (The Japanese did permit a fair amount of direct foreign investment, and every so often someone points out that if you deducted from the U.S. bilateral trade deficit with Japan the revenues of wholly owned or partly owned Japanese subsidiaries of U.S. companies—IBM, Fuji-Xerox, McDonald's, Disney—there wouldn't be a deficit. But, of course, what a foreign company makes on your soil is part of your GNP, not his, which is why Tennessee works so hard to win the Honda plants.)

Though only foreign banks had to get specific permission before making loans, domestic banks, too, found it wise to consult the authorities, especially about new loans (most bank lending, of course, is simply an extension of previous credits to the same customers). In a country that lacked energy resources, iron, copper, bauxite, cotton, lumber, the emphasis was always on export industries that could earn the foreign exchange that paid for essential imports. In collaboration with the Ministry of Finance, the Ministry of Trade and Industry (MITI) controlled the "window guidance"—the marching orders distributed with the loans from the discount window—given by the Bank of Japan. To the extent that a businessman needed to import industrial raw materials or machine tools or semifinished goods, moreover, the government could delay its approval of import licenses or limit access to foreign exchange. Companies that earned foreign exchange were supposed to repatriate it for allocation by MITI, and mostly they did. (It happened quite naturally: Less than 25 percent of Japanese exports in the 1970s were invoiced in yen, as against 90 percent of U.S. exports invoiced in dollars and 87 percent of West German exports invoiced in deutsche marks.) Japan's was not a centrally planned economy—businessmen with drive and persistence might find bankers they could convince, as in fact Honda did (the Ministry of Trade thought they were fools to make cars as well as motorcycles)—but the path of least resistance was what the government thought best.

Financial markets played a minuscule role in the allocation of capital resources in Japan in the 1960s, and it is fair to say that most politicians, bureaucrats, bankers, and businessmen saw no need for change. What was in the cards for the 1970s was an improvement in social services, from health and housing and education to retirement and workmen's compensation, which would be funded by the government's share of the nation's growing prosperity. Then, suddenly, the prosperity came into question. In 1971, Richard Nixon and John Connolly forced the first upward valuation of the yen (all the way to 308 yen to the dollar) to diminish what was seen as a competitive edge for Japanese products in the world economy; and in 1972, with an election pending, the Federal Reserve System in the United States led the world in an orgy of money creation. Prices for raw materials rose sharply throughout 1972, and then oil followed at the end of 1973. The Japanese realized that they had been riding a trend that for years had tilted the world's terms of trade to the benefit of manufacturers. Now everything was turned upside down. At the U.N. the "less developed countries" were trumpeting a New World Economic Order in which wealth would flow to the suppliers of raw materials. Japan might well be poor again.

The foreign banks certainly thought so. While they continued to make Finance Ministry–approved (now, in fact, Finance Ministry–solicited) "impact" loans, they charged the borrowers a premium, a "Japan rate" almost a percentage point higher than the Australians or the Scandinavians had to pay for their piece of the recycled OPEC profits. The Japanese belief that this penalty on their borrowing reflected racist attitudes is not necessarily wrong. The rising prices of imported raw materials coupled with a declining yen gave Japan an inflation rate that approached 25 percent in 1974–1975. But Japan is a ship that turns very slowly in the water. Swallowing hard, committing the nation's reserves to pay for the necessary imports and borrowing at home to support the increased cost of government, the leadership maintained its pledge to expand the nation's social programs. As a percentage of gross national product, government expenditures on social programs went from 3.9 percent in 1973 to 4.9 percent in 1974, 5.9 percent in 1975, 7.8 percent in 1979, 9.1 percent in 1981.

Over the years, the government had pretty much met its modest bills through taxes (with spending on defense limited to 1 percent of

GNP by the constitution the American occupying force imposed on the country and social services minimal, the Japanese had no serious problem balancing their budget); now there grew up an ever-increasing domestic deficit that had to be financed. At first, the government sold its bonds to the banks, which committed to hold the paper for at least one year. Eric Hayden of Bank of America in Japan described it as "a system of captive market and regulated interest rates," and noted that "the Ministry of Finance has been understandably reluctant to accommodate the growing pressures in Japan to establish a more efficient market for government bonds." Considering the fuss Americans made in 1987 about getting the opportunity to underwrite Japanese government paper, it's amusing to note Robert Alan Feldman's comment that one competitive advantage foreign banks had in the Japanese market in the 1970s was that they didn't have to bid for that stuff. As late as 1976, Federal Reserve Board governor Henry Wallich and Mabel I. Wallich commented that Japan had no money market because of "the virtual absence of public debt."

This was very soon to pass. Most of the government deficit has always been funded through the postal savings system, which historically has put its money into a Trust Fund Bureau that buys government paper. (In 1987, with government bond yields plunging well below 4 percent and some of its insurance and annuity products predicated—by law—on a return of 6.15 percent, the postal savings system began to look around for a better return, and scared the hell out of the banks by promoting consumer credit, a new idea in Japan.) As the quantity of paper the government had to sell increased, the banks required relief. They began with devices to bypass the *tanshi* brokers, taking short-term cash from their larger customers through the U.S. device of selling government securities under agreement to repurchase at a slightly higher price (this is in lieu of anything called "interest") tomorrow or next week or whenever. Because nothing called "interest" was involved, such transactions in the *gensaki* market were outside government bank regulations, and occurred at a market rate. Meanwhile, the asset books of the Bank of Japan, which had been based on paper related to economic production, clogged up with government bonds that could not as a matter of sensible economic policy be unloaded on the banks.

By 1981, with great reluctance, the government was forced to countenance a system whereby its bond issues were fairly quickly passed through the financial intermediaries to direct ownership by corporations and individuals, at prices set in a competitive market though not (as in the United States) by public auction. Though the similarity was not much noticed in either country, the Ministry of Finance in 1981, like the U. S. Treasury thirty years earlier, had been forced to admit it could no longer control the interest rates government paid when borrowing. Growing national debt at a time of growing industrial investment meant that the government would have to compete for long-term money against its own private sector, and that attempts to keep interest rates low by fiat would fail.

But the purposes of the money markets remain significantly different in the two countries. Americans, as Henry Wallich liked to stress, are themselves financial intermediaries—they hold liquid assets and they owe money, at the same time. People in the United States will borrow to buy a car or a refrigerator even though they have money in the savings bank that could cover the cost. The Japanese pay cash. Household and business alike, Americans put the check in the mail before they put the money in the bank, exploiting the "float" inherent in a debit-transfer payments system, where the person paid gets a tentative credit from his bank some time before the payer has the check deducted from his account. The Japanese find this shocking. Andreas R. Prindl of Morgan, Guaranty wrote in 1981, "The question of using float to one's advantage is a delicate one. As the Japanese have precise payments habits, it would be possible for a foreign company to suffer a loss of reputation were it to practice too aggressively types of payment deceleration common in the West." What Americans call "cash management," in other words, is out.

In proportion to their total financial assets, Japanese hold more cash than other people, more bank accounts, more bonds, and fewer stocks. They dislike the very idea of gambling: Chinese gamble, not Japanese. In finance as elsewhere, the Japanese have a bias toward doing things corporately, and because so many apparently independent companies are still to some degree affiliated with the *Zaibatsu* groups from which they were separated during the occupation, it seems reasonable to all that more than a quarter of the shares of Japanese companies should be owned by other Japanese companies. And that the government should be somehow involved. We cling to nurse for fear of finding something worse . . .

143

Organized securities markets start off as bond markets—it was not until the 1920s that stocks had anything like the importance of bonds on the New York Stock Exchange. In Japan, equity as a major source of capital got a somewhat earlier start, but was suspect because the *Zaibatsu* raised their money through their own banks rather than in a market. Even after the war, reliance on equity for capital was to be found most often at insurance companies, securities houses, and banks. Their raw material being debt, they could not use debt as foundation capital, too. To this day financial services corporations account for a far higher fraction of the value of stocks on the Tokyo Stock Exchange than anywhere else: When Morgan Stanley International Capital did a "Perspective" on world markets in spring 1986, it found that seven of the ten largest market capitalization stocks in Japan were financial services corporations, as against one in Britain and none in the United States.

Stocks as a recommended depository for people's savings did not arrive until well after World War II. As corporations are organized in Japan, shares are much more a claim on profits than evidence of ownership: Management runs the company, and will even hire goons (it is among the basic income sources of the criminal class) to put down any evidence of dissent at the annual meeting. "The stockholder is a subordinated creditor," the Wallichs wrote, "and management's long-run goals often sacrifice short-term profits." An American corporate raider—Marshall Cogan, one of the early partners in the firm that became Shearson Lehman Hutton—did take a run at a Japanese company in 1987, but he was beaten off with an angry ringing of temple bells.

The right to the share of profits, however, has been taken very seriously. Traditionally, in Japan as in England, new issues of common stock have been by subscription to existing shareholders at a price 15 percent below current market (leaving the investment bank truly in the position of "underwriter," taking up for resale only those shares for which the existing holders fail to exercise their rights). In a public offering where the price of the newly issued shares is above the book value of the existing shares, management is supposed to pay out the "profits" from the issuance to current stockholders. This gives corporations reason to raise equity by selling convertible bonds (which holders can convert to common stock at a price somewhere above current price) or warrant bonds (giving the holder the right to buy stock at a fixed price; the warrants are detachable and trade separately).

Both the banking law and the securities acts forbade banks access to the domestic securities business (except for government bonds) and forbade securities houses the exercise of banking functions in Japan. The matter was not significant until the 1980s, because the economic miracle was in fact financed by the banks. They were dignified and eminent, recruiting from the best families and the best universities. Securities firms were nothing of the sort. They had been the beneficiaries of the MacArthur democratization program, which sold off the stock of the Zaibatsu (about 40 percent of the value of all Japanese stock in 1947) to employees of the companies and the public at large. But such customers did nothing for the social distinction of brokers. "The banks defecated all over these guys for years," says William H. Brown, who left a post in corporate finance at Goldman, Sachs in Tokyo to become commercial attaché in the U.S. embassy in Tokyo. Hideo Matsumura, an old-timer at Nomura Securities, remembered his pleasure in a training program at Merrill Lynch: "The American stockbrokers didn't have any inferiority complex toward the banks. Working at Merrill Lynch was prestigious."

For most Japanese, brokers were fellows who ran prices up and down on the exchange, beat the drum to unsophisticated householders around the country to peddle stocks, traded for their own account in competition with their customers, and set up rigged deals for the benefit of politicians. As Bruce Roscoe wrote in spring 1987 in *Far Eastern Economic Review,* a weekly magazine owned by Dow Jones, "Japan's *kabuya* or stockbrokers have not been an envied lot. Their world was too dark, too beset with financial skulduggery. Relatives would not talk about the nephew who joined a securities firm. In fact, no graduates of the best universities, and possibly no graduates at all, would have wanted to become a *kabuya* until quite recently. Now," Roscoe added, "all that has changed."

What changed the perceptions was, of course, money. As late as the end of 1983, the market value of stocks in the Japanese market was about one-quarter of the value in the United States. By 1987, Japanese equity securities had a total market value greater than the total market value of American corporate equity. Much, maybe most, of this rise was the result of a change in the institutional preferences of Japanese savers: Only one-fifth or so of savings were in contractual savings (life insurance and pension funds, trust accounts and mutual funds) at the start of the 1980s, but about a third were so invested by 1987. That money was invested through securities houses, not through banks. The fraction directly invested by households in stocks other than mutual funds was probably up to about 9 percent as against 6.5 percent when the decade began.

And it was the securities firms that established a Japanese presence abroad (except in California, always a matter of special economic interest to Japan, where a number of banks had followed Sumitomo, a pioneer of the 1920s, to the other side of the Pacific). They rode a tidal wave of money pouring into and through Japan as a result of the country's immense trade surpluses. At the end of 1983, Japanese external assets were estimated by the Bank of Japan at $271 billion, and U.S. external assets were estimated by the Federal Reserve at $887 billion. By 1987, the United States was a net debtor, probably to the extent of $200 billion, and Japanese external assets at $600 billion or so net were greater than those of all of OPEC put together at the apogee of the oil cartel. The stockbrokers, the unclassy *kabuya,* were the people who advised the wealth-holders on what to do with this money, and who executed the transactions, worldwide.

In fiscal 1987, ending September 30, the largest Japanese brokerage house, Nomura, made a post-tax profit of better than $2 billion, and the three next largest, Daiwa, Nikko, and Yamaichi, made either just over or just under $1 billion after taxes. (These four among them do almost three-fifths of all the business on the Tokyo Stock Exchange.) These profits were greater than those of any other corporations in the financial services business—more than Dai-Ichi Kangyo bank, the world's largest, or Citicorp, or Merrill Lynch. In 1988, if one left New York out of the picture, the market value of the shares on the Tokyo Stock Exchange was greater than that of all the rest of the world put together. The numerical comparison is a little misleading, because something more than a quarter of that valuation represents cross-ownership among listed corporations, but even after the proper haircuts have been applied it's an awesome amount of money for a little more than 2 percent of the world's population on something considerably less than 1 percent of its habitable surface.

For institutions of such grandeur, the Japanese securities houses still live modestly indeed. At Yamaichi, for example, which almost went bust in 1965 and ever since has lived with special frugality, executive offices are near Tokyo Station, on the wrong side of the tracks. The visitor to a vice-chairman passes through a ground floor that looks rather like the bargain basement at a working-class American department store, full of people crowded together selling stocks, at the counters up front and at their desks and, of course, on the telephone. Even at Nomura—more dignified, a higher ceiling, marble floors, the desks behind the counter farther apart—the atmosphere has a kind of get-up-and-go very different from that of a Japanese bank, where the visitor rather expects to find Ramses II in the sanctum sanctorum, looking very good for a mummy and right at home amongst the stone trappings.

The home base of Daiwa is a nondescript steel-sheathed 1950s eight-story building between the hustle of Tokyo Station and the little bridge at Nihumbashi which was the center of Tokyo's predecessor village. Executive offices are on the fifth floor, right and then left around the short wall facing the single pair of elevators that serve the entire building. Broad stairs run beside them, and most employees walk. Reception is a small, square, windowless area from which doors at the left open to three large conference rooms, and a broad corridor at the right leads to corporate offices. Against the wall before the corridor opening is an armless red leatherette couch; just beyond the corridor is a high mahogany counter curved around in an L to provide some feeling of private space for the two young women who stand behind it, wearing the Daiwa uniform, a pleated fawn-colored skirt, beige blouse, and mannish maroon jacket with the Daiwa symbol, an abstract eagle, in the lapel. They step around the desk and bow from the hips, as only the Japanese can, to greet a visitor.

No one waits in the waiting room, of course, or sits on the leatherette couch. Japanese businessmen do not receive visitors in their offices: Anyone with an appointment will be escorted immediately, whether or not his host is ready for him, to a reception room with lace doilies over the backs of overstuffed chairs ranged around a table on which first green tea and then coffee are served by young ladies wearing the same uniform as the receptionists. Very senior executives, preserving their privacy, a very important privilege for very important people in crowded Japan, have their own reception rooms (which may even have windows), where the visitor waits until the other door opens. Below that level, people reserve time in one of a number of common reception rooms, which permits their employer to house them in open bullpens at considerable savings of space and money.

There may be other benefits from this system, too. One of the sources of Japanese efficiency, rarely noted, was the absence of a Japanese-language typewriter, which meant that executives had to take care of their own correspondence in their own calligraphy, and therefore were not insulated from reality by secretaries. Even now, after IBM in a clever act of cultural sabotage developed a Japanese computer keyboard, executives in Japan are more likely to live cheek-by-jowl in close communication with each other. "We have a large—well, 'sweat room,' " says Yasakuza Akamatsu, senior managing director of Daiwa International Capital Management Co. (DICAM). "All portfolio managers sit side-by-side, the chief investment officer is close. It facilitates exchange of information."

Behind the reception rooms, the bullpens at Daiwa are quite impossibly crowded, with traders and salesmen and technicians seated in narrow chairs at long picnic tables with spindly metal legs that seem fragile for the burden of screens and telephones. Away from headquarters, housing is even worse. Yukio Nakatsuka, a small, edgy, fast-talking (only in Japanese), chain-smoking managing director who runs Daiwa's equity trading operation, works in Kabutocho, Tokyo's Wall Street, about a mile away from headquarters, in a dark little room with dirty windows. By custom, all the market-related firms keep their trading and back-office operations here, near the Tokyo Stock Exchange. About two dozen feet from Nakatsuka's window, just above eye level, the trucks trundle along the inner-loop elevated highway that moves (or does not move) the merchandise of this crowded city. In yet another unimpressive building, closer to the railroad station, Isamu Miyazaki, a courtly, white-haired, grave man who is chairman of Daiwa Securities Research Institute, makes do with a section of a storeroom as his conference room. It was Miyazaki as much as anyone else who decided whether Daiwa would bid for, say, $2 billion of thirty-year U.S. Treasury bonds at the quarterly auction.

Daiwa has far more prepossessing quarters abroad, in keeping with chairman Yoshitoki Chino's injunction that when in Rome you do as the Romans do (which has a corollary that in Tokyo people should do as the Japanese do: In a speech at the Columbia University

Business School in spring 1986, Chino told an American audience that if they really thought the Japanese were in competition with them for the world's financial business it behooved them to learn Japanese as he had learned English). Those in New York, where Daiwa built rapidly in the mid-1980s to four hundred employees and cut back rapidly in 1988 to about three hundred, are high up in the same building of the World Financial Center that houses Dow Jones (and Refco), with wraparound views of the harbor and the Statue of Liberty and New Jersey; those in London, with about the same number of people, are in a handsomely redecorated building at St. Paul's courtyard. But in Tokyo all the securities houses are still rather belligerently utilitarian.

All of them are, to begin with, brokerage houses built on client lists of hundreds of thousands, even millions of small customers. Commissions are fixed on the Tokyo Stock Exchange on a sliding scale, which makes individual business very profitable. (The rates top out at roughly 1 percent on all trades with a value of less than $80,000.) Daiwa in 1987 took in something like $2 billion in commissions for trading on the TSE. And there are lots of customers out there. Income in Japan is fairly evenly distributed: The three middle quintiles of the Japanese income distribution have a far higher proportion of the nation's total income than their equivalents anywhere else. (The *wealth* distribution is nowhere near so level, being terribly skewed by the gap between those who do and those who don't own land, which has multiplied in value more than one hundred times in the last thirty years.) The *average* Japanese household has more than $60,000 in some form of savings account. Of Daiwa's three thousand salesmen, about two thousand are assigned to moving money from these savings accounts to securities.

It was not, in the mid-eighties, a hard sell. Interest rates on savings accounts dropped dramatically (*real* interest rates were okay, inflation in Japan being zero or even negative in the mid-1980s, but that's a pretty sophisticated concept). And the stock market went more or less straight up, with the average price per share more than quadrupling between the start of 1981 and the summer of 1987. "Japanese investors," said Takashi Nakayama, the lean and elegant general manager of Daiwa's investment advisory department, "used to be very conservative, they wanted to see earnings of ten percent of the price. But they were also kind of ignorant. Now they are getting kind of aggressive. It's because capital gains have been untaxed, which leads people not to pay attention to fundamental factors. So people shift money from savings to equities. And the proposed tax reform [this was 1987], which takes away the tax exemption from postal savings but leaves no tax on capital gains, will make investment in equities even more speculative." (Capital gains of corporations *are* taxed, with exceptions we shall note, but individuals are exempt on their first forty-nine transactions every year.) Even after the week of October 19, largely because the government moved heaven and earth to keep the market high, prices on the Tokyo Stock Exchange were still more than 10 percent up for the year 1987 and more than triple what they had been six years before.

Copying American custom, Yoshitoki Chino launched large-scale advertising campaigns, featuring a happy family of "Moodies," Smurf-like cartoon characters licensed from the Kent Toy Co., who prospered through investing. Rather than regarding the sales force as a special corner of the firm, he began to break in the trainees Daiwa recruited from universities by giving them a spiel and putting them into months of cold-calling, looking for accounts that could be opened via the telephone. (The accounts they developed, however, were definitely Daiwa's accounts, in the Japanese manner, and not the property of the "customer's man" who brought them in, as Americans have done this business.) Normal progression for a trainee is three to five years in sales followed by assignment to headquarters and then perhaps a return to sales for those who did well at it and liked it. The kids work very hard: Quotas are high, and if you don't meet them, you're out. Once the novices get past their apprenticeship, though there is no iron rice bowl, people who work for Daiwa in Japan are pretty much guaranteed a job for life. The training program also includes "study courses" in which the candidates learn how to read financial statements and prepare to take the examinations in bookkeeping given by the Japan Chamber of Commerce.

Compensation is a touchy subject, given the Japanese tradition that all members of an age cohort are paid the same until the time comes to appoint high executives, a tradition that does not consort well with aggressive selling. Nobuo Kiyota, assistant general manager of the personnel department, a confident young man who speaks Japanese at the speed of a machine gun, says that in the first three years the trainees must "face reality and take courses to cope with reality," but after that are judged by their performance, which means in the case of salesmen how much business they bring in. Everyone is on salary, of course, rather than on a share of the commission, "but twice a year like other Japanese companies we give bonuses, and the bonuses do not have to be the same for everyone." Branch managers are judged "principally," Kiyota adds, "on the basis of numerical performance, but also important is their efficiency in maturing juniors." In Japan as in the United States, a salesman earns the most brownie points by convincing customers to buy the securities the house is underwriting, distributing to the public on behalf of a corporate client. "Fees from brokerage and dealing are mandatory," says Shinichi Horii, general manager of the sales department. "They are planned at the start of the year. Underwriting profits are the windfall."

Well below the trainee and full-time salesman level, Daiwa, like Nomura, which had the idea first, employs housewives to work part time setting up Tupperware parties at which securities can be sold, first bonds, then mutual funds, and eventually, perhaps, trading accounts in stocks. Savings accounts in Japan are controlled by the lady of the house: Japan is notoriously a male-dominated society, but on the other side of that notoriety is the likelihood that the Japanese hands over his pay packet to his wife each week, leaving it up to her to pay the bills and make the investments. Other women, incidentally, are moving into more professional responsibilities at the Japanese securities houses, especially in the international divisions. Scott Pardee, vice-chairman of Yamaichi Securities (U.S.), reports that 76 of the 180 Americans that work for his company in the United States are women, some of them top people on the trading desk. My translator at Daiwa, seconded from the international corporate finance division, was Hiroko Tanaka, a young woman two years beyond a junior year abroad at UCLA, who was in the trainee program—as, she said a touch wryly, "an honorary man." Because most of the trainees in the Tokyo area live in dormitories (they couldn't afford anything else), and it was considered unsuitable to put a woman in the dormitories, Daiwa rented an apartment for its two women trainees to share.

In 1986, Daiwa extended its reach further into middle-class households by opening a "branch" among the counters selling costume jewelry and leather goods on the fourth floor of the Mitsukoshi Department Store in Yokohama. The counter is not unlike surrounding merchandise counters, but on the wall behind it is a blackboard with flipping orange numbers, telling the most recent sale and three most recent sales before that for the 130 most widely traded stocks on the Tokyo Stock Exchange. Daiwa saleswomen in uniform sell to shoppers who sit on high stools while looking over the literature (which includes, for example, a brochure for the Dreyfus Fund, in Japanese, a hand holding forth for the purchaser the Statue of Liberty and the lower Manhattan skyline; this is, however, a *Japanese* Dreyfus Fund, separately incorporated: Japanese law places strict limits on the sale of foreign mutual funds in Japan, which Americans cannot complain about too loudly because U.S. law prohibits entirely the sale of non-American mutual funds in the United States). The branch is open during store hours, including Saturday afternoon and Sunday when the market is closed, but not including Monday and Tuesday when the market is open; telephone orders will be taken from the opening of the market at nine in the morning on the other days, however, even though the store is closed until ten.

Mailings were sent to the store's list of 18,000 customers and drew about 1,800 responses. "Most people in this store," said Daiwa's branch manager Mieko Tanaka, a square-shouldered woman with hair pulled back in a tight bun, "should have savings about three times the national average, which means we should do an average transaction of about ten million yen [$80,000]." One gentleman came up to the fourth floor of the Mitsukoshi Department Store to Ms. Tanaka's counter, where nobody had ever met the man before, and plunked down $700,000 to buy securities. "People have so much money around here," sighed Ms. Tanaka. Chino defends the investment judgment of people who buy through this system: "Japanese housewives realize the importance of difference in interest yields. They know about mutual funds. The national newspapers tell them about foreign securities."

And in fact, of course, most of what Daiwa's customers buy is on Daiwa's recommendations, and the firm prides itself on its research capabilities. Every day shortly before eight in the morning one of the senior managers in the headquarters sales division consults with a senior trader, and with stock and bond analysts from the equities and bond departments as well as the Daiwa Securities Research Institute, and at eight on the dot he turns on a microphone that carries his voice over permanently leased lines to loudspeakers in the managers' offices of Daiwa's 105 branches scattered all over the Japanese islands. His message is an analysis of the action on the market the day before, and a "suggestion" of some stocks of the day that the salesmen should push at their customers. By nine o'clock, when the Tokyo Stock Exchange opens, Daiwa will have orders piled up for delivery to the post where these stocks are traded, and it is not to be doubted that the stocks will open strong. All four of the big houses do this sort of thing, to the despair of "efficient-market" theorists. Nomura is famous for pushing just one stock every day in this way, and a running gag in the industry speaks of the bribes others are willing to pay to get accurate advance information on what Nomura will be touting.

Daiwa's research is also available in printed form. All active customers receive a *Daiwa Weekly* with thirty or so stock recommendations, and larger customers receive a monthly report on economic conditions worldwide. The firm publishes and sells an annual 1,300-page *Analyst's Guide,* in English and Japanese (but mostly in numbers), ranking all industries other than the financial sector itself, and 953 companies within the industry categories, by criteria of sales, profitability, known and hidden assets, etc. The most ambitious of Daiwa's research products is an on-line Portfolio Management System, which is available to Daiwa's dealers (about two dozen of them, who buy and sell for the firm's own account) and traders (160 strong, who buy and sell for the accounts of institutional customers) and fund managers (for the $80 billion or so Daiwa had under management or "guidance" of one kind of another in mid-1987). This electronic guide to the Japanese stock market is also sold to foreign merchant banks, doubtless on a basis that gives Daiwa some access to their research in their home markets. Daiwa Securities Research Institute, which employs about 160 analysts, including a handful in New York and London, was spun off in 1982 as a juridically independent but wholly owned entity in the Daiwa Group. It does a good deal of international research, some of it vetted by a distinguished group of occasional visitors on retainer to the company—among them, for example, former German chancellor Helmut Schmidt and Wharton School econometrician Lawrence Klein, who exchanges equations with the computer wonks in Tokyo.

4

"As wearily expected," wrote the market commentator for the *Japan Economic Journal* (the English-language weekly of *Nihon*

Kezai Shimbun, the Japanese *Wall Street Journal*), describing activity on the Tokyo Stock Exchange for the week ended April 4, 1987, "it was another week in which internal imperatives ruled the corrupt roost. Wall Street looked okay even if the yen didn't, and these are the only two external items of even lukewarm interest to Kabutocho nowadays. Other than that it was the same sleazy scene of wholesale manipulation revolving around financings, window dressing, Euro-dollars and other warrants, personal greed, commission churning, face, and just plain fear, to name only some of the ulterior motives. Ignoble."

Things go on in Tokyo that would be highly improper, not to say illegal, in the United States. In spring 1987, the *Asian Wall Street Journal* reported an incident in which a Daiwa institutional sales-man spread a rumor that a product made by the Japanese food-processing concern Ajinomoto was about to be approved by the U.S. Food and Drug Administration as a medication for AIDS. The supposed sources for the rumor, which was a work of fiction, were never revealed. Japanese investors from the first diagnosis of the plague have been great enthusiasts for the business possibilities opened up by Western obsession with this subject (at this writing the disease itself has scarcely appeared in Japan, though given the behavior of Japanese tourists in places like the Philippines the reprieve will probably be brief). Over the next week, the price of the stock rose by 20 percent. Daiwa's agents on the floor of the Tokyo Stock Exchange rapidly accumulated the stock, purchasing 1.1 million shares Tuesday, 1.9 million Wednesday, 2.4 million Thursday, 6 million Friday, and 6.3 million in the half-day session on Saturday (meanwhile the firm was selling, day by day, 296,000, then 842,000, then 2.1 million, 2.5 million, and on Saturday 6.5 million shares, at progressively higher prices). Asked about this scandal, deputy general manager Takatoshi Okuyama said quite unashamedly, "We have to speculate sometimes. Once it's confirmed by a press announcement, it's too late to do any business."

The way the Tokyo Stock Exchange operates makes these practices even more troublesome. In the United States, brokers, except in the case of large block orders, are required to present bids or offers to the open marketplace. If Merrill Lynch has a buy order for AT&T and a sell order, it must take both to the market separately and expose them to other brokers at the specialist's post for execution, and cannot simply "cross" them upstairs. Transactions are done at arm's length, with other agents for other purchasers. In the Chicago futures and options markets, "crossing" off the floor in the Japanese manner is considered an especially heinous sin, for it makes possible the large-scale occurrence of "wash sales," by which brokers trading with each other by prearrangement can push markets up or down at their convenience.

In 1987, a Japanese securities house—not Daiwa—was accused of washing sales in Chicago, and was perplexed, for it had meant and done no harm, and such upstairs crossing is perfectly proper and routine in Tokyo. "We call it 'cross-trading,' " says Daiwa's Yukio Nakatsuka, helpfully. And the way the Tokyo Stock Exchange works, each trade presented by a broker as a fait accompli results in the acquisition or disposition of stock by the broker himself. The *saitori* who keep the books of orders not yet executed for customers (because the price they had specified had not been reached by the market since their order arrived) do not themselves make markets. They merely insist that anyone executing a trade at their post take from the books the orders at the price of the trade, in the order of their arrival. Let us now assume a broker arriving at a post with matched orders to buy and sell 42,000 shares of some security at, say, 675 yen (a moderate number—prices per share tend to be low in Tokyo, and the "round lot" for a standard transaction, 100 shares in New York, is often 1,000 shares in Tokyo). He finds at the post unfilled orders to sell at that price totaling 26,000 shares. To clear the matched trades for 42,000 shares, the broker will have to acquire 26,000 shares at a price of 675 for his own account.

Information passes from clerk to broker and back on the TSE by hand signals. The clerk is on an open line to the home office, and the flow clearly goes two ways. "The two functions in the trading department," says its boss, Nakatsuka, of Daiwa's operation, "are to execute orders and to gather information in the market." The broker tells headquarters what the result of bringing this transaction to the floor will be, in terms of the stock the firm will acquire or be forced to sell. And the price at which headquarters crosses the trades can be influenced by their impact on the firm's own position. The orders being crossed are, after all "market orders," to be executed at the current price. If the brokerage house knows that at 685 it will dispose of stock at the *saitori*'s desk while at 675 it will acquire stock, the price its customers pay or receive on their orders could be influenced by the firm's desire to accumulate or distribute the shares of this stock for its own account. "The Tokyo Stock Exchange," says Nakatsuka, "doesn't know if it's a trader's order [for Daiwa's own account] or a customer's order." So when Ajinomoto goes through the roof on a rumor, Daiwa's purchases may have been for customers, for its own mutual funds, for the trusts it "advises," for the traders personally, or for the firm.

Historically, "pools" that push prices up and down have been commonplace in Tokyo. In Japan, individuals own only one-quarter of the stocks but do more than one-third of the trading (before 1986 it was more than half the trading; by contrast, Americans as individuals own almost three-quarters of the stock in listed corporations, but do less than half the trading). As a result, many issues have a very thin float, because most shares are locked up in the vaults of institutions and other companies that would not dream of buying or selling shares without first consulting the company involved. Thus relatively small orders orchestrated by one or more brokers can move a stock some distance. One hears of "lantern stocks," stocks which lead the way up that wise observers can follow, and of "hospital stocks" that restore to health valued customers who have taken a loss on one of a firm's recommendations; both of these are considered suitable tips to politicians.

Securities houses may also be the beneficiaries of good tips from within companies. "Sony Corporation," says Shusako Toda, who ran the Daiwa equities research unit in New York, "has an American listing and follows American rules—it gives information to everyone, in the open. Not so other Japanese companies." And such information is always, of course, a path to temptation. The custom of crossing upstairs leaves the securities house with the option of shifting stock from one portfolio to another so that favored customers can be assured of buying on the upswing. The victims of this switch can later themselves, if they complain, become the beneficiaries of a "hospital" stock.

In any event, the government has looked with much favor on a rising stock market, especially in the 1980s, when the decision to "privatize" some key state-owned industries—telecommunications, the national airline, and the railroads, for starters—has given the Ministry of Finance a direct stake in how high the prices for certain securities can be set when the time comes to issue them. Tax policy worked to boost stock prices by taxing dividends to individuals but not their capital gains. "Here," said Tomohiro Abe, director of

Daiwa's international division, "a low dividend means a higher p/e ratio." Takatoshi Okuyama, deputy general manager of Daiwa's International Investment Services Division (a separate operation), says, "We believe in fundamental research, but now you can't use it in the Japanese market; all you can do is look at assets."

When it turned out that the policy of taxing the capital gains of corporations was becoming a drag on their participation in the market, the government in December 1980 approved the formation of "Specified Money Trusts," called *tokkin* as an acronym of their Japanese name, which in effect could pay taxes on a basis of last in, first out (LIFO), permitting corporations to play the market in shares they already owned without incurring tax liabilities on the sales. This of course gives further encouragement to corporations not to pay out money at a time when the government should by rights have been encouraging consumption rather than accumulation. Among the extraordinary benefits given the money managers in the original *tokkin* legislation was a privilege permitting such trusts to continue carrying at book rather than market shares that had in fact gone down in price, which invited them to advertise themselves as more successful than in fact they were. These rules were to be phased out in 1988, but in the aftermath of Black Monday the Finance Ministry decided that keeping the balloon aloft was more important than honest accounting: Holders of shares in investment trusts might be tempted to sell them, increasing the supply of stock in the market, if they were told they were losing money . . .

All sorts of fiddling about the marketplace were tolerated. It was not until 1988, for example, that the Ministry announced that consideration would be given to enacting a law to define and prohibit insider trading. This was about time. Among the sources of discomfort among observers of the Japanese stock market in the 1980s has been the growing closeness of the relationship between the investment houses and their corporate clients. The immense boom in exports has made the corporations cash heavy, and they have relied for increasing proportions of their income on a game the Japanese call *zaitek*, which may derive from the words for "investment" and "management" or from the American "high tech"—different translators give different answers. The aim is to leverage the low-cost money Japanese companies can borrow anywhere in the world into high-multiple returns on short-term capital investment.

Securities houses make money on both ends of *zaitek,* underwriting and selling the Eurodollar or Euroyen paper in London, designing the swaps by which customers who want yen assets give bargains in other currencies, and then advising the corporate client on investing it. Daiwa in 1987 reorganized to take advantage of the growing importance of this business, establishing a division that does nothing but client contact with corporations. The man who does the client contact, says Shigeru Uemura, an older Daiwa executive, once head of the New York office, who supervises such solicitation, "motivates the client." Then the actual work is farmed out to the other departments. "The policy," says sales manager Shinaichi Horii, hitting his fists together in a startling gesture, "is to control the total relationship with clients."

The recurrent emphasis on "control" when Japanese talk about markets leaves in the end a certain feeling of immaturity. Tolerance of ambiguity is the beginning of wisdom. From 1937 through 1965, the Japanese government operated a succession of semi-public agencies that bought stocks when the market was going down to protect securities houses and their customers from the consequences of folly. A form of window guidance provided similar results in 1987. Though the Brady Commission and other American observers expressed a degree of admiration for the ability of the Japanese to moderate the drop in share prices after Black Monday on Wall Street, the fact remains that rigged markets tell lies. By suppressing sales (volume on the Tokyo Stock Exchange, which had run beyond 1.5 billion shares a day in the spring of 1987, frequently fell under 300 million shares in the fourth quarter), the Ministry managed, at least for the time being, to pretend that nothing serious had happened.

But the imbalances that produced the 1987 crash are Japanese imbalances, too—inordinate land prices, overly expensive distribution systems for goods, overvaluation of financial assets as a multiple of the income stream that derives from them. The desperate scramble to keep the market up—the orders to the securities houses and the insurance companies not to sell and to absorb sales by their customers—may mean only that the Ministry needs time to think through what the Japanese government should do. But it may also mean that the Japanese, like the stalwart incompetents of the Reagan administration, really believe that they can somehow restore the status quo ante.

Still, the increasing involvement of Japanese financial institutions in foreign markets has multiplied the sources from which the

Japanese can draw good information. From a Japanese point of view, as John Plender has pointed out in *Financial Times,* what the deterioration of the dollar means is that Americans will not pay for the pensions of a rapidly aging Japanese work force. The Japanese save so much in large part because they are planning for a time when their longevity (the average life span is now eighty for men, eighty-six for women) will demand immense flows of investment income to sustain a huge community of retired people. They invest in American paper because they believe earnings on U.S. investments are the best source of such income, but the fact is that investment in American paper will yield fewer yen than planned for a community that spends yen. And the flight of foreign capital from the Tokyo Stock Exchange in October and November, despite the excellent prospects of the yen, was a reminder to the Japanese that there is much they cannot control.

The British had to send the flower of their educational system to administer the colonies and the United States had to exile its businessmen and foundation executives and soldiers to create the pax Americana. Now the Japanese must pay for their saliency on the economic scene by sending money. Black Monday—following as it did upon the collapse of the bond markets in spring and summer—definitely did teach the Japanese the dimensions of market risk in market economies. The question is what they will do—what they can do—with the lesson. They have admitted foreigners to their markets and they have gone abroad, after all, not because they wanted to but because they had to.

8

Tokyo: 2. The Money Dragon at Large

"June will be a good month in New York. You see, the Japanese pension funds will receive major payments in June and they will need a place to put the money."

—Kazuki Adachi,
Merrill Lynch in Tokyo, 1987

"Of course the Japanese are in. Market's up. Only time market goes up is when the Japanese are in."

—floor member, New York Stock Exchange,
June 1987

"A friend at Kidder, Peabody here told me that when GE took over the message came through from New York that GE isn't number two or number three in any of its businesses. They expect to be number one. I said, 'If you want to do that, you need an office of two hundred people in Tokyo to source capital there.'"

—Peter Gottsegen,
Salomon Brothers (London), 1986

1

Paul Aron, who retired in early 1988 as vice-chairman of Daiwa Securities America but remains as a senior adviser, first came to the financial markets in 1969, when he was already over forty. He had been a businessman with a specialty of turning around the less successful components of conglomerates: "I worked for the big fish who swallowed the little fish." A mutual friend who thought these talents could be profitably employed in the securities business introduced him to Howard Stein of Dreyfus Fund. Stein, basically a marketing man who has left investment decisions to his staff (he came up under Jack Dreyfus, who definitely made investment decisions himself), thought, as Stein will, that he didn't have much to lose. Dreyfus has been built on the philosophy of, Let's try it and see what happens. "Stein hired me at an attractive pay," Aron recalls from his avuncular senior status, an overweight man with thinned-out white hair and a matter-of-fact manner. "Then he took me to a bare desk and said, 'There's your telephone. If you're so smart, you'll find out what to do. I'll see you in six months.'"

This is not, however, a way to give a man a position in an organization. Aron's desk was in the research department, and the others in the department informed him that all American industries were already covered. So he looked around for investment opportunities that were not American industry, and he found one. "Everybody thinks Perry discovered Japan," Aron says. "I did." The problem was an "interest equalization tax," imposed originally by President John F. Kennedy to staunch a leak of American investment capital abroad—a leak so great that it was acting as a brake on the economic and military assistance funds the U.S. government could spend abroad without weakening what was then an almighty dollar. The tax was 11-¼ percent, which, all other things being equal, would cut the value of an investor's stake by that proportion the minute he put his money into a fund that specialized in Japanese securities. The tax had pretty much destroyed a small but growing market in "American Depository Receipts" (evidences of ownership of foreign shares registered with the SEC though the shares themselves were not) for companies like Sony, Tokyo Marine & Fire, and Fuji Film. Aron proposed to go a step further, purchasing Japanese shares in Japan. Stein was intrigued, and once again gave a very general license: "Go ahead—buy some things in Japan."

"In those days," Aron remembers, "if it were known that a U.S. investor was interested in a Japanese stock, the price would go up. I had to find a broker who would keep it absolutely secret. Nomura was too big, had its own fish to fry. Nikko was tied in with the Japan Fund, which meant we would get second-best advice. Yamaichi had

had troubles. Daiwa had no clients in America, and it was very aggressive. I told them, 'The moment I see a story in the U.S. papers about your working for us, you lose the business.' Nobody leaked. After we'd bought, of course, I told them to announce what we'd done." We arrange publicity to push up the price of the stock, naturally *after* we've bought it . . .

Aron's contact turned out to have major career benefits for the individuals involved in Japan. Chino was then head of the firm's small international division. Katushiko Fujimoto, the salesman who introduced Aron to Chino, became Daiwa's man in the Middle East through the OPEC ascendancy and made twenty-five round trips to Saudi Arabia, and now is in charge of all issues managed by Daiwa for foreign corporations, worldwide. Shigeru Uemura, an older man with a large gray head, now Daiwa's senior managing director for capital markets, was the delegate who picked Aron up at his Tokyo hotel on his first visit. (Uemura today supervises all underwriting activities in any market for Japanese corporations; he describes Fujimoto's job, which he once held, as "looking for blue-eyed borrowers.") Jiro Yamana, now deputy president for international operations, a long-headed, firm-jawed man with a large, ingratiating smile, was Aron's interpreter on his first visit to Osaka.

In the early 1970s, Aron moved over to the College Retirement Equity Fund (CREF) to manage an international securities department, and continued as a Daiwa customer. In 1976, Chino came to him with an offer of an executive vice-presidency in what was then a thirty-man Daiwa office in New York. "My job," Aron said, "was to be Mr. America, to explain what this meant, what that meant. In 1977 and 1978, I also went talking to people in Phoenix and Lincoln, Nebraska, and Wilmington, Delaware, wherever they'd have me. People remember I was out there beating the bushes when nobody else was doing it. And I was teaching at NYU. Now I have all these students working for companies all around the country."

Well into the 1980s, Daiwa did a good business selling Japanese securities to American investors, thanks in good measure to Aron's experience as a purchaser in the Japanese markets and his cleverness as an expositor for them. (In one brilliant paper, Aron managed not only to lower the apparently monstrous p/e ratios on the Tokyo Stock Exchange by—quite correctly—demonstrating the accounting differences that made Japanese earnings look lower than they would look by American accounting standards, but also—quite outrageously—to explain away the considerable remaining difference as a factor of the lower interest rates in Japan. If the interest rate on one-year Treasuries in the United States was 7.5 percent and the equivalent paper in Tokyo yielded 3.75 percent, Aron argued, then a 13.33 p/e ratio in the United States was the same thing as a 26.67 p/e ratio in Japan. It should be noted, however, that the people who bought Japanese paper on the strength of this argument made money.) Aron also lured his friend James Rosenwald, who had been following Japanese casualty insurance companies since the 1950s, to retire from Nikko Securities and become a counselor to Daiwa, advising Daiwa clients (usually from his estate in Trinidad, hooked into the world's information ganglia by satellite dish) on the best buys in Japanese financial services stocks.

Meanwhile, Aron was also preparing the ground for the time when the money would flow the other way. From Aron's pioneering comes some of Daiwa's lead in listing American securities on the Tokyo exchange and trading them for Japanese accounts—of the thirty-three U.S. corporations listed on the Tokyo Stock Exchange at the end of 1986, fifteen had been "introduced" by Daiwa, a list that includes IBM, Citicorp, Sears, Proctor & Gamble, McDonald's, Kodak, Chrysler, and DuPont. Today the firm routinely combines tourism and business, introducing Japanese investors to American corporations and vice versa under conditions of good cheer and fellowship. One such trip in January 1987, for example, started in Houston Thursday morning with visits to American General and Tenneco, continued that afternoon in Dallas with Tandy Corporation, city government officials, and then dinner at Kobe Steak House, followed by visits the next day to Texas Instruments and Trammel Crow. Friday afternoon everyone went to New Orleans for dinner at Antoine's and a visit to "Jazz Music Halls," with a sightseeing tour of New Orleans, then on Saturday golf at Chateau Country Club or a "River Cruise from Hilton Riverside," dinner at New Orleans' World Trade Center, and a return to New York on Sunday. The result is supposed to be a slight case of what the Japanese call *giri,* or obligation, on the part of the fund managers, and an inside track for Daiwa if Texas Instruments or Tenneco decides that it wants a Tokyo listing.

Daiwa's ambition was to use the lever of Japanese money to move the world of American finance, establishing a large place for itself in the United States. Daiwa America, separately incorporated, was to function as an American investment house with an advantage in its access to Japanese accounts. Its first specialty as a domestic firm was fixed-income paper. Daiwa became one of the first foreign-owned primary dealers in U.S. government securities, recognized by the Federal Reserve, and in most of the quarterly Treasury auctions in 1986 and 1987 it was the largest purchaser of long-term bonds. Sixty percent of its business in Treasuries by then was for U.S. rather than Japanese clients. Its attempts to become a big-league under-writer of corporate securities won it two bond issues of some size, one for GTE of California, which was distributed at a profit, and one for Rockwell International, which was too finely priced, as they say, and cost Daiwa a bundle (plus some reputation, because the trade be-lieved Daiwa had "bought" this business, deliberately taking a loss to gain entry). Daiwa International Capital Management Co., or DICAM, became money managers for a fair number of U.S. institu-tional investors, most notably the Oregon Public Employees' Retire-ment System. (This is still more a way for foreigners to invest in Japan than a way for Japanese to invest abroad. As of September 1986, DICAM's $12 billion under management came 53 percent from "overseas clients," but only 10 percent of the assets in which the money was invested were overseas assets.) In 1987, which was the wrong year, the firm established a presence in Collateralized Mortgage Obligations (CMOs—remember GNMAs); when interest rates rose in the spring and summer, the firm took a beating.

No doubt all this was very disappointing to Tokyo, where all four big securities houses feel that theirs is not—certainly should not be—a speculative business. In Japan, brokerage commissions on a fixed schedule pay the bills and everything else is gravy; in London, the Japanese securities companies have an inside track on the mas-sive new issues of Euromarket paper by Japanese corporations and yen paper, either Euroyen or "Samurai" (in Japan itself), by Euro-pean corporations. "We have the largest market in Tokyo," says Minoru Mori, the very tall managing director and general manager of Daiwa Europe in London. "Our industry is wealthy. Our investors are wealthy. We can offer very good advantages in service. In Tokyo it takes two or three months to complete a deal, preparation and translation and a one-month cooling period at the Ministry; here you can do it in three or four days."

New York, under SEC regulation, cannot compete with Lon-don. Daiwa America gets all the commission revenue when Japanese insurance companies buy directly in the New York market, as they do, and the firm's internal bookkeeping allocates to New York five-eighths of the commissions generated by Japanese customers who enter orders in Tokyo for trades to be executed in America. As these commissions are paid in yen, the fall of the dollar has helped Daiwa America pay its bills. Competitively, and this sort of measurement has its own vitality in Japan, the American venture has been a success: Though its Japanese customer base is only half as big as Nomura's, Daiwa does the largest share of U.S. securities business. But in 1987, even before Black Monday, the U.S. operation lost money.

"We have a unique situation in New York," says Takura Isoda, a compact, handsome, graying man in his fifties, who has spent nineteen years abroad for Daiwa (two of them as adviser to the sultan of Brunei). "London office depends three-quarters on Japanese stocks and bonds, and issues for Japanese companies. Here, three-quarters of what we do is U.S. business; we are already a local company. We have to compete with Goldman and Salomon and Merrill and First Boston, and London does not have to compete with Kleinwort and Warburg and Hill Samuel. If London loses business, it doesn't matter; if we lose, we disappear. We have developed an overdependence on fixed-income product, and we have invested too much on work in mergers and acquisitions for American companies. Tokyo has to understand that here we must take risks. If we are wrong, we disappear—but if we don't take risks, we will also disappear."

In the end, however, it was the rising tide of Japanese money that made Daiwa America more than ten times as big in 1987 as it had been in 1975, and paid for the handsome offices in the World Financial Center. "This firm," Isoda admits, "was built on our knowledge of what kind of securities our clients in Japan are fond of." Though its U.S. Treasuries trading operation, headed by an American, was one of the most sophisticated in Wall Street, the heart of the venture was the regularly scheduled conference at midnight in Tokyo on the days (actually, thanks to the International Date Line, the days *after*) the U.S. government was auctioning notes and bonds. New York participated in that conference by telephone, but it was the researchers and especially the salesmen in Tokyo who decided how much should be bid for at what price. The demonstration that Japanese advice carried more weight than American was the refusal of the Japanese houses to purchase or sell on the "when-issued" market, where domestic participants hedged through the week prior to the auction. The Japanese analysts didn't understand that—they call the when-issued market a "gray market," as though it were something underhanded—and what the Japanese don't understand, they don't do.

For several cycles, American competitors took advantage of Japanese neat habits in maintaining the maturity of their bond holdings, rolling over their investments by selling in the secondary market on a predictable schedule some of what they had acquired in previous auctions to finance their bids for the upcoming auction. A number of U.S. dealers got into the habit of shorting the older paper a week or so before the auction, with confidence that they could buy in their positions cheap from the Japanese. Then in spring 1986 the Japanese allowed their American agents to run a trap. By holding on to the older paper the wise guys had sold short, the Japanese firms created a squeeze in the market on those maturities and pushed up the price of the series. The eventual cost to the American shorts was something more than $50 million.

In May 1987, the Japanese houses even trapped the Federal Reserve System, buying at the auction (largely because the Ministry of Finance had ordered them to buy), and then selling out within three days. The Fed held a more or less formal meeting with the Japanese representatives in New York to suggest that this had better not be done again. Then in August 1987 the system got even: An auction that had been postponed because Congress was screwing around with the debt limit occurred by accident a day before the announcement of an unexpectedly large U.S. trade deficit. This pushed down the price of the bonds and the value of the dollar, and left the Japanese purchasers with immediate losses measured in the hundreds of millions of dollars. To the extent that this paper remained on the books of a U.S. subsidiary that had to mark its holdings to market every night, the losses destroyed even the hope that U.S. operations could be profitable in 1987. The experience was a pretty bitter one even for those who succeeded in transferring the paper to the books of the home company, which could continue to carry the holdings at cost by Japanese accounting principles, balancing those losses internally against the inventories of common stock holding on which profits had never been declared.

The carnage was even greater for the customers. Between September 1986 and September 1987, the Japanese insurance companies which had been the ultimate repository of the U.S. Treasury paper purchased by the securities houses lost almost 4 trillion yen—about $33 billion at 120 yen to the dollar—on their investments. About two-thirds of this had been compensated for by the difference between Japanese and U.S. interest payments on longer term paper. But the liabilities of insurance companies, of course, mount at an actuarially predictable rate whether investments show a profit or a loss. They did not have to publish these losses, but they had to keep track of them and explain them to the government. If the government wished to be generous, of course, it could look at their investment results another way, as the device by which Japan had funded the exports on which its economy relied. The losses of the Japanese insurance companies on their U.S. securities holdings could be said to have paid for half the U.S. bilateral trade deficit with Japan. Nevertheless, the observed results of acquiring the bonded indebtedness of the world's greatest economic power produced in Japanese institutional investors a strong feeling of Never Again. In September 1987, the Japanese for the first time became net sellers of American fixed-income paper, a development that was by no means unrelated to Black Monday.

As early as January 1987, however, Japanese investors had begun to shift portfolio strategy—to buy more equity and less fixed-income paper. Roughly 4 percent of Japanese purchases in 1986 had been equity, but now the ratio rose to an admitted 10 percent and a more likely 15 percent. (As investments can be made through London, where they have not had to be printed on any screen or reported to the Japanese Securities Dealers Association, and can be made in "free yen," which does not have to be reported to the Ministry of Finance, official and industry figures about Japanese overseas purchases are likely to be seriously misleading.) In February, Daiwa customers, to the firm's astonishment, bought more stocks than bonds in the United States. On the basis of directly acquired information, I have reason to believe that Japanese purchases accounted for at least 10 percent of all the buying at the New York Stock Exchange in the first half of 1987. The Tokyo offices of both Salomon and Merrill Lynch said they did by themselves 1 percent of the purchasing on the NYSE; both Morgan Stanley and Goldman said they did better than Sali or Merrill, there are other U.S. houses in town, and each of the four big Japanese houses is unquestionably bigger than any U.S. house in terms of the volume of orders by Japanese customers.

"These guys have tons and tons of money," said Geraldine Rigby, a large lady sent out from New York by Merrill to invent a "transactions desk" to coordinate the firm's work in Tokyo for Japanese corporations. "When I first became involved with the Japanese, when they were calling me in New York at two in the morning, they said, 'I'll buy U.S. government paper, other sovereign paper, U.S. banks because we know them, and public utilities because they're regulated.' They said, 'Here's my yen bond coupon, I'm looking to do better.' So they went into corporate bonds, interest rates went down, and the bonds were refunded on them. Japanese don't like that: They tend to buy and hold. They bought big in Ginnie Maes. Their losses from the drop of the dollar were mind-boggling. So now they're all interested in equities."

Most orders from Japan arrived in New York before the opening of the markets, not because the Japanese "like to buy at the opening" but because they like to buy if possible during their own business hours, which do not overlap at all with business hours in the United States. And a number of U.S. brokerage houses, incidentally—it isn't only the Japanese who "buy business"—accommodated them for most of 1987 by taking positions themselves, planning to lay them off in New York the next morning. This proved unwise, because Japanese institutions typically did not go to just one U.S. brokerage house with these orders, but spread the business around several of them. When the floor traders for the U.S. brokerage houses joined "the crowd" around the post at the New York Stock Exchange the next morning, they not only found their rivals waiting on the same mission, but not infrequently someone acting as agent for the Japanese institution, still doing what it started doing the night before.

According to a Salomon Brothers calculation, no less than 77 percent of the price movement from close to close on the New York Stock Exchange in 1987 came at the opening, reflecting overnight orders. Some of those orders were from Europe (though Jean-François Bernheim of Gruntal & Co., whose clientele is exclusively European, says that his clients, while they like to be able to talk with him in what is the very early morning in New York, tend to be much more active in the U.S. markets after noon, when their own markets have just closed and they are free to turn their attention across the Atlantic). Most of them were from Japan.

Several institutional changes in the 1980s facilitated the expansion of Japanese equity investment abroad. From the point of view of the individual investor, the most important change was probably the triumph of book entry as the means of holding and transferring securities in Japan. Such a system had been available since 1967, but Japanese investors liked the idea of holding stock certificates. As foreign certificates were either unavailable or legally questionable in Japan (a condition that also holds in the United States, which is the reason foreign corporations trade here under the cover of American Depository Receipts), there was a wide divide between buying domestic stocks and buying foreign stocks even after legal restrictions on individuals were lifted.

From 1985 on, however, Japanese law required that evidence of ownership of securities be maintained on computers, and individual investors were no longer given the option of receiving certificates. Instead, they receive confirmations from their broker that so-and-so-many shares of such-and-such a corporation are held by the brokerage house in their name or for their benefit. This obviously speeds the settlement of transactions (only three business days now elapse between a purchase or sale and the receipt of the security or the money), and it also means that from the customer's point of view the nationality of the company in which he is acquiring shares no longer makes any difference: His evidence of ownership is the same whether he buys a Japanese or British or American security. "We now divide our analytical staff simply into industries," says Isamu Miyazaki, chairman of Daiwa Securities Research Institute. "We no longer recognize national boundaries. One analyst compares General Motors and Toyota, another compares IBM and Mitsui."

By U.S. law, the Japanese brokerage houses needed a trustee to certify that *cestui que trust* was right to be trusting, and most Japanese firms that do business in the United States make arrangements with high-profile banks like Morgan and Chase for such services. Daiwa, which needed a bank of its own anyway in 1987 for its origination of collateralized mortgage obligations, secured a charter as a trust company in New Jersey and saved the money it had previously paid the banks.

Meanwhile, starting in 1981, the Ministry of Finance continuously liberalized the fraction of their assets that insurance companies and various trust funds could keep in foreign securities and in equities—and the government created the *tokkin* trust, which had something for everybody in its end run around Japanese accounting principles. Insurance companies under law, for example, can pay dividends only out of the interest and dividends paid them on their investments; capital gains must be segregated and held in a separate fund. All money paid out by a *tokkin* trust, however, qualifies as a dividend, including that fraction derived from capital gains. And this benefit carries no cost: While taking capital gains as income, *tokkin* trusts, as noted in the previous chapter, do not have to mark their assets to market and need register capital losses only after a sale. For nonfinancial corporations, which are taxed on their capital gains—and it should be remembered that such corporations own about 28 percent of all shares on the Tokyo Stock Exchange—the *tokkin* trust offers an opportunity to play the market without paying profits on established positions, because the trust is taxed as a separate entity. In effect, securities can be sold through a *tokkin* trust on a last in, first out (LIFO) basis. Finally, because all purchases and sales by a *tokkin* trust are done in the name of the trustee, companies and people can act in the market anonymously, an important consideration in Tokyo, where selling the stock of a company with which you do business may be regarded as an unfriendly act.

The *tokkin* trusts got off to a slow start, and as late as March 1984 there was only $6 billion in all of them put together. Then the appreciating yen squeezed much of the profitability out of manufacturing, and the big Japanese corporations came to rely increasingly on short-term securities profits for their earnings. No longer investing in new plant and equipment, they were cash rich; disgruntled bankers spoke of "the Toyotabank" and "the Matsushita Bank." Where once they had borrowed from the banks to build, now they borrowed from the market, especially the Euromarket, to invest in other paper. European and American investors hungry for yen-denominated assets bought the bonds of Japanese corporations at rates well below the rates in Japan itself.

When the bonds came with warrants—rights to purchase new stock in the Japanese company—the best names were actually able to borrow in early spring 1987 at negative interest rates. By selling purchasers of the bonds the right to buy stocks for a fixed number of dollars, they could borrow dollars at a fixed rate of 2 percent, then swap their dollar obligation for a much smaller yen obligation of a similar term because the market was certain that the yen in the future would be worth more dollars than it was at the time of the swap. Such deals could be made even when the price specified in the warrants was considerably above the present market price of the stock. The popularity of these warrant bonds, incidentally, produces a confusion in the world's view of the relationship of foreign investors to the Tokyo exchange. Every year the figures show foreigners as net sellers of Japanese common stocks, but in most years (not 1987, when they fled Tokyo in the crash), they are in fact net buyers. What happens is that the Eurodollar purchasers—especially the Swiss banks—take the stock they can acquire through converting their bonds or exercising their warrants as soon as such activity becomes profitable. This is not reported to the Finance Ministry, but when the banks take their profit by selling the stock on the exchange the Ministry reports a sale by foreigners.

Tokkin trusts received most of this money raised by the securities houses for corporations through the sale of Eurocurrency paper. In January 1987, valuing the yen at 120 to the dollar, there was $105 billion in *tokkin* trusts. By January 1988, there was $234 billion. In March 1984 just under 9 percent of the money had been invested in equities, with .3 percent in foreign securities; by January 1987 the ratio was 34 percent in equities, and 13 percent in foreign securities. One notes that some of this numbering misreports reality, because the securities acquired in spring and summer 1987 were still being carried at cost in January 1988, though October 19 had greatly reduced their market value.

Trust companies (which in Japanese law are neither banks nor securities houses) do this business, but most of them rely on the securities houses to provide investment advice and, of course, execution. In 1987, the securities houses through their London branches also arranged to provide most of the money: In April 1987, warrant bonds issued for Japanese borrowers in London totaled more than $3 billion. In the compilation of issuers of Eurobonds by the London gossip magazine *Euromoney,* the Japanese houses easily led the list of "bookrunners" in the first half of 1987. And even before the explosion of *tokkin* and warrant bonds, the Japanese houses had been major players in London. In 1986, Nomura was the most heavily capitalized foreign firm in Britain, with Daiwa second and Credit Suisse–First Boston third. Growth had been quite spectacular throughout the decade. "In 1981 I was told to go to London and be managing director of Daiwa Europe," said Katsuhiko Fujimoto, "and I stayed until 1986. When I made my farewell speech in London, I was unable to recognize many of our English personnel."

Japanese houses also have an edge in Southeast Asia. Chicago's Refco decided against trying to become a major player on the Singapore Monetary Exchange because the Japanese houses were so dominant. (It makes an interesting comment on how severe the panic was in Japan the week of Black Monday, and how effective the Finance Ministry was in repressing it, that one of the markets where the Japanese houses were central, Hong Kong, had to close—and in the other, Singapore, the price of the Nikkei-Dow index futures dropped by almost 80 percent.) Part of that edge, says Takatoshi Okuyama of Daiwa's international investment services, is an understanding of the money cultures of Southeast Asia, where there are no institutions: "Nobody knows who is actually controlling the money. We have to dig . . . go and find out where the clients are." And, of course, Asians' money can buy real property and buy or start businesses in America, while the Japanese still pretty much restrict foreigners to portfolio investments that have to be made through the securities houses.

Some of the Japanese presence abroad—how much of it, even now, is by no means certain—vanished in the crash. In early 1988, they were still frozen. Meanwhile, the money piles up: The Bank of Japan buys the dollars from the exporters to keep them out of harm's way, and begs those who take the yen not to put it into real estate.

2

Though very few Americans and (thank God) even fewer Japanese see it this way, the financial markets of the 1980s could be portrayed as a systematic and successful effort to swindle the Japanese out of their economic triumph. They have lost money on virtually everything they have bought abroad. Even something so safe as the floating-rate perpetual note—a permanent (but marketable) loan at what would always be a market rate of interest, to an entity absolutely guaranteed to service its debts, like the government of Sweden or a money-center U.S. bank so big that the Federal Reserve would be sure to sustain it—went sour once the Japanese became the major purchasers, losing a horrifying 12 percent of its market value in two short months in London in fall 1986. "We believed we understood credit risk," said Nobuya Hagura, president of Dai-Ichi Kangyo, the world's largest bank (speaking, by the way, in English). "We knew we understood interest-rate risk. We have now paid to learn about market risk." Implied was the statement, We shall not have to pay again.

To some extent, the Japanese have lost money through the poor-boy syndrome writ large. When the Kuwaitis were buying, back in the 1970s, they went to depressed Atlanta and Orlando and Phoenix and Boston, the places that were really on their backs, and picked up depressed property very cheap. The Japanese have ignored Houston and Dallas and Denver and Miami and have bought in booming New York and Washington, Los Angeles and Las Vegas (not to mention Hawaii, which is a special case), and paid top dollar, accelerating the rise in what were already pricey real estate markets. At the stock exchange, they are purchasers of blue chips, and AA-rated bonds, and government-guaranteed instruments. "They are not bottom fishers," says Scott Pardee of Yamaichi, who has tried unsuccessfully to convince them that bargains are good investments. They want "the best"—but in the market context "the best" is what's already overpriced, because everybody knows it's "the best." The host market being bathed in Japanese money finds its internal distortions magnified and its traders' worst instincts rewarded.

The Japanese have learned and play by all the written rules in the markets they have invaded. Their own markets, as noted, are full of hanky-panky, none of which they export. On the whole, they take "compliance" more seriously than many American firms, and much more seriously than the visiting British. "I am charged," Aron said while still vice-chairman of Daiwa America, "with the integrity of the firm. If one of our people comes to me with a suitcase a customer has given him, containing one hundred thousand dollars in bills, I tell him to take the money back, we run a brokerage house here, not a laundry. The Japanese accept it. In Japan, they don't account for unrealized losses, but we mark to market every day. They may not like it, but they accept that these Americans have crazy rules." No doubt Yamaichi and Nikko hired former Federal Reserve officials rather than hotshot Wall Streeters as their American vice-chairmen in part because public-sector employees were not so outrageously overpaid (especially by Japanese standards), but they were also making a statement. Not for attribution to an individual, the Securities and Exchange Commission certifies that in all the investigations of insider trading that followed on the Dennis Levine/Ivan Boesky revelations, there was only one instance in which a Japanese firm was even accused—and then the accusation was false. And in Japan, as noted, insider trading has never been a cause for censure, let alone criminal punishment.

The Japanese securities firms have bought understanding in the best way, by sending their young people to study for a year or two in British and American universities, especially American business schools. (Some have also worked the other side of the street: Nikko, for example, recruited a score of students at Harvard, Yale, and Princeton to spend a summer with Nikko's own trainees in Tokyo and learn something about the Japanese securities business; two of them stayed on to work for Nikko.) When rules are not written, however, when they are merely an internalized code of behavior in the market, the older generation of Japanese still tend not to notice them. Those who are most meticulous in meeting what Anglo-Saxon lawyers would call every jot and tittle of their obligations to those with whom they have some accepted relationship will cheerfully swindle any Samaritan who carelessly wanders down the pike.

It does not occur to the investment strategists of a Japanese insurance company that one should not hustle a customer's man to do executions at 2¢ a share, or buy net from five different firms without telling them that one is also buying from the others. *Sauve qui peut*—if they're prepared to buy our business, we'll sell it. They'll probably find some way to get it back from us—we do, when we buy business. One does not in the Japanese world owe obligations to strangers. And the victor in battle owes nothing to the vanquished. After a year when Daiwa Securities made more profits than any of the Japanese banks, Tomohiro Abe of its international division said scornfully, "If a person is a big boy here, the small boy can't do anything about him because he is protected by the sheriff. So we have to go abroad because there the sheriff cannot protect him."

"Fundamentally," says Ambassador Nara at Merrill Lynch Tokyo, "my thesis is that the Japanese don't change and Americans don't know that. Americans always change, and the Japanese don't know that." But he makes an exception for emergency situations, when Japanese behavior can turn on a dime and stay turned. History shows remarkable examples; my own favorite is the total Westernization of the criminal justice system in the 1880s, to deprive the powers of their claim for extraterritorial jurisdiction over the bodies of their nationals—a claim enforced well into the twentieth century with predictable long-term hatred for foreigners in places like imperial and republican China, the shah's Iran, and Panama. Much of the long-standing goodwill toward the United States in Japan—and there is such; it was not the least of the reasons MacArthur could make the occupation work—derives from the prompt American decision to renounce special privileges for its citizens following this reform (a decision very reluctantly followed by the European powers, who liked their special status in nineteenth-century China, thought they should be permitted a similar status in Japan, and regarded the Americans as wimps).

What is being asked of the Japanese now in the economic context is something culturally more difficult, for it is a change that must be volunteered and cannot be forced—to admit that they've won, loosen the chin strap, and join the club. It is probably fair to note that they might make more progress in this if they were ever given any indications that they were being invited to join a little for themselves, and not only for their money.

9

Frightening the Horses in London

"There are two kinds of research—theoretical research and practical research. Say your problem is to send a blindfolded man across the street. With theoretical research, you hire a team of people to observe the traffic at different hours, time the traffic lights and determine their influence on the flow past this spot, and so forth. At the moment when you know the traffic will be lightest, you send your man across. With practical research, you send a number of people walking across the street blindfolded at different hours, determine the fraction that arrive safely at each moment, and then decide when your man should go. The London Stock Exchange believes in practical research."

—John Forsyth,
Morgan, Grenfell & Co., 1986

1

*I*n February 1988, the International (née London) Stock Exchange and the Bank of England reported their findings on the behavior of the British financial markets during the week of Black Monday, and it was *la vie en rose.* Yes, there had been an occasional problem getting through on the telephones and the spreads between bid and asked had widened somewhat, but really the British markets had behaved better than those of any other country, and everybody ought to come do business in London. We'd love some more portfolio insurance and index arbitrary business, too.

This had been the plan. A week before the so-called Big Bang

176

of October 1986, when the London Stock Exchange had abandoned its traditional way of doing business and invited banks and insurance companies and foreign corporations to come own broker/dealers in London, Stephen Raven of S. G. Warburg, London's point man on international coordination in the clearing of securities trading, had claimed that "the International Stock Exchange will embrace all the major players in the world, all together in one exchange to make real-time prices in all stocks. Everything listed around the world can be traded here. The great band of the world will be able to deal in our market for immediate execution. Today our institutions go to the American market for IBM, purchase or sale, but once we have our new market we will have a price in size [that is, willingness to buy or sell large numbers of shares at the bid or asked on the screen]."

So they tried that, and it didn't work. British broker/dealers did a good deal of business with American firms and in American securities before the New York market opened on October 19, but it was because American mutual funds (especially Fidelity) were jumping the gun and American broker/dealers who dealt for their own account were doing business where they didn't have to print their trades or tell their own self-regulatory organization (the New York Stock Exchange) what they were up to. There is also some reason to believe that Japanese institutions, having been told not to sell into New York that day, dumped American securities in London for the same reasons of anonymity. The British firms, however, immediately laid off on New York all they had bought in London (this is why the market opened so catastrophically down); even the London Stock Exchange and the Bank of England had to admit through their glowing optimism that the British jobbers had not increased whatever their positions in U.S. securities.

Britain had adopted the American NASD system for trading through computer screens. One of the quirks of that system was that it locked if people put into the machine a bid equal to an offer already there, because those bids and offers had priority and they weren't being executed. This happened a lot in London. When the London Stock Exchange staff began to detect such shenanigans more quickly, the British dealers reduced the size for which their bid was good from the tens or even hundreds of thousands of shares (British share prices are lower than those in the United States, and the round lot even before Big Bang was a thousand rather than a hundred shares) down to a few thousand. Even then the phones were off the hook a lot.

Eventually, the LSE put into action a "fast market" exception like the ones in the Chicago pits, which released the broker/dealers from the obligation to live up to the bids they had put on the screens if someone actually got through and hit them. The dealers did, force majeure, wind up with £250 million of additional inventory on Monday—but they sold it all off to credulous customers on the even steeper drop on Tuesday.

Worst of all, the market in the hours it was open was very nearly irrelevant: More than two-thirds of the drop in prices in the two days was at the openings, when the dealers frantically marked down (all together, oddly enough) what they would pay for stocks. The governor of the Bank of England, Robin Leigh-Pemberton, noted smugly that "we cannot discount altogether the possibility that some of our domestic markets, perhaps as a by-product of improved liquidity, globalisation and technological change, have become permanently more volatile." John Plender commented in *Financial Times* that "Other observers may nonetheless be drawn to more revolutionary trains of thought, namely: what was the point of investing so heavily in making London's already sophisticated financial markets more sophisticated, if the result of Big Bang is simply to cause prices to take a more drunken lurch at the first sign of trouble?"

Both domestic and foreign consumers of the financial services offered in London were amazed by the reports, which were presented as a suitable contrast to what had been emerging in America (self-flagellants, these Americans: Look at Watergate and the Iran-Contra hearings). A few days before these reports were published, Hans-Joerg Rudloff, vice-chairman of London-based Credit Suisse–First Boston, told a meeting of portfolio managers in Zurich that among the "illusions" shattered October 19 was that an International Stock Exchange in London "could trade shares of multinationals such as Nestle and Daimler-Benz better than their local markets." Some observers felt renewed sympathy with the historic positions of the French and the Irish, that when there's money to be made the English are absolutely shameless.

2

In the Thatcher years in England, oil and financial services have been the two great earners of foreign exchange. It is hard to decide which would have been more astonishing to the ardent socialists whose government displaced Winston Churchill's at the end of World War II. Socialist Britain despised markets, and indeed the socialists still do. British Labour was committed to public ownership of the commanding heights of the economy and to fairly tight political control over virtually everything that wasn't publicly owned. And austerity was cultivated for its own sake. Until a year or two before my own first visit in 1954, restaurants had been forbidden to charge more than seven shillings and six-pence (about a buck in those days) for a meal, which had made dining out for the well-to-do English a movable feast indeed: One went to one restaurant for hors d'oeuvres at seven-and-six, another for a main course at seven-and-six, and a third for dessert and coffee at seven-and-six.

In Chicago the markets arose from the wit of half a dozen imaginative individuals, pulling with them an institutional structure that had been set in place for other purposes. In Tokyo the markets grew because government purpose could not be served without them. In London the most important markets were essentially "for others." The banks and securities houses that flocked to London from the 1960s on were allowed to do only a very small business in domestic pounds. (There was a category of previously expatriated pounds, like the Japanese free yen, which could be invested in foreign securities.) But U.S. dollars were piling up abroad, some because antagonists as well as friends of the United States needed dollars to buy dollar-denominated commodities but did not dare hold their money where a hostile U.S. government could seize it, some in the hands of governments and central banks that used interest-earning dollars rather than sterile gold in their reserves, some simply the product of American payments deficits (which had started in the late 1950s, when the costs of foreign aid and of the American military presence abroad became more than the nation's then-invariable trade surplus could carry).

In July 1963, President John F. Kennedy made those dollars already outside the United States especially valuable by announcing plans to impose (as of the date of the announcement) an "interest-equalization tax" to stem the flight of capital from the United States by taxing away the benefits of higher interest rates abroad. In effect, this discouraged money from being repatriated, for anything that was abroad and stayed abroad, or went abroad to pay for imports, was exempt from the tax. As usual with currency controls (which does not mean they should never be attempted), the interest-equalization tax invited Americans to find legal or undiscoverable ways to get their money abroad.

In 1962, the British firm of S. G. Warburg (part owner of the American Kuhn, Loeb) had pioneered the issuance of what one of the stockbrokers that distributed the paper to customers called "Eurobonds." This was a $15 million six-year note designed in fact to help finance the modernization of Finsider, the government-owned Italian steelmaker. When it appeared that the market did not like the looks of Finsider, Warburg blithely switched the issuing authority to Autostrade Italiana, proprietor of the great new Italian expressways, and a sibling of Finsider in the Mussolini-originated corporate bundle Istituto Recostruzione Industriale. Jacques Attali neatly summed up what had happened: "an exotic contract, drawn up according to British law, signed in The Hague, for a loan quoted in Luxembourg, issued in dollars in order to finance investment paid for in lire by an Italian company that was not the borrower!"

Loans that had been previously made to European firms from New York now became much more economical to make from London. Paris, which might well have had a chance at this business (for Britain was not then inside the Common Market), blew it because the Banque de France was not willing to see loans made in a foreign currency by firms operating within French borders. The Bank of England had decided early on, a year after the Suez debacle of 1956 had put an end to imperial ambitions, that it did not wish to see the pound used as a vehicle for international finance, and equally did not wish to see its control over the domestic money supply demolished by floods of foreign money freely converting into and out of pounds. But unlike the French, the Bank of England saw no objection to having London used as a home away from home for financial institutions that for whatever reason were peddling the currency of their own country.

"It doesn't matter to *me,*" said James Keogh, who as Cashier of the Bank of England was responsible for regulating the immigrants, "whether Citibank is evading American regulations in London. I wouldn't particularly want to know. If the Comptroller's people [the reference is to the Comptroller of the Currency, which chartered and regulates Citibank in the United States] feel they can make their jurisdiction run in London, I say, 'Good luck to them.'" Or, as an American banker who would still like to be anonymous put it in the early 1970s, "The Bank of England doesn't care what you do in London, so long as you don't frighten the horses."

American banks slowly but at an accelerating rate took up the invitation. There were only ten of them in London in 1960, and some of those were restrained by long-standing correspondent relationships with British banks. Six years later there were fifteen, and when I was in London in 1973 working on my book *The Bankers* there were thirty-eight. They flocked to Europe in part because their American customers were investing in Europe and it seemed risky to abandon their international business to others, and in part because the margins in England looked even more inviting than the costs looked menacing. In the United States, banks had to keep reserves at the Federal Reserve; in Britain, all of a dollar deposit could be lent out if a bank wished to put all the money at risk. In the United States, banks had to pay fees for deposit insurance; in Britain, there was no such thing. In the United States, banks were barred from the securities business by the provisions of the Glass-Steagall Act; in Britain, they could conduct through "merchant banking" affiliates whatever securities activities they wished, so long as everything they did involved foreign suppliers and takers of foreign funds.

Particularly after OPEC prices made borrowers of all the world—for nobody could cut consumption of other things fast enough to pay the escalating cost of oil, and in any event the Arabs needed places to put what was more money than they could spend—the international banks based in London became the conduit for the money. They could book the loans wherever they would pay the least taxes on the proceeds (the Bahamas were a favorite residence, though Luxembourg had many admirers). The work was most easily done in London because it was London and Samuel Johnson's comment is still true, that the man who is tired of London is tired of life; because the communications were good; because the time zone was convenient; and because the regulatory authorities saw and heard and spoke no evil.

The British willingness to let anybody do anything in London so long as they weren't corrupting the British markets was especially influential in getting the Eurobond business centered in London, for Eurobonds were "bearer" paper, so nobody except the bank that bought it for a customer knew who owned it and nobody buying it on the secondary market asked any questions about where it came from. "The Eurobond market," *The Economist* wrote with flat finality in 1987, "was built on tax avoidance." As a Conservative MP

Christopher Tugendhat put it, "It is difficult to generate much enthusiasm about the people who purchase Eurobonds." *New York Times* correspondent Jeff Gerth points out that when a U.S. company that has issued Eurobonds goes into Chapter 11, many of the bonds are not represented on the creditors' committee—their holders would rather not take the chance of being discovered.

Eurobonds became the instruments of choice for capital flight from the third world and laundering by criminal elements in the United States. When reform was in the air in early 1987, David Watkins of Goldman Sachs in London told Matthew Barrett of *Euromoney* that the market would have to resist disclosure: "If they insist that a customer has to disclose the beneficial owner, that would be too much and our clients would walk. There's no way a Swiss bank would let some London auditor pry into its business."

Success in this market was in large part a function of what was politely called "placing power" and impolitely called "stuffing power." Underwriters were far more profitable if they had trust customers or managed investment funds to which they could sell the paper at a price better than what they had bid for it, even if nobody in the outside world wanted to pay that much. When the Japanese came, their banks could not compete because they didn't have trust powers, but their securities houses could assault the citadel because they had major money under management for which they did not have to account. The Swiss, of course, had the greatest edge: "They charge you a large commission for buying you the wrong stock," Jocelyn Hambro of Hambro's Bank said in 1973, when his was the largest merchant bank in London, "and the chap can't complain because he shouldn't have had the money there anyway." American firms were somewhat disadvantaged in this game because their books are a little more public than those of European and Japanese firms (only a little: mustn't exaggerate), and because the SEC rules forbid them to make firm contracts for the sale of any paper to American clients until the date of issue.

American corporate issuers of such paper were bound until 1984 by a requirement that they deduct a withholding tax on interest paid to foreigners. But there were a couple of "havens" with which the United States had a tax treaty that permitted American corporations to pay interest without withholding taxes. A favorite, because it also had rigid bank secrecy laws, was Netherlands Antilles. Such bonds could not be bought by Americans, to prevent their use for the evasion of U.S. taxes, but of course the world has a free market for such paper and once the initial issue had been distributed it was easy enough for Americans to purchase it. In 1987, as part of the hunt for evidence on the insider trading types who had surfaced on Wall Street, a functionary in the U.S. Treasury Department decided to revoke the tax treaty with Netherlands Antilles, provoking screams of rage from American "investors" who had, it turned out, acquired this stuff. It is a measure of the decline of any feeling for honesty in the press as well as in the markets that this decision provoked howls of outrage not only from the tax evaders who saw their paper decline in value, but also from all the reputable organs of opinion. The Treasury expelled the man who had made the decision, and restored all the benefits to all the thieves.

Someone is going to pay a price for this anonymity eventually. So long as Eurobonds were couponed and the coupons were cashed quarterly or semi-annually, companies could hope to keep track of whether the Mafia or whoever was forging paper, but with the introduction of zero-coupon bonds in the early 1980s the invitation to fraud became irresistible. Courts are going to have a good time in the early years of the twenty-first century sorting out who is liable to whom for what when more paper than was ever issued floods in for redemption. But by then everyone connected with its issuance will have moved on to better jobs and knighthoods or to an ultimate reward.

Once these bonds were issued, they traded in a market that left no fingerprints. London has a stamp tax on securities transactions, so all purchases and sales are ostensibly concluded elsewhere. The two clearinghouses, Euroclear and CEDEL, are in Brussels and Luxembourg, respectively. Between the two of them, in 1986, they settled roughly 60,000 transactions a day (more than the total on the London Stock Exchange) worth more than $15 billion a day (three times the total on the New York Stock Exchange). Though the paper is still allegedly bearer bonds and anonymous, in fact all of it is now held in the form of book entry, with the bonds themselves—$350 billion worth—deposited in a trust account and transfers made inside the computer. The market is totally opaque. Bids never appear on screens anywhere, and except in the clearing machinery, which is protected by bank secrecy laws even more rigid than those of Switzerland, there is no record except in the banks' and brokers' own books of who bought what from whom at what price at what time.

"The international market," said Jay Stearns of the Canadian brokerage house Wood, Gundy, chairman of the International Securities Regulatory Organization in 1986, "has never had reporting. It's a dealer-to-dealer market."

Euroclear, which settles two-thirds of the Eurobond trades, goes back to 1968, when the market grew so big that participants began to feel the disadvantages of not being able to net out debits and credits with a single payment and delivery or receipt. Morgan Guaranty began the clearinghouse as a proprietary service, but decided four years later that cooperative ownership would be the better part of valor, and essentially gave away the system (for $1.75 million, undoubtedly less than it cost to set up) to what were then 125 significant participants. In 1987, another two thousand participants were invited in to take a little piece of the ownership.

Morgan retained, however, the contract to operate the clearinghouse and also—not by its own volition, its executives assured John Duffy of *American Banker,* but by the intricacy of Belgian law—the exclusive right to make the loans of money and securities that enable the market to clear every night. Its fellow big banks get some piece of the lending action through supplying letters of credit that back the lines Morgan extends to the smaller firms clearing trades through Brussels. In the absence of such letters of credit, Morgan will allow smaller firms a line only twice as large as their deposit with Morgan—that is, $20 million against a $10 million deposit—to complete their customers' purchases and sales through Euroclear. "Morgan doesn't just make things hard for the little guy," one such says in London, "it eliminates him. One fail uses up my line of credit, and then all my other trades for that day fail, and I have to pay interest to my customers. Merchant banks don't have that problem: They can use institutions' funds to buy the shares on a deal, and then indemnify the managed account so they don't lose money."

Prior to late October 1987, when volume undoubtedly receded, Morgan's loans to participants in Euroclear involved at least $5 billion a night in either money or securities, or annual revenues that cannot have been much less than half a billion dollars. Euroclear has more than five hundred multilingual employees and rooms full of computers, and under the circumstances one assumes that the fees Morgan as operator charges for the service do not cover all the costs. Indeed, one of the ways Morgan keeps the smaller participants from rebelling is by rebating at the end of the year most of the fees the system itself has collected. Even so, knowledgeable observers believe that at least $150 million a year drops down to Morgan's bottom line.

Stanley Ross of Deutsche Bank in London told John Duffy, "I think it's cheap at half the price. When the mother and father of all Eurobond crashes comes, as I believe it will, and you have a rush of people trying to get out of the market, who is going to be left holding the baby?" On Black Monday, when the world expected and more or less got a flight to quality, Morgan stock, always the class of the banking group, took the worst pasting of all. It appeared that the reason was a rational concern over what might be happening at Euroclear, but on Morgan's complaint the New York Stock Exchange censured Spear, Leeds for its performance as the specialist in Morgan's stock, and Spear, Leeds resigned what had been a very profitable franchise, so there must have been other reasons.

Eurodollar trading is not a market outsiders can penetrate: In recent years, the Japanese securities houses have led the "league tables" in underwriting new Eurobonds, but they have never been much of a force in trading them. (In fairness, the language of this trading is English and relatively few of the customers on the buy or sell side are Japanese: The Japanese put bonds in the mattress and wait for them to come due.) The trading game is played very rough, like rugby, where if one of your players is injured you play on with one man less. Especially in the case of new issues, the sharks are forever looking for a trace of blood in the water, a bit of evidence that the issue has been overpriced and cannot all be stuffed into customer portfolios. "There are occasions when you wind up owning an entire issue," said Peter Gottsegen of Salomon Brothers. "You own more than the entire issue, because you also own the shorts." If you do in fact own all the bonds and all the shorts, of course, you can squeeze the shorts mercilessly for whatever price you wish, assuming the issuer doesn't care—and usually he'll be on your side.

In the British system, the underwriter is exactly that: He agrees to take at the published price what existing shareholders don't. When the markets collapsed on Black Monday two weeks before an $11 *billion* issue of shares from the British government's holdings in British Petroleum, four large American firms were left facing losses that totaled more than $350 million. British underwriters by and large had laid off their risk, but American firms couldn't do that in their home market and really didn't want to, anyway, because in previous privatization sales by Mrs. Thatcher's government they had made a good business of returning to British hands at a premium (through resale in the United States, avoiding British stamp tax) the shares the government had hoped to place in the United States. But the real reason the government proceeded as planned, despite what Treasury Secretary James Baker mistakenly thought was a dignified *public* appeal on behalf of these nice Republicans, was resentment in the City about the great enthusiasm these firms had shown in squeezing shorts during the previous two years.

By fall 1987, the Securities and Investments Board set up to supervise the securities markets in Britain was supposed to have enforced on the Eurobond dealers and traders a requirement that they present their bids and offers on screens for the world of potential purchasers and sellers to see. The Association of International Bond Dealers vigorously protested. The bankers and securities firms didn't want to publicize their games beyond what they chose to tell the tame and dazzled young journalists of *Euromoney* and *Institutional Investor,* they disliked leaving an audit trail tax authorities might be able to follow, and they feared, as the *Euromoney* article put it, "the inevitable narrowing of spreads that would ensue." In March 1988, the British government announced that the power to compel such disclosure was being withdrawn from the SIB. If foreigners wanted to run an opaque market in securities not denominated in British pounds, that was fine with Mrs. Thatcher. Just don't frighten the horses.

3

Though the Eurobanks and the Euromarkets were by far the most important financial activity in London, commanding by the mid-eighties something more than $2 trillion in total assets/liabilities, the English for a long time regarded them as curiosities of interest mostly to Americans. The London Stock Exchange especially continued as it had always been, a private club where transactions were expensive for the public, in part because the government imposed a 2 percent stamp tax on all sales of stock, in part because commissions were fixed and high. The principle of its organization was "single capacity." Some firms were strictly jobbers, dealers who stood at their "pitch" on the floor and bought and sold for their own account only from and to other members of the exchange. The other firms were strictly brokers, executing orders for public customers, forbidden to buy and sell for their own account. "Dual capacity," the governors of the London Stock Exchange had decided in 1840, was "highly inexpedient and improper." In 1912 fixed commission schedules were imposed, and the system was set in concrete.

In theory jobbers competed with each other; in fact there were a number of "joint books" confidentially approved by the exchange—plus, the Monopolies Commission found in 1978, no fewer than 269 "price spread agreements" by which supposedly competing jobbers arranged to quote the same prices at the pitch. All this was hush-hush: Nobody except people on the floor knew what Americans called the "spread" and British called the "touch" between bid and asked at the pitch. In an illiquid market with low volume and collusive jobbers, though, it had to be high. The New York Stock Exchange bragged that most specialists quoted a spread of only an eighth of a point, which on an average-priced share was a little less than three-tenths of 1 percent of the price, but a study by the London Stock Exchange itself in July 1986 showed an average touch of four-fifths of 1 percent of the price on the "Alpha" group of the 60-odd most actively traded stocks, almost 2 percent on the "Beta" group of 400-plus less active stocks, and well over 3 percent on the 1,240 least active. On top of that came commissions fixed as late as 1986 at a rate of .58 percent on the first £100,000 of a transaction— and a stamp tax that was 2 percent until 1983 and still 1 percent until fall 1986. Among the results of these spreads and fees and taxes was that a considerable proportion of trading in the stocks of the best-known British companies migrated from London to New York. By 1985, on the artificial American Depository Receipt vehicle that saved British companies from registration with the SEC, New York traded more shares than London did in Jaguar, Imperial Chemical, the pharmaceutical concern Glaxo, and several others. Jobbers in England could not handle large volumes of orders, because their total capitalization was only about £300 million.

Not much could be done about it under the rules as they existed up to the mid-1980s. Stock exchange member firms had to be partnerships, which meant that anyone sinking capital into them also sunk (as the "names" did at Lloyd's) a possible risk of unlimited personal future liability. And partnerships by British tax laws had to distribute their entire revenue at the end of each year. But the result was, as Jacob Rothschild, scion of a great house, pointed out in 1983, that the total profits of all London Stock Exchange firms put together were less in 1982 than the profits of one American house, Salomon Brothers. Rothschild did not point out, however, that the Salomon Brothers trading floor in New York bought and sold securities, equities, corporate bonds, and government bonds, to a value several times as great as the value of all the trading on the London Stock Exchange.

What enabled the jobbers to survive was a unique settlement system, the "account" period. In Chicago, everybody marks to market every day, and pays or collects tomorrow. In New York, trades are settled five business days after they occur, so that what you buy on Tuesday you pay for and receive next Tuesday (barring a holiday); what you sell on Tuesday you deliver and collect for next Tuesday. In the British system, however, there are twenty-five account periods, usually two weeks though at least two are always three weeks. Settlement is a week from the Monday that follows the close of the account period. In a normal two-week account, for example, if I buy something on Wednesday of the first week, I will not be called upon to pay for it until nineteen days later. "Market makers can run much bigger positions with this system than with a five-day rolling settlement," said Stephen Raven of Warburg. "And within the account period the market maker doesn't pay stamp duty." Even so, on the day the account period settled the larger jobbers on the London Stock Exchange were likely to be in debt to the banks for anywhere from thirty-five to sixty times their capitalization.

"The jobbers thought they were market makers," said Warburg's Sir David Scholey, who had worked some years in the United States when Warburg was linked with Paribas (the Banque de Paris et du Pays Bas) and the American house of A. G. Becker in an effort to establish a major presence in New York and Chicago, "but the jobbers could deal only with the brokers, and eight or ten brokers did all the business. The system was doubly cushioned and cartelized, and real market makers aren't cushioned."

There was even—at this writing, still is—considerable question about exactly what had settled. Because the market was so tightly cartelized, it was possible to run the London Stock Exchange settlement to some extent along the lines of the clearing corporations in Chicago. Through the institution known as "cash and new," favored participants were permitted to roll over their positions from one account period to another, paying up the difference between what the prices had been at the time of their bargain and what they were at the end of the account period. And the "cash" part of this settlement could of course be an advance to the luckless fellow whose losing bet was being carried forward. "You always have this worry in the back of your head," said Sir Kenneth Berrill, chairman of the Securities and Investments Board, "about what some young man on the telephone may have said to a customer." But it was the fact that the jobbers themselves could play with house money during the account period and if necessary go on a "cash-and-new" basis at settlement that made possible a single-capacity market where £300 million of capital bought and sold £500 million of equity securities every day. The one little fault the Bank of England thought there might be in the British markets was the account system, which exposed brokers to big risks of customer default and did not mesh well with the rest of the world. No doubt it will go at some point, too, because one of the major sources of income for U.S. brokerage houses is margin interest on their customers' borrowings, and the account system gives British customers a free ride. But the British brokerage firms themselves have been used to getting a free ride on the account, and they like it.

4

In February 1979, to everyone's surprise, a Tory government through the Director General of Fair Trading brought suit against the London Stock Exchange for "restrictive practices." This greatly upset and exercised the Bank of England, for the London Stock Exchange was the locus of trading for British government debt as well as the market for corporate shares. ("Gilts," for "gilt-edged," a reference to the original printing of British government bonds years before, were traded for next-day bilateral settlement, however, not within account periods and not through a clearinghouse.) On consideration, however, the Bank of England saw merit in the idea of restructuring the LSE. "We wished to protect the stock exchange from itself," says one of the officers who worked on the problem, "keep it from becoming irrelevant. Their trading volume had become only a fraction of the Eurobond volume, and they didn't entirely understand what was happening. We wanted them out of the Restrictive Practices Court, not so they could keep going as they were—far from it—but so they could realize where their own best interests lay.

I think the phrase 'Big Bang' originated here, because the question in our minds was whether the changes should be phased in or done all at once in a big bang."

The 4,600-odd members of the stock exchange were far from eager for change. Though volume was low by American standards, the profitability of the Housemen, as the oldtimers called themselves, was entirely satisfactory. There was money to be made by riding the tails of the takeover artists, a business pioneered in London as long ago as the 1950s by Charles Clore and Oliver Jessel and Jim Slater, who "ramped" shares, to use the British term of art for manipulation, and bought companies like the 1980s American raiders, for their breakup value rather than their future cash flow. Money flowed from individuals, who had owned 80 percent of the shares of British companies before World War II, to institutions, which by the mid-1980s owned 70 percent, leaving behind commission revenues on the sales. The big brokerage houses managed the money for the institutions. "While they made no direct charge for this service," John Plender and Paul Wallace write, "they enjoyed commissions on all the transactions, so putting themselves into a curious position where they were both user and provider of their own broking service. The resulting potential conflict of interest gave an incentive to 'churn' clients' portfolios—that is, to deal actively in shares to generate a higher commission income." Merchant banks running trust accounts could buy for a number of them at the lower wholesale commission rates and then charge each customer the higher commission for small purchases and sales. "This turn," Plender and Wallace note, "sometimes called the retail-wholesale split, gave the merchant banks a powerful incentive to deal actively." No government agency policed this sort of swindle; no law prohibited it.

The logjam broke in 1983, when, essentially under the aegis of the Bank of England, the secretary of state for trade and industry and the chairman of the stock exchange reached agreement that if LSE procedures relating to minimum commissions and limitations on membership could be changed, the stock exchange rule book might qualify for exemption from the rules against restrictive practices. The changes the Bank of England set up were a sweetheart deal for the London Stock Exchange, as the Labour opposition insisted; worse, they were not going to slow the decline of the exchange as the location of choice for the trading of securities that could also be bought and sold in New York. Various participants returned to battle, and by the time the dust settled, the new structure looked very different from what London had known before.

Insistence on the partnership form of organization would go: Corporations would be permitted to own 100 percent of LSE member firms. The ownership of such corporations would be opened to banks, savings associations, and insurance companies. Foreigners, too: a very new idea. Foreign firms had never been permitted at the London Stock Exchange, as the Japanese, typically, had been too polite to mention when Mrs. Thatcher was threatening death and damnation to Japanese firms in London unless the Tokyo Stock Exchange found room for English brokers. The barrier was especially interesting in the light of London's history because, as Hamish McRae and Frances Cairncross write, "Of the fifteen accepting houses, the City's top merchant banks, all but one (Robert Fleming) are directly descended from banks formed by immigrants—and the original Robert Fleming was a Scot from Dundee."

Single capacity would go: All members could become market makers, whether or not they did business with the public, and market makers would be permitted to take brokerage commissions. And fixed commission rates would go: All commissions would be negotiable, as they had been in the United States since 1975. Market makers would have to print their bids and offers on screens available to all members, and at least for the "Alpha" stocks the exchange would publish every day the volume of trading, the opening price, the high price, the low price, and the closing price. The per-share stamp tax would be reduced to one-half of 1 percent, but would apply (as it had not before) to sales within the account period even if they were reversed before settlement. The account period system would be kept intact.

On the old stock exchange, brokers strolled from jobber to jobber, looking for a better price or whatever they looked for. Donald Cobbett remembers that they were called "squirts," because they were "always squirting around the market in pursuit of the closest possible price basis." Newcomers didn't get much help, he adds: No badges identified the jobbers, price boards did not display the name of the firm, and in the 1930s there was no *Industrial Jobbers Index* to tell the neophyte "which jobbers dealt in what shares." In the new world, with markets being made by banks and brokers as well as jobbers, bids and offers would have to be presented to the world at large, simultaneously from all market makers, on screens. Stock exchange floors, seen as a system, are "order driven"—that is, the action begins with an inquiry at the post by a broker with an order to fill. Screen-based systems are "quote driven"—from the point of view of the participants, the action begins when a market maker solicits business by putting his bids and offers before the public.

A model for a quote-driven exchange already existed in the National Market System of the National Association of Securities Dealers in the United States. Gordon Macklin, a brisk, businesslike former dealer and stock salesman who had moved over from the board of NASD to be its president at about the time NASDAQ began sending quotes to computer terminals in 1972, made several trips to England and convinced Sir Nicholas Goodison of the stock exchange that "the more transparent the market, the greater the volume." Delegates from London roamed the NASD facilities in Washington, D.C., the computer center in Trumbull, Connecticut, the trading rooms of the big dealers, and they bought the system, which they called SEAQ—Stock Exchange Automated Quotation. Not the least of the advantages offered was the ease with which National Market System and stock exchange securities could be cross-listed and cross-quoted on each other's screens. By 1984, the first such internationally shared stock quotes began to appear on what was called SEAQ International. Macklin had also been chairman of the National Securities Clearing Corporation, which now developed an International Securities Clearing Corporation subsidiary to interlink with the TALISMAN system in use in London. "The whole thing," Macklin said shortly before his retirement in spring 1987 (another great market timer), "was tied to the potential of linking their market with ours."

Among the unexpected complications arising from the end of single capacity was a perceived need for increased investor protection in a market where the brokers who were supposed to be their representatives might actually be the counterparty in the trade. The solution was to be a requirement of "Chinese walls" to separate the brokers from the dealers. The gradual descent of the London market into legalisms can be illustrated by the definition of "Chinese walls" given in 1988 in the *Licensed Dealers (Conduct of Business) Rules:* "Chinese walls means an established arrangement whereby information known to persons in one part of a business is not available (directly or indirectly) to those involved in another part of the business and it is accepted that in each of the parts of the business so divided, decisions will be taken without reference to any interest which any other such part or any person in any such part of the business may have in the matter." The merchant bankers were not impressed.

How does one enforce good behavior at a stock exchange? The answer given in the United States in 1934 was a Securities and Exchange Commission, and the American model has intrigued British commentators from its beginnings. Professor L. C. Gower of the University of London did a study for the Department of Trade in 1983 and recommended an Investor Protection Act that might indeed establish a commission. Once again the Bank of England intervened, appointed its own committee chaired by Sir Martin Jacomb of Kleinwort, Benson, and brought to the Tory government the proposal that finally carried the day—a private body, a Securities and Investments Board, responsible to the Department of Trade, empowered to license "self-regulatory organisations" like the stock exchange that would have their own rules satisfactory to the SIB and would enforce them. Time was now short—under the terms of the deal by which the government withdrew its case against the stock exchange, the new LSE rules had to come into effect on October 27, 1986. So the Bank of England itself put up the money for the proposed SIB before it had any juridical capacity whatever, and the Department of Trade appointed to head it Sir Kenneth Berrill, a small, perky man in his sixties with wispy hair and an iconoclastic self-image, who had been the chief of the "Think Tank" in the prime minister's office for both Conservative and Labour cabinets, and had left government to run the international brokerage house Vickers da Costa, which was then in the process of being acquired by Citicorp. More than a thousand amendments to the bill were introduced in the House of Lords, and many carried. The ombudsman contemplated in the original legislation, for example, was made more independent of the SIB than had at first been planned (he would be supervised by a Financial Services Ombudsman Bureau, Ltd.)—but his rulings were made less binding on the parties. That sort of thing. Finally, on November 6, ten days *after* Big Bang, the bill received its third reading in the Commons and the Royal Assent, and it became possible to make rules.

The stock exchange was seeking international business, and the Eurobond dealers were beginning to deal in equities. Gordon Macklin had originally gone to London as a consultant to the Association of International Bond Dealers (which had its headquarters in Zurich) and to the International Primary Market Association. A number of members of these organizations expected that when the stock exchange was restructured they would be able to acquire memberships at reasonable prices, but in June 1985 the leaders of the LSE failed to secure the 75 percent vote they needed to alter their Deed of Settlement. "The backwoodsmen," said the man from the Bank of England, "wanted to make new memberships so expensive nobody would join, and when the leadership showed signs of yielding to them, we had to be on the other side." But it wasn't, as the British say, on: Being a member of the London Stock Exchange wasn't worth all that much. There was a reason why there hadn't been a new firm buying a membership in the old House since the end of World War II. In the end, the LSE charged the new foreign members about $60,000, 1 percent of what the Tokyo Stock Exchange charged, and 7 percent of what it cost to become a member in New York. By early 1987, no less than a quarter of the firms in the House were or were owned by foreigners.

Because the new law required securities dealers that were not members of a self-regulating organization like the stock exchange to register directly with the Securities and Investments Board and accept direct supervision, the Association of International Bond Dealers and International Primary Market Association members after their initial rebuff at the stock exchange formed what they called ISRO, the International Securities Regulatory Organization. Slowly but eventually with a great bright light it dawned upon the members of the stock exchange that if ISRO members wished to trade away from the exchange the stocks that were their bread-and-butter, they might starve to death. Early in 1987, after more than 75 percent of the stock exchange members voted to go along, the stock exchange and ISRO were merged to form the International Stock Exchange on terms that left ISRO dominant, but quietly so.

Virtually ignored in all this foofaraw was the fact that the new law, while mandating a species of deregulation on the rule book of the stock exchange, was for the first time ever subjecting the Eurodealers of ISRO to the long arm of government control. Once the law was fully implemented, which still has not happened as of March 1988, a Morgan, Stanley, to suggest a name, would no longer be able to move a block of New York Stock Exchange listed stock from one set of hands to another in London with nobody in the United States ever the wiser. Bids and offers now made entirely dealer-to-dealer on the telephone, by people whose ability to do favors for each other is absolutely unconstrained, would have to be exposed to public view. "Bargains," to use the term the British prefer to "trades," would have to be printed on the screen, at least the prices of the shares if not the sizes of the actual trades (the new stock exchange, while permitting *Financial Times* to market the first tickertape report of activity, has still fought off any requirement that the size of trades be made public, ostensibly because the jobbers are worried that predators would learn their positions).

The number-two man in one of the five most active houses in the Euromarket, speaking only with a guarantee of anonymity, denounced the "cruel irony of a deregulation that regulates a market that has been unregulated for twenty-five years without a serious scandal or failure and with an unparalleled record of innovation. But we could generate zero support from our Continental or American brethren in our desire to fight. We do two hundred billion dollars a day in this market; the domestic market is a peanut next to this. There is no domestic financing here; British corporations do their financing through us. But no one wanted to take the hassle. They'll write their own rules and then they'll apply them to us, and maybe it will take and maybe it won't. Who's to say what is meant by 'carrying on business'? Suppose we're doing it through the Amsterdam office? But we are physically captive here. The real bang you hear may be the door closing if they regulate us so we can't live here."

Jay Stearns of Wood, Gundy and ISRO was philosophical. "You can't spit in the wind forever," he said. "ISRO dealt last year in three thousand, four hundred different dollar equities, in London. It's a vast turnover that has been going on outside any stock exchange. The change will codify what's been happening, and give reporting." Speaking for Barclay's Bank, which was a player in the international securities markets as well as international lending but was never able to escape regulation by the Bank of England, Sir Martin Jacomb described the integration of the London Stock Exchange and ISRO as "a *tremendous* achievement. It will greatly facilitate the supervision of the market." It was supposed to happen in 1987.

Not everyone thinks London will be as important to the future of finance as it has been in the past, because so much of what was done here was done by foreigners who may well begin to find the grass greener at home. Quite apart from the shakeout in the broker-age business, which is worldwide, there are fewer American banks in London in 1988 than there were in 1983. "Like the postwar politicians who yearned for a far greater role on the international stage than Britain's new status as a second-rate power actually justi-fied," John Plender and Paul Wallace wrote in the book derived from their TV series *The Square Mile.* "Britain's financiers aspired to a more grandiose position than was justified by the post-imperial status of sterling in the world financial system. If they succeeded, it was very largely thanks to the enterprise of foreign firms."

"There will be closer and closer linkages between Tokyo and New York for the cash markets," said Tone Grant of Chicago's Refco in fall 1986, "and closer and closer linkage between Tokyo and Chicago for futures and options. Very tight relationships among Tokyo, Chicago, and New York. London will be for off-hours trad-ing, with some residual business in Singapore."

In the run-up to Big Bang, everybody spent as though the City had become Golconda. Three of the four giant British "clearing banks" acquired both a jobber and a broker (Barclay's took the biggest); Warburg bought the biggest brokerage firm, Mullen's, which had been the Bank of England's agent in distributing gilts, plus the second-largest jobber. From the United States, Citicorp, Chase, Security Pacific, Merrill Lynch, and Shearson Lehman ac-quired big-time brokers; Goldman, the two Morgans, and Salomon decided they would do it for themselves. Merrill built its own nine-story headquarters building in a pleasantly conservative wide-win-dowed style near the northern edge of the City; Salomon Brothers built a trading floor the size of two football fields, larger than the famous Room in New York, over the trains at Victoria Station, some miles away. At its peak, the Salomon office had more than six hun-dred employees.

Among them, the expanding British and the arriving foreigners (twelve European banks acquired brokers) bid up the price of traders and well-connected institutional salesmen by a factor of ten, until men who three years before would have been delighted and amazed to be paid $70,000 a year were taking home $700,000; they bid up the rental of office space not only in the City of London but actually across the Thames (one house started its own ferry service called "the horizontal elevator"). Per square foot, rentals were soon half again as much as those in the most expensive blocks of New York. What can only be described as fast-food architecture sprang up through the Square Mile as what color had survived on the street—furled umbrellas, bowlers, striped pants—disappeared into shirtsleeves before screens upstairs. Out toward the estuary in Dickensian Canary Wharf the Canadian property developers Olympia and York, builders of the Battery Park offices in New York, began a construction project four times as large as anything previously built in Europe.

The beginnings of Big Bang were a terrible mess. At the Saturday rehearsal ten days before, dealers failed to update their quotes on the screens, reached with alacrity for their phones when the button that lit up indicated a call from Prudential Insurance and failed to pick up the call at all when it was from a little brokerage house, and neglected to inform the exchange when bargains were struck. Yielding to frantic demands from the smaller brokers, who could yell their way to attention at the pitch but felt disabled at the end of a telephone wire, most jobbers agreed to continue to make a market on the floor of the exchange while they moved the A-team upstairs. For the first week, they were glad they had done so, because the computers went down: Though the London Stock Exchange had never done as much business as the U.S. over-the-counter market, the combination of novelty and inexperience at economizing on the consultation of screens led British brokers and dealers to demand almost three times as many peeks at the data as NASDAQ had to handle for the same volume of actual trades. But the bugs worked out, some new Tandem computers were rushed from Silicon Valley, and by the end of November more than three-quarters of all trading was upstairs. In December less than 5 percent of the business was being done on the floor, and in February the floor was abandoned.

For the stock exchange in the first fifty-one weeks after Big Bang, both benefits and costs flowed as predicted. The Bank of England in its quarterly for February reported that average commissions on very large trades were down about 50 percent, but of course a lot of institutional business was being done net, without commission, on the direct lines between the market makers and the institutions. By summer, volume was more than double what it had been before, and the technical problems had moved over to the settlement system, which was holding more than $6.4 *billion* worth of trades that, even with the ease of netting through the account system, the TALISMAN program had failed to clear. The abandoned stock exchange floor had been made into a clerks' warren because no other room available to the exchange was large enough to hold all the paper.

Profitability was variable. Barclay's, thanks to the inherent strength of the jobber it acquired and the managerial skills of Sir Martin Jacomb, made money; the other clearing banks did not, and Midland dropped its most important acquisition, the institutional broker W. Greenwell. (This did not greatly surprise the people at Greenwell's. "When we were first taken over by Midland Bank," said chemicals analyst Stuart Wormsley a week before Big Bang, "we had three hundred and fifty people. Now we have five hundred and fifty. I'm glad it's not my money any more.") Even before the market fell out of bed the week of October 19, the American invaders were cutting back pretty drastically. The systemic problem, which Blaise Hardman of Morgan, Grenfell saw even before the game began, was that "traders will grab an unsustainable portion of the reduced costs."

The Eurobond market was beaten up by the dramatic interest-rate fluctuations of spring and summer 1987, and underwriting profits disappeared under the onslaught of Japanese firms slashing their way to the top of what everyone called "the league tables" after the organization of British football competition. The money was supposed to be in organizing the swaps after the underwriting—the arrangements whereby borrowers arranged to receive one currency and pay another, or change variable interest rates into fixed interest rates, or both. Not infrequently, these swap arrangements left the bank or broker that did them holding one side of the deal while waiting hopefully for a customer to pick it up. "The American banks," Hardman observed, "are booking profits saying they're trading profits when they are really credit exposure. They say they've solved the Latin American debt problem in the swap market. What they don't understand is that the swap market *is* the Latin American debt problem of the 1990s."

A visitor to London with the right friends at home sees mostly brilliant people who take limited responsibility for the nuts and bolts.

At the close of the day, it is impossible for an outsider to estimate how resourceful the City really is. The birth of financial futures was a difficult labor here, and the open interest at the French MATIF quickly came to exceed the overnight positions at the London International Financial Futures Exchange (or LIFFE). Options, now traded on the stock exchange itself, seem more the British speculator's and even hedger's cup of tea, and as Chicago has now learned, that's not over time the right business.

One of the reasons the American firms began cutting back in the summer of 1987, even as the markets boomed, was the difficulty of selling to the English techniques that had been honed to profitable perfection in New York. "A man from Prudential passed through here," said Peter Gottsegen of Salomon Brothers, "ready to do mezzanine financing and equity financing for leverage buyouts. He said to me, 'It's like selling shoes in Africa—lots of barefoot people, but they don't want shoes.' " This reluctance to experiment with fancy finance may turn out to be a safety net rather than a restraint, but for plain vanilla finance the staffing levels got awfully high.

"The real worry," said Sir Kenneth Berrill at the Securities and Investments Board, "is not that prices will fall, but that this will be followed by a drop in volume. If turnover fell by a third and stayed down for six months, a very serious squeeze would come." As these words are written, volume has been down by more than a third for five months, with little apparent prospect for revival. The moral hazard will be considerable. John Brew of the brokerage house Grieveson, Grant said before Big Bang that if commissions turned out disappointing "the obvious way to compensate for a loss of income on the introduction of negotiated commissions was for broking firms to take positions in the shares that their analysts were about to recommend." In its rush to modernity, London gave up both of its most important protections against misbehavior in the market: single capacity, which put a real (not just Chinese) wall between activities that inescapably create a conflict of interest, and the unlimited liability of partners in the broking and jobbing entities.

The Guinness scandal of 1986, involving not only efforts to push up the price of stock Guiness was offering as payment in a takeover deal but also efforts to push down the price of its rival's stock (Ivan Boesky did some of the dirty work), was a reminder of how little the rules of the new game have been internalized in London. The 1985 scandal at Lloyd's, where one of the promoters clearly cheated his "names" and was merely rapped on the knuckles for his fiddling, has shown how deep the tendency lies to excuse one of our own for actions that would be heavily punishable if the miscreant were an outsider. Markets policed that way lose the confidence first of participants and then of the larger public.

Experience in the United States argues that when the partnership form goes, so does the sense of fiduciary responsibility and continuing relationship. It is probably significant that the first fruit of the downturn after Black Monday was a serious campaign by the larger houses to have the Department of Trade and Industry deny Sir Kenneth reappointment when his term ended in May 1988. "The costs faced by investment firms of having to ensure that all their employees understand and comply with hundreds of new, complicated rules have been estimated at as much as £100 million," Clive Wolman wrote in *Financial Times*. "The cutback now threatening many securities firms has added a twist to the resentment caused by the additional costs, administrative burdens *and restrictions on business-getting* [emphasis added] and has intensified the search for the culprit." If Ronald Reagan was able to install at the SEC the chairman of a brokerage house who was openly concerned first of all with what he considered the inadequate profits of Wall Street, some very prominent Englishmen couldn't see why Margaret Thatcher should make them put up with an unaffiliated intellectual like Sir Kenneth Berrill.

As in the United States, these tensions will never disappear. Because they are new in England, there is no way to predict the forms they will assume when they surface. In February, Britain got off to a bad start, with a Department of Trade announcement that Sir Kenneth would indeed be retired at the end of May, despite a leader in *Financial Times* two days before the announcement urging the government to think to the lady's reputation. His replacement was a man from the Bank of England, coming on loan. As the Bank's strength has never been regulation—from the disaster of the property lenders in the early 1970s to Johnson, Matthey in 1986 it has been easily blindsided by sharp operators—the signal given is highly discouraging.

10

New York: The Buck Stops Here

"The goose that lays golden eggs has been considered a most valuable possession. But even more profitable is the privilege of taking the golden eggs laid by somebody else's goose."

—Louis D. Brandeis, 1914

1

What one notices first, browsing the floor of the New York Stock Exchange, is how much older on average the personnel is, by comparison with Chicago and Tokyo. The clerks of course are mostly kids as they always were (and now at least a third of them are women, which they never were), but the brokers who actually bid and offer and transact, even those whose seats are rented for them by their firms, are thirty-five and up, sometimes way up. One of the repetitive stories in the New York papers tells of the geezer who started as a runner on the floor seventy-six years ago and just celebrated his ninetieth birthday by doing another day's work at the post where he was a specialist in the days when the pools were rigging RCA. If they aren't the old-timers themselves, quite a lot of the members are the sons of old-timers, particularly specialists and floor brokers—$2 brokers, so called, because their commission historically was 2¢ a share per round lot of 100 shares, paid by the firm that used them to execute its customers' trades. These days, with the average hand-executed trade up over 3,000 shares, it's closer to a penny a share for a routine "market order."

About a third of those on the floor are $2 brokers, and at a little better than a penny a share for routine executions, nearly all of them in 1987 took home a commission income in six figures. All the paperwork associated with their trading is done by a firm that "clears" for them, they have no special need for office space, and their necessary expenses are not much more than comfortable shoes. Stanley Abel, a silver-haired, hard-selling former Lehman Brothers partner whose discount brokerage firm of Abel/Noser serves large institutional clients as both broker and analyst (different jobs for different fees), argues that executing large trades on the floor should not cost a pension fund or mutual fund more than 2¢ a share: "We have two Rolls Royces in garages down here," he says, "to testify that you can get rich at two cents a share." This is a minority view; a few days earlier Martin Kaplan of Merrill Lynch, who runs all the firm's equity trading for itself and its customers, had talked of chewing out almost to the point of dismissal a young trader who had agreed to do big business for a Japanese insurance company at 2¢ a share. Dealing with individuals the firms charge a great deal more, anywhere from 12¢ on thousand-share orders by the less expensive "discount" brokers to half a dollar or more at the full-service houses where the customer gets someone to hold his hand. Dividing total shares by total commission revenues in the New York Stock Exchange figures, one comes up with about 15¢ a share for each side of a trade, on average—about two-fifths what commissions were in 1971. Anybody whose advice is worth having—and there are such— is of course worth a lot more.

Though the volume of trading even after the crash is literally sixty times what it was when I first visited in 1951, the floor is if anything less agitated. The members who walked around a lot at a fast pace then were the floor traders who played for their own account and searched out the action wherever there was a burst of noise. There were then more than three hundred of them, but only a handful survive, thanks to 1977 reforms that really required the crowd at the post to fill orders from off the floor before dealing with members openly trading for their personal accounts. (These reforms had been publicly urged on the Exchange by the SEC as early as 1963.) Brokers walk back and forth between the sixteen free-standing kiosks called "posts" and their clerks at the phone desks that line the walls, picking up order slips and reporting executions; specialists stand beside their posts, not infrequently leaning against the counter (people can sit inside the kiosk, but nobody sits on the trading floor); reporters who work for the stock exchange stand close by at the counter with sheafs of stiff IBM cards on which three pencil marks (the stock, the price, and the number of shares) will give the information that flashes around the world within fifteen or twenty seconds of the instant the card drops into a slot in the counter.

A forest of screens darkens the sky even in the big room with its white stone walls and cathedral windows, and about a quarter of the membership now works in dark windowless annexes off the main floor. Here and there in front of the eight-sided posts there are active crowds of brokers yelling at each other and the specialists, but mostly people stand around and chat, waiting for action. More than fifteen hundred stocks are traded on an ordinary day, but three-fifths of the trading is in two hundred of them. Only about a tenth of each day's volume, perhaps a seventh of the transactions, passes through the old system of clerk writing ticket for floor broker to execute at post. Half the trading by volume is accounted for by three thousand or so daily sales of blocks of ten thousand shares or more, most of which are arranged upstairs on the telephone and merely carried to the post to be printed on the tape. In another 40 percent of the volume, one side or the other of the order arrives at the post through the electronic delivery system the Exchange introduced in 1976.

Prior to the 1984 extension of this Designated Order Turnaround (DOT) system to make it usable for larger orders, there were moments of frantic activity when clerks grabbed preprinted order slips out of shoe boxes to distribute to hordes of $2 brokers hustling off to posts to execute a "program" of buying or selling the upstairs computer had just recommended. If the Exchange maintains its restrictions against brokers using electronic communications to the posts for their own trading after the market has moved more than 50 points, the shoe box brigade may be reactivated.

Thirty-odd years ago, when a clerk needed his member to come pick up a message from the office, he had the member's number posted on a board high up in a corner of the trading room. The clapping sound of these numbers mechanically hitting the board could be heard through the room, and people looked up to see if they were needed. Now, of course, floor brokers carry beepers, which in the general noise are too soft to be noticeable any distance away.

Unlike the New Bedford fish auction, the New York Stock Exchange can't permit brokers and clerks to use walkie-talkies, because there aren't enough frequencies in the world.

Agitation is common twice a day: when trading starts at 9:30 and when it ends at 4:00. Orders bunch at the opening, some overnight from Tokyo and Europe, some simply the morning's mail from the brokers, some from domestic strategists who for their own reasons send in "Opening-Only" orders. This is the one block trade where nothing is prearranged and the crowd at the post is actively involved. Nothing is left over from last night, unless orders have been left for execution on the specialist's book. The fifteen hundred stocks to be opened are handled by about four hundred specialists working as part of fifty-three specialist firms, nearly all of which are in effect partnerships.

The specialist's most important single function is the choice of the price at which trading begins, with a single transaction that lumps together all the orders prior to 9:30. There is always some degree of "imbalance," which may or may not be remedied by changing the price ("market orders" presumably will be executed at whatever price the specialist sets). Wherever he opens the stock, the specialist buys up any sell orders that cannot be matched with buy orders, or sells from his own inventory whatever stock is necessary to meet buyers' demands. As much as a quarter of the day's trading may sometimes be done in the first half hour. If a specialist proposes to open the stock at a price more than two points or 10 percent away from last night's closing price, he is supposed to get approval from a member of the board of the Exchange.

In fact, such movements are not uncommon. Eugene Rotberg of Merrill Lynch, formerly the man who raised the money internationally to support the World Bank, once took the price at which a stock opened the year, added up all the up moves and down moves of the stock from each opening to each closing bell, and calculated what the change in price to the last trade of the last day should have been if movement in stock prices had occurred only during the trading day. He found that he accounted for less than half the year's actual change in price by adding up the changes that occurred in each day's trading. More than half the movement of prices of exchange-traded stocks had occurred overnight, which meant it was determined by the price at which the specialist opened the stock.

The *Special Study* of the markets done by the SEC after the

1962 market break found a number of instances where the specialist opened a stock higher than it had closed the night before even though he had more sell orders than buy orders (and vice versa), and recommended a rule the Stock Exchange did in fact adopt, that the specialist be permitted to change prices at the opening only in the direction indicated by the balance of overnight orders. One of the things that worried sophisticated students of these subjects in the 1970s, perhaps correctly, was the decision of the newspapers and the Associated Press to substitute a figure of the price/earnings ratio calculated on today's price for the old report on opening price in the familiar tabular presentation of each day's activity.

Again at the close there is a rush of orders, some associated with traders' desires to hedge their overnight exposures in the futures or options markets, or just to square off and go home and sleep, and some (as noted in Chapter 3) probably related to games being played between the stock market and one of the index futures markets. The advertised price for a stock in tonight's reports and tomorrow's paper, after all, is the closing price. Until the day after the crash, when the rule was suspended to help reduce fear and trembling, brokers handling orders from companies buying back their own stock were required to cancel them half an hour before the close of trading, to diminish the danger of manipulation. Orders from anyone other than a company buying back its own stock may be marked "MOC" for "market on close," which does not hold the broker to the absolutely last sale, but something near it. One of the reasons the price of a stock moves so much overnight is that it moved so much in the last half hour of trading the afternoon before.

Market orders from the public through the electronic system can arrive either as IBM cards spat out by one of eight printers at the post and passed to the specialist by his clerk or through direct transmission to a screen at the post. The specialist normally asks the brokers in the crowd if anyone wants to fill the order at the existing bid or asked, and if no one does he fills it. Though there are variants from stock to stock, the usual rule has been that if an order received on DOT is not filled within three minutes, the specialist sells or buys the stock out of his own inventory at the current bid if it's a sale or offer if it's a purchase.

The specialist has on another screen, from the Intermarket Trading System mandated in the mid-1970s by the SEC, the bids and offers for this stock on any other regional exchanges where it may be traded. This includes the so-called Cincinnati Stock Exchange, a computerized order-matching service to which a number of over-the-counter dealers belong. If the stock that has been ordered through DOT can be purchased in any of those markets at a lower bid or sold at a higher offer, the specialist is obliged to either send the order to that exchange or match the price. With rare exceptions, however, prices on the New York Stock Exchange are better than those elsewhere. Much of the business other exchanges do in NYSE securities involves companies that are "in play" and traders who want to escape margin requirements. The ITS serves as a way for specialists and brokers elsewhere to lay off their positions in New York.

As noted in Chapter 3, the mechanical rules associated with the execution of DOT orders can disrupt the human adjustment to unbalanced order flows on bad days on the Stock Exchange. Where live brokers in the crowd can "participate-out" an order on the other side, each buying (or selling) only part of what he has been instructed to buy (or sell), the DOT orders must be executed in their entirety. Nor is there any way out of it: No one would be willing to risk giving a specialist discretion to fill only part of an order from the DOT system so that an order on the other side could be divided up among a number of his clamoring customers.

The specialist position, combining broker and jobber, was and is the keystone to the New York Stock Exchange. Since World War II, each stock has been assigned to a single specialist, by a committee of his fellow members. The specialist agreed to remain all day (in person or by prearrangement with another member in his own firm) at the post where "his" stocks were traded. He kept a book in which he maintained a record of orders brokers had left with him because they could not be filled on arrival at the post and the broker had other business elsewhere. Usually these were "limit" orders, to sell at a price higher than the present price, or to buy at a price lower than the present price, though they might also be orders to be executed on an opening or a close. At about a third of the posts on today's New York Stock Exchange the same book hangs on the same hook on the pillar that supports the little marquee above the desk. It is long and narrow, with pages ruled along the horizontal for entries to show the number and size of the orders at each price, and the symbol of the brokers who left them. The other two-thirds of the specialists now have computerized books that come up on a screen with the touch of a button.

One of the things that has changed out of all recognition in the last generation is the role of the specialist's book. In the 1950s it was the holy of holies, the very font of inside information. Now it pretty much just hangs there. Being in the right company, I was permitted on a recent visit to look into the books several specialists kept on several active stocks. They were to all intents and purposes empty. Electronic order systems mean brokers are less likely to leave with the specialist an order now "off the market," because they no longer have to worry about the time and possible expense involved in making sure an order gets to the post where the stock is traded when it approaches the limit price at which a customer wishes to buy or sell. Now an upstairs computer can be programmed to send the order through automatically when the screen shows the stock bid or offered at the desired price.

Meanwhile, the existence of an active options market has cut back the "stop-loss" orders that once filled specialists' books with odd-looking requests to buy at higher prices (for people who had gone short and wanted to get out if the stock moved up) or sell at lower prices (for people who owned stock and wanted out if it began dropping). One should note that these people were not necessarily losers—they could keep changing the prices at which their stop-loss orders were to be executed if the stock moved as they hoped, so that in effect the "stop-loss" order became a way to lock in a profit. There is still some reason to worry that a trader aware of such orders will "gun the book," driving a price down knowing he can buy for less (or up knowing he can sell for more), but computerized records make such behavior riskier than it used to be.

When a broker arrives in the crowd at the post and inquires the bid and asked prices on a stock that interests his customer, it is the specialist who quotes the prices. The broker reveals whether he has a buy order or a sell order only after hearing the spread: "Three-quarters for two thousand!" if buying; "two thousand at three-quarters!" if selling. In either case, a broker on the other side accepting the trade will say "Sold!" Each makes a note of the other's firm (a broker acting for another one will "give up" the name of the firm that gave him the assignment), and presently will hand the slip of paper to his clerk to confirm the trade to the customer and get a record of it on the computer in the office. At a very modern market like NYMEX, where they trade the petroleum futures, clerks put in a running record of the trades their principals think they've made, and the computer matches the records, giving each trader and broker information in a matter of minutes, while memories are still fresh, of busted trades that will have to be reconciled. At the New York Stock Exchange, where for generations people have not had to settle their transactions until the fifth working day after the trade, specialists and brokers will normally verify the trades they did with each other soon after the close of the trading day. Brokers may not find out from each other until the third day after the trade that they have problems with QTs (for questioned trades, with disagreements about price or size, or which broker was on which side) or DKs (for don't knows, where one party says he has no record or recollection of doing this trade at all). Executions on DOT are locked into the computer matching system immediately.

One person the brokers cannot appeal to in case of a disagreement is the specialist: Trades that are made in front of him are not, officially, his business. There's no way he could remember them all. If there is no buy order close to the price of the most recent sale when an order arrives with a broker, however, the specialist must bid for his own account; if there is no sell order at a nearby price, he must offer from his own account. He has taken an oath to "maintain a fair and orderly market" in the stocks assigned to him. He is not, however, required to commit suicide—if the market is collapsing, and all the orders are on one side, he can rapidly lower his bids in hopes of discouraging sell orders or raise his offers to discourage buy orders. If worst comes to worst, after receiving the consent of a governor of the exchange, he can close trading in the stock temporarily while he and his friends look around for orders on the side not now represented at the post. The less active the market, the more likely the specialists are to be involved in the trading. During the 1930s and 1940s, it was by no means uncommon for specialists to be on one side or the other in half the trades. Today the proportion is closer to a quarter (the figures say 11.6 percent, but that's of gross business—of 35.7 billion shares bought in 1986, specialists bought only 4.1 billion, but they also sold 4.2 billion of the 35.7 billion sold).

In markets where nothing out of the ordinary is happening, specialists unquestionably smooth out very successfully the movement of prices in the more heavily traded stocks. The SEC report on the 1987 crash selected nine heavily traded stocks, and found that in September, the month before the crash, six of them moved in price by only one-eighth of a point or did not change at all from the previous sale on more than 95 percent of the trades—including more than 95 percent of trades involving a thousand shares. Even on October 19, all but one of them had more than half its sales either at the same price as the previous sale or only an eighth away—and two stocks (General Motors and Exxon) moved an eighth or stayed at the same price on more than 90 percent of the trades.

The Stock Exchange likes to measure how well the specialists are maintaining their markets by the number of times they sell on a rising price and buy on a falling one, supposedly smoothing out market movements, and by that measure the current cadre delivers better than a 90 percent "stabilization rate." But of course the normal market-making function—the specialist selling at 40-⅛, buying at 40, then selling again at 40-⅛, making $125 per thousand shares each time around—counts as a series of stabilizing trades. Moreover, it gives the specialist credit for helping to stabilize the market if he rushes to sell what he has acquired in a crash, or buy what he has sold in a fast-rising market, even if his precipitous sale or purchase aborts what might have been the start of a trend back toward equilibrium. Like everybody else, the specialist is forbidden to make a short sale unless the last sale at a different price was at a lower price: the "up-tick rule." When the Brady Commission and the SEC investigated specialist performance in the Great Crash, they found that though the specialist community as a group had manfully bought when no one else was buying and had suffered unrealized losses of a third of their capital on October 19, almost a third of those who had agreed to maintain their markets wound up with reduced long positions or even with short positions as the result of their day's work: That is, they had on balance joined the mob pushing the prices down. As of March, with more to come, the Exchange had taken four stocks away from their former specialists.

This was not a surprising result to historians of finance. Studying the May 1962 break in stock prices (which ended with a selling climax day when 14,750,000 shares changed hands, the second highest number to that time in the history of the Stock Exchange), the SEC found that the specialist in IBM had lightened his inventory considerably during the period just before the stock fell out of bed, and continued to be a net seller through most of the avalanche. "There were times," he admitted, "when our position was probably a little on the small side, yes."

"When would that have been?"

"Well, that was during the end of May, when the break was strenuous in IBM."

"How did you end up with a small position in a period of a break?"

"Well, self-preservation."

Every time the market has broken in this century, there have been calls for "reform" of the specialist system. The SEC study of the 1962 episode concluded, "Whatever other lessons may be drawn from the May 1962 market break, the results of this study indicate that both the tests of specialists' performance and public presentation of the test results are in need of revision." The SEC study of the 1987 break used about the same tests that had been used a quarter of a century before to measure the performance of specialists in selected high-volume stocks, and came up with roughly the same conclusions, especially on the inadequacy of the NYSE measurements: "The Commission has urged the NYSE to adopt relative performance measures so that specialists who were regularly among the lowest ranked specialists would be subject to performance reviews. . . . A NYSE task force headed by then NYSE Chairman Batten on the specialist system in 1976 made findings consistent with the Commission's views. Nonetheless, the NYSE has retained its absolute measures."

Historically, the specialist's monopoly position has occasioned a good deal of discomfort. The SEC's *Special Study* in 1963 worried about the specialist's "ability to outbid and underoffer his customer." A limit order in the book, if it had some size, made a floor under the stock, and only the specialist would know about it. If he agreed with the customer that a stock down that low was a good buy, he could stand guard at an eighth of a point above that price, acquiring an inventory with the certain knowledge that if his judgment was wrong, he could dispose of the stock only an eighth of a point down—which in the days of fixed commissions still yielded him a profit, because he was paid for executing the order left in his book. From 1910 to 1922, out of concern for such possible shenanigans, the NYSE forbade specialists to be the counterparty on trades executing orders in the book. But this if anything stimulated what was at the time a common attitude about the legitimacy of brokers scratching each other's backs, and it also meant that orders at price limits in the book could easily be passed without execution as the market plunged or soared through them. Today, of course, with the book a less significant factor, these concerns are reduced.

An obvious problem with specialists from the beginning was that they were undercapitalized. To give depth to a market, a specialist presumably would have to be able to hold in inventory something not far off a day's trading in the security, long or short. If he can do it without knocking down the price ahead of time, consistent with his obligation never to sell except on an up-tick, a specialist who comes into a very down day short does the community of the Exchange as well as himself a favor, because he will be able to absorb that much more of the stock offered him. Similarly, if the price is going to go sharply up, a market maker is in much better shape to serve the market (as well as himself) if he comes in with a large supply of stock.

In general, NYSE specialists do not take a view of where a stock is going over time. They are in business not to maximize the value of their inventory but to maximize the turnover of their capital. Some of them do not read the annual reports of the companies whose shares they trade, though there are also a few who send associates out to do the sort of visiting that upstairs securities analysts do. They will of course want to know as fast as possible any piece of news that will influence the bidding and offering for their stocks, but the inside information that counts for them, day by day, is what order flow is backed up behind the crowd at the post. The ability of both specialist and broker to do their jobs right often depends on the degree of trust between them.

A $2 broker, for example, may have an order to sell more than 100,000 shares of, say, Ford, which its owner has decided to feed onto the floor for execution in pieces rather than giving it to a big firm to be gobbled as a block. The broker is not obliged to tell the specialist he has an order of this size, and if he doesn't do so, the specialist may take more into his own inventory than he would if he knew there was that much more to come. On the other hand, a broker arriving at the post to "cross" a large block that has been bought and sold upstairs may have completed the transaction in his office, or may have wound up positioning some part of the block, long or short, in his own inventory in order to close the deal. If he has had to take a position, he will as soon as possible on whatever strategy he can find put that position into the market, which forms a ceiling on the near-term price (if the broker is long and must sell) or a floor (if he's short and must buy). Whether or not the specialist will get that information depends on his other relations with this broker, and how badly they need each other.

At the same time, the broker who comes to the post with a "clean cross" (all the shares he has to sell from one customer matched with a buy order from another) can find the specialist insisting that "reasonably anticipated needs of the market require him" to take some part of the deal for his own position. The regional exchanges in Chicago, San Francisco, and Philadelphia live to some extent on the business the brokers execute there rather than in New York because they are not on good terms with the specialist in New York. The Stock Exchange is still a club, in other words, despite the presence of 300–400 brokers who rent seats, because in a lot of ways it really is a club—even if the leaders of the club don't think so. People get blackballed, in effect, every day.

This club, however, takes in $10 billion a year in commission revenues and supports the employment of perhaps a quarter of a million people around the country in more than six thousand offices. And it has astonishing survival capacity. John Brooks in 1973 quoted Donald Regan, then head of Merrill Lynch, as asking, "When all the electronic gear is in place, will we still need a New York Stock Exchange? Probably not in its present form?"—and Brooks suggested that his might be "one of the last books to be written about 'Wall Street' in its own time." Two years later, casting a gimlet eye on the likely result of computerization and the change from fixed to negotiated commissions, Chris Welles wrote a book called *The Last Days of the Club.* But it's very much still there, larger than life, and in the aftermath of the 1987 crash, when its antiquated procedures performed better than much that was more up-to-date, arguably stronger than ever.

2

Cities have functions, even more in their folklore than in reality. London and Peking administered empires; Pittsburgh and Birmingham made steel; Paris and Rio de Janeiro and Havana made whoopee; and New York priced things. Not just financial instruments—all sorts of things. Literature and musical talent and art. Coffee and sugar, from quite early on. Cotton, after the Civil War.

Transportation, after the 1890s, when J. P. Morgan decided to "rationalize" the nation's railroads. Ideas. To the extent that "the truth" for Americans was determined by what Justice Oliver Wendell Holmes called "the power of the thought to get itself accepted in the competition of the market," that market was located in New York. For intellectual New Yorkers, the 1970s was a miserable decade not so much because the city went bankrupt as because they saw the locus of decision making moving from the place where the world was priced to Washington, D.C., where they printed the money. The 1980s remedied some of that, and the progressive weakening of the government returned authority to the market.

When people say "the market," what they are likely to mean is the Dow-Jones average, which is the price of thirty of the most heavily capitalized industrial (non-transportation, non-utility, non-financial) companies traded on the New York Stock Exchange. This is a nineteenth-century construct of Clarence Dow, a scholarly journalist of great energy and confidence (told when he applied for a job at the Providence *Journal* that they didn't have anything for him to do, he said that was all right, he knew what news was, he'd find things to do, and for five years he was the paper's star reporter). When he started Dow, Jones & Co. on Wall Street in 1882, the stock auction at the four-story New York Stock Exchange Building was like the gold fixing in London, a twice-a-day call through the listed stocks. The prices from those two calls were transmitted electrically through a telegraphic printing ticker perfected by the then-unknown Thomas A. Edison, and the news Dow and Jones uncovered and distributed was written by a strong hand with a well-pointed copper stylus through twenty-four sheets of carbon paper onto twenty-four flimsies, which were then hand-delivered around the Street. In May 1884, the company acquired its first printing press; in July, Dow took his first crack at creating a representative list of stocks that could be priced and averaged (no weighting were assigned) and followed as a market proxy. The *Wall Street Journal* itself, so called, came five years later.

There were eleven stocks in the Dow average at first, then twenty and then thirty, because customers were complaining that the list was too narrow. All were, of course, traded in New York. In 1896, Dow broke out a separate industrial list. Those who think one can put stocks in a drawer for one's grandchildren might be interested in it: American Cotton Oil, American Sugar, American Tobacco, Chicago Gas, Distilling & Cattle Feeding, General Electric, Laclede Gas, National Lead, North American, Tennessee Coal & Iron, U.S. Leather (preferred), and U.S. Rubber. It is perhaps worth noting that Dow was one of few people to write about the New York Stock Exchange who had hands-on experience as a member, though it appears he joined as a favor to his son-in-law's brother, an Englishman who could not be a member himself until he was naturalized an American citizen. The Japanese had lots of precedent in excluding foreigners from a stock exchange.

Even when the official market consisted of two calls a day, brokers had continued trading between and after them, much as the gold market does now. As J. P. Morgan and his friends refinanced American industry, they usually kept the senior debt for themselves and leaked out to a credulous public the watered stock that had little if any value at the time of its issuance. Publicized and acclaimed, the markets boomed, the auction became continuous at the New York Stock Exchange, and individual brokers became specialists in different stocks. Within the membership, any number could play; most stocks had multiple specialists who might or might not collude with each other on the prices they offered. The market mixed honest auction pricing with rampant manipulation, some of it casual conspiracy on the floor by "pools," some of it more purposive rigging arranged to serve the "distributions" arranged by the Morgan interests, the Rockefeller interests, and their allies.

Thomas Lawson organized a $35 million profit for the Rockefellers in the creation of Amalgamated Copper (with zero risk to the sponsors, who indeed never put in a penny of cash themselves). Later he wrote a best-seller called *Frenzied Finance* in which he described how he was mobbed as he entered the dining room of the old Hotel Waldorf. Not only the guests and diners but the waiters and room clerks and bellboys wanted his advice on how to buy Amalgamated. "I lost sight of the terrible seriousness of it," he wrote, "and I chuckled as one does when one sits on the cool grass under the apple trees and watches myriads of ants hunting and jostling and bumping over each other to get away with what to humans is but a tiny grain of dirt." The book gave to the language what would become an important term: "the system," which Lawson was the first to use to describe what Stewart Holbrook called "roguery and corruption by large financial and industrial interests."

Government first intervened to supervise what went on in this place only after the crash of 1907, when J. P. Morgan single-handedly kept the action on the floor from bankrupting the country, playing the role the Federal Reserve would play eighty years later. The next year, Theodore Roosevelt in his penultimate State of the Union message demanded federal regulation of stock exchanges to stop speculation, and in New York, Governor Charles Evans Hughes sent forth to investigate the practices of the Exchange a committee chaired by Horace White, an old-time journalist who fifty years earlier had reported the Lincoln-Douglas debates for the Chicago *Tribune.* Like the SEC Division of Markets looking at the interplay of index futures and stock trading nearly eighty years later, the committee reported back that it was "unable to see how the State could distinguish by law between proper and improver transactions, since the forms and the mechanisms used are identical." But it did recommend the establishment of a minimum 20 percent margin to slow down the practice of pyramiding, by which speculators used their paper profits to buy more stock: With margin at 10 percent, a 10 percent rise in price allowed the plunger to double his holdings with no additional investment. It urged the Exchange to enforce its rules against prearranged "wash" trades brokers could use to give an appearance of prices moving up or down. And it suggested an end to the practice of opening branches "luxuriously furnished and sometimes equipped with lunch rooms, cards and liquor . . . [which served] to increase the lure of the ticker by the temptation of creature comforts." Read 'em and weep.

The assassination of Archduke Franz Ferdinand in Serbia on June 28, 1914, provoked an accelerating flow of sell orders from holders of American equities in Europe, moving their assets from paper to gold. When the czar mobilized Russian forces on July 30, all the markets of Europe closed, and the next morning before the opening of the New York Stock Exchange, despite an original intention to soldier on, Morgan and his allies decided they could not contain the flood. There simply wasn't enough gold in New York to buy the paper from Europe. Stocks would not trade again at the Exchange until mid-December, by which time some of the overhang had been worked off (at much reduced prices) in the informal "gutter market" that formed in the streets of downtown New York. The organized Curb Exchange, now the American Stock Exchange in its own building on the other side of Trinity Church graveyard from the top of Wall Street, then traded on Broad Street itself, and was closed with the New York Stock Exchange (thus the "gutter market," which was in the gutter rather than on the curb).

Waves of demand from the European combatants and then from a mobilizing America drove all prices higher, eventually including stock prices, and activity rose to the point where in 1917 the Stock Exchange suffered its first paper crunch. "The larger wire houses presented the appearance of gambling hells in the morning," Robert L. Smiley wrote in *The Magazine of Wall Street*, "just before the cards and chips had been swept away by the attendants. Very few brokerage firms had any conception of just how they 'stood.' " Then in 1918 the Liberty Loans to finance the war vastly expanded the network of salesmen for investment paper and the fraction of Americans whose assets included such paper, building the preconditions for the giant boom in the securities markets in the 1920s.

This was still to a considerable degree a rigged market. "Manipulation of some sort," wrote Edwin Lefevre in 1923, recounting the exploits of an alleged Larry Livingston whom all the world knew to be the plunger Jesse Lauriston Livermore (to whom the book was dedicated), "enters into practically all advances in individual stocks. . . . Such advances are engineered by insiders with one object in view and one only and that is to sell at the best profit possible. However, the average broker's customer believes himself to be a business man from Missouri if he insists upon being told why a certain stock goes up. Naturally, the manipulators 'explain' the advance in a way calculated to facilitate distribution." It will be noted that in a market where specialists ran the posts and participated in a high fraction of the trades, these pools could operate only with the knowledge and consent of the specialist, who was, indeed, almost always a player in them.

But the rigging was easy: People were optimistic, and major new products like the radio and the automobile were in fact generating huge industrial investments in a Schumpeterian, innovation-driven upward thrust of the business cycle. What did them in, as always—it is, of course, the most frequently observed parallel between 1929 and 1987—was the acclerating greed not only of the participants but of the outsiders increasingly sucked into the vortex. As the cycle aged and the market should have topped, stock prices rose still higher. Frederick Lewis Allen in his book *Only Yesterday*, published in 1931, gave a most modern explanation of what had levitated the market—a decision by the Federal Reserve in 1927 to expand the money supply. He printed a table showing price changes between March 3, 1928, and September 3, 1929: Anaconda from 54-½ to 162, General Electric from 128-¾ to 396-¼, RCA from 94-½ to 505, Union Carbide from 145 to 413-⅝. Of course it blew up.

Twice during the decade of the 1920s, the Stock Exchange would close on a day when the rest of the country was working. The first such was September 16, 1920, when a bomb went off in a horse-drawn wagon at the corner of Wall and Broad streets. "It killed thirty people outright and injured hundreds," Allen wrote eleven years later, "wrecked the interior of the Morgan offices, smashed windows for blocks around, and drove an iron slug through the window of the Bankers' Club on the thirty-fourth floor of the Equitable Building." William H. Remick, president of the Stock Exchange, was at the call-money post in the corner when the immense noise and shock struck, and the broken glass dribbled down through the heavy silk curtains. "I guess it's time to ring the gong," he said, and went to the rostrum and closed trading for the day. The market had been rising; when it reopened the next morning, it was still rising. The second time the NYSE closed was on Thursday, October 31, 1929, two days after the worst drop the market had ever known (until October 19, 1987). Prices had turned up on Wednesday, October 30, and at 1:40 in the afternoon, vice-president Richard Whitney, Morgan's man on the floor, later to be president of the Exchange and convicted of stealing from the Exchange's own employees' Gratuity Fund, announced that the Exchange would not open until noon the next day, and would be closed both Friday and Saturday; and people cheered.

The Exchange was then quite literally a private club (it was not incorporated until 1971), and all its member firms were partnerships with no obligation to report results to anyone. The Securities and Exchange Act of 1934 made this private club, in effect, an agency of the government, which was not easy for either side. Under the new law, the Exchange was required to impose on trading within its walls whatever regulations the Securities and Exchange Commission might dictate. It was a long time before anyone on Wall Street really believed that. In his history of the Exchange Robert Sobel reports without vouching for it a story that when SEC chairman William Douglas traveled to New York to meet with Stock Exchange leaders, in fall 1937, he told them, "The job of regulation's got to be done. It isn't being done now, and, damn it, you're going to do it or we are." The lawyer for the board commented that the Exchange had 150 years' experience running this thing as a private operation, and that Douglas, upon taking it over, might find "some things you will like to ask us." Douglas thought there was one thing: "Where do you keep the paper and pencils?" It was in part to demonstrate that he was not bluffing about his willingness to exercise the SEC's powers that Douglas in early 1938 imposed upon the exchange the up-tick rule, the requirement that short sales (which Douglas somewhat naively would have liked to prohibit entirely) can be made only if the most recent previous sale at another price was at a lower price.

Not until William McChesney Martin, Jr., became president in 1938 at the age of thirty-one did the Exchange have a salaried executive (though Martin, later to be chairman of the Federal Reserve Board, had been a member, too, a floor broker for A. G. Edwards of St. Louis). Martin saw the Exchange through its slough of despond, after the arrival of war in Europe failed to generate the burst of volume the World War I experience would have predicted. Sobel paraphrases an article by a broker who had been around since 1907, which appeared in *The Exchange* in April 1940: "Business remained uncertain, there was a lack of prospects for substantial profits, although taxes were sure to go up, and the war news remained unclear. The New Deal regulations and rules prevented chicanery and manipulation, and this was to the good, but at the same time they necessarily decreased interest in stocks and bonds."

Under these circumstances, Martin sought to eliminate competition to the Exchange, real or potential. There were small exchanges around the country in most major cities, trading the securities of local companies, but also trying to build themselves as markets for the stock of major corporations already traded in New York. Martin, to the outrage of the SEC, promulgated a rule prohibiting member firms from doing business in listed securities anywhere but on the floor of the NYSE. After a full proceeding complete with hearings, the SEC announced its support for competing markets on the regional exchanges, warning prophetically that in their absence such trading would not remain on the New York floor but drift off to the over-the-counter market. Martin, who could be stubborn, neither consented nor appealed, but stopped attempting to enforce his rule.

In 1941, Martin was drafted into the army, served for a while as a sergeant, and wound up a colonel. (Thirty years later, having retired from the Federal Reserve Board, he would return to chair a committee that brought back very conservative recommendations on what should be done to preserve the auction market in the age of the computer.) His successor in 1941 found life no easier: The percentage of the total number of shares listed on the Exchange that traded during a year reached its historic low in 1942 at 9 percent. In 1986, the ratio was over 64 percent.

In fact, however, from the early days of the war, the Europeans had been selling, though not quite as they had sold a quarter of a century earlier. This was an era of total war, and one of the first things the allied governments had done was demand that citizens make their foreign assets available to the state. It was the British and French governments, not private parties, that were selling the accumulated foreign investments of their populations to pay for the sinews of war. They did not believe that the New York Stock Exchange could fairly price their holdings in an auction market. In 1915 the Europeans had sold into a declining market, which bowed down before the weight of their sales even though economic conditions in the United States were improving, thanks largely to sell orders from the combatants who were dissipating their patrimony. This time around, they expected to get some benefit from the prosperity their purchases were creating. They went to the leading brokers and investment bankers and asked them to find purchasers off the floor. And despite Martin's never-revoked rule, the brokers went around to the insurance companies and mutual savings banks and the handful of pension funds to make particular sales away from the market.

Prior to the Great Depression, the membership had been mice properly deferential to the great bankers, who provided liquidity. Now the commercial bankers were gone, chased away from the securities business by the Glass-Steagall Act, and the investment bankers were busy selling utility bonds to insurance companies. The political fights within the Exchange in the 1930s had been over how hard to struggle against government regulation, and those had been lost with the disgrace of Richard Whitney, who had once called the Stock Exchange a "perfect institution."

The majority of members were traders for their own account, specialists, and odd-lot dealers. This last category, now vanished, included more than two hundred members, affiliated with one of two firms that worked all the posts, who lived by buying and selling at slightly higher commission rates public orders involving less than a "round lot" of 100 shares. (Odd lots accounted for more than 13 percent of the volume in 1940, as against less than 1 percent today. In 1976, with the installation of the electronic order system, specialists began handling odd-lot purchase and sales in their stocks, and the former odd-lot dealers became part of specialist firms or $2 brokers.) Unlike the old guard, who had been bankers, the floor members had to make their living from the Stock Exchange. In 1940, trading had dropped to 207 million shares (less than the trading on scores of *days* in 1987, with almost as many mouths to feed on the floor as there are today). And now the floor members were told that their fellows with upstairs brokerage offices planned to use those offices to distribute to big purchasers blocks totaling millions, perhaps tens of millions, of listed shares.

The floor contingent mobilized, and for the next generation it was their representatives who controlled the board and the administration of the stock exchange. In the Harry Truman age of accelerating democratization, the New York Stock Exchange was more a private club than ever. The floor members did not, however, control what happened in the outside world. With help from the Clayton Anti-Trust Act and the SEC, against the complaints of the floor membership, the brokers with orders from the British and French sold their big bundles of stocks off the floor, over the counter. A pattern was set for the postwar development of the Exchange.

Minimum commissions would continue to be fixed by the Exchange at so much per 100 shares, and orders for more than 100 shares would pay the appropriate multiple of that commission—ten times as much for a 1,000-share order, a hundred times as much for a 10,000-share order. The Exchange would seek to cultivate the small customer, whose business it could handle. Individual specialists merged into larger specialist firms to give them the capital they would need to handle larger orders. Very large blocks of stock, still uncommon, could be brought to the floor as part of a "special" offered for sale at a fixed price, and separate from the auction market; members might earn extra commissions from the seller by placing pieces of such blocks.

In the 1950s, the Exchange set its face against the growing mutual fund movement, which recruited small investors who wanted professional management of their money and the safety of diversification. Instead, its president G. Keith Funston promoted a Thatcherite people's capitalism, a "Monthly Investment Plan" by which brokers would sell individuals shares of stock in the nation's largest corporations much as the government had sold them savings bonds, by regular deductions from payroll. Even at the sales loads common in the 1950s—8.5 percent of the retail price, which means 9.3 percent of the money actually invested, was not uncommon—mutual funds looked to most householders like a better bet. Mutual funds, corporate pension funds, and accounts administered by bank trust departments were by far the most rapidly growing categories of savings in the 1950s. In 1945, mutual funds had less than $1 billion in assets; by 1965, they had more than $35 billion. The Stock Exchange was well behind the power curve.

In fact, the membership was of two minds about the threat from mutual funds. Such funds traded more often than individual shareholders did—indeed, some of them were virtually churned to generate large commissions, in a few cases for brokerage houses associated with the funds. (This came to be prohibited by law.) The fixed commission based on 100 shares provided bonanzas when mutual funds traded thousands of shares, and the funds were often willing to allocate this business to brokers according to how many shares of the fund they sold. (This also came to be prohibited by law.) Banks allocated orders to brokers according to the deposits the brokerage firms left in checking accounts that paid no interest.

As the public grew more sophisticated and mutual funds began to advertise their investment performance, their managers began to seek out ways to avoid unnecessarily large commission payments. Block business began to be done over the counter by dealers working on small margins, often on a basis where they were "riskless principals"—that is, they pre-sold the blocks they bought. A dealer could charge both buyer and seller less than a commission system that might impose costs of more than $5,000 to move a $500,000 block (both sides, remember, paid commission). As dealers cultivated their contacts with the mutual funds and pension funds, they became willing to undertake such transactions even when they were at risk— when they had to "position" some of the block themselves, and sell it off later, taking the risk that the price would move against them. Especially when conducted by well-capitalized investment banking firms like First Boston, Blyth, and Morgan Stanley that were not members of the stock exchange and not bound by its commission rules, this "Third Market" might well deliver not just a cheaper but a better product than the New York Stock Exchange.

For almost twenty years, the Exchange under the leadership of its floor members fought back. In 1955, while blocks were still very uncommon, the board passed Rule 394, prohibiting member firms from dealing with nonmembers, as principal or agent, in the purchase or sale of listed securities. The SEC could have imposed the result of the multiple-trading case of 1941 to assure the access of over-the-counter dealers to this business, but it didn't. In 1962, arguing that this alternative market was contrary to the public interest and survived only because it poached information from the ticker tape and quote machines operated from New York, the Stock Exchange removed the private wires that connected two Dallas houses to New York member firms and to the ticker system. They sued, and in 1962, in *Silver v. New York Stock Exchange,* they won in the Supreme Court, at least on their case (the principle was left murky). And, of course, the regional exchanges had always been protected. Blocks sold (sometimes positioned) by member firms became their most important source of profits. "When I first came here in 1971," says Arnold Staloff of the Philadelphia Stock Exchange, "this place existed mostly on gimmicks: We found ways for institutions to avoid the fixed commission rates in New York."

The Exchange hung on to fixed commissions and kept most though by no means all the business, in large part because a handful of member firms led by Salomon Brothers became aggressive bidders for blocks. Salomon especially used its commission revenues as a cushion against losses on positions to bid better prices than the over-the-counter dealers would risk. Then, in 1965, the bank stock dealer Morris Schapiro, who had for years made a market in the stock of Chase Manhattan with member firms of the New York Stock Exchange among his customers, sued the Exchange to prohibit it from ordering its members to stop dealing with him after the stock was listed on the big board. Lyndon Johnson was president, and had appointed Manuel Cohen, a Brooklyn lawyer, as chairman of the SEC. Cohen's wife, John Brooks reported, "characterized her husband's job by saying, 'If I were doing it, it would be called nagging.'" Cohen leaned on the Exchange, and Rule 394 went the way of William McChesney Martin's anathema against the regionals.

But what really did in the Exchange's effort to fence off a monopoly in large blocks at fixed commissions was the sheer, visible scandal of it. Fund managers and brokers alike had grown fat on what came to be called "soft dollars." Floor brokers would be directed to split their commissions with others, research could be bought (and anything could be qualified as research), sales commissions could be boosted, and extravagant and exotic luxuries could be arranged for those who controlled business. Bernie Cornfeld's I.O.S., which had very successfully sold outside the United States a "Fund of Funds" incorporating a number of established U.S. mutual funds, began its own "proprietary funds," allegedly to give its investors access to the hottest money managers in the United States, but actually to direct the tens of millions of dollars in commissions its orders generated.

Meanwhile, the Exchange had failed to organize itself to handle the quantity of business generated by the bull market of 1967–1968. Volume rose above ten million shares a day on a floor barely geared to accommodate six million. As many as 25 percent of the orders on a busy day produced "fails" at the clearinghouse five days later, and the banks fell weeks behind on the manual transferring of stock certificates from one ownership to another. A firm as eminent as Lehman Brothers was threatened with the loss of its license to do business because of its inability to locate customer securities left with it for safekeeping and to segregate its customers' cash. The Stock Exchange and its members began a crash program of computerization, which did not work (first efforts in that direction, of course, rarely do). And the market turned down, in what would be, from 1968 to 1970, the worst drop (more than one-third) since 1929–1931. As always happens in a bear market, volume shrank. A number of what had been the hot stocks of the 1960s dropped precipitously, and some turned out to have been crooked. There were scandals in the unpublicized issuance of "letter stock," shares that had not been registered with the SEC and could not be sold to the public but could be carried as assets by the brokerage houses and mutual funds that bought them. Major brokerage houses began to lose money.

In early 1970, the bells began to toll for the bankrupt. McDonnell & Co., a brokerage house closely associated with the Henry Ford family; Hayden, Stone, with 90,000 public customers (rescued, after much panic, by the little house of Cogan, Berlind, Weill & Levitt that would grow into Shearson Lehman); Goodbody & Co., fifth largest house on Wall Street, with 225,000 customers (absorbed, at a price paid by others in the brokerage community, by Merrill Lynch); Francis I. DuPont, rescued by H. Ross Perot, making his debut on the national scene. Congress in December 1970 set up a Securities

Investors Protective Corporation that would insure moderately rich investors (up to $500,000) against losses from the bankruptcy of the brokerage houses that held their securities. A study of institutional investors was launched. And Robert W. Haack, president of the New York Stock Exchange, without clearing his speech with any of his board, called for a rationalization of business on the floor, including an end to the protective tariff of fixed commissions.

Richard Nixon's SEC had received a public mandate from him to ease off on the Stock Exchange, and initially had encouraged an increase in commission rates to make up for the declining profitability of the institution. But 1970 was too dramatic an experience. Under the leadership of William J. Casey, later of the CIA, the SEC rather to everyone's surprise began to pressure the Exchange. By 1971, institutional trading accounted for 28 percent of the volume and 42 percent of the value of all trading on the Exchange, and over-the-counter dealers were making increasing inroads. Don Regan of Merrill Lynch urged his colleagues to face up to the ease with which an automated over-the-counter market could do what Exchange members did on the floor. The Exchange bowed partway, and negotiated with the SEC an arrangement whereby commissions would be negotiated after April 1971 on block sales of $500,000 or more; after 1973, on sales of $200,000 or more; and after May 1, 1975, on all trades. For four years, the Exchange wriggled, hiring its old president Bill Martin to write a report recommending continuation of its basic rules, seeking to win legislation from Congress that would prevent the arrival of May Day.

Fully negotiated commissions arrived in a bad year, when stock prices were lower than they had been since 1966, and volume was down from the early 1970s. And the worst fears of some of the brokers were quickly realized: Competing against each other for institutional business, they drove commissions to one-third and even one-quarter of what they had been. But the business did indeed return from the over-the-counter market to the member firms, and SEC approval of Rule 390, which required members to bring their blocks to the floor to be crossed at the specialist's post (and printed on the tape—there was a high order of public interest here), kept the floor members involved. (Not everyone approves: William Brodsky, president of the Chicago Mercantile Exchange, whose father worked on the New York Stock Exchange floor for J. W. Seligman and would have worked there himself except that "I was automated out of a job," says scornfully that "without Rule 390 the specialist would be an odd-lot dealer, and the whole market would be better off.")

As the market turned around, so did volume. A better grade of computers, more knowledgeably programmed, moved the share transfer system out of the signed-certificate age and into book entry, kept track of the trading for all the brokers, and performed 98 percent of the settlements at the touch of a button. Commission revenues bottomed in 1977 at about 10 percent less than their previous high. And from 1977 to 1987, they quadrupled. Total volume passed five billion shares a year for the first time in 1976; by summer 1987, volume was running at a rate of more than forty billion shares a year, half of it from big institutions trading in blocks of more than 10,000 shares, and everyone was making a bundle.

But this was a Faustian bargain: The Exchange had sold its soul. Prior to 1975, the struggle had been to keep the institutional business in a framework built to serve (sometimes to swindle, but usually to serve) individual investors. Prices did reflect the hopes and fears—and, yes, the information—of literally millions of people, who like Isaiah Berlin's fox knew many things. Needs, desires, ambition, greed, brains, luck, force, vanity, deviousness, money, contacts, credit, fantasy, analysis—all met in the marketplace, all influenced the prices of investments. Now the world of the stock market is full of hedgehogs who all know the same thing, which is basically what the other hedgehogs are doing.

"We were brought up," says the French broker J. de Berteigny, a dignified man in middle age looking over the roofs of Paris, "with the idea that the stock market anticipates what will happen in the economy. That's still true here, but it's not true any more in the United States." Fred Alger, who ran money as a gunslinger in the 1960s and as a computer wonk in the 1980s (though he still fondles a slide rule as he talks), says, "This business has gone from one guy reading tea leaves to systems and analysis. You can have much more confidence now in doing what you're doing." But if the result of all the curve fitting in the computer is that one triumphs at predicting what one's fellow money managers will do, the markets become efficient as agents of perversion. Volatility is the least of it. The Stock Exchange has accommodated itself to the vagaries of the lumpy market, but the economy that is supposed to benefit by the efficiency of market-based decisions has not been performing well.

In 1972, Richard Nixon's friend Bunny Lasker, chairman of the

Exchange, having lived through the drought years, said, "I can feel it coming, S.E.C. or not, a whole new round of disastrous speculation, with all the familiar stages in order—blue-chip boom, then a fad for secondary issues, then an over-the-counter play, then another garbage market in new issues, and finally the inevitable crash. I don't know when it will come, but I can feel it coming, and damn it, I don't know what to do about it." We could have used that kind of conservative attitude fifteen years later.

3

One further function in New York must be noted: the creation of instruments related to corporate money raising. Though the simple-minded junk bond promoted by Drexel Burnham—high risk, high rate—was essentially a California operation, and much of the trading in the more elaborate schemes was done in London, the locus of invention was New York. Salomon Brothers was especially fruitful under the leadership of Robert Scully, a brisk man in his late thirties who pioneered the idea of "segmenting value. We sit around all day, concocting ideas that give value for our customers and advantages to the buyers, and make money for ourselves," he said in 1986. He was happy at Salomon then, but eighteen months later, after his investment banking department had willy-nilly participated in the losses of the traders on and after Black Monday, he would be among the self-severed limbs leaving the firm.

Some of these ideas concocted on Wall Street became generally known. Salomon's STRIPS, for example, were divisions of U.S. Treasury bonds into a coupon instrument that yielded steady income (some of which was a return on your capital, for at the end you would get nothing back) and a zero-coupon bond that paid no interest at all until it was cashed in, some years later, for its face value, which was a multiple of the price you originally paid. For people with tax-free IRA accounts, who could accumulate without interference from the IRS, the zero-coupon bond with its exact statement of what you would have in ten years was just what the doctor ordered. For Japanese insurance companies and others who wanted income streams, the severed coupons were ideal. A bond that might have sold for 101-½ when whole could easily sell in its pieces for, say, 102, with overnight investment of capital—in a wholly safe instrument—

by the underwriter. The same sort of thing could be done, at higher risk and higher reward, for private issuers.

Then there were collections of warrants that could be attached to bonds. Salomon invented "harmless warrants," which allowed the purchaser of a bond to get more of the same in five years if the rates were then attractive; if not exercised on that date, the warrants expired. It was a minor gamble for the issuer, in that he could be compelled at some future time to sell more bonds at an interest rate higher than the then-prevailing market. But the potential benefit to the purchaser was such that he was willing to accept a slightly smaller rate here and now. A variant of this approach gave the buyer a dated warrant at a price, with a guaranteed cash refund if on the day the warrant could be exercised the price was unattractive.

There were currency swaps of all dimensions (these were conducted mostly in London), by which a company with a better credit standing in Japan than in the United States could sell bonds in yen and swap the proceeds into dollars, or a company with a desire to pay floating interest rates could swap a fixed-coupon obligation for a floating-rate loan. There were "Heaven & Hell" warrants, which required the issuer to pay more in one unlikely set of circumstances or allowed him to pay less in another equally unlikely set of circumstances. On March 18, 1986, for example, Salomon sold an issue of yen bonds for the Kingdom of Denmark, with the yen at about 170 to the dollar. Denmark would have to pay back more yen in 1991 if the yen were weaker than 263.55 to the dollar, and would be permitted to pay back fewer yen if the yen were stronger than 90.01 to the dollar. Similar bonds were issued for American Express, IBM Credit, the Republic of Austria, the Province of Saskatchewan, and a U.S. Federal Home Loan Bank . . .

Everyone got into this act. "Today," Scully said in 1986, "a company raising money calls in a bunch of bankers from around the world and runs a beauty contest. We compete with ideas. Companies like IBM and GM are besieged with people from all over the world with ideas on how to raise money. The half-life of a new idea in this business is about half a heartbeat. A few years ago, Shearson Lehman originated the capped Floating Rate Note [a note with varying rates that cannot go above a certain limit]. They did five billion dollars in the first month, even though we developed our own variant of it the afternoon we heard about it."

Merrill Lynch, looking toward public customers, developed a menagerie, TIGERS (like the Salomon STRIPS), and an original called LYONS, for "Low Yield Option Notes." This was the creation of Lee Cole, older than Scully, no sharp edges, round-faced and cheerful, who had come to Merrill from Bank of Boston, where he was an options specialist. "Lots of clients need income plus security of capital," Cole says. "There were two camps on Wall Street—traders who knew about options but knew nothing about corporate finance, and investment bankers who knew bonds and stocks and maybe convertible bonds, but not options. Merrill now has twenty-five billion dollars in Cash Management Accounts, and needs product for these people. Our strategy was to tell people to put their money in a safe place. What we wanted was an instrument with little principal risk that pays a little interest and offers a possible gain." A LYON is a zero-coupon bond that on expiration offers the purchaser either what are now below-market interest rates, or stock in the company at a price fixed the day the bond is issued. If the company's stock does well, the bondholder activates the option and makes a stockmarket profit; if the company's stock does poorly, he cashes the bond and takes the lower interest rate. Like any zero-coupon bond, this instrument works best for IRA accounts, but Cole reports that he can sell any Lyons that a well-regarded company wants to issue.

None of these instruments is meaningful unless it can be bought and sold subsequent to its original issue, and all the houses that invent such paper also make a market in them—ideally, with other houses. Such secondary markets for junk bonds have been a major activity for Drexel Burnham. The problem for the firms has been that the apparent expansion of the market for paper with segmented values at the moment of its issuance can turn into a severe contraction for half the issue. The best advertised example came in the area of "collateralized mortgage obligations," bonds like Ginnie Macs backed by pass-through payments from householders.

Salomon and Merrill both offered immense quantities of this paper, in the tens of billions of dollars, some of it segmented into instruments of "interest only" (IO, like bond coupons) and "principal only" (PO, like zero-coupon bonds). Valuation here was extremely complicated, because when interest rates turn down people prepay their mortgages, channeling more money more quickly to the owners of the PO strip and reducing the payments to the IO strip;

when interest rates turn up, the market price of the PO segment will turn down not only because all bond prices drop on rising interest rates but also because the normal expectation of prepayment on the mortgages is diminished. The risk, in other words, is a multiple of what it would be on either instrument alone. Merrill Lynch forgot about this in spring 1987, and took an advertised licking of more than $350 million.

In short, it turned out that there was no Holy Grail. No doubt the efficient-market theorists greatly exaggerated how accurately markets find prices at any given moment, but over time reward does indeed track risk. And every generation, apparently, must learn the lesson anew.

11

Technology and Illusion

"It might have been supposed that competition between expert profession- als, possessing judgment and knowledge beyond that of the average private investor, would correct the vagaries of the individual left to himself. It happens, however, that the energies and skill of the professional investor and speculator are mainly occupied otherwise. For most of these persons are, in fact, largely concerned, not with making superior long-term forecasts of the probable yield of an investment over its whole life, but with foreseeing changes in the conventional basis of valuation a short time ahead of the general public. They are concerned, not with what an investment is really worth to a man who buys it 'for keeps,' but with what the market will value it at, under the influence of mass psychology, three months to a year hence."

—John Maynard Keynes, 1935

1

*I*n 1968, the National Advisory Commission on Civil Disord- ers, chaired by Governor Otto Kerner of Illinois (who was soon to go to jail for his piece of the profits on a racetrack scam in that state), reported back to President Lyndon Johnson on the riots that had torn the country and dominated the television screens the previous summer. "White racism," the Report concluded in a sentence written by a Rumanian immigrant with an academic's knowledge of the United States, "is essentially responsible for the explosive mixture which has been accumulating in our cities since the end of World War II." With that sentence went some of the hope for major improvement in the condition of our urban centers and for the reduction of racial disparities in the United States. There was unquestionably white racism in the country, and it impeded all serious efforts to set the feet of the black population on the path they wished to follow, but other harms and hindrances were more "responsible" and other harms and hindrances were more susceptible to remedy. By concentrating public and official attention on a slogan, the Kerner Report wasted one of what were never going to be many opportunities to move a step here, a step there toward widely sought goals.

All presidential commissions and panels—I have sat on two—are subject to this sort of distortion. Kentucky Fried Chicken can run on a KISS system (Keep It Simple, Stupid) because its leaders are resolving tactical rather than strategic problems. When the question is Tolstoy's "What to do?" intelligent answers require a tolerance of ambiguity and a willingness to confront the complexities of life. Unfortunately, measured responses and lengthy wrestles with reality are not what the president or the Congress or the press wants. The result usually is that the good stuff gets put in the back of the book, while up front the creative fellows looking to drum up support for changes they wish to make in, say, the public schools put something smashing like "rising tide of mediocrity" that is sure to catch the attention of the producers on the nightly news. The Presidential Task Force on Market Mechanisms, otherwise known as the Brady Commission, after its chairman Nicholas Brady of Dillon, Read, fell victim to this tendency. "From an economic viewpoint," its "Executive Summary" proclaims, "what have been traditionally seen as separate markets—the markets for stocks, stock index futures, and stock options—are in fact one market. . . . To a large extent, the problems of mid-October can be traced to the failure of these market segments to act as one."

The case is much stronger for the opposite conclusion, that these three are quite separate markets with different products merchandised in different ways and purchased for different purposes, with different settlement and clearance systems and different reasons for being. The problems of mid-October can be traced to the computer wizardry that permitted people to pretend that apples were oranges, that these separate markets were really one. It was because technology allowed participants to behave as though there were a single articulated market which offered them a choice of stalls at which to do the same business that the vacuum formed under prices in an unprecedented way. The Brady Report is an admirable piece of work, full of fascinating information, much of which was not previously available, and written with vigor and grace, a great credit to its authors and the commissioners. It benefits also from the good fortune that the president put on the panel two consumers of the products (Howard Stein of Dreyfus Fund and Roger Kirby of Guardian Capital) who knew how these things ought to work and would not be persuaded that a 508-point drop in one day—a 750-point drop in three days—was the way the ball ought to bounce.

As noted earlier, and as demonstrated in the hundred days after Black Monday, the market was more rationally priced at the end of that terrifying week than it had been at the beginning. And it is also true that nearly all the world's stock markets dropped in the fourth quarter of 1987 by roughly similar percentages. (Losses looked smaller abroad to an American investor because the dollar dropped by something more than 10 percent in the quarter, boosting the dollar value of foreign securities.) The damage done by the participants' faith that three markets were one was less in the 508-point one-day loss than in the 800-point rise spread over the first eight months of the year. Misinterpretation of the relations among the cash, futures, and options markets had produced an institutional euphoria before it produced the institutional panic of October 14–19.

The difficulty of running an auction market for very large bidders has been apparent since the 1960s, when changed investment philosophies at pension funds, bank trust departments, insurance companies, and philanthropic foundations led to substantial increases in the proportion of pooled savings invested in equity. Pension plans and insurance companies especially have actuarially derived obligations, to be met from the earnings of the funds. The assumptions as to those earnings over time determine how much money a corporation must take from its profits and sink into the pension funds, how much premium the insurance company must charge for a given policy.

In the sustained boom of the 1960s, as interest rates rose, conservative advisers who urged the funds to maintain their traditional 3 percent or lower estimates on earnings were easily pushed into the shadows by a generation—a book I wrote on them in the late 1960s, with pictures by Cornell Capa, called them a "New Breed on Wall Street"—who promised 8 percent, 10 percent, 20 percent; and sometimes, usually briefly, delivered. (One notes in passing with some amusement that several brokerage houses recommended companies as good buys at the top of the 1987 boom because their profits were going to be increased by reductions in the payments they made to a pension plan that had become "overfunded" because of the rise in the market value of their investments; in the world of financial analysis, the fact that the dog is chasing its tail does not alter judgments derived from the speed with which the dog is running.)

But the market turned down in 1969, and then, quite seriously, in 1974. From the rubble of disappointed hopes arose the phoenix of portfolio theory, "beta" measurements that claimed to give fund managers formulas that maximized return for a given risk, or minimized risk for a given return. Such measurements helped analysts for fund managers make the "asset allocation decision" that was the mystery at the heart of their work. Looking over the decades, the professionals had decided that it was safe to have substantially more money in stocks than their fathers would have approved—and the courts agreed, redefining the practical injunctions that limited the permissible actions of fiduciaries and "prudent men." Assuming for simplicity only two possible kinds of investment, in bonds and stocks, the question would be rational expectations of "total return"—interest, dividends, rise or fall in the price of the paper from the day you bought till the day you sold (or cashed in). Rising bond markets, by reducing interest rates, created enthusiasm for stocks; falling stock markets, by increasing dividend yields, might draw new institutional investors; falling bond markets, by raising interest rates, led institutional investors to commit more to bonds; and rising stock markets, by reducing dividend yields, led fund managers to question whether they wished to keep money in "fully priced" stocks. In theory the system was self-equilibrating.

Asset allocation moved with deliberate speed, and altered the degree rather than the kind of investment. By and large, the fluctuation varied from 60/40 to 40/60. But the sums of money were immense. If all institutions at once went from 40 percent in stocks to 60 percent in stocks, the demand even in the 1970s would have been for 8 percent of the market capitalization of the shares listed on the New York Stock Exchange, and today the total would be at least 15 percent. It is not too drastic a simplification to say that the bull markets and bear markets in stocks from the mid-1960s to the early 1980s reflected the gradual building or unwinding of equity positions by the great institutions. It happened, necessarily, fairly slowly. Even after the New York Stock Exchange permitted negotiated commissions, buying and selling large quantities of stock was an expensive and unwieldy business. The traders who worked for the fund managers had to proceed slowly and delicately to make sure that they didn't sabotage the profitability of the strategy by moving prices too far, too fast.

Meanwhile, the United States government sabotaged the actuarial base of contract savings by running its own affairs in ways that created immense swings in interest rates and (a phenomenon that would become increasingly related to interest rates as the nation's net asset position beyond its borders decayed) in the exchange value of the dollar. From the point of view of fund managers (and now the bag of managers expands to include people who run banks and thrift institutions as well as investors of contract savings), these interest-rate swings swept the prices of the Treasury paper in the portfolios down (if interest rates rose) or up (if interest rates fell). Even where the liabilities to be met from the funds are remote, rapid changes in the valuation of what should be the stable assets are disconcerting. Into this confusion, this demand by the markets that well-established theories be stretched to cover radical novelty, there came in 1977 Rich Sandor's T-bond futures contract and the chance to lock in a price and a yield on the portfolio of long-term Treasury bonds.

Moreover, to digress briefly, the T-bond futures contract was a benefit to all, because it created an instrument the investment world needed on a day-to-day basis, quite apart from the governmental fecklessness that created it. Prior to the creation of the futures market at the Chicago Board of Trade, different U.S. Treasury bonds might sell at rather different yields. Every piece of paper, after all, is worth what the market will pay for it. The actuaries who scheduled the obligations of the funds therefore also determined the bond maturities these funds would buy. Thus there was an essentially random distribution of demand, stronger for some "series," where the market would be robust, and weaker for other "series," where the market would be thin. And there were scores of different series, because the Treasury auctions off new bonds every quarter.

Both public and private purposes were served by the creation of a uniform proxy for the bond market, an artificial construct that represented the universe of T-bonds with more than fifteen years before their expiration. The arbitrage between this construct and the cash market for bonds was also, significantly, an arbitrage among the different issues. The seller of a T-bond futures contract could make money by remaining on the lookout for underpriced bonds that could be delivered in satisfaction of the contract. In the lingo of the trade, he "played the basis" (a basis point being 1/100th of a percentage point). By doing so he established much greater uniformity among the debt issues of the United States, and considerably increased their liquidity. The triumph of the market came in 1982, when the Treasury had planned an auction on Christmas Eve, and the Board of Trade decided to close on Christmas Eve. The Treasury postponed the auction. God bless us every one.

By the same token, heavy trading in the cash market kept the T-bond futures market from attempting to create too many synthetic bonds. In all commodity markets, one of the worries has always been that contracts as an abstraction from the physical commodity can be created ad lib by traders. As each contract holder can insist on delivery when the contract expires, a serious imbalance between the contents of the warehouse and the paper in the market can bankrupt honest men and disrupt production and consumption out in the real world. Most futures markets therefore put limits on the number of contracts any participant or group of participants can hold, and developed systems for alerting the markets and changing the rules near the date when the contracts expire (that is, permitting purchases only for purposes of liquidating short positions) if a serious imbalance develops between the deliveries that can be demanded by contract holders and the actual supplies of the commodity traded. It was the failure of the Hunts to understand this necessary self-protective reflex in futures markets that first drove silver prices above $50 an ounce and then drove the Hunt interests to various bankruptcy courts.

As a normal matter, prices in the futures market and prices in the cash market for real commodities are not tightly linked. As the contracts expire, of course, there is a "convergence," but with ninety or sixty or even thirty days to go the fact that what is in the cash market is there for consumption and must be sold and must be bought this week (even for storables it's a nuisance to move it back to storage) may mean more than the long-term reasoning that drives the futures prices. And the futures price, of course, can briefly spike because of rumors or fashions that have no economic logic at all, simply because buying and selling on a futures basis is something participants don't *have* to do today.

Economic logic says that a futures contract will sell for the cash price less the cost of carry. But in the agricultural commodities sellers create new product that need not be carried, and may not be willing to take a futures price reduced by the cost of carry if they expect the cash market to sustain current prices. The relationship between cash and futures prices is a function of the season of the year, and whether farmers will be making deliveries between the creation and the expiration of the contract.

A futures price well above the cash price will not necessarily tempt people to buy a commodity and store it. With perishables like pork bellies and feeder cattle it may not even be possible to buy and store, and with storables like wheat and corn players may find all sorts of reasons why putting some silos aside to be emptied ninety days hence will be inconvenient. And if you wish to unwind the transaction later and sell the commodity back to the cash market, there may be costs of finding a buyer, reinspecting the merchandise, trucking it from here to there, etc. (As a matter of trading technique, there seem to be big differences between futures contracts on perishables and futures contracts on storables. Observers have noted with amusement that the Chicago Merc has never succeeded with a storables contract and the Board of Trade has never succeeded with a perishables contract.) It is probably significant that even when all the paper involved is in the futures markets, when it's March wheat against June wheat, people do not talk about arbitraging contracts, which implies real equality of prices: They talk about "spreading" them, holding the differences within traditional dimensions.

Most of the time, divergences between the price of wheat reflected in a futures contract for 40,000 bushels and the price of wheat at the silo by the railroad track are resolved in time in the direction of the futures price. Futures markets are in truth an efficient and inexpensive way to "discover" what prices are going to be. Farmers get mad and declare themselves cheated when these markets predict lower prices; governments get mad when they predict inflation; speculators get mad when a market they think they understand swings back and forth and whipsaws them. Aberrations occur. But the information in the futures price is greater in scope and quantity (if less certain) than the information in today's price in the cash market for consumption. The economic value both producers and consumers find in locking up a price for something they will need to sell or purchase at a known time in the future means that society as distinct from ideologues or politicians normally does not begrudge the players in these markets the costs they add to the normal processes of getting and spending.

2

When the stock index futures began trading in 1982, institutional investors looked to see whether these contracts might offer managers of equity funds advantages comparable to those the managers of bond funds had gained from the T-bond contracts. There were, obviously, major differences. The stock index futures contracts contemplated cash settlement rather than possible delivery of an underlying commodity. On the day the contract expired, the price would be that of the index in the stock market that day. The buyer of a futures contract who had paid more than that price for the basket of stocks would pony up cash, and the seller who had sold for more would collect; the buyer of a futures contract who had paid less than the final day's price for the stocks in the index would win, and the seller who had sold for less would lose. There was no deliverable commodity against which the futures contract could be arbitraged.

Nevertheless, the fund managers could use stock index futures as the millers used the wheat contracts. An asset allocation decision to put a higher proportion of a fund into equities could be implemented initially with the purchase of an index contract, in effect guaranteeing the fund manager (as the wheat contract guarantees the miller) that he can purchase what he knows he will want at today's price rather than at the prices that may prevail some weeks or months away. Conversely, a fund seeking to reduce its equity exposure could sell a futures contract, then slowly "unwind" its holdings in the individual stocks over the succeeding months, selling on strength to gain the maximum price and moving the money into the now preferred Treasury bond or Treasury bill holdings. As in the agricultural markets, the price of the future might diverge from the theoretically "correct" current cash price (after calculating costs of carry), but as long as the medium-term movements of the futures contract and the index of stock prices went in the same direction at a more or less similar pace, which was pretty much guaranteed by the fact of ultimate convergence, hedgers could do their business in stock index futures as they did in wheat even when the futures market and the cash market did not track each other very closely.

There was, after all, no economic reason for the price of the futures contract and the price of the cash index to maintain a narrow parity. Unlike the T-bond arbitrage, trading the index futures against the underlying stocks serves no useful purpose. Because different bonds (like different grades of wheat) can be delivered against the T-bond contract, the arbitrage between futures and cash tends to equalize what should be equivalent yields among different pieces of paper issued by the same unimpeachable creditor. But the entire stock index has to be delivered against the S&P contract, and the ratio of value among the stocks in the index is predetermined by the proprietors of the index rather than by the market. Indeed, the fact that arbitrage activity could not influence the relative prices of the different stocks in the package was a central argument for permitting the stock index futures contract to settle with payments by losers and collections by winners rather than with actual delivery of the "commodity."

The existence of a hedging strategy for equities played back into the asset allocation formulas of the great institutions. Because the value of the stock portfolio could be hedged, and hedged quickly, it was no longer necessary to sweat over decisions that involved switching considerable chunks of money from one kind of investment to another over a period of time. Considerably larger stockholdings would be safe, because index futures contracts could be sold against those holdings (or index put options could be purchased) as soon as the market started to drop. This was an untested proposition, because both index futures and options on indices did not begin to trade until 1982, and did not achieve any substantial volume until after the market had begun its exponential rise of 300 percent in five years. But it came with excellent academic credentials, and fund managers wanted to believe it, so they did.

Institutional decisions to change their asset allocations had been, as noted, a central factor in determining when the stock market topped off and bottomed out. In 1987, that brake was disconnected from the vehicle. When stocks became what would once have been called "fully priced" in early 1987, and the gap opened between rising interest payments on bonds and shrinking dividend payments on stocks, many of the institutions that would once have begun moving a fraction of their riches from stocks to bonds instead relied on what their advisers called "portfolio insurance," a computer-generated program that would purchase hedges whenever the value of the equity holdings seemed in danger. "Dumbest idea ever accepted by any substantial part of mankind," says Howard Stein of Dreyfus Fund, a member of the Brady Commission. "How could anybody believe everybody could sell at the same time?"

Meanwhile, the options market also imparted an upward bias to stock movements, because of the asymmetry in options strategies for professionals dictated by the up-tick rule at the stock exchanges. The writing of naked calls—calls on stocks the seller of the call did not own—was a fairly safe way to go short for an insider, and odds-on profitable. Assume shares at 53, the call at 55, the premium at $300, and no commissions to pay. If the writer's judgment is wrong and the stock begins to rise, he can buy it in the market to cover the call at any price short of 58 and still show a profit on the premium; the worst that can happen to him is that he winds up owning a stock he doesn't much like if his initial judgment was right and the price now turns around. Thus the existence of an options exchange shifts potential short selling on the floor by professionals out to the options market, while retaining on the floor the potential for buying by professionals to cover what are in effect short positions.

Naked puts were much more risky for traders. A call could be covered in the market at any time by purchasing the stock on which the call had been written. Writers of puts were obliged to purchase at the contract price, and could hedge that obligation only by selling short. But the rules of the Securities and Exchange Commission and the Stock Exchange prohibited short sales except on an "up-tick," when the most recent sale at a different price had been at a lower price. As October 19 demonstrated, there could be days when such a thing happened so rarely even an insider might be trapped. Professionals frequently sold naked calls, adding to effective demand for stocks, while professionals rarely sold naked puts. The balance from the options market reinforced the bullish tilt from the change in institutional allocation strategies.

As noted in Chapter 4, the application for the S&P 500 futures contract submitted to the Commodity Futures Trading Commission in 1981 by the Chicago Merc—and the testimony of its officers before Congressman John Dingell in 1982—clearly indicated a belief that because of the complexity of putting together the 500-stock package and the cost of buying or selling small pieces of so many stocks, nobody would be able to arbitrage the futures contract against the cash market. Trading in the S&P futures, like trading in soybean futures, would tend to "discover" the prices some weeks or months ahead, but on a day-by-day basis the linkage between the futures price and the cash price would be no stronger than it was with agricultural commodities. There was no danger that the tail would wag the dog.

Even on those terms, there was something troublesome about a contract that allowed major customers to buy "the market" rather than individual stocks. It was one thing to offer the public "mutual funds" that permitted individuals to diversify their holdings far more broadly than ordinary people ordinarily could. Mutual funds bragged about their judgment as stock pickers. It was something else to deliver an inexpensive, prepackaged, no-brain shortcut to an institution that was investing the insurance premiums or retirement funds of thousands and thousands of employees. What made stock markets important in an economy, after all, was their transmission of investors' judgments as to which industries and which companies were most likely to thrive and thus should find it easiest to raise fresh money. For professionals to invest huge pools without exercising that sort of judgment subverted some part of the legitimacy of market capitalism.

Indeed, this is the ultimate argument against regarding the futures exchanges and the stock exchanges as "one market." *The Economist* wrote in a bumptious leader early in 1988, "If futures markets, soundly played, come to dominate share markets, so be it. That fate overtook the business of pork bellies long ago." But all pork bellies are more or less the same (or can be made identical by expert grading). Stocks are different one from the other in ways that make some of them at each point in time considerably better investments than others. Random-walk theories, like monetarist theories, were deeply misleading as a guide to the real world, and for the same reasons—because they substituted curve fitting for analysis. But for the very real-world reason that their fund managers were unable to "beat the market" with any consistency, institutions accepted the theory, and decided to buy "the market" rather than particular stocks. Funds that by mid-1987 had more than $160 billion under management were set up as "passively managed," investing only in the stocks that made up one of the major indices (usually the Standard & Poors 500), in proportion to their representation in the index. For this community, unfortunately, the futures contract was a close substitute for what they would otherwise buy in the cash market.

Then, as noted in Chapter 4, the mathematicians found a way to arbitrage the S&P 500 index futures contract against the stocks in the real market, and the New York Stock Exchange contributed the DOT system that enabled brokers to enter orders for however many stocks they thought they needed, simultaneously, with the push of a button. And now, if they are willing to look at what they are doing, all the participants are brought face-to-face with several significant differences between "index arbitrage" of the S&P stocks and "spreading" between futures contracts and cash purchases in agricultural commodities. First, we have no warehouse. In a cash settlement system it doesn't matter how many shares of stock exist; there can be as many contracts as anyone wishes to buy and hold. Second, there is no physical cost of carry, just some interest to pay or dividends foregone. Once the balance sheet of the arbitrage shows black numbers, there is no reason ever not to push the buttons and pocket the pennies. Third, the only transaction cost is a couple of pennies a share for stock, a couple of dollars per contract for futures, and a small fee to the Depository Transfer Corporation; in stocks, by contrast to agricultural commodities and even T-bond futures (for the basis relationship between different issues of Treasuries changes constantly), unwinding the arbitrage is as easy as putting it on in the first place.

For several participants, index arbitrage is a bonanza. It enables the managers of index funds to promise their patrons results that slightly improve upon the total return on the index as measured by the indexer. It permits the trading department of the broker/dealer to generate virtually certain revenues for the firm's own accounts. And it encourages the brokerage house that carries out such programs for others to generate commission revenue for itself and friends in New York by pushing the S&P pit in Chicago just a little further in the direction it wants to go anyway. In a more sinister possibility, the existence of futures and options contracts closely linked to the cash market permits the brokerage house to take any known large orders from large institutions for stocks that are significant in the indices and buy contracts or options or stock in a different market ahead of the customer's order, with near-certainty that prices will move in ways that assure the broker a profit on his own trades.

But all these are pathologies, not normal development. These instruments—stocks, futures contracts, even options—were designed for a time when people rode bicycles and only birds flew. They are pretty much the same instruments they were before, though much ingenuity has been invested in making them more salable. Trades that create the derivative instruments and trades that transfer ownership of the shares settle the same way only to the extent that all computer blips move in the same manner. The instruments are undoubtedly substitutes for each other at the margin, perhaps as much as polyester and wool, or gypsum wallboard and lathe-and-plaster, or television and opera. They should be priced in ways that reveal rather than conceal their differences, and in an institutionally well-ordered economy they would be. They look so much alike only because computers have eliminated the transaction costs that always kept them separate. But it is precisely in those areas where the hand is quicker than the eye that government regulates not to keep order but to prevent deception.

Leaving aside the question of whether back-and-forth transactions in derivative instruments and stocks helped drive the market too high and then pushed it down too quickly—though I think the evidence is overwhelming that they did—the present blurring of institutional distinctions leaves the investing public to watch intraday swings that frequently run 3 percent, which represent nothing more or less than the leveraging between markets of what would be trivial movements in any one of them. Individuals buy and sell at a moment in time, and every day a significant number of them find that they bought at the top of what was a meaningless intra-day price movement, or sold at the bottom. At recent yield ratios, the difference in the price the individual pays or receives because he purchased or sold at one hour rather than another may be greater than a year's dividend from the stock. Customers who have such experiences will go away; by the millions in the months after Black Monday, they did go away. Unfortunately, this goose has functions even more important than laying golden eggs for brokers. The risk premium people will demand if they are to invest their savings in productive enterprise will rise if they see the market becoming a casino.

Because the instruments really are different and the markets that trade them are different, there are indeed easy ways to prevent the sort of promiscuous trading back and forth that has created the present dilemma. We shall look at them in Chapter 12.

In January 1988, Shearson Lehman Hutton announced that it would stop doing index arbitrage for its own account, but would continue to offer the service to institutional customers. This momentous step was then advertised at immense expense during several breaks in the Super Bowl telecast, as Shearson's contribution to the reduction of volatility in the markets. One observer told the *Wall Street Journal* that this wasn't particularly meaningful, because Shearson had never been a real player; its profits from index arbitrage probably hadn't exceeded $3 million or $4 million a year. Bagatelle (truly—the advertising cost more than last year's profits). One commentator said he hoped Shearson's action wouldn't lead people to believe there was anything wrong with index arbitrage. The treasurer of the Rockefeller Foundation said with the arrogance of his kind that he welcomed Shearson's decision: "If other folks drop out for some reason or another, it may increase our opportunities." But the real question raised by Shearson's action was rather different. By its nature, index arbitrage must be done quickly, and brokers who do it for clients must have discretionary authority over the accounts. Member firms of the New York Stock Exchange have committed themselves never to permit orders for their own account to take precedence over orders for customers. If there is money to be made in index arbitrage, and the firm offers the service to customers, how can it conduct such activities for its own account?

One moves a step further. John Forsyth at Morgan, Grenfell observes that the money spent to gather information proves people don't really believe in random walks. Yet the pension and endowment fund managers on the average show results less good than the results of investing in an index. And the comparison has deteriorated with the passage of the years: Advisers do worse than they used to. Indeed, even real index funds tend to do less well than the index itself, which is why we get little bits of corruption in the market like "guaranteeing the close." And an inquiry for the Department of Labor by the firm of Berkowitz, Logue & Associates indicates that mutual funds, which have to sell on the basis of their results to people with whom they don't have lunch, do better than the funds where the owners are playing with other people's pensions. "Of course," says Howard Stein of Dreyfus Fund, "we have our own traders, who police what's done for us in the market."

One inquires further. Markets equilibrate. Who is making the money the investment funds seem to be losing? Where are the plus items that balance the minuses? Well, the income the big broker/dealers show on their own proprietary trading activities is way up in the 1980s. The New York Stock Exchange's *Fact Book 1987* shows "trading and investment" as the source for 27.4 percent of all the revenues of member firms (as against only 20.9 percent for commissions). Before 1982 there had never been a year when "trading and investment" revenues had exceeded commission revenues for the membership of the exchange. Correlations and causes? Maybe. The *Wall Street Journal* report on Shearson's action noted that "the in-house proprietary trading department of one Wall Street firm reportedly made $40 million during the week of the Oct. 19 stock market crash."

John Shad, a tall, dyspeptic gentleman rather slow of speech, came from E. F. Hutton in 1981 to be chairman of the Securities and Exchange Commission. One cannot help noting that he left behind him, though there is no reason to believe he was conscious of the specifics, the attitudinal climate that produced the check-kiting scheme for which Hutton would soon pay fines in the millions of dollars. In one of his earliest speeches as chairman of the SEC, Shad said the real problem in the markets was that prices were too low and investment houses were too unprofitable. He thought these deficiencies were impeding capital formation in the United States.

Among Shad's first actions to remedy this condition was a change in the SEC rules governing capital requirements for brokerage houses. Pre-Shad, brokerage houses needed capital of 4 percent against their net credits from customers (a rather peculiar proxy for total activity, endorsed by Congress in 1975 as an alternative to the old-fashioned system of requiring a ratio of capital to assets to guarantee that some fraction of the money a financial firm invested was its own). The purpose of capital adequacy rules, the SEC had told Congress early in its administration of them, in 1936, was to prevent a broker's "excessive trading for his own account." In 1982, despite what then seemed the most perilous economic environment since the depression (it was, in fact, the trough of a recession, but nobody knew that for sure), Shad's SEC reduced brokers' capital requirements to 2 percent, encouraging broker/dealers to trade more actively for their own accounts and hold larger positions.

The new SEC attitude that what counted was not the protection of the public but the profitability of the great brokers culminated in the no-action letter of December 17, 1986, that in effect exempted Merrill Lynch (and by extension, the other brokers who traded for their own account) from the up-tick rule that would otherwise have prevented them from completing index arbitrage operations by selling short into a declining market. Asked why on earth this had been done, Blair Corkran of the agency said, "The rule was impeding the efficiency of their index arbitrage." In reducing impediments to Merrill's profitability, at whatever potential cost, Corkran considered that he was carrying out the policies of Ronald Reagan's SEC. Maybe he was right.

Among the other restraints on broker/dealers that prevented them from large-scale trading for their own account in listed securities was a set of SEC rules governing the relations between brokerage houses and fund managements. In the days of fixed commissions, this relationship was admittedly dark and dirty. President Robert S. Haack of the New York Stock Exchange said in a speech in 1970 that "the securities industry, more than any other industry in America, engages in mazes of blatant gimmickry. . . . Deals are frequently involved, complicated and bizarre." After the move to negotiated commissions, per-share commissions on big institutional accounts dropped by two-thirds—but turnover in these funds tripled, so that the net commission income of the brokerage houses changed relatively little. And as the years passed commission income was increasingly supplemented by trading profits on block transactions where the house both took commission and made a trading profit.

In 1975, Congress specifically permitted institutions to pay more than minimum commissions to brokers who supplied research services as well as execution of orders, and told the SEC to police what these "soft dollars" were actually spent for. The *Wall Street Journal* in 1984 found one brokerage house using them for a "European Investment Seminar" for money managers in Paris, Madrid, and Milan, and another giving a group of money managers a trip to the Winter Olympics for meetings. This was troublesome to Shad's SEC, which relieved itself of the troubles in 1986 by announcing that it would no longer monitor the uses of soft dollars—these fellows were big boys, after all, and could take care of themselves.

Under Shad's leadership, the SEC also abandoned its computerized Market Oversight Surveillance System (MOSS), arguing budgetary limitations, so that even if the SEC had wished to police the behavior of brokers it lacked the most important tool it would need when doing so. But the Department of Labor was then in the hands of Secretary William Brock, whose people took seriously their duty under the Employee Retirement Income Security Act (ERISA) to verify the proper use of pension funds. Within a month of the SEC abdication, the Labor Department's Pension and Welfare Benefits Administration had ruled that fiduciaries were obliged "to assure that the [fund] manager has secured best execution of the plan's brokerage transactions and to assure that the commissions paid on such transactions are reasonable, in relation to the value of the brokerage and research services provided to the plan."

The Labor Department's intervention has generated a great body of research material, most of it gathered for worried pension-fund sponsors. The SEC has refused so far to look at this material, and the New York Stock Exchange has refused to release to the researchers one of the most important elements of the data in its computer memory—the identities of the firms on the other side of the trades brokers have executed on behalf of pension funds. The evidence is that some funds with some brokers pay higher commissions and get poorer executions than others. The suspicion is that the brokers involved with these funds may be scratching each other's backs, but in the absence of cooperation from the New York Stock Exchange, which the SEC and congressional committees could command but don't, the case can't be made.

In effect, necessarily, the big brokers who handle the institutional accounts deal with them as both principals and agents. The conflict of interest inherent in a single firm acting as both broker and dealer has been studied repeatedly over the years, including by me in 1975 in a report to the Twentieth Century Fund published as part of the Fund's compendious *Abuse on Wall Street: Conflicts of Interest in the Securities Markets.* But what worried us all in the past was the limited range of situations where the broker was also an underwriter (conflicted by his duty to get the highest price for the issuer and the lowest price for the customer), or a distributor of a secondary offering, a large block of existing stock sold as an underwriting (who made a considerably greater commission from such sales than on ordinary transactions, and not infrequently paid customers' men a bonus for peddling these goods rather than listed stocks), or an over-the-counter dealer (who might be recommending the stock to a customer for the purpose of unloading something undesirable from the firm's own inventory), or a block positioner (who set a price for the block that assured him a profit on the resale, and then charged his client a commission on top of his profit).

The *Institutional Investor Study Report* of the SEC in 1971 noted, "A potential conflict of interest exists when a block trade assembler places its discretionary accounts on the passive side of the block trades. [This] . . . allows the block trade assembler to avoid a very risky and often unprofitable activity, while at the same time increasing its commissions." I noted in 1975 a Wall Street partner who had commented that in these block transactions, which printed on the tape at whatever price the parties wished because they could choose whether or not to show a commission, "even the printed price doesn't mean anything, because you never know what the side deal is." And this business has expanded beyond all recognition. In 1975, there were on average only 136 trades a day that ran 10,000 shares or more; in 1986, there were 2,631.

Stanley Abel points out that most of these sales in block form were quite unnecessary, that the bulk of the trading by institutions is in stocks for which the market is so extensive and so active that 50,000 shares and more can be bought or sold without special arrangements, during a single day, quietly, in the crowd before the specialist's post. There is no need for the institutional investor to give a broker the potential advantages of dealing in block form. But now nobody worries about the ethical implications of putting clients in contexts where the house gets the biggest profit. Those of us who did the conflict-of-interest studies for Twentieth Century Fund were fairly cynical about the 1970s, but in our wildest dreams we could not have imagined that a brokerage house with fiduciary responsibilities to its customers would trade for its own account against them or ahead of them (which amounts to the same thing) in listed securities—or in options and futures that were proxies for listed securities.

An investment adviser who has institutional clients remembers that he had a fund manager in his office on Black Monday, and the man grew increasingly nervous as the day wore on. Finally, he decided he had to get some part of his fund out, too, and he put in a call to his broker, Goldman Sachs, in Philadelphia. The customer's man said to him, "Everything's backed up. There's one hundred fifty-two orders ahead of yours—you're number one-fifty-three."

The fund manager turned to his adviser and said ruefully, "You think if a Goldman trader puts in an order for the house account, that'll be number one-fifty-four?"

Making the situation even worse is the fact that between the moment the New York market closes at 4 P.M. and the moment it reopens at 9:30 A.M. even member firms are not obliged to report to anyone their transactions in listed stocks. *American Banker* estimates $900 million a day of unreported trading in foreign equities in London, in addition to roughly the same amount for which at least the prices now print on the *Financial Times* ticker reporting "bargains" at the International Stock Exchange. And there are firms like Jefferies in Los Angeles, not a member of any exchange, which does several million shares a day in block trades, some unquestionably for fellow brokers, and lays it off, perhaps with brokers who do business with Jefferies elsewhere after hours, through a securities house Jefferies controls that is a member of the New York Stock Exchange. "You don't make money today in markets," says John Forsyth of Morgan, Grenfell in London. "You make money *between* markets."

The part of this iceberg that shows has been "insider trading." When the firm regarded information about their customers' plans as a trust and would never have maintained trading positions beyond their needs as dealers with the thought of profiting by their customers' activity, then the people who worked for those firms had a standard of behavior to which they could repair when tempted—or be judged when seduced. Once the firms themselves are playing against their clients, then of course their employees will do the same to them. The defense when it comes boils down to a complaint that the institutions have squeezed the brokerage houses so hard on commissions that the only way they can make a living is by getting their own back in trading, but it's hard to see how once you buy this argument you can tell the stewards on Carl Icahn's TWA not to rip off the headphones kitty, or the underpaid cop not to deal a little cocaine on the side. Nor are the investment bankers without blame: Hans-Joerg Rudloff of Credit Suisse–First Boston in his Zurich speech in February 1988 made scornful reference to bankers who "sold hybrid securities to the public at premiums of 12 and 14 per cent, hiding their profits behind the sophisticated structure of their instruments."

Gene Rotberg at Merrill Lynch, who ran part of the SEC *Special Study* in the early 1960s and moved on to be the man who raised all the money for the World Bank, believes that the great houses have been hoist on the petard of their own publicity. "We try to act as if we are the market," he says, "but we aren't; we are the middlemen. We have great salesmen, we have great research, but we don't have wealth. We don't want to invest our capital; we want to turn it over." Martin Kaplan, a large man with a long head and big gestures, runs all Merrill's equity trading—for its own account and for customers. "This firm," he says, "has spent a lot of time building up its integrity. We have a compliance guy right on our trading floor. If one of our traders runs ahead of a customer's order, he gets fired. The money you make is never worth the publicity you suffer. If I think something is trading right, I may lean over my desk and say, 'Hey, Eddie—buy me twenty-five thousand XYZ.' But then a customer comes in, he thinks it's trading right, too; I cancel all my orders. The rule on the floor is, The customer gets priority."

Actually *cancel?*

Well, no. Just that the guys on the stock exchange floor, the same guys, are now notified that they're not buying for Merrill any more, they're buying for the customer. And if the price has gone up since the purchases made for the house account? Well, everything is time-stamped. But four days after Shearson Lehman had announced it would no longer perform index arbitrage for its own benefit, Merrill followed suit. Perhaps the no-action letter approving short sales without an up-tick and written for Merrill's benefit can now be sent to the dead-letter office.

There is no intention here to be critical of Merrill. This is the way the game plays, now. Charlie Merrill probably wouldn't have thought much of it, but he's long gone. His brokerage house is no longer a private partnership; it's a listed company. Like all such, it lives off its 10-Qs, the quarterly filings of income, expenses, and profits that heavily influence the price at which Merrill's widely traded stock sells in the market. One now has obligations to stockholders that seem at least on a par with those to customers. Irving Pollack while an SEC commissioner recalled an old-timer of the 1920s who said, "The brokerage business was built on the idea that the captain of the ship got off last." But the stockholders are widows and orphans: can't leave them on the bridge. Corporations, as I had occasion to observe in a book published in 1955, are soulless; when you cut them, they don't bleed, though sometimes—listen carefully—they will scream. The term "corporate fiduciary" is perilously close to an oxymoron—like "trust department" in a bank with target levels of profitability for each division.

"When the history of the financial era that has just drawn to a close comes to be written," Supreme Court Justice Harlan Fiske Stone wrote in 1934, "most of its mistakes and its major faults will be ascribed to the failure to observe the fiduciary principle, the precept as old as Holy Writ, that 'a man cannot serve two masters.' " It is by no means impossible that a similar comment will be made of the 1980s.

The Brady Report calls for review by "the appropriate authorities" of four items the commission could not explore. One of them is "Customer vs. Proprietary Trading . . . [when] broker-dealers and futures market makers can act as principal for their own account as well as execute customer orders." Another is "NYSE order imbalances . . . [ways to favor] public customers in execution over institutional and other proprietary orders through the DOT system."

Reporters cannot make such studies on their own resources. All they can do is testify that when speaking off the record the great majority of people in a position to know consider that proprietary trading by the broker/dealers in the 1980s has been a serious scandal and a serious contributor to the malaise of the securities markets. It's a pity that for reasons that have nothing to do with the merits of these Brady recommendations, neither the SEC nor the Congress seems likely to pursue them.

Until the next crash.

12

Fixing It Before It Breaks More

"All nations with a capitalist mode of production are seized periodically by a feverish attempt to make money without the mediation of the process of production."

—Karl Marx, 1861

1

The purpose of the marketplace is to create an all but automatic guidance for the allocation of scarce resources, human and physical. All markets when they work properly do that, from the fish market to the foreign-exchange market. High prices bring fresh investment, new people, new ideas. Low prices discourage producers and lead people to shift their efforts elsewhere. The benefits from correct allocation are sufficient to justify big rewards for the laborers in this vineyard. If the valuation systems go blooey, however—if the price of financial instruments comes to signify something other than prospective earnings, if the Common Agricultural Policy of the Common Market sets the price of wheat so high that German farmers plant it on hillsides never cultivated before, if the Japanese reward the accumulation of land by taxing everything else—the markets will do harm by sending resources where they will not be well employed.

In the sixties the American markets fed conglomerators; in the seventies they fattened the kleptocrats of the third world and the banks that floated on liquidity they had made themselves by exploiting the unregulated Euromarkets; in the eighties they gilded the takeover artists and junk-bond promoters who exploited a dishonest tax code and the near erasure of the line between money and credit. When markets generate such self-centered results, the rewards fall brainlessly on the just and the unjust, and it scarcely matters who gets them because they are in any event unearned.

Because markets are so important, especially to economists, there is a tendency to think that they have an independent existence. We say—I have just said—that markets do things, and of course it's only people who can do things: We remain in control of our machines. But our machines supply us with perceptions, and to the extent that these perceptions are different from reality we make bad decisions, especially in markets. It is a peculiarity of our universities that while the sociologists are telling us that news is a construct, and there is no real world out there against which reports may be tested, our economists insist that the market is "efficient," and the prices that come out of it embody all the information about the real world available at this moment in time.

To say the market is "efficient," however, is to make a statement in the realm of philosophy rather than that of economics. What is meant by "the efficient market" is nothing more nor less than Leibniz's famous postulate that this is the best of all possible worlds. And financial markets for sure are not the best of all possible worlds. Someone is always trying to beat them. The tax code makes unproductive investments seem profitable, inflation disguises value, any price is okay so long as the buyer believes there is somewhere a greater fool who will pay more. When all else fails, we can call upon creative accounting to conceal, for example, as the big banks did in 1987, the fact that the Internal Revenue Service makes us pay taxes on the income we say we have erased by increasing our loan loss reserve. Henry Hill, formerly of Price Waterhouse, editor of the *Journal of Accounting, Auditing and Finance,* points out that the change from "true" to "fair" in the accountant's certificate was something the New York Stock Exchange promoted, in 1933, when it first required listed companies to include auditors' statements in their annual reports to stockholders.

Why does the company look to be worth more dead than alive? Because we depreciated the physical assets a lot faster than their real depreciation. Why did we do that? Because every dollar shifted from profits to depreciation saved us 42¢ in taxes. Doesn't that in effect mean that we have to pay more taxes next year than we would have had to pay if we had depreciated the physical assets on a schedule reflecting their real loss of value? Yes, and that's why the stock sells at a lower multiple of earnings. Also, what with inflation bumping up the replacement costs, anyone who buys the company can write up the value of these assets on *his* books through "purchase accounting" and use them as a backing for the bonds he sells to pay him back for what he paid for the company. *Cui bono?* Get away from me, boy, you bother me: That's capitalism.

People who build information into prices, of course, have their own reasons for doing so. For experienced people on Wall Street, it's shooting fish in a barrel. "I do not have to inform the daily press as to the value of the stock or to work the financial reviews for notices about the company's prospects," Ernest LeFevre wrote in 1923 in his persona as Larry Livingston, explaining how a professional runs up the price of something he has already bought and wants to sell for much more. "When there is activity, there is a synchronous demand for explanations; and that means, of course, that the necessary reasons—for publication—supply themselves without the slightest aid from me." Thirty years later, someone from the SEC gave me an example from his own experience: "Take Graham Paige [then a known maker of auto parts]. . . . It was a real dog, selling around two points, with three or four hundred shares traded every week. Not every day—every week. Then, one fine morning, the stock opens with a five-thousand-share block, and there's a frenzy of activity, sales back and forth.

"All over the country people are sitting in funeral parlors [then a popular phrase for the brokers' offices that were open to the public], watching the ticker on Trans Lux screens, and suddenly they see GP, GP, GP, appearing over and over again. They go over to their customer's man, and they ask him, 'What about it? Why all the activity?'

"Now, no broker can ever afford not to know the answer to a customer's question. If he doesn't know the answer, it's sure the broker across the street does. The customer's man has been noticing the tape himself, and wondering about it, and guessing. So he makes up an answer. 'I've heard that there's a rumor in New York about a merger with Ford,' he says in his most secretive voice. The public comes roaring into the market to buy Graham Paige, because it's merging with Ford. The price soars, the floor traders sell out at the top for big profits, and the price and activity in the stock slowly settle down to what they were.

"A lot of money has been made on the floor, and a lot of money has been lost by the poor dupes in the funeral parlors. And there never was any reason for it at all."

Today it's perhaps even simpler. One of the first instructions given the greedy acolyte in Oliver Stone's film *Wall Street* is to call a code signal to a reporter on a financial newspaper. Even without the Foster Winans sort of crookedness, there is a symbiosis between news and greed. Few brokers see anything improper in putting out a buy recommendation for a stock in which their firm holds a position it will be winding down at a profit. And the rumor that starts with a self-interested whisper in a commodities pit will in a matter of minutes be heard on trading floors all over the world and in brokers' offices and in people's homes through the news retrieval and cable television services.

It is this information that the efficient-market economists insist is perfectly embedded in the price. So what?

2

We move in circles that if not concentric get wider as we go. The problem that caused the most concern in early 1988—the use of program trading and index arbitrage between the futures and cash markets for securities—is the narrowest and simplest. There is no reason why the futures market has to be a more efficient price discoverer in stocks than it is in soybeans. Players do not constantly arbitrage the bean futures against the bean, mostly because of the nuisance of reselling real beans once bought and delivered. The stock market lends itself to tight arbitrage against the futures contract, so that spikes in one resonate against spikes in the other, multiplying both, because by accident technology virtually eliminated the costs of reversing transactions on the New York Stock Exchange. There are virtually no transaction costs. As noted in Chapter 11, the real question is not how to regulate the supposed "one market" that couples these very disparate instruments, but how to increase transaction costs enough to make the computers stop pretending that apples are oranges.

In my first article on this subject, in *Barron's* the first week in

December 1987, I suggested an automatic delay in registering the arrival of program trading orders. Planning their arbitrage activity, the rocket scientists at the brokerage houses and investment advisory shops calculate a "breakage" from the movement of prices between their decision to enter the orders and the execution on the floor. Increasing the time between order and execution would multiply the risk that the arbitrage would lose rather than make money. That's still a good idea, but a specialist (who would not care to be named in this connection) found a better one: Bring back the transfer tax.

New York State until the early 1970s had a 5¢ per share tax to be paid by all sellers of stock, on an exchange or over the counter. Troster, Singer, as noted in Chapter 1, moved across the Hudson to escape it. The new tax would have to be federal to make sure dealers can't escape it, and given the inflation since the early 1970s it should be 10¢. The execution of an S&P 500 arbitrage involves the purchase of 3,500 shares or so, which at 10¢ a share means on the round-trip a tax of about $700. One hears the chorus of objection: That will send American business overseas. But both Britain and Japan already have a transfer tax (the British call it a "stamp tax," as they did in the days before the American Revolution). If you applied the British tax, which is one-half of 1 percent ad valorem, the basket of stocks to be bought to serve as proxy for the index would at this writing require a round-trip payment of about $1,250.

At 10¢ a share at 1987 trading volumes, the tax would yield the federal government about $4 billion, but of course there would be less trading. Say the government would make about $2 billion. Every little bit counts. And the feeling of a close link between the futures and the cash would be little by little dissipated, discouraging institutional investors and their advisers from ducking out on their obligation to invest their money rather than "buy the market."

What we want ideally is something that resembles the relationship between the futures contract for the Nikkei-Dow index traded in Singapore and the prices of the stocks in the index as traded in Tokyo. On Wednesday, October 21, 1987, the Nikkei-Dow futures in Singapore, which had stood at about 23,000 on Monday (Tuesday the market was closed) opened just over 5,000. It then moved up rapidly to about 19,000, which was still 2,000 yen below the price in Tokyo. Commodity futures markets tend to spike, very sharply, up and down. People who play them get used to it. People who play stock markets do not have to get used to it—and won't. On balance, over time, the index futures markets and the T-bond futures markets and the currency futures markets probably will predict the price some months ahead with better accuracy than the usual Ouija boards, maybe 80 percent of the time. But people who want to use them to push around today's cash price should be discouraged in the one way that discourages them, the creation of a climate in which they are more likely than they used to be to lose their money.

In addition to these possible advantages, a transfer tax would give a certain bonus in the form of an end to the embarrassing business of "dividend recapture" that now clogs up the stock exchange systems for no economic purpose. Under Japanese accounting rules, insurance companies can show profits and pay dividends to their stockholders only from the premiums, interest, and dividends paid to them. Capital gains and losses must be sequestered in a separate fund which serves as a hidden reserve. Assume a U.S. public utility paying a 55¢ per share quarterly dividend to stockholders of record on Tuesday. The Japanese insurance company buys a million shares at $34 a share in time to collect the dividend, simultaneously selling the million shares at 33-3/8 for delivery the day the stock goes "ex-dividend." The fund that sells the stock at 34 and buys it back at 33-3/8 gets 62.5¢ less 2¢ brokerage and clearing costs, and makes 5.5¢ per share over and above the dividend, risk-free. No problem finding sellers. The Japanese insurance company pays 64.5¢ (including brokerage and clearing) for 55¢—but the 55¢ is on income where everyone can see it and say, My, what a profitable insurance company; while the 64.5¢ loss is out in cloud cuckoo land where only God and the Ministry can find it.

In early 1988, there were days when such plays accounted for something approaching one hundred million shares a day on U.S. stock exchanges. "You look on the screen," says Shearson's Herb Freidman, "and it says the market traded two hundred fifty million shares, which is absolutely misleading; really it was dull all day." At the end of March 1989, we are told, the Finance Ministry will let the insurance companies declare their trading and investment profits without tax penalty. But this is not guaranteed: The U.S. brokerage houses will be out in force trying to persuade the Japanese government that this idiocy, on which they make a few bucks a week, is really one of the sources of Japan's strength, and, wishing to be courteous, the Japanese may well consult the Treasury Department about what they should do—and then it all depends on who is

Secretary of the Treasury, and how much he believes that it is a matter of first importance for him to help the profits of American brokerage firms. A transfer tax would prevent such an embarrassment by making the operation visibly unprofitable.

3

The losses the markets suffered from program trading, financially and in reputation, were significant and will endure. But the distortions introduced by proprietary trading are more serious, because they strike at the trust between principal and agent that is central to the ethical conduct of finance.

Before dealing with conflicts of interest, one should note an old question of whether even those members of exchanges who do no business with the public—and thus have no agency obligations to place ahead of their self-interest—should be permitted to profit by their advantages in being present on the floor where public orders are exposed.

In 1945, what was then the Division of Trading and Exchange at the SEC requested the commissioners to prohibit exchange members other than specialists performing their function from trading on the floor for their own account. The fear in those days was that these guys would form pools, as they had in the 1920s, or corrupt brokers to learn what customer orders were waiting to be filled, giving them opportunities to get in on the ground floor. Their interest in the market was almost entirely in the promotion of volatility, and their purchases and sales would exaggerate short-term trends. And they tended to flock together.

But the floor traders contributed what was in the 1940s a badly needed liquidity, and they were amusing fellows (one said to me in 1952, when asked what he did for a living, "I listen for the bell that tells me the streetcar is coming, when it comes I get on, and when I feel it slowing down, I get off.") The $2 brokers performed important functions in acting for member firms that could not serve public customers if their own members had to carry every order to every post, and these fellows would have to up their charges (at additional price to the public) if they couldn't supplement what they made as $2 brokers with a little trading for their own account. Ditto for the odd-lot brokers. By agreement with the Division of Trading and Exchange, the exchanges imposed strict rules on what floor traders

257

could and could not do—and then relaxed them when the SEC turned its attention to other things. Now, of course, people who want to trade for their own account inside a market go to Chicago, anyway. Sonny Kleinfield in his book on traders tells a story about one who went off to Chicago saying, "I want to play with the man-eaters."

And, not surprisingly, the most obvious violations of ethical market behavior went with them to Chicago. For some years, the single most indefensible activity in American markets was the practice of many who stood on the top ring of the active financial pits to buy and sell for their own account. Only people who do a public business and need to see signals from the telephone clerks are permitted to plant themselves on those tiers. But anyone there, observing the orders flashed not only to himself but to everyone else who stood on that side of the pit, could also buy and sell for his own account ahead of the public order. The result was that public orders for an S&P futures contract in Chicago or a gold or silver future at New York's COMEX were rarely filled at a price more favorable to the customer than the price of the most recent trade. If the possibility of such a price arose, a member of the exchange took the money and ran. Leo Melamed urged his board in late 1986 to forbid members on the top ring to buy and sell for themselves, but for some months the reform hung fire. In April 1987, Melamed (without much help from the Commodity Futures Trading Commission, which has not taken an interest in this question) bulled through his Board a rule, prohibiting a member who executes an S&P futures order while standing on the top ring from trading such contracts for his own account later in the day.

Conflicts arising from shifting roles in the relation between broker and customer are more subtle and more difficult. When the Securities and Exchange Act was first passed in 1934, Congress left open the question of whether the markets should have to take the loss of liquidity that would result if brokers were prohibited from performing dealer functions. Could a customer get good advice from a broker who could offer him either an exchange-traded security on which the broker would make a small commission or an unlisted security on which the broker as dealer made a much larger markup? The law requested a study which the SEC delivered in 1936. By then the mainspring of reform had wound down a bit, and it was easy to say that the study advised against segregating the broker and dealer functions, though in fact it was a balanced document that on perusal more than fifty years later appears to lean a little on the side of segregation.

Indeed, the SEC study even lanced the sacred cow of these discussions, in case some congressional toreador really wanted to kill it. In a passage that sounds very modern in the aftermath of Black Monday, the staff cast doubt on the all but universally accepted idea that more liquidity always makes better markets: "The prominence of the quality of liquidity increases the inclination, already too prevalent, of buyers of securities to think in terms of the appreciation of the value of the security rather than the promise of continued and substantial earnings. This inclination impairs the value of the market as an accurate barometer of investment opportunities and thus tends to vitiate the judgments of even those buyers who do think in terms of underlying worth."

Regardless of what might be desirable—and one notes that the British, who did have this segregation into "single-function" firms, have abandoned it—the eggs are now scrambled. We want brokerage houses with many public customers to participate in underwritings and secondary offerings, to compete in making markets for over-the-counter securities, and to take the pressures of block trading away from the specialists, who don't have anything like the capital to handle them. One part of the disaster of Black Monday was the disappearance of upstairs market making and block trading, with the result that orders which normally come to the floor with buyer and seller already crossed were dumped onto the specialist for sale.

Nevertheless, it remains good law and good ethics that a man cannot sell his agency, that he cannot make money for himself beyond his contracted fee by executing transactions in which he enters as an agent for someone else. Over-the-counter dealers who sell to and buy from the public are not permitted to charge a commission in addition to their markup on the merchandise, and it is hard to see why the fact that a security is listed on an exchange should alter that rule. If a firm is an "upstairs market maker" (even if the phrase really means nothing more than that it is trading for its own account and wants the market maker's privilege of borrowing a higher fraction of the necessary capital), it is in effect functioning as an over-the-counter dealer. Stock exchange rules prohibit a broker/dealer from filling a customer's order out of its inventory, carrying the cross to the floor, and charging a commission. But the rule has an opening the size of a triumphal arch in the exemption of block trades where the firm is working down its position—and it is hard to see why a customer should ever pay a commission when part of what his buy order does in the market is to maintain or increase the price his broker receives selling the same security on the same day for the broker's own account.

In the early days of the computer, the law professor Harry Kalven worried that through its operations "mankind will lose its benign capacity to forget." The other side of that coin is that when you want the records, they're there. With securities and money now moving as blips permanently registered on magnetic disks, we can retrieve with the push of a button knowledge of whether a firm's inventory diminished on a day when its customers bought or rose on a day when they sold. The proper control of trading in listed securities by broker/dealers is simply an extension of the rule that governs over-the-counter trades. On any day when the customer in effect has bought from or sold to the broker, he may not be charged commission. That would concentrate everyone's attention mightily, because the immediate loser would be the customer's man whose customer would not pay a commission, almost certainly reducing the customer's man's income.

The need for direct policing of proprietary trading derives in part from the growing success of the big brokers, especially Merrill Lynch, in selling customers a package of services that ties them to the house rather than, as was the custom of the country until the 1980s, the individual who services their account. Prior to the cash management accounts and the home equity loans, the customer's man expected that his customers would follow him if he for any reason went to another brokerage house. His list was his treasure, his guarantee against unemployment. If the firm for which he worked did things that he thought might piss off his customers, he had clout when he complained. The purpose of the cash management account that Merrill pioneered was to break the hold of the registered representative over his clients (and for this reason it was a hard sell when new: Merrill had to run its first-ever contests for customer's men, vacations in the Bahamas and such, to get them to sell it). With the decline in the authority of the customer's man, the need for outside examination of what happens in proprietary accounts became pressing.

A rule that prevents the broker from trading against his customer does not police intermarket trading, where a broker acts in his own interest in the Chicago pits or on the New York floor or over the wires to Tokyo or London in response to his advance knowledge of what his customers are doing. Here again, as usual in potential conflict situations, what is wanted is greater transparency. The name, address, and serial number of all customers and all counterparties, with times of the arrival of orders and their execution, should be on file where all regulators (and through the regulators, who should have the right to refuse access for specified cause, the press) can retrieve the information. The commodity exchanges and the CFTC, because they are protecting their clearing corporations and have to worry about squeezes, are already much better at this than the stock exchanges and the SEC, which will not even disclose the identities of the brokers. And, of course, every firm that wishes to do a securities (or banking) business in the United States should be required to make such records available to U.S. authorities individually or via their own domestic authority on some basis acceptable to the United States.

Non olet, the Roman emperor Vespasian said of money: It doesn't smell. That was Vespasian's money: gold coins. A lot of ours stinks. Not one of our great banks and brokers today, or law firms, for that matter, would turn down the account of a Colombian drug king or an African tyrant or a corrupt American highway commissioner or a thieving East European bureaucrat. They might if they thought it could be on the front page of the newspapers tomorrow. We wouldn't have anywhere near so much third world debt or busted banks or mergers-and-acquisitions agitation if the law made our markets more transparent. When the next crash opens the door for new legislation, let's hope there will be enough congressmen with a sense of smell to make a difference.

4

Since the 1950s, our markets have been wrestling with monster institutions, and losing, with serious consequences. Of all the reasons that can be adduced for the virtual disappearance of productivity growth in the American economy, the misallocation of capital from the domination of our markets by institutional investors is, I think, the most convincing. The immense influence of this constituency, with its low time horizons, contributes to the choices of CEOs and their attitudes toward their work. It is because so high a proportion of corporate shares are in such hands that the takeover games can be operated as they are. The manager of an institutional fund is measured by his performance quarter by quarter, and the edge he can get parking stock for a raider, or lying in wait with the highwaymen for the arrival of the greater fool, may make a significant difference in the fees he gets next year.

In general, institutional money managers are judged by reference to the average, which contributes to mediocrity and conformity, close adherence to fashion. Or, worst of all, to the decision not to invest, to "buy the market," and seek to improve on the average performance of the market through trading. Institutions trade, of course, with a great weight of money, at very low commission rates, with computer-designed hedging strategies—and without taxes on their profits. Even the mutual funds do not pay taxes themselves but merely pass on to recipients, most of whom do pay taxes, the profits from the trading.

The use of these funds for passive investment in stocks, "buying the market," presents a profound problem in public policy. I go back far enough to remember when Paul Cabot as treasurer of Harvard (and head of State Street Fund) was using endowment money to build the electronics industry along Route 128, and Carl Hathaway at J. P. Morgan was finding growth stocks for that bank's trust department to place in pension funds. No small part of the social purpose of professional investment of such money were the judgment and information skilled managers with able research personnel would bring to the decision on which enterprise to back. Who is to play this role if the salaried advisers of the institutions will not? But if your performance is to be judged by the quarter, you have little incentive to look for long-term winners.

One of the interesting "what-if" questions looking back over the last few years guesses the good or ill that would have resulted if either the Board of Trade or the Merc had succeeded in marketing their futures contract on an index of over-the-counter stocks. One went with NASDAQ's National Market System index, one with the SPOC (Standard & Poors over-the-counter index). Each exchange spent something more than $10 million structuring and promoting its own contract, and neither was able to drum up any business. Both Leo Melamed and CBT chairman Cash Mahlmann now say the expenditure was worth it, because it kept the other guy from developing a big asset; the reader can decide whether this is the essence of cut-throat or just sour grapes.

I like to think, being at heart a romantic, that the contracts failed because at the institutions someone said, "Wait a minute. The purpose of buying developing companies in the over-the-counter market is picking the Haloids that turn into Xeroxes. The reason for being there is that a million dollars invested in just the right place over the counter may make more than twenty million in the industrial averages on the exchange." Under those circumstances, buying the market is nutty, like betting on every number on the roulette wheel—but it might have happened, diminishing the social utility even of this market, if the two exchanges hadn't got everybody so confused they quit. The success of an index contract might well have brought more money into over-the-counter stocks as a group, but giving investment managers the notion that they could buy this market and did not have to pick among its components might well have left the more promising ventures enfeebled with thirst like the Ancient Mariner in a sea of liquidity that did not nourish them.

"Most investing," the *New York Times* opines just a touch smugly, "has now come to be done by institutions, and most institutions have grown too large to be able to profit from buying modest stakes in small numbers of companies. Instead, they have been reduced to buying and selling 'the index' of highly capitalized companies, hoping to beat the averages by carefully timing when they buy and sell." In fact, all institutional investors together still own no more than 25 percent of the shares of listed stocks on the New York Stock Exchange, and no one of them owns as much as one-half of 1 percent. And the largest split up their business among a number of managers. Restricting any one management firm to a maximum size of, say, $10 billion, which is a little less than one-half of 1 percent of the valuation of traded stocks, might persuade these firms to return to choosing industries and companies.

Obviously, one cannot stop institutions or fund managers from trying to gain what they consider the higher yields of stocks (because the prices rise) while securing the safety of Treasury bills. The strategy of "buying the market" and then timing sales and purchases through the derivatives in Chicago harmed the institutions themselves as well as the market mechanisms, but the same people are still running these funds and managing the money, and like everyone else fund executives are highly motivated to prove somehow they were right though it came out wrong.

A transfer tax on stocks would discourage these destructive strategies, but it's probably not enough. The public interest calls for the long-term investment of savings, not their use for trading purposes. Thus the tax exemption now given to all the earnings of pension funds, endowments, and such should be withdrawn from trading profits. If institutions want to trade, let them do it on a level playing field with traders and companies and households. Define "short term" as less than nine months, because that's the maximum length for commercial paper to be sold without an SEC registration statement. All profits on paper held less than nine months should be taxable at the rate applied to corporate earnings, whatever the organization that receives the profit. The rule would also apply to mutual funds, which currently can pass-through all their earnings to shareholders without tax, on the sensible argument that the shareholders have to pay the taxes. But we don't want taxable funds trading in and out, either. As demonstrated on October 19 and 20, institutions that have become traders bring neither stability nor liquidity to problem markets. Let us discourage their participation in any capacity other than that of investors.

5

The changes in domestic policy that will be needed before the market becomes sturdy again are beyond the scope of a book of this kind, and little I have to say on the subject is original, anyway. Keynes in 1931 said about the British government exactly what most American economists said in 1987 about theirs: "The objects of national policy, so as to meet the emergency, should be primarily to improve our balance of trade, and secondarily to equalize the yield of taxation with the normal recurrent expenditure of the Budget by methods which would increase, rather than diminish, output, and hence increase the national income and the yield of the revenue, whilst respecting the principles of social justice. The actual policy of the Government fails on each of these tests."

But one corner of tax policy seems crucial to my subject: the distinction now made between interest on term debt, which is a tax-deductible expense, and dividends on equity, which can be paid only from post-tax income. The waste of American cleverness on the construction of schemes to move income from taxable to nontaxable exceeds the waste on the construction of military scenarios, and the result is obscene in Justice William Joseph Brennan's famous formulation: It is utterly without redeeming social value.

Learned fellows, mostly in the pay of the securities industry, tell us of the services done by takeover artists and leveraged-buyout specialists in dislodging stuffy management and assuring that property sells for its replacement cost. (Nobody ever says why property should sell for its replacement cost: Would anyone in his right mind buy Chrysler stock because it would cost so-much to replicate the giant AMC plant at Kenosha the company is closing down because nobody can make money producing cars there?) The process is tautological: The market failure that has valued the stock of a company for less than the price at which an investment banker with a story can sell it means the company has been badly managed. Therefore we need a theatrical production of paper creation, at the end of which the same company, often enough with the same management, faces its tasks with a much heavier burden of debt.

No less a tough guy of the Euromarkets than Hans-Joerg Rudloff, deputy chairman of Credit Suisse–First Boston, told a Euromoney meeting of portfolio managers in Zurich in early February 1988 that much of the blame for the international malaise of the markets rested on (to quote the *Financial Times* story on the speech) "[r]aiders who, with the complicity of investment bankers, rated companies by liquidation values rather than by earnings and dividends." Note the echo of the comment on liquidity in the SEC broker/dealer segregation study of fifty-two years before.

What happened in America, most of the time, was that the Internal Revenue Service inadvertently filled the coffers of the investment banks. The game is most easily illustrated with numbers. Assume $10 of pre-tax earnings and a corporate tax rate of 40 percent. With equity, $6 is available for distribution to stockholders or retention as surplus; if the firm has junk bonds instead of equity in its capital accounts, $10 is available for interest payments. Assume a 14 percent interest rate. Ten dollars of payments supports $71 of bonds. Whenever the price/earnings ratio on the stock gets under 11:1 (that is, the stock sells for less than 66), there is money to be made by selling junk bonds and buying out the stockholders. The promoters of this process, who have nothing to do with making or selling anything but paper, keep the difference.

And through this orgy of restructuring, productivity has risen more slowly in America than in any other industrial country. No doubt existing management and the mercurial faddishness that has characterized business school instruction in the past generation bear most of the blame. But the areas where the investment bankers have been most active are also the areas where productivity has risen most slowly. We have created markets that misallocate resources, and in the process, adding insult to injury, generated monstrous rewards for the miscreants.

The way you stop it is by changing the definitions that underlie the tax code. As the accountant and accounting theorist Henry Hill argues, we would be best off going back to the original Adam Smith, who divided the sources of funds to an enterprise between what he called "circulating capital" (we would say "working capital") and "fixed capital." Interest paid on working capital is an expense. Interest or dividends paid to fixed capital is a return on investment. All returns on investment should be equally taxed or not taxed. (Hill prefers the latter; I am more or less indifferent.) The important thing is to stop the distortions of the markets that result from inappropriate definitions.

Thanks in large part to these tax distortions, the 1980s have seen a vast growth of corporate debt and an actual shrinkage of corporate equity. The result is an economy that is both domestically and worldwide far more fragile than it should be or need be. There is a case to be made that start-up and smaller companies that must pay premium rates to borrow should be able to deduct interest costs from income before taxes, but there is no case whatever for the deductibility of interest on junk bonds or on utility bonds or on the equipment trust certificates that finance the purchase of boxcars and airplanes. A Congress that in 1986 summoned up the courage to take away the tax deductibility of consumer installment interest payments should be able to do the same to soulless corporations. The end result need not increase the total tax burden on corporations, because rates can be pushed way down. And the savings in payments to accountants, lawyers, and investment bankers would be spectacular.

6

Perhaps the greatest menace to the markets right now is what the futurists like to call "globalization." Once a market moves upstairs and becomes a collection of transmissions from computers to screens, players in Calcutta, Rio, Perth, and Calgary are all equal, provided they have recognized banking connections. The comment by Warburg's Sir David Scholey that technology has separated IBM from the dollar and ICI from the pound and Fiat from the lire states a truth of potentially enormous importance. Fortunately, its time is not quite yet in the markets, and with a little luck we may be able to keep it from gaining on us.

As noted in Chapter 1, there is at this writing only one fully international market: foreign exchange, on the Reuters screens. It runs twenty-four hours a day, with participants passing on their "book" to the next time zone as the hands move on the clock. And it is essentially an interbank market, though a number of securities houses and multinational corporations play in it. There is a real daily demand for the "commodity" (paying for cross-border trade requires shifting about $12 billion a day from one currency to another), and financial flows—transnational credits and purchases and sales of securities—run at least twice and perhaps three times as much. Euroclear, it will be recalled, handles $10 billion to $20 billion of transactions all by itself, much of it by people who do not do their other business in dollars. There is an active futures market in Chicago and options markets in Philadelphia and Montreal, but an even larger "forward" market operated by the banks themselves, in which companies that know they will need deutsche marks or lire or pounds or dollars or yen on a certain day can contract for them now. And the Reuters screens are backed up by the world's best funds-transfer communications system, SWIFT, the Brussels-based Society for Worldwide Interbank Financial Telecommunications, with CHIPS, the Clearing House Interbank Payments System computer in New York, available for final settlement.

Every time interest rates fluctuate domestically in one of the countries with currencies actively traded on a cash or future or forward basis, the exchange rates of the currencies will change. So the messages dart back and forth, and trading probably totals (nobody knows) $200 billion a day. Not the least of the reasons why banks commit major resources to this market is the fact that you can book the profits wherever the taxes are lowest. There is no more liquid market in the world, but the fact is that it doesn't flow smoothly, and prices often move by 1 percent or more as traders reinforce trends. Securities broker Stanley Abel asks a good question:

"If Bankers Trust made three hundred thirty-five million dollars trading foreign exchange in the last quarter of 1987, who lost it?" To which the only answer is: "Bankers Trust's customers, directly or indirectly." The daily fluctuations in exchange rates are a burden on international trade and investment, quite apart from the large longer term movements that disable industrial planning by the corporations that rely on foreign supplies or foreign orders.

Sixty-odd years ago Max Beerbohm entered a contest to write an advertising slogan for the world convention of advertising men in London. "Buy advertised products," ran his entry, "and help pay for the advertising." Customers shell out a steep risk premium on the profitability of their international trade these days to pay the costs of twenty-four-hour-a-day, worldwide foreign-exchange trading.

For the rest, there is no twenty-four-hour trading—yet. One can buy or sell IBM in England on the American five-day rolling settlement basis, but British customers would rather buy it on their own account period basis, and British market makers won't position it. The International (that is, London) Stock Exchange report on Black Monday unwittingly demonstrated the extent to which the British market served as a place to which foreigners could take their dirty laundry to be shipped home as the property of a London dealer rather than as the property of the trader who did his deals in London rather than at home.

Nothing can be traded in the United States that is not registered with the SEC, which means that foreign securities, with a handful of exceptions, are traded on the basis of American Depository Receipts, which are subject to different taxes in their home countries. Different juridical systems of ownership and different customary systems for settlement prevent large-scale cross-border investing in either debt or equity securities. And should.

Once again, however, Chicago is leading the way to trouble. The CFTC will not stand forever against the opening of a pit to trade the Nikkei-Dow index at the Merc, which has made arrangements with Singapore to trade this contract. The Board of Trade T-bond contract already trades at the London International Financial Futures Exchange (LIFFE), and on its own floor at hours convenient to Tokyo. And Reuters, as noted, has signed up with the Merc to offer on its screens and through its computers all the contracts traded in the Merc's pits. One assumes that in this case the Reuters computers, which keep no record of who did what in foreign-exchange trading, will be programmed to supply a full record of who bought what from whom at what price, and who the ultimate customers are behind the brokers. If the arm of the CFTC does not now reach far enough to force such recordkeeping, Congress should change the law—and, just in case, write the law so the CFTC is compelled to enforce it.

New York is in the act, too. Early in 1988 well-advanced negotiations between NYMEX and the London Petroleum Exchange, by which London would have gained the right to trade the New York contracts (under license, at a price), fell through, to the horror of the British traders. The reason was that NYMEX had opened negotiations with Reuters, to make arrangements for round-the-clock trading of its energy contracts similar to the arrangements Reuters had made with the Merc. There is handwriting on this wall.

Richard Sandor of Drexel, Burnham and of the Board of Trade argues that "Henry Ford ran his factories twenty-four hours a day at the start of the industrial revolution. Now we have to keep the financial factories open twenty-four hours a day. Why build a factory and keep it open only twenty-five percent of the day? We have five thousand people in Chicago who are exchange members and we throw off one hundred thousand jobs. If we keep it going twenty-four hours, we'll employ five thousand people at night, and we'll have another twenty thousand jobs. Why shouldn't the United States export its technical know-how; if that's what you're good at, sell it."

Maybe. Worldwide twenty-four-hour trading eliminates the most important and effective limit on price movements—in Brady Commission terms, the "circuit breaker." As noted in Chapter 10, over the course of an ordinary year in New York, the net movement of stock prices reflects overnight changes more than changes during the trading day, which usually means prices return to normal after the excitement of the close. One of the reasons the foreign-exchange market swings so widely even with central bank intervention to smooth the price movements is the fact that the actors never get a chance to sleep on the results of what they did yesterday: The situation on the screens when they come to work is so different from what it was yesterday that they have to start from scratch. Computers are wonderful machines, but they never stop to think.

Beyond that, our experience is that when the world's governments coordinate their economies we get ghastly inflation or major recession. What is needed for stability worldwide is that some countries should be doing rather well at the same time that others are doing rather poorly. In 1972, all the central banks put the pedal to the metal at the same time to celebrate the conclusion of the Smithsonian Agreement that was going to assure currency stability in our lifetimes. This was followed as the night the day by an ascendant OPEC and the sort of inflation that punished everyone for the next ten years, and could be broken only by the sort of concerted action that produced the deep recession of 1981–1982.

If there is going to be a genuine free market in currencies, then nations will have to accept the limits on their sovereignty imposed by their inability to insulate the domestic value of their legal tender from the consequences of government policy. The combination of high deficits and tight money that Reagan and Volcker ran in the early 1980s would be impossible with free markets, because the rules of the game would have to forbid the central bank to hold down the growth of the money supply by sterilizing the inflow of funds drawn by high interest rates. Economic historians will note the irony that the United States plunged into a course of unrestricted foreign borrowing just as the disasters of the Latin American economies demonstrated the folly of using international credit to avoid the consequences of domestic mismanagement.

True management of the world's economies by political authority requires at all times that some countries more or less voluntarily accept the discipline of reduced consumption and (at least temporarily) reduced employment. How difficult it will be to get the leading power to accept such discipline can be seen by the wrigglings and squirmings of the second Reagan administration. What Black Monday said was that Ronald Reagan's morning in America was at best a false dawn. At best.

In fairness, the international economy went as wrong as it did because the Europeans and the Japanese found it convenient to feed American appetites even at their own expense—for the dollar-denominated financial assets they acquired in return were greatly diminished in value as the 1980s wound down. As Jack Bennett, treasurer of Exxon, said as long ago as 1979, "There is no doubt that holdings of U.S. Treasury bills by foreign governments are higher than they would have been if they had not chosen to promote their exports and deter their imports." But even internationally, in the absence of enforceable law, creditors have rights and remedies, often painful to debtors.

In the end, then, no one really wants free markets internationally, because no one wishes to accept the limits on his own country's decision-making power that free markets inevitably impose. In his Zurich speech, Hans-Joerg Rudloff of Credit Suisse said that "globalisation of markets puts the onus on the governments which had opened the way for the free flow of capital round the world. It meant that countries' economic performances would be tested by the free movement of capital and by the verdict of investors, however hard some governments might now find it to live with the situation." But the fact is that governments profoundly influence the "verdict of investors," both their own and others', especially when money must flow across national boundaries to express the verdict. Moreover, the most common reason for international diversification, whatever the portfolio theorists in the universities may say, is always going to be distrust of one's own currency. If international markets are to be less honest than national markets, and everything we know says that they will be, players will demand greater risk premiums before using them. The limits to private international investing in foreign corporate equity (as distinguished from capital flight) are a lot narrower than is usually admitted; the real question is whether they will be discovered before or after they are exceeded.

7

The capitalist, free world—and the two adjectives are, I cautiously agree, linked—has been lucky in its enemies. In 1925, John Maynard Keynes cited a conversation with two "Communist ironsides" who had come to a meeting accompanying Zinoviev. " 'We make you a prophecy,' they said. 'Ten years hence the level of life in Russia will be higher than it was before the war, and in the rest of Europe it will be lower than it was before the war.' Having regard to the natural wealth of Russia and to the inefficiency of the old regime, having regard also to the problems of Western Europe and our apparent inability to handle them, can we feel confident that the comrades will not prove right?"

The French philosopher Bertrand de Jouvenel remembered a day soon after the end of World War II when he was part of a delegation waiting to welcome Georges Bidault, then the French foreign minister, back from a trip to Moscow. As the train slowed down in the station, a railroad worker ran alongside the minister's carriage, calling up to the window, "Monsieur le Ministre! Monsieur le Ministre! Is it true they have a workers' paradise in the Soviet Union?" And in 1962, Nikita Khrushchev told John F. Kennedy, "We will bury you," that by the 1970s the standard of living would be higher in the Soviet Union than it was in the United States. Not a Frenchman survives who thinks the Soviet Union is a workers' paradise, and if Mikhail Gorbachev echoed Khrushchev, even the Russians would laugh.

Market systems had the run they did in the 1980s because of the overwhelming proof that the advertised alternative did not work. Albert Woljinower of First Boston was in Peking on October 20, 1987, and found his hosts terribly concerned: Did the crash mean that the Russians were right and the market economies would collapse? The Chinese leaders had no great love for markets, but they knew beyond doubt that nobody, not the Russians, not themselves, could make a command economy work beyond the rather primitive phases of capital accumulation. What would be left for them?

People unquestionably expect markets to deliver more than they can. The one certain truth about markets, as J. P. Morgan observed to the Pujo Committee eighty years ago, is that they fluctuate. The great advantage they offer is that they routinely compel the recognition of error. Samuel Johnson observed in 1775 that "there are few ways in which a man can be more innocently employed than in getting money," but the values of the market discipline are greater than that. Greed was already going out of fashion before October 19, and there can be no question that it is a vice—but it is the cleanest of vices, the one most easily and publicly rebuked by reality.

One never need worry about an adequate supply of greed; like all the vices, it's always there. The willingness to acknowledge error, however, is always scarce. What went wrong in the 1980s was the constant construction on Wall Street, in Chicago, in Washington—and, to rather different ends, in London and Tokyo and Frankfurt—of labyrinthine structures difficult to penetrate and understand that permitted the politicians and bankers and traders and investors and business leaders to deny the reality of their own mistakes.

October 19 should have chilled the fantasies. It did, but only briefly. The losses have been taken but not internalized. The denials persist.

Notes

PROLOGUE

Malkiel quote: Burton Malkiel, *A Random Walk Down Wall Street,* W. W. Norton & Co., New York, 1973 (1985 edition), p. 123.
Malkiel writes "past movements": Malkiel, *Random Walk,* p. 128.
Call options quote: Joel A. Bleeke, "Portfolio Insurance: When, Not What," *Wall Street Journal,* 12/11/1987, p. 24. (Italics added.)

CHAPTER 1

Kontos at noon cut maximum order: The October 1987 Market Break, A Report by the Division of Market Regulation, U.S. Securities and Exchange Commission, Washington, D.C., February 1988, Chap. 9, p. 17.
Truman quote: Bob Tamarkin, *The New Gatsbys,* William Morrow, New York, 1985, paperback edition, p. 123.
Berger story: Donald Cobbett, *Before the Big Bang,* Milestone Publications, Portsmouth, Hants, England, 1986, p. 88.
Unnamed dealer: Marcia Stigum, *The Money Market,* revised ed., Dow-Jones Irwin, Homewood, Ill., 1983, p. 305.
"some of these 'cyphering cits' ": Charles Mackay, *Extraordinary Popular Delusions and the Madness of Crowds,* Farrar, Strauss & Giroux ed., p. 71.
Samuelson quote: "The Role of Energy Futures," in *Perpectives on NYMEX, 1986–87,* the annual report of the New York Mercantile Exchange, New York, 1987, unpaginated.
Robinson quote: James Tanner, "As OPEC's Members Produce Above Quota, Big Data Gap Widens," *Wall Street Journal,* 11/24/87, p. 1.
Rothschild scene: Donald Cobbett, *Before the Big Bang,* p. 55.
Kennedy quote: Arthur M. Schlesinger, Jr., *A Thousand Days,* Houghton-Mifflin Co., Boston, 1965, p. 654.

CHAPTER 2

"the forces of supply and demand": William M. Clarke and George Pulay, *The World's Money: How It Works,* George Allen & Unwin, Ltd., London, 1970, p. 82. It is probably worth noting in passing that the gold fixing was resumed in 1954 as a service the British commonwealth could perform for South Africa.
Marx quote: Karl Marx, *Capital,* Volume I, translated from the German edition by Samuel Moore and Edward Aveling, Charles H. Kerr Co., Chicago, 1906, p. 144.

NOTES

Gilbert letter: George S. Moore, *The Banker's Life,* W. W. Norton & Co., New York, 1987. p. 217.

"I don't want the full commission—": Martin Mayer, *New Breed on Wall Street,* Macmillan, New York, 1969, p. 33.

CHAPTER 3

Harry Bennett quote: As told to Paul Marcus, *We Never Called Him Henry,* Gold Medal Books, Fawcett Publications, New York, 1951, p. 47.

Galbraith quote: John Liscio, "The Galbraith Speculation," *Barron's,* 12/7/87, p. 8.

Treasury official on Silva Herzog: Karin Lissakers, "Dateline Wall Street: Faustian Finance," *Foreign Affairs,* Summer 1983, p. 160.

"equities and options have been acting": Anthony G. Delis, "When Stocks Trade Like Commodities, History Says There's Big Trouble Ahead," *Barron's,* April 13, 1987, p. 67.

"In a correction": Alan Abelson, "Up & Down Wall Street," *Barron's,* 10/19/87, p. 1.

"no one is forecasting": Tim Metz and Beatrice E. Garcia, "What Next? The Plunge in Stocks Has Experts Guessing About Market's Course," *Wall Street Journal,* 10/19/87, p. 1.

"specialists on other exchanges": Nicholas A. Giordano, "Too Many Regulators Spoil the Markets," *New York Times,* 11/1/87, Section 3, p. 3.

An SEC rule: 17 CFR 240. 11b–1(a)(2).

Specialists: Robert E. Norton, "Specialists: Special at Exactly What?" *Fortune,* 2/1/88, p. 22.

Specialist performance October 19: Report of the President's Task Force on Market Mechanisms, Washington, D.C., January 1988, p. 49.

Program trading, 1:10–1:50: The October 1987 Market Break, A Report by the Division of Market Regulation, U. S. Securities and Exchange Commission, February 1988, Chap. 2, pp. 38 and 39.

CHAPTER 4

Soros: "A Bad Two Weeks," *Barron's,* 11/2/87, p. 35.

Nov. put contract at 195: See SEC 1987 Report, Chap. 8, pp. 12–13.

Panic of 1907: Vincent P. Carosso, *The Morgans: Private International Bankers, 1854–1913,* Harvard University Press, Cambridge, 1987, pp. 540–541.

Findings: A Review and Evaluation of Federal Margin Regulations. A Study by the Staff of the Board of Governors of the Federal Reserve System, Washington, D.C., December 1984, pp. 167 and 166.

"share for share": Federal Reserve Board Regulation T, Section 220.12(b) (2).

"Professionals. . .": Brady Commission, p. 65.

"effective 20–25%. . .": SEC Report, Chap. 3, p. 20.

Bank behavior: SEC Report, Chap. 4, p. 32.

CME margin figures: Commodity Futures Trading Commission, *Follow-up Report on Financial Oversight of Stock Index Futures Markets During October 1987,* Washington, D.C., 1/6/88, p. 39.

MMI report: Division of Trading and Markets, Commodity Futures Trading Commission, "Analysis of Trading in the Chicago Board of Trade's Major Market Index Futures Contract on October 20th, 1987," Washington, D.C., January 4, 1988, p. 15.

Notes

Brady on MMI: Brady Commission report, Section VI, p. 68.

Binns quote: Testimony of W. Gordon Binns, Jr., to the House Energy and Commerce Committee, Subcommittee on Telecommunications and Finance, July 23, 1987, mimeo, p. 6.

"the up-tick rule": Division of Economic Analysis and Division of Trading and Markets, *Interim Report on Stock Index Futures and Cash Market Activity During October 1987,* Commodity Futures Trading Commission, Washington, D.C., November 9, 1987, p. 61.

"index-related futures trading": Securities and Exchange Commission, *The Role of Index-Related Trading in the Market Decline of September 11 and 12, 1986,* Washington, D. C., 1986, Executive Summary, p. 1.

SEC Report: Chronology at Appendix B, pp. 33–40; "unable to quantify" in footnote, Chap. 3, p. 26. One notes with amusement that the Report cites a *Wall Street Journal* story about my article in *Barron's* that first called this scandal to public attention, but not my two *Barron's* articles themselves. Shucks.

Leland quote: "Prospects: Brady's Market Plan," *New York Times,* 1/17/88, Section 3, p. 1.

CHAPTER 5

Nickel: Bob Tamarkin, *The New Gatsbys,* William Morrow, New York, 1985, paperback edition, p. 241.

"Tight margin manufacturing": David Gilbertson, "The London Metal Exchange," in *The Square Mile in 1986,* De Montfort Publishing Ltd., London, pp. 135 and 138.

Friedman quote: The United States Balance of Payments, Hearings Before the Joint Economic Committee, 1963, p. 459.

Nixon quote: Martin Mayer, *The Fate of the Dollar,* Times Books, New York, 1980, p. 202.

.06 of 1 percent: Value Line Futures, Kansas City Board of Trade, 1987, p. 5.

CHAPTER 6

Friedman party: Bob Tamarkin, *The New Gatsbys,* William Morrow, New York, 1985, paperback edition, p. 239.

CRT material: "Intermarket Interview: Gary Ginter and Joe Ritchie," in *Intermarket,* Sept. (Part 1) and Oct. (Part 2) 1985, p. 4 et seq.

" 'price discovery' feature": SEC Report, Chap. 3, p. 6.

CHAPTER 7

Dulles quote: Robert Alan Feldman, *Japanese Financial Markets: Deficits, Dilemmas and Deregulation,* MIT Press, Cambridge, Mass., and London, 1986, p. 142.

"Dollar-raising capability": Eric W. Hayden, "Internationalizing Japan's Financial System," *An Occasional Paper of the Northeast Asia–United States Forum on International Policy,* Stanford University, Palo Alto, December 1980, p. 19.

Savings figures: Japan Financial Statistics 1986, Federation of Bankers Associations of Japan, Tokyo, p. 13.

Government expenditures on social programs: Robert Alan Feldman, *Japanese Financial Markets,* p. 6.

NOTES

"government bonds": Eric W. Hayden, *Occasional Paper,* p. 5.

"public debt": Henry and Mabel I. Wallich, "Banking and Finance," in Hugh Patrick and Henry Rosovsky, eds., *Asia's New Giant: How the Japanese Economy Works,* Brookings Institution, Washington, D.C., 1976, pp. 251 and 276.

"payment deceleration": Andreas R. Prindl, *Japanese Finance: A Guide to Banking in Japan,* John Wiley & Sons, Chichester and New York, 1981, p. 102.

"subordinated creditor": Henry and Mabel I. Wallich, "Banking and Finance," p. 253.

Matsumura quote: Bernard Wysocki, Jr., "Big Dealer: Top Japanese Firm Grows in Importance in Securities Markets," *Wall Street Journal,* 4/1/87, p. 1.

"Japan's kabuya": Bruce Roscoe, "Markets/Stocks: Suddenly *the* Place for Everybody to Be," in special section "Japan Banking and Finance" in *Far Eastern Economic Review,* Hong Kong, 4/9/87, p. 65.

Japanese and U.S. 1983 external assets: Hirohiko Okumura, "Japan's Financial Markets," p. 52.

Play the market: I own a million shares of Matsushita, acquired at $4 a share. They are now worth $40 a share. If I sell, I owe tax on my $36 profit. If I begin a *tokkin* trust, I can acquire another million shares at $40 and sell them at, say, $44. My average cost per share is $22, and thus in traditional accounting my profit on the sale of the million shares is $22 million. By using a *tokkin* trust, I can reduce my taxable profit to $4 million.

Semi-public agencies: Paul Aron and Laurie J. Aron, "Japan: Equity Markets," in A.M. George and I.H. Giddy, *International Financial Handbook,* John Wiley & Sons, New York, 1983, Section 6.7, p. 5.

CHAPTER 9

"revolutionary trains of thought": John Plender, "Lombard. The Fetish of Liquidity," *Financial Times,* 2/12/88, p. 11.

Rudloff quote: William Dullforce, "Rudloff Castigates World's Bankers," *Financial Times,* 2/5/88, p. 23.

Attali summary: Jacques Attali, *A Man of Influence,* Adler & Adler, Bethesda, Md., 1987, p. 247.

Keogh quote: Martin Mayer, *The Bankers,* Weybright & Talley, New York, 1974, p. 457.

Flat finality: "Euromarkets: Now for the Lean Years," *The Economist,* 5/16/87, pp. 5 and 7.

Tugenhadt: Richard Spiegelberg, *The City: Power Without Accountability,* Blond & Briggs, London, 1973, p. 95.

Watkins: Matthew Barrett, "Is the Party Over for the AIBD?", *Euromoney,* May 1987, pp. 45 and 46.

Hambro: Martin Mayer, *The Bankers,* pp. 445–446.

Howls of outrage: Save one—my "A View From Outside" column in *American Banker* for 7/13/87 was entitled "Lesson from the Antilles" and was most enthusiastic about what the Treasury had done.

Ross quote: John J. Duffy, "Morgan Bank Quietly Profits Operating Euro-Clear System," *American Banker,* 6/18/87, pp. 1 and 15.

Fear: Euromoney, May 1987, p. 49

"Dual capacity": W. A. Thomas, *The Big Bang,* Philip Allen, Oxford, England, 1986, p. 3.

"retail-wholesale split": John Plender and Paul Wallace, *The Square Mile: A Guide*

to the City Revolution, Hutchinson Business, London, 1985; paperback edition, 1986, pp. 77 and 78.

Fleming: Hamish McRae and Frances Cairncross, *Capital City: London as a Financial Centre,* Methuen, London, 1984 edition, p. 9.

Squirts/jobbers: Donald Cobbett, *Before the Big Bang,* Milestone Pub., Portmouth, Hants., 1986, p. 31.

"Chinese walls": W. A. Thomas, *The Big Bang,* p. 134.

American model has intrigued British commentators: My book *Wall Street,* with a British subtitle of *The Inside Story of American Finance,* was published in London in 1959, four years after its U.S. publication; its publisher Max Reinhardt bought the English rights to gain the rights to my subsequent *Madison Avenue, USA,* which was, thank God, a best-seller on both sides of the Atlantic. Being a super publisher who really sold books, he proceeded to win considerable attention and surprisingly good sales for what he had considered an ugly duckling, using a publicity campaign built around the question "Does Britain need an SEC?"

"more grandiose position": John Plender and Paul Wallace, *The Square Mile,* p. 243.

John Brew: John Plender and Paul Wallace, *The Square Mile,* p. 155.

"search for the culprit": Clive Wolman, "City Policeman Under Fire," *Financial Times,* 1/5/88, p. 14.

CHAPTER 10

Brandeis quote: Hurd Baruch, *Wall Street: Security Risk,* Acropolis Books, Washington, D.C., 1971, p. 24.

"self-preservation": Dialogue between SEC and IBM reported in Robert Sobel, *NYSE: A History of the New York Stock Exchange, 1935–1975,* Weybright & Talley, New York, 1975, p. 271.

"tests of specialists' performance": 88th Congress, 1st Session, House of Representatives, *Report of the Special Study of the Securities Markets of the Securities and Exchange Commission,* Washington, D.C., 1965, Part 2, Chap. 6, p. 121.

"relative performance measures": 1987 SEC Report, Chap. 4, pp. 28–29.

"ability to outbid": 1963 SEC *Special Study,* Volume 2, p. 143.

"reasonably anticipated needs": "Code of Acceptable Business Practice for Specialists," 3.e, in *The Specialist and His Job,* New York Stock Exchange, undated.

Regan quote: John Brooks, *The Go-Go Years,* Weybright & Talley, New York, 1973, pp. 356–357.

1896 Dow: Lloyd Wendt, *The Wall Street Journal,* Rand McNally & Co., New York, 1982, p. 68.

Thomas Lawson: Stewart H. Holbrook, *The Age of the Moguls,* Doubleday & Co., Garden City, N.Y., 1953, pp. 172–173.

Horace White: Vincent Carosso, *Investment Banking in America,* Harvard University Press, Cambridge, Mass., 1970, pp. 133–134.

"gambling hells": Robert L. Smiley, "Wall Street's Red Tape," in *The Magazine of Wall Street,* 2/3/17, p. 592, cited in Vincent Carosso, *Investment Banking,* p. 234.

"Manipulation of some sort": Edwin Lefevre, *Reminiscences of a Stock Operator,* Pocket Books edition, New York, 1968, p. 237.

Bomb: Frederick Lewis Allen, *Only Yesterday,* Bantam Books edition, 1946, pp. 64–65.

William Douglas: Robert Sobel, *NYSE,* pp. 34–35.

NOTES

"decreased interest in stocks and bonds": Ibid, p. 79.
Manuel Cohen's wife: John Brooks, *The Go-Go Years,* p. 150.
Bunny Lasker: John Brooks, *The Go-Go Years,* p. 355.

CHAPTER 11

Keynes quote: "Adam Smith," in *The Money Game,* Random House, New York, 1968, p. 217.
"White racism": Report of the National Advisory Commission on Civil Disorders, Bantam edition, New York, 1968, p. 10.
"one market": Report of the Presidential Task Force on Market Mechanisms, Washington, D.C., 1988, p. vi.
Bumptious leader: "Wall Street's Fevers," *The Economist,* 1/16/88, pp. 17–18.
Rockefeller Foundation treasurer: Beatrice E. Garcia and Douglas R. Sease, "Shearson Scales Back Program Trading in Effort to Restore Confidence in Market," *Wall Street Journal,* 1/25/88, p. 3.
Trading revenues: New York Stock Exchange, *Fact Book 1987,* p. 61.
"$40 million": Beatrice E. Garcia and Douglas R. Sease, "Shearson Scales Back," *Wall Street Journal,* 1/25/88, p. 3.
Robert S. Haack quote: Hurd Baruch, *Wall Street: Security Risk,* Acropolis Books, Washington, D.C., 1971, p. 293.
"block trades": SEC, *Institutional Investor Study Report,* House Doc. 92-64, 92nd Congress, 1st Session, Washington, D.C. March 10, 1971, Volume 4, p. 1596.
"side deal": Martin Mayer, "Broker-Dealer Firms," in Roy Schotland, ed., *Abuse on Wall Street: Conflicts of Interest in the Securities Business,* a Twentieth Century Report published by Greenwood Press, Westport, Conn., 1980, pp. 433 and 460.
$900 million: James R. Kraus, "London Takes Lead Role in Global Equity Swaps," *American Banker,* 12/18/87, p. 9. *Rudloff quote:* William Dullforce, "Rudloff Castigates World's Bankers," *Financial Times,* 2/5/88, p. 23.
Soulless corporations: Martin Mayer, *Wall Street: Men and Money,* Harper & Bros., New York, 1955.
"fiduciary principle": Justice Harlan Fiske Stone, "The Public Influence of the Bar," *Harvard Law Review,* Volume 48, 1934, p. 8.
Further study: Report of the Presidential Task Force on Market Mechanisms, Washington, D.C., 1988, p. vii.

CHAPTER 12

Marx quote: Karl Marx, *Capital,* Volume II, translated from the second German edition by Ernest Untermann, Charles H. Kerr Co., Chicago, 1933, p. 64.
"true" to "fair": Henry P. Hill, *Accounting Principles for the Autonomous Corporate Entity,* Greenwood Press, Westport, Conn., 1987, p. 15.
Runs up the price: Ernest LeFevre, *Reminiscences of a Stock Operator,* Pocket Books edition, New York, 1968, pp. 203–204.
"funeral parlors": Martin Mayer, *Wall Street: Men and Money,* Harper & Brothers, New York, 1955 revised edition, 1959, pp. 64–65.
"man-eaters": Sonny Kleinfield, *The Traders,* Holt, Rinehart & Winston, New York, 1983, p. 10.
"Underlying worth": Securities and Exchange Commission, *Report on the Feasibility and Desirability of the Complete Segregation of the Functions of Broker and Dealer,* Washington, D.C., June 20, 1936, p. 100.

Notes

" 'the index' ": "The Crash and Its Best Students," editorial, *New York Times,* 2/4/88, p. A26.

Keynes on British government: John Maynard Keynes, *Essays in Persuasion,* W. W. Norton & Co., New York, 1963, p. 163.

Rudloff on international malaise of markets: William Dullforce, "Rudloff Castigates World's Bankers," *Financial Times,* 2/5/88, p. 23.

Jack Bennett quote: Martin Mayer, *The Fate of the Dollar,* Times Books, New York, 1980, pp. 244–245.

"globalisation of markets": William Dullforce, "Rudloff Castigates World's Bankers," *Financial Times,* 2/5/88, p. 23.

"Communist ironsides": John Maynard Keynes, *Essays in Persuasion,* p. 305.

A Useful Small Glossary of Important Terms, with Examples

Arbitrage   Assumes the existence of two separate markets in which the same or equivalent objects are traded. By purchasing in one while selling in the other, the **Arbitrageur** equalizes the prices in the two markets.

The obvious example and most active market is currencies. Assume the pound selling at $1.7545 in London and $1.7540 in New York. Buying pounds in New York and selling them in London yields a certain profit of $5/100$ths of a cent on every pound. For each million dollars, which is the minimum such order, the profit would be $285.06 less transaction costs. Thus traders hang over screens worldwide, looking for such discrepancies and quickly erasing them.

A slightly more complicated arbitrage looks at the current exchange rate, the interest rates in the two countries, and the "forward" exchange rate for a purchase of pounds, say, ninety days from now. The "spot" market arbitrageurs have done their work, and the price is now $1.7542 for pounds in all markets. The annualized ninety-day interest rate in pounds is 8 percent; in dollars, 6 percent. A million dollars put into pounds at $1.7542 and held a quarter of a year at 8 percent would give its lucky possessor 581,461.63 pounds. A million dollars put into a 6 percent certificate for a quarter of a year gives $1,015,000. That number of dollars buys that number of pounds at an exchange rate of $1.7456. If the ninety-day forward rate is $1.7540, a person with a million dollars has an interesting choice: He can lend in the United States and get $1,015,000 in three months, or he can buy pounds and lend them in Britain and buy the forward contract to return to dollars with the certain knowledge that when he reconverts his money he will have $1,019,883.68. Here the arbitrage will not necessarily bring either interest rates or currency rates into line, and may be carried on for some time if, for example, the United States is committed to keeping its interest rates lower than English rates or England is committed to higher rates.

In the stock market context, arbitrage classically has been practiced on convertible bonds. A bond with the right to convert to 50 shares of stock is worth $1,250 if the price of the stock goes to 25. Should the price of the bond fall *below* $1,250, an arbitrageur can buy the bond, sell the stock, and pocket a certain profit. Again, in such situations other arbitrageurs will be following similar strategies, and the price gap will vanish.

In the agricultural futures pits, significantly, the term "arbitrage" is not used, because futures contracts are not the same thing as commodities—indeed, futures contracts for delivery of different months are not the same thing. Instead, the term used in the futures markets is **Spreading,** which keeps *like* objects *similarly* priced.

Basis In interest rates, a basis point is $1/100$th of 1 percent. If the money being borrowed is large enough, this is not trivial: On the U.S. national debt, for example, a basis point is $200 million a year.

In futures trading, the basis is the difference at any moment between the price in the futures market and the price for the commodity in the cash market. The word expresses the fact that in the futures context one cannot arbitrage but merely spread. In arbitrage, there is no risk. In spreading or hedging, there remains a "basis risk."

Block In the stock market, a large number of shares to sell; today, conventionally, 10,000 or more. Blocks may be inconvenient to sell in the course of an auction market, because the heavy supply presses the price down. Brokers for the holder of the block (usually some fund or institution) thus try to sell it away from the market, over the telephone, to known possible large customers. If the stock sells, the broker is usually paid commissions on both the buy and the sell side. Large brokerage firms will often complete such deals by purchasing a part of the block for themselves, **Positioning** it until another purchaser can be found. When blocks listed on a U.S. stock exchange are sold in this manner, brokers who are members of the exchange must bring the transaction to the attention of the **Market Maker** at the exchange, and cause the sale to be published on the ticker tape or the computer screen like the sales accomplished by normal bidding in the open market.

A block already traded upstairs and carried to the exchange floor as a done deal is said to be CROSSED. If all the shares have been bought by public customers, rather than the broker himself, it is a "clean cross."

Call *see* **Options**

Clearing Trades made in financial markets are legally registered in a "clearing," where the representatives of the parties accept their obligation to live up to the terms of the trade.

In the stock market, this is followed by a "settlement" at which the buyer pays and the seller delivers his shares, and the contract between them becomes a historical curiosity.

In the futures markets and the options markets, where what are traded are contracts of a fixed duration, a "clearing corporation" interposes itself between buyer and seller and becomes the counterparty in every trade. The practical significance is twofold. Strangers can safely trade with each other, because at the end of the process the assurance that obligations will be met is that of the market as a whole rather than that of the other side of a trade. And the holder of a futures contract can always **Extinguish** his contract by purchasing an opposing contract and presenting it to the clearing corporation.

If you have agreed to accept delivery of 40,000 bushels of soybeans in two months, you can escape by purchasing a futures contract obliging you to deliver to someone else 40,000 bushels of soybeans in two months. The clearing corporation will then annul both contracts. If the price of beans has risen since you "bought" them (by purchasing a contract to accept delivery), you will make money because you can "sell" the beans (by purchasing a contract to make delivery) at a higher price. If the price of beans has dropped, you will lose money. But you won't have to accept delivery of the beans.

Cross *see* **Block**

Dealer   Someone who fills orders to buy and sell, either directly or through brokers, making a profit by the spread between what he pays to acquire and what he receives when selling. If a dealer maintains an inventory of what he sells, buying into and selling from his own **Positions** rather than merely going out to buy his customers' needs or lay off their orders on wholesalers, he is a **Market Maker.** If he buys and sells on his own initiative rather than in response to public orders, he is a **Trader.** Most dealers seek to do a maximum number of trades at a small margin, turning over their capital (and what they can borrow) as rapidly as possible. A broker who positions blocks is a dealer while disposing of his position. In the United States, most brokers are broker/dealers.

Derivative Instrument   A tradable contract to buy or sell a financial asset that trades independently. Ultimately, the value of a derivative instrument depends entirely on the value of the asset, though its price will vary from that value because it is separately traded. Options and futures contracts are the major derivative instruments.

Eurocurrency   The original "Eurodollar" market was a product of the cold war and of the deficit in the American balance of payments from foreign aid and overseas military expenditure that exceeded what was until the 1970s a consistent American trade surplus. The dollars that went abroad were held there, first because they were useful for the purchase of commodities (most significantly, oil) that were sold for dollars in the world market; second because the United States had a nasty habit, most recently displayed in the Panamanian imbroglio, of seizing the American bank deposits of disliked foreigners. By keeping dollar-denominated accounts in banks outside the United States, foreigners got the use of the currency without the political risks. Dollars were an extremely convenient currency because they could be turned quickly into any other currency. Until the 1980s, moreover, dollar interest rates were lower than those in most currencies because the United States was a creditor nation and creditors always borrow cheaper than debtors, domestically or internationally.

And Eurodollar interest rates were cheaper than U.S. dollar interest rates, because dollars held in U.S. banks at home were subject to reserve requirements by the Federal Reserve (and a deposit insurance fee), while all of a bank's dollar deposits could be lent in countries where the local currency was not the dollar. Eventually, the success of bank dollar lending outside the United States provoked the issuance of bonds denominated in dollars, and the growth of **Euromarkets** in which these bonds—there are now something like $2 *trillion* worth—could be traded. Despite their prestige and the immense sums devoted to them and made in them, Euromarkets remain unregulated, not reporting their trades, creators of "bearer bonds" in an age when everything else is held in book entry form in the name of the owner, havens for money acquired in ways that will not bear examination.

In recent years, with the decline of the dollar, the Euromarkets have turned increasingly to lending in yen, marks, pounds, various francs, and the antipodean dollars (Australia and New Zealand).

Extinguish *see* **Clearing**

Futures Contracts   As the name implies, contracts for the future purchase or delivery of something, at a price and on a date set in the contract. Such contracts can be traded in the United States only upon approval of the Commodity Futures Trading Commission, a government agency. A futures contract is an obligation: Someone with a contract for delivery must either make delivery on or near the last day (delivery terms are in the contract) or must purchase a contract to accept delivery to cancel his earlier contract.

The overwhelming majority of futures contracts are extinguished rather than used as a mechanism for purchase or sale of the underlying commodity. But because the contract can be used as a device for purchase or sale, its price on the day it expires must be virtually identical to the underlying price of the commodity. Thus someone who knows he will need wheat or oil or copper in sixty days can in effect lock in a price for it by purchasing the futures contract: If the price goes up and he has a contract to take delivery, he reduces his effective price in the "real" market by his profit when the contract is extinguished; if the price goes down, the effective cost of his purchase is what he pays in cash for the commodity plus what it costs him to extinguish his contract.

Nevertheless, until 1981 it was considered essential that the *possibility* of delivery of the underlying commodity be part of the valuation of the futures contract. Without the discipline of an ultimate relationship between the quantity of the commodity produced and consumed and the quantity of contracts written for its delivery, the contract could become a simple crap shoot of no economic value. In 1981, however, the Commodity Futures Trading Commission approved a contract that bought and sold million-dollar Eurodollar loans at set rates of interest, and such loans could not be delivered in Chicago. They were therefore settled with a cash payment at the moment of expiration, if they had not previously been extinguished. The next year, cash settlement was also approved for stock **Index** futures contracts, on the grounds that it would be too complicated to deliver all the stocks in the index. When improved technology at the New York Stock Exchange made it possible to buy or sell all the stocks in the index, the contract expanded and offered its holders an additional, unanticipated opportunity for profit.

Anywhere from a third to two-thirds of the trading in futures contracts is by speculators and traders in the pits, who of course never take delivery of anything but provide the liquidity the market requires by incessant trading with each other and with the producers and consumers who use the underlying commodity. Activity in the pits tends to be a function of price volatility: If the price of the contracts rises and falls often and fairly far (too far is no good), there will be a lot of traders. If the price moves little and rarely, the trading pits will stand deserted.

Hedging   A generic term for an activity which seeks to match instruments that have prices likely to move in different directions under a common stimulus. Holding a contract to accept delivery of March wheat, one could buy a contract to make delivery of June wheat. If the wheat price rises, the March contract goes up in price (because you have a bargain), and the June contract goes down in price (because the price in your contract is less than the price someone with wheat to sell can get in the cash market). Between the two, you're safe. Experienced people can **Spread** the **Basis** between these two contracts, and hope to make some money out of the pair: Hedging seeks to avoid loss, sacrificing some but by no means all the potential profit.

An investment banker planning to underwrite bonds for a large corporation will hedge his underwriting profits by selling in the Treasury-bond futures market, while buying the bonds from the company. If interest rates go up, the investment banker may lose money on the inventory of corporate bonds he has acquired from the company—but he will make it back on the increased value of his T-bond futures contract. This is not something underwriters *can* do, by the way; it's something they *do* do, all the time.

Hedging against the movement of stock prices is a relatively recent phenomenon, first developed in the newly created **Options** exchanges in the 1970s. Owning a stock, one can purchase a **Put Option** that gives the right to sell it at a price fixed in the options contract. If the price in the market goes down, the stock can still be sold at that price; its value is hedged. When stock indices began trading, academic theorists advised fund managers that it had become possible to hedge entire portfolios of stocks. By selling futures contracts on the stock indices in a declining market according to a prearranged program, the funds could recoup their losses on their stocks through the gains on their contracts. This entirely theoretical safeguard to the value of investments was given the brand name of **Portfolio Insurance**.

Index Fund A pool of money invested in the list of stocks priced to determine the value of one of the popular averages or indices—most commonly, the Standard & Poors 500. Each stock is held in the fund proportionate to the weighting it receives in the index.

Index Arbitrage Futures contracts on various stock indices have been traded since 1982. Because the stock exchanges have developed very efficient electronic order systems, the **Basis** between the futures contract for the index and the cash price of the underlying stocks has become much smaller than it is in agricultural commodities. Thus, it has become possible (easy for **Index Funds,** which already own all the stocks) to perform actual arbitrage between the cash-settlement contract and the calculated value of the index itself. This result was accidental and aberrational. See Chapters 4 and 11.

Long The condition of owning. If you are "long," you benefit from rising prices of the things you own.

Margin A term of art related to borrowing, unfortunately used in different ways:

1. In the stock market, to express the fraction of the purchase price of a stock that the buyer must put up in cash. Under law, this margin requirement is fixed by the Federal Reserve Board; for the past twenty years, it has been 50 percent. Any losses of course come entirely from the customer's stake. Individual brokers then set a "maintenance margin" below which the customer's equity will not be permitted to fall, usually 25 percent. If the price drops to the point where the customer's investment no longer covers 25 percent of the price in the market, the broker sends a "margin call," and if more money is not posted, usually in two or three days but sometimes sooner, the broker will sell the stock, using as much of the proceeds as

necessary to pay back the loan that financed the purchase, and crediting the rest to the customer. In the language of the business, alas!, "margin" can also be used to refer to the loan itself, so that an account where the customer's margin in fact is rather light will be referred to as "heavily margined" because there are large loans outstanding.

2. In the futures market, to express the performance bond a purchaser of a contract must deposit with the clearing corporation that substitutes itself as the counterparty to both sides of the trade. The purpose of the bond is to guarantee that if the market moves against a customer, he will still have enough money on deposit with the clearing corporation to enable the clearing corporation to pay the owner of the contract that has gained in value. Note that no money is borrowed or lent. For most futures contracts, there is a maximum daily price move before trading in that contract is suspended overnight, and the margin is about twice that maximum move.

Every night, all contracts are **Marked to Market** (that is, revalued at today's closing price). On a contract to accept delivery (a purchase), a rising price will increase the value, and the owner will be permitted to take his winnings, withdrawing what is now an unnecessarily large "margin." If, however, the price has gone down, so that the contract has lost value, the owner's deposit will be reduced by the extent of his loss, and if it drops below a prearranged floor he will receive a call for "variation margin," which must be posted within an hour (if it's a call made during the trading day because prices are moving very fast) or overnight when the clearing corporation marks to market at the close of the trading day. On a contract to make delivery (a sale), falling prices produce a profit. Margins on the futures exchanges tend to run between 5 and 10 percent of the value of the contract, normally closer to 5. For political reasons, the margin on the S&P 500 futures contract is at this writing 12 percent. By law, margins are set by the clearing corporations themselves, though the Commodity Futures Trading Commission can *in an emergency* temporarily raise them.

Market Maker   A dealer who buys and sells from his own inventory against orders from the public or (more commonly) from other broker/dealers. A "recognized" market maker is one who has accepted responsibilities to maintain a continuous market, standing ready to buy or sell even in markets where the price seems to be going one way. On the U.S. exchanges, market makers are called **Specialists,** and they have franchises on stocks assigned to them by the administration of the exchange: Nobody else on the trading floor can hold himself out as a market maker in those stocks. In return for their monopoly, they pledge to maintain a "fair and orderly" market.

Open Interest   The futures contracts that have not been extinguished in the day's trading and survive overnight as obligations of the clearing corporations. The depth of a futures market—its ability to absorb large orders without large price changes—is determined by the size of the open interest more than by the volume of trading. The relationship between the open interest and the quantity of the underlying commodity available for delivery is an assurance or an alarm bell for administrators and regulators of exchanges. If the open interest is high and the quantity of the commodity available for delivery is low, there is a danger of a "squeeze" on delivery day, and the exchange may take steps to eliminate trading that could create additional open interest. The Commodity Futures Trading Commission permits traders to create an expanded appearance of open interest by buying and selling identical contracts and holding them to create a "synthetic option."

Options A contract conveying the right but not the obligation to buy something (a CALL option) or to sell something (a PUT option) at a price established in the contract. In a European option, the right exists only on the day the option expires. In an American option, the right can be exercised on any day prior to expiration.

Traded options in the United States are written for **Strike Prices** set by the options exchange. For any stock or index, there will be at least half a dozen of these for each expiration date, normally set 5 points apart. With a stock selling at 70, for example, there might be options to buy or sell at 55, 60, 65, 70, 75, 80, and 85. An option to buy at 55, a 55 call, is "in the money" to the extent of $15 a share—by exercising the option today and selling the stock delivered, the owner of the option will make $15. That means he can sell it for something more than $15, so he probably will not use it as a way to take delivery (some professionals and funds will). An option to buy at 80, an 80 call, is "out of the money," and will expire worthless when its time comes unless the price rises above 80 in the interim.

The price of an option is called its "premium." Sellers of options—in the language, "options writers"—receive the premium. It is calculated in an auction market by bids and offers, just as the price of a futures contract is set in open outcry. **Covered Options** are options written by people who own the security (in some cases, commodity or currency) that will have to be delivered if the purchaser exercises the option. Thus someone who owns a stock can sell a call and pocket the premium with the knowledge that the worst that can happen to him is that he will have to sell his stock at the strike price of the call even if the price in the market has gone higher. Someone who has a **Short Position** in a security can safely write a put, knowing that if the price goes down, his profit on his short sale matches his loss on the put, and he has gained the premium.

Naked Options are options written by people who do not own the security that will have to be delivered against a call, and are not short elsewhere in the market to hedge the put they have written. Potential losses are now unlimited, for the call writer may have to purchase a stock at a price much higher than the strike price to fulfill his contract, and the put writer may have to pay for stocks that have become much cheaper than they were when he agreed to the strike price.

The purchase of options offers great leverage—a play on a hundred shares at 100 that would cost $5,000 on 50 percent margin at the Stock Exchange may be available for a few hundred dollars in an out-of-the-money option. As is usual in highly leveraged situations, the odds are against the player, especially one who must pay retail commissions (on sale as well as purchase, if the option proves to have a value) in addition to premiums.

Positions   The trader's or dealer's holdings. These may be an inventory of securities or buy contracts or call options (**Long Positions** that benefit by a rise in price) or they may be an inventory of obligations to buy stock that the trader has already sold and must return to the lender, or futures contracts to make delivery, or put options (**Short Positions** that benefit by a fall in prices), or some combination of the two (**Hedged Position**). A broker may acquire a long or short position in the process of putting together a block trade. A market maker usually has a position on one side or the other of a market.

Primary Market   The first market into which an issue of securities is sold by the underwriter, before trading begins. All subsequent buying and selling of securities occurs in a **Secondary Market.** In general, securities are very difficult to sell to their initial buyer unless he has good reason to believe there will be a secondary market into which he can resell if he needs the money. A "secondary offering" is a distribution, usually of stock, handled as though it were a sale in a primary market.

Program Trading   Buying and selling securities according to a prearranged "program," normally the product of a computerized strategy, rather than according to anyone's judgment of the value of the individual stocks being acquired or sold.

Proprietary Trading   Trading by brokers, who presumably are representing customers in the market, for their own account rather than for the accounts of their customers.

Put *see* **Options**

Short   The condition of owing. If you are "short," you benefit by falling prices. A **Short Sale** establishes this condition, though an equivalent condition can also derive from the sale of a call option, or the purchase of a put option, or the purchase of a futures contract to make delivery of a commodity at a fixed price on a certain future date. In the stock market, the short seller borrows stock from someone and sells that stock in the market. He stands liable to the lender for any dividends it earns, he may pay a borrowing fee, and he must return it, usually on demand after notice of a few days. Customers who have margin accounts and borrow to make their purchases must usually agree to let their brokers lend their stock to short sellers. The broker rather than the owner of the stock receives whatever fees are paid on the borrowing.

Specialist *see* **Market Maker**

Spooz   The Standard & Poors 500 futures contract, from the ticker symbol SPZ.

Spread   In the market, the difference between the "bid," what someone is prepared to pay for a security or a contract, and the "asked," what an owner (or short seller) is prepared to sell it for. Also, **Spreading.**
   see also **Arbitrage** and **Hedging**

Trader   Specifically, someone who operates in a market entirely on his own behalf, not filling public orders or accepting obligations to anyone but himself. Many market participants who also have other functions trade for their own accounts on the side. The defense, not necessarily a bad one, is that all markets need liquidity, and traders provide it.

Index

INDEX

INDEX

Index

INDEX

Index

INDEX

Martin, William McChesney, Jr., 218–19, 222, 224
Marx, Karl, 33, 251
MATIF, 133, 199
Matsumura, Hideo, 145
meat market, wholesale, 14–15
Meilke, John, 92–93
Melamed, Leo, 9, 22, 27, 59–60, 89, 258
  background of, 104–6, 129
  currency futures and, 107–10
  on governmental relations, 129
  index futures and, 111–13, 130, 262–63
  on limits to pit trading, 132
  stock market crash and, 62, 80, 104
  T-bill futures and, 110–11
Merrill Lynch, 6, 60, 75, 145–46, 154, 202, 204, 212, 223, 248–49
  cash management accounts pioneered by, 228, 260
  commodities business of, 92, 98–99
  corporate money raising instruments created by, 228–29
  international trading by, 23–24, 136, 160, 167, 174, 196
  up-tick rule exemption granted to, 86, 245, 249
Merrill Lynch, Pierce, Fenner & Beane, 105, 111
Michigan, University of, xxix
MidAmerica Exchange, 90–91
Midland Bank, 198
Midwest Stock Exchange, 71
Milan Stock Exchange, 24
Miller Tabak Hirsch, 130
Minneapolis Grain Exchange, 100
Mitsopoulos, Gus, xxxii, 124, 133
Mitsui, 169
Mitsukoshi Department Store, 151–52
Miyazaki, Isamu, 148, 169
Mocatta Metals, 107, 109, 129
monetarist theories, 240
money-market mutual funds, xxi–xxiii
money markets, 142–43
money supply, xx, 216
Monopolies Commission, 187
Moore, George S., 3, 21, 33
Morgan, Grenfell & Co., 176, 243, 248
Morgan, J. P., 50, 80, 213, 215, 217, 262, 272
Morgan Guaranty, 13, 132, 143, 169
  in Eurobond clearing, 184–85
Morgan Stanley, 39, 60, 62, 167, 196, 198, 221
Morgan Stanley International Capital, 144
Mori, Minoru, 164
Motherwell, Robert, 124
moving averages, xx
Mullen's, 196
Mussolini, Benito, 180
mutual funds, 177, 240
  in Japan, 152, 156
  NYSE resentment of, 220–21, 223
  stock market crash and, 62, 80
  tax exemption of, 262, 264

Nakatsuka, Yukio, 148, 155
Nakayama, Takashi, 149
naked options, xxix–xxxi, 49, 74–75, 239
Nara, Yasuhiko, 136–37, 174–75

National Advisory Commission on Civil Disorders, 230
National Aeronautics and Space Administration (NASA), 47
National Association of Securities Dealers (NASD), 177
  National Market System of, 192
National Association of Securities Dealers Automated Quotations (NASDAQ) market, 3–4, 192, 197, 206, 224
  companies traded on, 5–6
  growth of, 4–5
  indexes of, 262–63
  resiliency of, 10
  rules governing trades at, 259–60
  stock market crash and, 5, 9–10, 64
National Futures Association (NFA), 92, 95
National Market System index, 262–63
National Securities Clearing Corporation, 192
Netherlands Antilles, 182–83
New Bedford Seafood Exchange, 27–28
  bidders on, 29
  description of, 28–31
  gold-fixing markets compared with, 31–33
  NYSE compared with, 203–4
New Deal, 218
New Gatsbys, The (Tamarkin), 93
New York, N.Y., 212–13
New York Commodity Exchange (COMEX), xxv, 18, 21, 89, 258
  CRT's success at, 128–29
  failure of Volume Investors at, 98–99
  petty cheating at, 130
New York Mercantile Exchange (NYMEX), xix, xxv, 106, 131
  oil futures traded on, 16–18, 23, 207–8, 269
New York Metropolitan Opera, 21
New York Produce Exchange, 106
New York Stock Exchange (NYSE), 5, 7, 19, 57, 71, 101, 112, 130, 132, 144, 177, 194, 201–29, 254, 263
  British shares traded at, 187
  Chicago markets compared with, 91
  commission schedule of, 38–39, 201–2, 212, 220–25, 233–34, 245–46
  computerization of, 223, 225
  electronic order-delivery system at, 59, 113, 203, 205–6, 208, 219–20, 241, 250
  employees' Gratuity Fund of, 217
  government regulation of, 214–15, 217–19
  history of, 213–26
  influence of futures markets on, 135
  Japanese investment at, 160, 167–69, 226
  legal infrastructure of, 35
  market making on, 36–37, 39–40, 62–66, 80, 87, 202–12, 214, 216, 219–20, 224
  member firms of, 34–35, 219–22, 224, 243–44, 248
  order imbalances at, 250
  personnel at, 201
  reforms for, 202, 218, 220, 222–24
  regional exchanges and, 218–22, 224
  regulating arbitrage activity at, 255
  requirements for listings on, 34, 252
  Rule 10-a of, 84–86, 209, 218, 239

Index

Rule 390 of, 39, 63, 76, 224–25
Rule 394 of, 222
Rule 431 E-5 of, 76–77
scandals at, 223
settlement system of, 208, 225
stock market crash and, 62–67, 69, 75–80, 82,
  87, 185, 205, 208–10
survival capacity of, 212
trading at, 37–40, 202–12, 214, 219–20, 225,
  234
up-tick rule of, 84–86, 209, 218, 239
New York Times, xx, 65, 88, 182, 263
Nihon Kezai Shimbun, 153–54
Nikkei-Dow index, 23, 40
  futures on, 133, 172, 255–56, 268
Nikko Securities, 146, 161–63, 173–74
Nippon Life, 134
Nixon, Richard M., 100, 224–26
  gold standard abandoned by, 50–51, 107–9
Nomura Securities, 138, 146–47, 153, 161, 165,
  171
Norton, Bert, 109–10
Norton, Carol, 109

odd-lot dealers, 219–20, 224, 258
oil market, xxvi, xxvii, 7, 25
  on NYMEX, 16–18, 23, 207–8, 269
  posted price and, 18
Okuyama, Takatoshi, 154, 157, 172
Olympia and York, 197
one-decision stocks, xvii
onions futures, 105
Only Yesterday (Allen), 216–17
Opening-Only orders, 204
open interest, 96
  relationship between real inventory and, 17–18,
  43
  in S&P futures, 70
  in T-bond futures, 71
open-outcry auctions, 45, 91, 132
  trends in, 127–28
options, xxvii–xxxii, 241, 267
  buyers vs. sellers of, 47, 49
  definition of, xxviii
  duration of, xxix–xxx, 48–49
  European vs. American, 48
  futures compared with, xxviii, xxx, 47
  price and, xxix–xxx, 48–49, 242
  purpose of, xxix
  in stock market context, xxviii–xxix, xxxi
  on T-bond futures, 46
Options Clearing Corporation, xxx–xxxi, 74,
  82
options markets, xxviii–xxix, 196, 198–99, 207,
  239
  abuse in relations between underlying stocks
  and, 130
  CRT's operations and, 127–29
  stock market crash and, 49, 71–82, 133
Oregon Public Employees' Retirement System,
  164
Organization of Petroleum Exporting Countries
  (OPEC), xxvii, 16, 18, 88, 141, 162, 181, 270
Osborne, Bruce, 78–79
out-trades, 68–69, 131

over-the-counter market, *see* National
  Association of Securities Dealers Automated
  Quotations market

Pacific Stock Exchange (PSE), 36, 68
  SCOREX electronic order system of, 64
  stock market crash and, 64, 75
panic of 1907, 75, 217
Pardee, Scott, 25, 151, 173
Patman, Wright, 51
performance bonds, xxiv–xxv
Perot, H. Ross, 223
perpetual floating-rate notes, 172–73
Phelan, John:
  on dynamic hedging practices, 82, 85
  stock market crash and, 79–80
Philadelphia Stock Exchange, 36, 222
  stock market crash and, 65
pit scalpers, 8–9
Plender, John, 159, 178, 190, 196
Pöhl, Karl Otto, 61–62
Pollack, Irving, 249
pork-bellies futures, 106
portfolio insurance, xxxii
  at LSE, 176
  rational strategies for, 125
  S&P 500 futures and, 83–85, 125
  stock market crash and, 67, 69, 77, 82–83,
  86–88, 125, 238–39
portfolio theory, 233–34, 271
positioning, 9
postal savings system, 139, 142, 150
Prechter, Robert, xix
premiums:
  on options, xxviii–xxx, 46, 48–49
  on S&P options, 73–74
Presidential Task Force on Market Mechanisms,
  see Brady Commission
prices, xvi
  availability of, xvii
  discovery mechanisms for, 14–16, 19, 134–35,
  236–37, 240, 252, 254
  of futures contracts, xxvi–xxvii, 235–38
  in futures vs. cash markets, 235–38
  importance of, 10
  information built into, 253–54
  inside, 4–6, 10, 20–21
  at LSE, 177–78
  options and, xxix–xxx, 48–49, 242
  predicting movement of, *see* technical analyses
  of stocks at morning opening, 204–5
  technology and reporting of, 19–22
  at TSE, 155–56
Price Waterhouse, 252
primary markets, xviii–xix
Princeton/Newport Partners, 7
Princeton University, xvii
Prindl, Andreas R., 143
program trading:
  regulation of, 254–57
  stock market crash and, 82, 86–88
proprietary trading, 120, 257–61
  need for policing of, 260–61
  profits made on, 244–45
  of T-bond options, 122

299

INDEX

Prudential Insurance, 98, 197, 199
Pujo Committee, 272
Pulay, George, 32
put options, xxviii–xxxi, 49
  naked, xxx, 74–75, 239
pyramiding, 215

Quantum Fund, 70

racism, 230–31
random-walk theories, 240
Raven, Stephen, 24, 177, 188
RCA, 201
Reagan, Ronald, 50–51, 61, 200, 245
  stock market crash and, 82, 87, 158, 270
Reed, John, 77
Refco, xxxii, 12, 27, 92–93, 98, 149, 196
  basis risk assumed by, 118
  commissions charged by, 120–21
  CRT compared with, 126–27
  Dittmer and, 114–17, 119–21, 124
  educational training programs of, 121–24
  efficiency of, 120–21
  employment philosophy of, 124–25
  Grant's analysis of and program for, 116–17,
    120, 133
  growth and diversification of, 117–18
  international operations of, 133, 172
  naming of, 114
  primary dealer status of, 118–19
  revenues of, 119
Regan, Donald, 212, 224
Remick, William H., 217
Renfrew, Glen, 21–23
repurchase-agreements (repos) markets, 19
Reston, James, xx
Reuters, 4–5, 267
  CME and, 22–23, 110, 268–69
  in foreign-exchange markets, 20–21, 25
  price reporting by, 20–22
  trading and, 22–23
Reuters Alert, 22
Reuters Monitor, 21–22, 25
*Review and Evaluation of Federal Margin
  Regulations, A,* 76
Rich, David, 68
Rigby, Geraldine, 168
Rio Tinto, 12
risk-transfer devices, xxxi–xxxii
Ritchie, Joe, 126–29
Robinson, M. S., 18
Rockefeller, John D., Sr., xviii, 214
Rockefeller Foundation, 243
Rockwell International, 164
Roosevelt, Franklin D., xv
Roosevelt, James, xv
Roosevelt, Theodore, 215
Roscoe, Bruce, 145
Rosenberg, Steve, 21
Rosenthal, Leslie, 14, 98, 100, 102
Rosenwald, James, 163
Ross, Stanley, 185
Rostenkowski, Dan, 61
Rotberg, Eugene, 204, 248–49
Rothschild, George, 24

Rothschild, Jacob, 187–88
N. M. Rothschild & Sons, 31–32
Ruder, David, xxix
Rudloff, Hans-Joerg, 178, 248, 265, 271
Rugnetta, Joe, 29–31
Rutz, Robert, 71, 96, 114

Salomon, William (Billy), 46, 110, 119
Salomon Brothers, 46, 54, 59–60, 69, 160, 165
  commission revenues of, 222
  corporate money raising instruments created
    by, 226–28
  overseas operations of, 167, 185, 196, 199
  profits of, 187–88
  T-bill futures and, 110–11
Salzman, Jerrold, 112
Samuelson, Paul, 15
Sandburg, Carl, 91
Sandner, Jack, 9
Sandor, Richard, 45, 269
  on limits to pit trading, 132
  Ginnie Maes and, 89–90, 100–104
  T-bond futures and, 103–4, 234
savings, savings accounts:
  by Japanese, 139, 144–46, 149–52, 159
  money-market funds compared with, xxii–xxiii
Schapiro, Morris, 222
Schlesinger, Arthur, Jr., 26
Schmidt, Helmut, 153
Scholey, Sir David, 25, 188, 267
Schultze, Charles, 53
Schumer, Charles, 119
Charles Schwab, 74–75
Scully, Robert, 226–28
secondary markets, xix
Securities and Exchange Act, 217, 258
Securities and Exchange Commission (SEC), xxii,
    xxix, 38, 66, 103, 130, 165, 182, 187, 200,
    225–26, 249–50, 268
  British intrigued by, 193
  CBOE supervised by, 90
  conflicts of interest and, 247, 258–59, 261, 265
  establishment of, 217–18
  insider trading investigated by, 173–74
  Market Oversight Surveillance System (MOSS)
    of, 245–46
  Market Regulation Division of, 86, 136, 215
  NYSE reforms and, 202, 218, 220, 222, 224
  pro-brokerage house rulings of, 244–46
  on relationship between derivative and equity
    markets, 135–36
  specialist performance investigated by, 209–10
  stock market crash and, 10, 67, 76, 80, 86,
    208–10
  on stock openings, 204–5
  Trading and Exchange Division of, 257–58
  up-tick rule and, 84, 86, 218, 239, 245
Securities and Investments Board (SIB), 186, 189,
    193–94, 199
Securities Dealers Association, 167
Securities Investors Protection Corporation,
    223–24
Security Pacific, 196
Seibert, Muriel (Mickey), 35
J. W. Seligman, 224

Index

Senate, U.S.:
Ways and Means Committee of, 61
see also Congress, U.S.
Shad, John, 130, 244–46
Shakespeare, William, 38
Shearson Lehman Hutton, 21, 70, 96, 144, 196, 223, 227, 243–44, 249, 256
Shell International Trading, 18
Shepherd, Mary, 131
short positions, xxiii–xiv, xxv, xxxi
short sellers, xxi, xxiii–xiv
Shubik, Martin, xvii
Sieger, Joseph F., 105
Silva Herzog, Jesus de, 52
Silver, David, 41–42, 66
silver, Hunts' attempts to corner market in, 15, 17–18, 128, 235
Silver v. New York Stock Exchange, 222
Singapore Mercantile Exchange (SIMEX), 22–23
Singapore Monetary Exchange, 133, 172
Slater, Jim, 190
Smiley, Robert L., 216
Smith, Adam, 266
Smith, Adam (George J. W. Goodman), 40, 60
Smithsonian Agreement, 107–9, 270
Sobel, Robert, 217–18
Society for Worldwide Interbank Financial Telecommunications (SWIFT), 267
Sony Corporation, 156
Soros, George, 70
Southeast Asia, Japanese edge in, 172
South Sea Bubble, 13, 68
Soviet Union, 271–72
Spear, Leeds & Kellogg, 37, 185
specialists:
books kept by, 206–7, 210–12
CRT as, 127
market making role of, 36–37, 39–40
at NYSE, 36–37, 39–40, 62–66, 80, 87, 202–12, 214, 216, 219–20, 224
stabilization rate of, 209
stock market break and, 204–5, 209–10
stock market crash and, 39–40, 62–66, 80, 87, 209–10, 259
undercapitalization of, 211
Specified Money Trusts, 157
speculators, 11, 13, 225–26
spreads, spreading, xxvii, 6, 24
CRT and, 127–28
index arbitrage and, 241
at NYSE vs. Chicago markets, 91
at NYSE vs. LSE, 187
on petroleum contracts, 17
on wheat contracts, 236
Square Mile, The, 196
squeezes, 17
Stallone, Sylvester, 117–18
Staloff, Arnold, 222
Standard & Poors (S&P) 100 index, options on, 47, 71–74, 80, 130
Standard & Poors (S&P) 500 index:
futures on (Spooz), 7, 8, 23, 43, 59, 62, 66–67, 69–70, 72, 80, 83–84, 86–87, 93, 104, 111–13, 125, 132, 238–41, 258
overvaluation of, 56

Standard & Poors (S&P) over the counter (SPOC) index, 262
State Street Fund, 262
Stearns, Jay, 184, 195
Steele, Sir Richard, 13
Stein, Howard, xxii, 161, 232, 239, 243
Stigum, Marcia, 12
stock brokers, stock brokerage firms, xx–xxi, xxvii, 11
accounting policy and, 256–57
bankruptcies among, 223
buy vs. sell recommendations of, xiv
at commodity exchanges, 92
conflicts of interest of, 246–50, 258–61, 265
of Japan, 119, 145–58, 162–67, 169–74, 182, 185
at LSE, 177–78, 190–92, 196–200
margin lending profits of, 76–77
NYSE trading by, 37–38, 201–4, 206–8, 210–12, 214–16, 219–23, 225
in options trading, xxx–xxxi, 72, 74–75, 241
petty cheating by, 130–33
proprietary trading profits of, 244–45
rumors spread by, 253–54
SEC leniency toward, 244–46
stock market crash and, 56–60, 63–66, 69–70, 72, 74–75, 80–81, 86, 244
Stock Exchange Automated Quotation (SEAQ) International, 192
stock market break (1962), 204–5, 209–10
stock market crash of 1907, 75, 214
stock market crash of 1929, 217
stock market crash of 1987, 13, 104, 272
banks and, 70–71, 75–80, 82, 185
Brady Commission on, *see* Brady Commission
damage done to new companies by, 5
fuel of, 50–67, 167
as institutional panic, 87–88
LSE and, 62, 176, 178, 200, 268
NYSE and, 62–67, 69, 75–80, 82, 87, 185, 205, 208–10
options markets and, 49, 71–82, 133
Reagan and, 81, 87, 158, 270
Refco and, 119
results of, 68–88, 232, 242, 259
role of portfolio insurance in, 67, 69, 77, 82–83, 86–88, 125, 238–39
SEC and, 10, 67, 76, 80, 86, 208–10
specialists and, 39–40, 62–66, 80, 87, 209–10, 259
stock brokers and, 56–60, 63–66, 69–70, 72, 74–75, 80–81, 86, 244
surviving, 9–10
technology and, 65–66, 86–87, 231
TSE and, 40–41, 62, 157–59, 172
victims of, xxxi, 5
stock markets:
as cash markets, xx–xxi, xxiii
for direct investment, xxi
economic importance of, 225–26, 240
efficiency of, xvii, 252–53
Japanese attracted to, 54–55, 58
manipulation of, 56–60, 247
options in context of, xxviii–xxix, xxxi
technical analyses of, xviii–xx

301

INDEX

Index

303